REVIEW

FOR THE

PROFESSIONAL
ENGINEERS'
EXAMINATION

FOR

INDUSTRIAL ENGINEERS
REVISED EDITION

REVIEW

FOR THE

PROFESSIONAL
ENGINEERS'
EXAMINATION

FOR

INDUSTRIAL ENGINEERS

REVISED EDITION

DONOVAN YOUNG, PH.D., P.E.

ENGINEERING & MANAGEMENT PRESS
INSTITUE OF INDUSTRIAL ENGINEERS
NORCROSS, GEORGIA

Library of Congress Cataloging-in-Publication Data

Young, D. (Donovan), 1936-
    Review for the professional engineers' examination for industrial engineers /
Donovan Young.
        p.   cm.
    Includes bibliographical references and index.
    ISBN 0-89806-134-2
      1. Industrial engineering--Examinations, questions, etc.
    2. Industrial engineering--Problems, exercises, etc. I. Title.
T56.24.Y68   1993
670.42'076--dc20   93-28424
                                                      CIP

Printed in the United States of America.

ISBN 0-89806-134-2

99 98   6 5 4

Additional copies may be obtained by contacting:
Institute of Industrial Engineers
Customer Service
25 Technology Park/Atlanta
Norcross, Georgia 30092 USA
(404) 449-0460 phone
(404) 263-8532 fax

Quantity discounts available.

Table of Contents

7. Work Measurement, Human Factors, and Ergonomics 301

8. Management and Safety 337

Foreword

Many industrial engineers have found it worth their while to become registered as professional engineers. There are several reasons: 1) *Full membership in the profession of engineering*. No engineering credential is as widely accepted in engineering as the PE. 2) *Preparation for career unpredictability*. No one knows the future course of their career. Also, if you leave engineering work for a year or more (this applies particularly to women), the PE will help you regain employment later as an engineer. 3) *Admission to practice of some occupations*. In most states, you cannot offer your services as a consulting engineer without being licensed as a PE. In many organizations, particularly utilities and government agencies involved in technical work, engineering registration is helpful or even necessary for advancement. 4) *Mobility and job security*. The PE can help you move to a new job because of its universal recognition as a technical credential. 5) *Public benefit*. Your registration also benefits the public. Because you have a public license to practice engineering, the public is assured that you have passed a rigorous set of procedures chosen to safeguard the health, safety, and welfare of the public.

Most states use two examinations to qualify a candidate for professional registration: the Fundamentals of Engineering (FE) Exam for engineer-in-training (EIT) status; and a discipline-specific examination, such as the PE. These exams are prepared under the direction of the National Council of Examiners for Engineering and Surveying (NCEES) and are the same throughout the country. The purpose of the FE Exam (also called the EIT Exam) is to insure that anyone claiming to be an engineer has demonstrated competence in engineering fundamentals; its topics cover the first two years of an ABET-accredited engineering program. The purpose of the PE Exam is to demonstrate competence in some recognized branch of engineering; its topics are determined by NCEES after a survey of engineering practice and are reviewed periodically.

Because all engineers in the same discipline take the same EIT Exam and PE Exam, taking the exams in one state avoids the necessity for taking them in another state, and it is easy to become registered in additional states. Registration requirements are governed by the states, however, and they usually differ somewhat between any two states. The best source of information on the requirements that affect you is the board of engineering examiners for your state.

The EIT Exam is usually taken in the last year before graduation from college; if you have already graduated, the nearest university offering an engineering program will usually have review courses for the EIT Exam. The PE Exam usually requires that a person have four years of engineering experience beyond the BS degree, and some review is imperative. In the four or more years since graduation, most industrial engineers will have forgotten a number of their academic skills and will not have practiced industrial engineering in the breadth needed to pass the PE Exam. Studying for the exam will also enable an engineer to come up to the current level of the field. The specifications for the exam are updated about every five years, so it is important to know what topics will be on the current test.

This review text serves a number of purposes for the person taking the PE Exam. First, it gives examinees an idea of what topics the test will cover. Second, it presents a good review of the material in each of those topics. Third, it provides the test taker with a good test-taking strategy. Finally, it is, and will continue to be, a good overall reference for industrial engineering topics.

Good luck on the test!

W.J. Kennedy, Ph.D., P.E.
Former IIE Director of Professional Registration

Preface

If you are an industrial engineer who intends to take the Professional Engineers' (PE) Examination as the final step in achieving professional registration, this book is for you. Probably you have earned an accredited degree in industrial engineering and have gained experience from several years of professional practice. No review book can substitute for education and experience, but it can help you freshen and consolidate your mastery of the tools of your profession.

Your experience may not have been as varied as you would like, and as a result you may be out of practice in areas where you once were confident. This book can help you brush up on those areas and regain your lost skills. Or your experience may have outpaced your education; perhaps you are routinely using statistics techniques that were not taught in school when you were a student, or perhaps you are doing things with computers that were beyond the state of the art when you were in school. This book, and the references it cites, can help you fill in some educational gaps.

You may be undecided about how best to organize a time-limited review effort. This book tells you exactly what the IE PE Exam authors expect you to know, and how the exam will test you. With this book's help, you can budget your review time wisely and perform triage: decide which skills to polish, which skills to brush up lightly, and which skills you can safely ignore.

The first chapter of this book is about the PE Exam itself: what to expect and how to do your best.

The second chapter gives ten realistic problems similar in both form and coverage to the eight problems that you will actually solve on the IE PE Exam, although these problems are probably somewhat tougher, on the average, than the actual problems will be. Every problem in the exam concerns doing something specific (designing something, deciding how best to operate something, etc.) about a particular situation in an application area such as facility design, facility operation, manufacturing, production planning and control, inventory control, work design and measurement, safety, quality control, management, or computer and information systems. For each kind of problem, the solutios in the second chapter give examples of correct approaches and illustrate applicable methodologies and techniques.

The exact procedures, format, and structure of the IE PE Exam are available in a separate supplemental book from Engineering & Management Press: *Authentic Practice Exam for the Professional Engineers' Examination for Industrial Engineers*. As its title implies, the book provides a realistic dry run of the exam, in its current (1996) form, complete with solutions and scoring guides.

The methodologies and techniques—knowledge areas—that must be mastered to do well on the IE PE Exam are the subject of the remaining chapters. In these chapters, the 100 most important industrial engineering technical procedures, algorithms, and methods are reviewed. Each technique is illustrated with one or two solved examples, and literature references are given to indicate an authoritative source of more detailed information.

The organization and contents of this book are based both on the 1996 specifications for the IE PE Exam and on a comprehensive survey by the National Council of Examiners for Engineers and Surveyors (NCEES) of what industrial engineers do and what they need to know. This survey is the one used by the Professional Examination Committee of IIE (Dr. W.J. Kennedy, Jr., chairperson) to guide the contents of the exams. The exam specifications used in compiling the exams are open information and are summarized in chapter 1.

For many helpful suggestions, criticism, and technical help, grateful acknowledgement is due to Dr. W.J. Kennedy, Jr., who served until recently as IIE Director of Professional Registration, to Dr. Thomas G. King at NCEES, to Forsyth Alexander of Engineering & Management Press, to consulting engineers Yadollah Sayan and Dr. William V. Harper, and to the many industrial engineers who submit, edit, review and score IE PE Exam problems as a service to their profession.

Donovan Young

Chapter 1
The Professional
Engineers' Examination

The purpose of the Professional Engineers' Examination for Industrial Engineers (the IE PE Exam) is to help guarantee that registered industrial engineers have the competence to practice engineering in a manner that will safeguard life, health, and property and promote the public welfare. Having earned an accredited engineering degree, passed the Fundamentals of Engineering Examination (formerly known as the Engineer-in-Training Examination), and practiced for several years, you certainly have the potential for passing this final requirement for registration as a professional engineer. This book will help you review your skills and become confident of performing well.

This chapter outlines the exam structure (1.1), the application areas covered by the exam (1.2), the skills tested by the exam (1.3), a recommended strategy for planning your review effort (1.4), and some hints on test-taking tactics (1.5). Chapter 2 will show the kinds of problems that can be expected in each application area, and the remaining chapters will give a detailed review of the skills needed to solve the problems.

1.1 Exam Structure

The PE Exam takes a full day. You will solve four essay-type problems in the morning and four sets of multiple-choice questions in the afternoon. Each essay-type problem is scored by a human scorer and is assigned a raw score of 0, 2, 4, 6, 8, or 10. A raw score of 6 converts to a score of

70%. Each set of multiple-choice questions is scored by machine and is assigned a raw score of 0, 1, 2, 3, 4, 5, 6, 7, 8, 9, or 10. Again, 6 converts to 70%. An overall average of 70% constitutes passing; this is achieved when the total raw score is 48. For example, if a candidate's work is scored 8, 4, 6, 4 for the morning and 7, 7, 8, 4 for the afternoon, the candidate passes.

1.1.1 Essay Problems

An essay-type problem is presented in the examination pamphlet—one or two problems to a page—as a *Situation* followed by one or more *Requirements* labeled (a), (b), and so forth. Sometimes, a problem contains more than one situation, each followed by its requirements. Tables or figures often accompany the situation. Typical problem statements for essay problems are given in examples E1 and E3 in chapter 2.

You are to write your responses to the requirements for an essay-type problem in the solution booklet given to you with the examination pamphlet. It generally takes three or four pages to respond to a problem's requirements, although some candidates can pack a high-scoring solution onto a single page, and others may use eight or 10 pages. Scratch work, which the scorer will not see, can be done on the left-hand pages of the solution booklet; responses are written on the right-hand pages, which are lightly ruled in 0.20-inch squares. If you need a second solution booklet to complete your work, you will be given one.

Essay problems are designed so that approximately 40 minutes is the standard time for a qualified engineer to read all parts of the problem, organize an approach, perform calculations or execute design tasks, and write a well-documented set of responses with supporting work.

Each essay-type problem is scored 0, 2, 4, 6, 8, or 10 points, with 6 points intended to represent minimum required competence. Consequently, up to 40 of the required 48 raw points can be earned in the morning, and 24 is a passing pace. Scorers' expectations for essay responses are discussed in section 1.5.2.

1.1.2 Machine-scored Problems

A multiple-choice problem is presented in the examination pamphlet as a *Situation* followed by 10 *Questions*, each with four alternative answers labeled (A) through (D). Typical problem statements for multiple-choice problems are given in examples E2 and E4 in chapter 2.

For each question in the problem, responses are marked on an answer sheet by blackening the response block that corresponds to the one best answer. Often calculations or design tasks will need to be performed to choose the best answer; such work, which can be written in the exam booklet, will be ignored in machine scoring.

Approximately 40 minutes is the standard time needed for a qualified engineer to read the situation and all 10 questions, calculate and design, choose answers from the alternatives, and mark answers on the mark-sense form.

The three incorrect alternative answers to each question, called *distractors*, are intended to appear correct to a candidate who commits a specific error or misinterpretation expected of unqualified engineers, takes a shallow view, or just guesses. (However, the questions are not intentionally tricky; see 1.5.2 for a discussion of how they are developed.) The score on each machine-scored problem is 0 to 10 points—the number of correct responses. Consequently, up to 40 of the required 48 points can be earned in the afternoon session of the examination.

1.2 Application Area Coverage

The application areas covered by the IE PE Exam continually evolve as the profession evolves. In the report, *Analysis of Professional Activities and Requirements of the Engineering Profession*, published by the National Council of Examiners for Engineering and Surveying (NCEES) in 1989, the results of a large-scale study of what engineers do on the job and what they need to know were released. Exams given through October 1992 contained broader coverage than today. Then, candidates selected eight out of 20 problems, distributed as follows:

Former Application Area	*Number of PE Exam Problems*
Facilities	4
Management Systems	3
Manufacturing Systems	4
Production Planning and Control	2
Inventory Planning and Control	1
Quality Assurance and Safety	2
Work Methods and Measurement	1
Human Factors	1
Computer Information Systems	2
	20

A significant change in the IE PE Exam format was made for 1993. There is no choice of problems; the exam has eight problems to be solved by all candidates. The application-area coverage (with broader definitions of application areas than before) is:

Application Area	Number of PE Exam Problems
Facilities	2
Information and Management Systems	1
Manufacturing	2
Production and Inventory Systems	1
Quality Assurance	1
Work and Safety	1
	8

W. J. Kennedy, the director of professional registration for the Institute of Industrial Engineers, published the detailed format of the IE PE Exam in the article, "New Professional Engineering Exam Format for 1993," in the December 1992 issue of *Industrial Engineering* magazine. The format is shown in table 1-1.

1.3 Knowledge Coverage

The knowledge areas covered on the exam closely follow those skills and abilities identified as most important in the NCEES's 1989 report. The 15 most important knowledge areas are:

Rank	Knowledge Area
#1	Cost analysis
#2	Probability and statistics
#3	Systems design and analysis
#4	Management principles
#5	Computer software
#6	Measurement and instrumentation
#7	Manufacturing processes
#8	Operations research
#9	Work methods and measurement
#10	Human engineering
#11	Codes and standards
#12	Reliability and failure analysis
#13	Statistical quality control
#14	Ergonomics
#15	Computer hardware

Table 1-1. IE PE Exam Format (starting with October 1993 Exam).

Problem	Application Areas	Knowledge Areas
#170: Facilities Morning; essay type	Any of: site selection, plant layout, equipment, material handling or waste management, packaging, capacity analysis, utility requirements	Two to five from: probability and statistics, codes and standards, operations research, systems design or analysis, cost analysis and engineering economy
#171: Manufacturing Morning; essay type	Any of: products, manufacturing processes, maintenance procedures, operations sequencing, machine grouping, robotics, automation, value engineering	Two to five from: probability and statistics, measurement and instrumentation, operations research, manufacturing materials, manufacturing processes, systems design or analysis, cost analysis and engineering economy
#172: Production and Inventory Systems Morning; essay type	Any of: forecasting, production scheduling, project scheduling, production control, inventory control, resource planning, logistics and distribution	Two to five from: probability and statistics, computer software, operations research, work methods and measurement, manufacturing processes, systems design or analysis, cost analysis and engineering economy
#173: Work and Safety Morning; essay type	Any of: work analysis and measurement, incentives and payment plans, workplace design, human-machine interfacing, industrial hygiene and safety	Two to five from: probability and statistics, measurement and instrumentation, codes and standards, management principles, ergonomics and human engineering, work methods and measurement, systems design or analysis, cost analysis and engineering economy, reliability and failure analysis
#470: Facilities Afternoon; multiple-choice, 10 questions each with 5 possible responses	Any of: site selection, plant layout, equipment, material handling or waste management, packaging, capacity analysis, utility requirements	Two to five from: probability and statistics, codes and standards, operation research, systems design or analysis, cost analysis and engineering economy
#471: Manufacturing Afternoon; multiple-choice, 10 questions each with 5 possible responses	Any of: products, manufacturing processes, maintenance procedures, operations sequencing, machine grouping, robotics, automation, value engineering	Two to five from: probability and statistics, measurement and instrumentation, operations research, manufacturing materials, manufacturing processes, physical and mechanical properties of materials, systems design or analysis, cost analysis and engineering economy
#472: Quality Assurance Afternoon; multiple-choice, 10 questions each with 5 possible responses	Any of: quality assurance plans, reliability analysis, control procedures, capability analysis, quality aspects of design	Two to five from: statistical quality control, probability and statistics, computer software, electrical theory, measurement and instrumentation, codes and standards, ergonomics and human engineering, cost analysis and engineering economy, reliability and failure analysis
#473: Management and Computer Information Systems Afternoon; multiple-choice, 10 questions each with 5 possible responses	Any of: organization design, staffing plans, productivity, human resources, computer systems analysis and design, specification of computer equipment, computer communication protocols	Two to five from: probability and statistics, computer software, computer hardware, computer systems, codes and standards, operations research, management principles, ergonomics and human engineering, systems design or analysis, cost analysis and engineering economy

1.4 PE Exam Review Planning

Now that you know how the IE PE Exam is structured and generally what it covers, you should pause and plan your review effort. This book is not intended to be read from cover to cover. If you simply plunge in and plow through, you could waste time in two ways: rehashing what you already know and trying to learn what you should not be bothered with.

Determine the number of hours that you can commit to reviewing for the exam. Eight to 10 hours would be two afternoons or four evenings. Do not commit to more than 60 hours, which would be 20 or 30 sessions spread over two or more months. For many engineers, about 20 hours is an appropriate commitment.

To make best use of this finite block of time, perform a sort of triage (a term used for sorting battlefield casualties into those who will survive without treatment, those who can survive with treatment, and those who will not survive—first priority is given to the middle group). You can most safely skip reviewing those skills that you use regularly. On the other hand, there is little benefit, per unit of study effort, in trying to learn any complicated skills you did not learn in school or have not needed on the job. This is a review book; it is not intended to teach skills from scratch. Concentrate on the middle group of skills—those you learned in school but have not needed on the job, or those you sometimes use on the job but do not feel expert in.

Chapter 2 will familiarize you with both kinds of problems appearing on the exam. A realistic and up-to-date vehicle for a timed dry run is available in a separate book, *Authentic Practice Exam for the Professional Engineers' Examination for Industrial Engineers,* published by Engineering & Management Press. In addition to scorer-approved solutions, that book also contains scoring guides, exam administration rules, and specimens of actual exam materials.

The remainder of this book, chapters 3 through 8, contains supporting material for the bulk of your review effort. It is organized by specific skills and contains more than one hundred solved examples. Plan to spend most of your review time honing your skills in these chapters. Skip everything that seems too easy or too hard.

1.5 Doing Your Best

This section reviews exam-taking tactics. It should be reviewed a day or two before taking the exam.

1.5.1 Time Management

Industrial engineers, of all people, should be good at time management. Nevertheless, solution booklets for the IE PE Exam often exhibit unmistakable signs of poor time use. A candidate may score eight or 10 points on one or two problems, then two or four points on others, writing incomplete solutions and ending with an "Out of time!" scrawl. Obviously the most basic principle of time management is simply to be aware of time and be in control of how you use it. You should set aside the first few minutes to scan all the problem statements. Then start on the easiest part of the easiest problem, intending to spend at most 45 minutes on any one problem.

To maintain control of how you use your time, envision *points earned* versus *time spent* as having the diminishing-return relationship illustrated in figure 1-1. Every problem will have a different curve of the same general shape. Use figure 1-1 to envision how to balance your efforts. If two problems had the same curve, you would earn more points by working up to point A for each of them than by working up to point B for one and point C for the other. This shows that if all problems and parts of problems had diminishing returns per unit of time spent, and any setup time required to shift from one task to another were ignored, it would always be best to work on the easiest (greatest points per unit time) task that remains to be done.

Of course the real situation is closer to that of figure 1-2 in which points come in "chunks," and the easiest parts cannot always be done first. For example, in figure 1-2 the candidate had to spend five minutes on some setup work worth two points before being able to earn four more points in only two minutes. Nevertheless, the general principles of being aware of time, doing the easiest problems and parts of problems first, and balancing your efforts still hold. It is not suggested that you actually estimate points per unit time for problems; the easiest-first doctrine can be applied when you have only a rough feel for relative difficulties of various parts of the exam.

Strict easiest-first tactics would make you skip around more than you really should. Test takers are often advised, in the spirit of balancing effort, to move on when they get stuck and come back if they have time. But it may cost several minutes to get back into a detailed, complex problem. Leave a problem only if you feel further effort will be nonproductive, not simply because you are faced with 10 minutes of tedious computations while an easy first requirement of another problem beckons. Along with the principle of balancing your effort, which leads to the tactic of answering the easiest problems first, it is advisable to avoid skipping around.

Two final suggestions for good time management are to plan quickly and to avoid chasing rabbits. Chasing rabbits is doing interesting work that does not need to be done, and it is surprising how many candidates waste time investigating side issues that are not directly addressed in the requirements. No matter how interesting a side issue may be, remember that it has zero productivity and should be, literally, the last thing you spend any time on. Time spent in planning—selecting problems, estimating difficulty of pieces of work, and altering the order of work—is overhead time that does not directly earn points. While working on a problem, give full attention to the problem itself (although not to the extent of losing track of time). Work on the requirements of a problem in their natural order unless you feel that one requirement, or part of it, may need to be omitted.

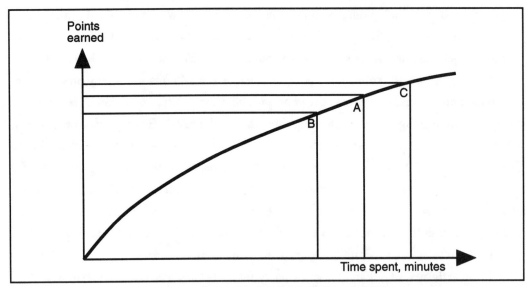

Figure 1-1. Smoothly Diminishing Productivity.

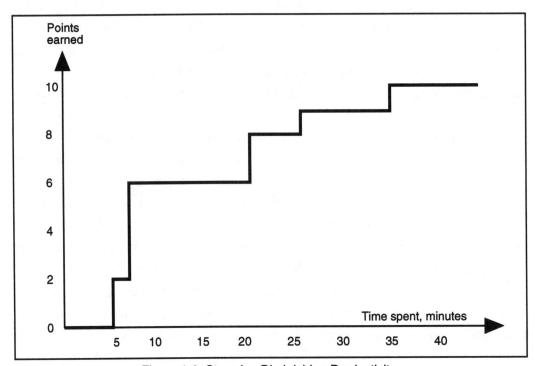

Figure 1-2. Stepwise Diminishing Productivity.

1.5.2 Scorers' Expectations

For essay problems, scorers work from an Item-Specific Scoring Plan (ISSP). The ISSP is developed by first listing aspects of a qualified engineer's approach to the problem at hand: What valid assumptions should be made? Which effects should be considered, and which ignored? Which formulas, algorithms, or techniques are applicable? What degree of accuracy is appropriate? What effects should the engineer recognize as posing possible danger or unreasonable financial burden? Once these characteristics of a qualified response are understood for a specific problem, descriptions are prepared of typical responses that would earn 10 points, eight points, six points, and so forth.

In practice, the resulting scores are not very different from those that could be assigned by an ordinary point system—so many points earned or deducted for doing this or that. The main differences are in liberal treatment of unusual or unexpected responses, unequal weighting of requirements, rational handling of partial credit, and emphasis on supporting work.

Essay problems tend to examine approaches to complex situations. You can be asked for a layout or a line balance or a workstation design, for example, where there is no one best answer; your design or approach might even be better than that of the problem author. An ordinary point system would be biased toward the expected, ordinary response.

If an essay problem has five requirements, each requirement is not necessarily worth two points. Under a carefully developed ISSP, setting up the problem before answering any requirements is often scored more heavily than cranking out the answers, and not all answers are equally weighted in indicating a candidate's qualifications.

Under the ISSP, scorers give partial credit: after a penalty is exacted for an error, subsequent work is scored without further penalty for the consequences of the error. That is, the scorers try to avoid letting an error have a domino effect. However, if an error or unwarranted assumption trivializes subsequent responses, the trivial responses are scored as wrong. (See section 1.5.3, pointer 3.) Scorers expect to see clear, well-organized paths to responses. Most of the test-taking pointers listed below concern supporting work rather than bottom-line answers. Emphasis on supporting work is built into each ISSP because your approaches and methods indicate your qualifications much more surely than whether your answer agrees with that of the problem author.

Some skills do not involve creativity, however, and some situations are narrowly enough defined so that every qualified engineer would take the same approach and achieve the same result. These are the kinds of skills and situations that are examined by the machine-scored problems in the afternoon session of the exam.

Machine-scored problems are edited to remove ambiguities and make distractors attractive without making the question tricky or unfair. The questions are also edited to be independent of each other, so that an error in one will not have a domino effect. The questions are then administered to sample groups of engineers. When too many people give a wrong answer to a question, it is reexamined to determine the cause—ambiguous wording in the question or responses, valid interpretations under which a distractor is correct, trickiness, or simply that a distractor is a good one. Except in the last case, changes are made. Changes are made also if a question is negatively correlated with the rest of the exam (the better one does on the exam, the worse on the question) or if a question is negatively correlated with qualification (better qualified engineers do worse on the question). Finally, after the exam has actually been administered, remaining discrepancies can be resolved by rescoring the question to allow more than one response to be scored as correct.

Because the scoring procedure simply counts the number of correct responses, it is never wise to fail to mark a response to any of the questions in a machine-scored problem. Even if none of the distractors can be identified as incorrect, there is a one-in-five chance of earning a point by answering. In fact, as will be demonstrated by example E1 in chapter 4, if you could eliminate an average of $3\frac{1}{3}$ distractors from each multiple-choice question, you could expect to pass the afternoon portion of the exam!

1.5.3 Pointers for Exam Taking

The following 10 pointers should help you put your best foot forward on the IE PE Exam.

1. High face accuracy is reassuring.

In these days of computers and hand calculators, rightmost digits no longer imply a false claim of precision, because they are useful as a tracer. For example, linear regression is a fixed procedure: If the scorer expects $y = 2.674832 + 13.75543x$ and gets it from you, it is impossible for you to have committed an error, but a rounded-off $y = 2.7 + 13.8x$ could have been given by an unqualified engineer who could not perform linear regression but could sketch the points to scale and draw a straight line through them. As another example, suppose you report $Q = 69.2820$ as the bottom-line answer to an economic order quantity problem where the scorer expects $Q = 20$. The scorer can easily spot that you mixed yearly and monthly figures in the square-root formula for Q, since the ratio of the wrong to right answer is the square root of 12. However, reporting the less accurate $Q = 69$ could hide the source of the error. It is to your advantage for scorers to trace sources of errors because the engineer who did something mysterious and unfathomable is far down the ISSP list.

2. Second-best judgment is second-best.

A qualified time-study engineer will adjust for performance pace first to get a normal time, then adjust for allowances. Doing it backwards gets the same answer, but raises competency questions even if there is no immediate need for knowing the normal time. For example, if an operation has a 3% scrap rate, do you feed it 1.03 times as many parts? Close, but not the $1/(1 - 0.03)$ answer that would be given by a better qualified engineer.

If you get an unreasonable result and cannot identify what went wrong, at least point out its unreasonableness. If you mix time units and report an economic order quantity as 69 when the correct quantity is 20, you will lose points. But if the problem conditions are such that a quantity as great as 69 should be recognized as too high, don't compound the damage by failing (or pretending to fail) to remark that your answer is unreasonably high.

3. Never trivialize.

The most costly assumption is a trivializing one—one that makes easy what was supposed to be difficult, thereby robbing you of a chance to demonstrate your competence. For example, in a statistical hypothesis test, if you inappropriately assume that two variances are equal, you might lose the opportunity to show that you can handle the more complicated test that applies when variances are unequal.

In a project scheduling problem, if the critical path you compute is shorter than the correct critical path, this may prevent you from showing that you can "crash" the critical path. (This is an example of trivialization by error rather than by assumption.)

In a material requirements planning problem, if your economic order quantity is 69 rather than the correct 20, you may lose the chance to show that you can plan the timing of further shipments, because the 69 units already satisfy all future demand.

One classic kind of trivialization by error trips up a few candidates on nearly every IE PE Exam. A requirement calls for a subtle choice—an investment is barely justified or a hypothesis is almost accepted—but earlier errors make the choice an obvious one. If the point of the requirement is to see whether the candidate can recognize tie-breaking intangibles or identify further needed data, the candidate loses the chance to demonstrate these abilities.

You can catch and correct most errors or assumptions that trivialize further requirements simply by remembering the *tinstaafl* principle ("there is no such thing as a free lunch"). If a requirement turns out to be ridiculously easy or obvious, go back to your earlier work to see why; certainly the problem's author did not intend to give you a free lunch.

4. Avoid ad-hoc methodology.

By brute force, anyone can solve a 3×3 assignment problem, schedule two jobs on two machines, or find the critical path in a very small project network. The scorer cannot distinguish reliably between a candidate who ignores an opportunity to demonstrate competence and one who fails to recognize the opportunity. When you see more than one way to do a problem, discard the ad-hoc method that works only because it is a "toy problem" and choose the method that would work best on bigger, more realistic problems.

In a recent exam, one candidate wrote, "I could set up the matrix and invert it, but it is obvious A is cheaper than B." Since the point of the requirement was to see if the candidate could set up the matrix and invert it, the scorer had to assign the appropriate score. (The scorer claims to have written in reply, "What do you want, an engraved invitation?")

5. Provide traceability.

There is a legend about an engineer who, when pressured for a critical cost estimate, gave as his entire report the figure $3,790,415.56 centered on a sheet of bond paper and bound in a blue folder.

Think of the scorer as a client or technical supervisor who is checking your work in detail. Anything unclear will be questioned, and the scorer's only way of questioning is to reduce your score. No number or conclusion should appear as an answer or in a formula or table without its ancestry being clear. Remember: The scorer is more interested in how you proceeded than in the bottom-line answer.

6. Neatness counts.

(Actually it is good organization that counts, not neatness per se; neatness is an issue only if it is difficult for scorers to interpret what you have written.) Some candidates seem to be sloppy on purpose, almost as if they hope the scorer will move past the indecipherable mess and assume it is correct. More likely, a scorer forced to go through a response with a fine-toothed comb will find some nits to pick.

Not only is good organization among the hallmarks of a qualified engineer, but it is a central issue in certain requirements when the response involves descriptions, subjective comparisons, identification of key factors, or advocacy. One valuable tactic is to put all your false starts and initial scratchwork on the left-facing scratch pages provided in the solutions booklet, or at least cross out such work. Let the scorer read only the neat, properly organized, correct work. (Crossed-out matter is completely ignored by scorers; in the sense of page appearance, neatness really does not count.)

7. Never change the question.

Always answer the question that you judge the author is trying to ask, not what you think should have been asked instead. The context governs. "Per hour" might mean "per machine-hour"; "crash cost" might be for maximal crashing or for crashing for one time unit, and it might be the extra cost or the total cost—whatever is reasonable in context. "Best" might mean "least cost" or "greatest profit" or (if a time spread is involved) "greatest net present worth."

Faced with red herrings (distracting, irrelevant facts), misprints, inconsistencies, or poor wording, the more qualified engineer will brush them aside while the less qualified engineer will choke.

8. Avoid telegraphing incompetence.

For some reason, many candidates waste one or two solution pages copying down or paraphrasing the situations and requirements. This smacks of marking time while mentally floundering, or of trying to lull the scorer ("Duh, two pages so far and nothing incorrect yet; good candidate!"). If iterating the data helps fix the problem in your mind, fine—but you should put the meaningless copy work on a scratch sheet. In general, the best-qualified engineer's solution will show only valid progress.

If 40 data points are given and you decide it is relevant to compute their sample mean and standard deviation, use your hand calculator and report something like in figure 1-3 (where 30.7 is the first datum and 19.1 is the last):

Mean: $\dfrac{(30.7+...+19.1)}{40} = \underline{21.7944}$

Sample variance: $\dfrac{(30.7^2+...+19.1^2)-\dfrac{1}{40}(30.7+...+19.1)^2}{40-1} = \underline{196.7006}$

Sample standard deviation: $\sqrt{196.7006} = \underline{14.025}$

Figure 1-3. Sample Solution.

This shows, without writing all 40 numbers, exactly how the quantities were computed. Some candidates simply give the name of the calculator whose routine was used, as if to imply that it is the calculator's fault if the result is incorrect. What this really says to the scorer is that the candidate is probably ignorant of some detail such as whether the calculator's sample variance function uses n or $n-1$ in the denominator.

Another telltale sign of ignorance is to give overly elaborate references for an unimportant procedure, such as a textbook page citation for a standard engineering economy compound interest factor. Dilution, whereby the candidate gives more than one answer, is usually taken as a sign of ignorance. The qualified engineer will give the right answer only; if a candidate gives n answers, with the right one among them, the scorer should award $1/n$ of full credit.

In general, you will lose any game you try to play with the scorers. The engineer who manipulates emphasis in technical reports to divert attention from the truth is the kind of engineer the process is designed to stamp out, not license.

9. Do not unnecessarily complicate things.

The well-qualified engineer realizes what the problem is mainly about and does not find it necessary to invent side issues. For example, if you are given that hourly labor costs of $21.60 include overhead and fringe benefits and that there is time-and-one-half for overtime, and if the problem is about balancing an assembly line rather than about wage administration, you can bet that $1.5 \times \$21.60 = \$32.40$ is the appropriate hourly overtime cost. Some fringe-benefit items are omitted from overtime, and some overhead items are different as well, but to make a correction for this you would need to assume two fringe benefit rates and two overhead rates. If that can of worms were meant to be opened, the data would have been given.

The qualified engineer respects traditional practice. It seems unnecessarily pedantic to give a year 365.25 days instead of the traditional 365. All you will accomplish by doing so is to make your answer look slightly wrong at first glance. Cash flows are traditionally treated as occurring at the end of a year rather than continuously throughout the year, even when the latter is more realistic. An economic comparison on the basis of future worth in a situation in which it is traditional to use present worth or equivalent annual cash flow may confuse a scorer; even if it does not, a qualified engineer does not indulge in unnecessary complications.

10. Manage time and select familiar problems.

Even if the exam you take is not one in which you choose which problems to solve, time management and problem selection are critical. As discussed earlier in this chapter, you can best be sure of performing up to your actual qualifications if you use your time where it earns the greatest number of points. And if you must choose which problems or requirements to solve, it is best to choose on the solid basis of your existing skills and knowledge rather than on an illusory basis of perceived difficulty, brevity, or straightforwardness.

Chapter 2
Major Application Areas

This chapter reviews the application areas included in the exam and discusses the skills most often needed to solve problems in each area. Ten problems are presented that are typical of those actually appearing in the IE PE Exam.

2.1 Facility Design and Operations

Specifications for the 1994 IE PE Exam call for two problems in the general area of facilities, one problem being of the essay type and the other being a set of 10 multiple-choice questions, each with five choices. The possible application areas for both problems are listed as site selection, plant layout, equipment, material handling and waste management systems, packaging equipment, capacity analysis, and power service and other utility requirements. In practice, most facilities problems concern facility location, facility layout, material handling design, or facility operations.

2.1.1 Facility Location

Facility location problems frequently are conceived by the problem author as an application of a particular methodology and will be presented either straightforwardly (e.g., "formulate and solve the linear program that will identify the best location") or in a thin disguise, where you will be expected to recognize the problem structure and select the appropriate method. Many such methods are those reviewed in chapter 6, particularly section 6.3.3.2.

E1.   At the Epaulet oil refinery in West Texas, there are six process plants $P_1, ..., P_6$ currently served poorly by the central process water system. It is desired to drill new wells to serve some of them better and relieve load on the central system. The potential demands for supplemental water for the six plants are 200, 400, 400, 500, 300, and 400 gpm respectively. Four sites $W_1, ..., W_4$ have been identified at which wells could be drilled, having capacities to supply 300, 400, 400, and 500 gpm, respectively. Any well drilled will be connected by underground piping to one plant, will serve that plant only, and must be adequate for that plant's entire potential demand. The equivalent annual benefits of supplemental water for the six plants, in thousands of dollars, are 25, 30, 30, 35, 35, and 40, respectively. The costs of drilling a well, connecting it to a plant, and operating it have been estimated and converted to equivalent annual costs in thousands of dollars:

Equivalent annual cost if serving plant...

Well site	P_1	P_2	P_3	P_4	P_5	P_6
W_1	15	19	25	11	5	9
W_2	22	15	24	12	7	12
W_3	14	12	26	10	17	18
W_4	17	12	20	9	7	13

Determine which wells should be drilled, if any, and which plants they should serve.

This problem has the structure of an assignment problem (see section 6.3.3.3) and can be solved by the assignment algorithm. The initial cost table, where M is a large cost to prevent assignments of inadequate wells, and the negative costs are the benefits, is

	P_1	P_2	P_3	P_4	P_5	P_6
W_1	$-25 + 15$ $= -10$	M	M	M	$-35 + 5$ $= -30$	M
W_2	$-25 + 22$ $= -3$	$-30 + 15$ $= -15$	$-30 + 24$ $= -6$	M	$-35 + 7$ $= -28$	$-40 + 12$ $= -28$
W_3	$-25 + 14$ $= -11$	$-30 + 12$ $= -18$	$-30 + 26$ $= -4$	M	$-35 + 17$ $= -18$	$-40 + 18$ $= -22$
W_4	$-25 + 17$ $= -8$	$-30 + 12$ $= -18$	$-30 + 20$ $= -10$	$-35 + 9$ $= -26$	$-35 + 7$ $= -28$	$-40 + 13$ $= -27$

The most negative cost (greatest profit) in the cost table is –30. To get all nonnegative costs, add 30 to every element in the table. Let 30 plus a large number M be another large number also called M. Add two dummy wells with all-zero cost rows.

	P_1	P_2	P_3	P_4	P_5	P_6
W_1	20	M	M	M	0	M
W_2	27	15	24	M	2	2
W_3	19	12	26	M	12	8
W_4	22	12	20	4	2	3
W_5	0	0	0	0	0	0
W_6	0	0	0	0	0	0

The cost table is ready to begin solution by the Hungarian algorithm. Subtract the minimal element from each row. (The columns all already have zero elements.) Make as many zero-relative-cost assignments as possible.

	P_1	P_2	P_3	P_4	P_5	P_6
W_1	20	M	M	M	(0)	M
W_2	25	13	22	M	0	(0)
W_3	11	4	18	M	4	0
W_4	20	10	18	2	0	1
W_5	0	0	0	(0)	0	0
W_6	0	0	(0)	0	0	0

Only four assignments can be made. Cover all zeros with four lines:

	P_1	P_2	P_3	P_4	P_5	P_6
W_1	20	M	M	M	0	M
W_2	25	13	22	M	0	0
W_3	11	4	18	M	4	0
W_4	20	10	18	2	0	1
W_5	0	0	0	0	0	0
W_6	0	0	0	0	0	0

The minimal uncovered element is 2. Subtract 2 from the uncovered elements, add 2 to the line-intersection (doubly covered) elements, and again make as many zero-relative-cost assignments as possible.

	P_1	P_2	P_3	P_4	P_5	P_6
W_1	18	M	M	M	(0)	M
W_2	23	11	20	M	0	(0)
W_3	9	2	16	M	4	0
W_4	18	8	16	(0)	0	1
W_5	0	(0)	0	0	2	2
W_6	0	0	(0)	0	2	2

Five assignments can be made. Cover all zeros with five lines:

	P_1	P_2	P_3	P_4	P_5	P_6
W_1	18	M	M	M	0	M
W_2	23	11	20	M	0	0
W_3	9	2	16	M	4	0
W_4	18	8	16	0	0	1
W_5	0	0	0	0	2	2
W_6	0	0	0	0	2	2

The minimal uncovered element is 2. Subtract 2 from the uncovered elements, add 2 to the line-intersection (doubly covered) elements, and again make as many zero-relative-cost assignments as possible.

	P_1	P_2	P_3	P_4	P_5	P_6
W_1	16	M	M	M	(0)	M
W_2	21	9	18	M	0	(0)
W_3	7	(0)	14	M	4	0
W_4	16	6	14	(0)	0	1
W_5	(0)	0	0	2	4	4
W_6	0	0	(0)	2	4	4

Six assignments can be made. The optimal assignments are for wells to be drilled at all four sites and assigned to plants as follows: W_1 to P_5, W_2 to P_6, W_3 to P_2, and W_4 to P_4. Plants P_1 and P_3 will not receive supplemental water. To recover the net benefits we can go back to the original cost table and mark the corresponding assignments:

	P_1	P_2	P_3	P_4	P_5	P_6
W_1	−25 + 15 = −10	M	M	M	−35 + 5 = −30	M
W_2	−25 + 22 = −3	−30 + 15 = −15	−30 + 24 = −6	M	−35 + 7 = −28	−40 + 12 = −28
W_3	−25 + 14 = −11	−30 + 12 = −18	−30 + 26 = −4	M	−35 + 17 = −18	−40 + 18 = −22
W_4	−25 + 17 = −8	−30 + 12 = −18	−30 + 20 = −10	−35 + 9 = −26	−35 + 7 = −28	−40 + 13 = −27

The overall equivalent annual net benefit is $102,000, consisting of $140,000 of equivalent annual supplemental-water benefits realized in the plants, less the $38,000 equivalent annual cost of drilling and connecting the wells.

2.1.2 Facility Layout

Facility layout problems, especially those that can be solved by using activity relationship charts (see section 6.3.3.1), frequently appear in the IE PE Exam. In addition, layout issues often appear as sidebars in material-handling problems.

2.1.3 Material Handling Design

Material handling is so central to industrial engineering that its issues can play a part in almost any problem. When material handling is the main theme of a problem, the problem is likely to test engineering judgment more than methodology. An essay problem can, for example, give a detailed description of an operation and ask you to identify the material-handling principles that are being violated and to propose improvements. Or, it could ask you to design a layout based on material handling considerations. Machine-scored material-handling problems are likely to be more quantitative.

E2.   The soup division of a food processing plant is laid out in four functional kettle areas having the following capacities in numbers of 2000-gal batches of soup processed per kettle per day:

Area	Capacity
Heater kettle	14
Mixer kettle	8
Slow kettle	8
Evaporator kettle	6

The plant produces 100 batches of soup per day. Batches for the various recipes are pumped from kettle to kettle along one of the following kettle routes:

Route	Kettle sequence	Load, batches per day
1	Heater, Mixer, Evaporator	20
2	Mixer, Slow	14
3	Mixer, Slow, Evaporator	10
4	Heater, Mixer, Evaporator	12
5	Heater, Mixer	20
6	Heater, Mixer, Slow, Evaporator	24

(Two of the routes are identical, but are treated separately for reasons that need not concern us.)

The physical arrangement of the four functional areas is one of the five layouts shown below (H, M, S, and E label the heater kettle area, mixer kettle area, slow kettle area, and evaporator kettle area, respectively):

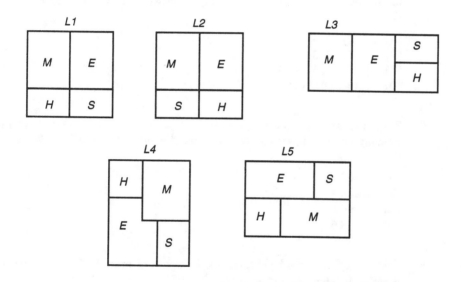

The layout uses the minimum possible number of kettles, but the pumping of material between kettle areas may be excessive. You are to investigate the possibility of converting to a three-cell, cell-manufacturing layout with each cell covering one or more of the existing routes. Pumping between areas would be particularly economical if all the pumps and lines could be of the standard 40-batch-per-day capacity.

QUESTIONS 1–10

1. Rank the alternative functional layouts *L1* through *L5* from worst to best:

   (A) *L3, L2, L1, L5, L4*
   (B) *L4, L3, L1, L2, L5*
   (C) *L4, L5, L1, L2, L3*
   (D) *L1, L2, L3, L5, L4*

2. The number of heater kettles, mixer kettles, slow kettles, and evaporator kettles currently in use, respectively, is presumably

    (A) 1, 1, 1, 1
    (B) 5, 10, 7, 12
    (C) 6, 13, 6, 11
    (D) 8, 13, 13, 17

3. If the kettle manufacturer offered as a free demonstration to modify one kettle in one area so as to increase its capacity by four batches per day, which kind of kettle should it be?

    (A) Heater
    (B) Mixer
    (C) Slow kettle
    (D) Evaporator

4. If kettles were rearranged into cells, each cell handling all of one or more routes, which of the following route compositions of cells would be most attractive both in staying within a 40-batch-per-day capacity and in requiring the fewest kettles?

    (A) (1, 3), (2, 6), (4, 5)
    (B) (1, 5), (2, 3), (4, 6)
    (C) (1, 5), (2, 3, 4), (6)
    (D) Either (B) or (C)

5. There exists one three-cell layout that uses as few machines as the functional-area layout does. It has two cells that handle only one route each. Which are those routes?

    (A) 1 and 3
    (B) 2 and 4
    (C) 3 and 5
    (D) 4 and 6

6. Under the functional layout, the total amount of material handling between areas, in batches per day, is

    (A) 100
    (B) 190
    (C) 290
    (D) 310

7. Under a cell-manufacturing layout with cells made of routes (1, 5), (2, 3), and (4, 6), the total amount of material handling between areas, in batches per day, is

    (A) 0
    (B) 24
    (C) 100
    (D) 190

8. Under the functional layout, the total amount of material handling within areas, in batches per day, is

    (A) 0
    (B) 24
    (C) 100
    (D) 190

9. Under the cell-manufacturing layout with cells made of routes (1, 5), (2, 3), and (4, 6), the total amount of material handling within areas, in batches per day, is

    (A) 0
    (B) 24
    (C) 100
    (D) 190

10. It is desirable for cells to be specialized to minimize scheduling, training, and maintenance within cells. If the goal is first to maximize specialization, next to minimize the number of kettles, and third to stay within standard pumping capacity, which of the following cell-manufacturing layouts should be chosen?

    (A) (1, 4), (2, 5), (3, 6)
    (B) (1, 5), (2, 3, 4), (6)
    (C) (1, 3), (2, 6), (4, 5)
    (D) (1, 5), (2, 3), (4, 6)

ANSWERS:

Question 1 can be answered by activity-relationship analysis (section 6.3.3.1). The relevant interactions between areas are the total flows from one area to another. The flow H → M, for example, appears in routes 1, 4, 5, and 6 and the total is 20+12+20+24 = 76 batches per day. The other interactions and total flows are: M → E, 32; M → S, 48; and S → E, 34. Layout L1 provides poorly for the 48 batch-per-day flow M → S. Layout L2 provides poorly for the 76 batch-per-day flow H → M. Layout L3 provides very poorly for both of those flows. Layout L4 provides well for every flow. Layout L5 does almost but not quite as well as L4, having a shorter common boundary for the flow M → E. Thus the ranking from worst to best is that given in answer (A).

Question 2 can be answered by determining how many kettles of the various kinds are necessary to handle the current load. Heater kettles process each batch that takes route 1, 4, 5, or 6; there are 20+12+20+24 = 76 such batches per day, and each heater kettle can process 14 batches per day, so the number of kettles is 76/14 rounded up, or 6. Similarly the numbers of kettles of the other types are 100/8, 48/8, and 66/6, rounded up, respectively. Answer (C) is correct.

Question 3 really asks, since we have no basis for assuming one kind of kettle is more expensive than another, how many kettles could be decommissioned as a result of the capacity increase. If the four-batch-per-day increase were implemented on a heater kettle, we would need enough kettles to process 76–4 = 72 batches per day, requiring 72/14 = 5.14 → 6 kettles compared to 6 previously. Similarly, for mixers, slow kettles, or evaporators we get 12 compared to 13, 5.5 → 6 compared to 6, and 10.33 → 11 compared to 11, respectively. Of these alternatives, only the capacity increase in a mixer kettle will make a kettle redundant. Answer (B) is correct. If the increase is misconstrued as applying to *all* kettles of a given kind, it would appear that the most beneficial capacity increase would be for evaporator kettles, leading to selection of the incorrect answer (D).

Question 4 can be answered by determining for each set of cells whether each cell processes 40 or fewer batches per day (all of them do) and the sum of the numbers of kettles required. The first cell in answer (A), for example, which combines routes 1 and 3, must process 20 batches per day in its heaters, 30 in its mixers, 10 in its slow kettles, and 30 in its evaporators. The cell as a whole processes 30 batches per day. Dividing by the capacities (14, 8, 8, and 6 batches per day, respectively) and rounding up, we see that the cell requires 2, 4, 2, and 5 kettles of the respective kinds. Similarly the second cell in answer (A) processes 38 batches per day and requires 2, 5, 5, and 4 kettles of the respective kinds; and the final cell in answer (A) processes 32 batches per day and requires 3, 4, 0, and 2 kettles of the respective kinds. The total number of kettles is 38 (one more heater and one more slow kettle than were required in a functional-area layout). The cells in answer (B) stay within 40 batches per day and require only 37 kettles; and the cells in answer (C) stay within 40 batches per day and require 37 kettles. Thus answers (B) and (C) both give the most attractive route compositions of cells, so that answer (D) is correct.

Question 5 has correct answer (D):

Routes in Cell	Batches per day	No. of heaters	No. of mixers	No. of slow kettles	No. of evaporators
1, 2, 3, 5	64	3	8	3	5
4	12	1	2	0	2
6	24	2	3	3	4
		6	13	6	11

This layout uses only 36 kettles, the same number (and the same number of each kind) as was used by the functional layout. No other 3-cell layout achieves this. Note that the first cell processes more than 40 batches per day and will require more pumping capacity than is provided by a standard 40-batch-per-day pumping system.

Question 6 can be answered from the data developed for question 1 or from the raw data. From the raw data, the 20 batches per day taking route 1 flow twice from area to area, the 14 batches per day taking route 2 flow once from area to area, and so forth. The total is 190 batches per day; answer (B) is correct.

Question 7 is easy to answer since in a complete cell-manufacturing layout there is flow only within cells, not between cells. Answer (A) is correct.

Question 8 is also easy to answer since in a functional layout there is flow only between areas, not within areas. Answer (A) is correct.

Question 9 asks for the total flow within cells, which is the entire 190 batches per day; answer (D) is correct.

Question 10 requires load-balancing computations of the kind already performed for questions 1 and 5. But first, note that the layouts given in answers (A) and (D) are the only ones that exhibit cell specialization to the extent of having two cells that contain only three of the four kinds of kettle; for example, cell (1, 5) needs no slow kettles and cell (2, 3) needs no heaters. The other two layouts can be eliminated because they each have only one cell with any specialization. Of the two highly specialized layouts, balance computations show that the layout of answer (A) needs 40 kettles, whereas the layout of answer (D) needs 37 kettles. Answer (D) is correct. (Pumping capacity would be considered only if the two candidates needed the same number of kettles.)

2.1.4 Facility Operation

As contrasted with facility-design problems, most facility-operation problems on the IE PE Exam can also be characterized as operations research problems—that is, applications of optimization or queueing theory. However, pure facility-operation problems do occur occasionally. For instance, an industrial engineer who in in charge of the operation of facilities is frequently the person who pays utility bills, negotiates rates, and adjusts operations to minimize utility costs. Recognizing this, an appropriate problem would be to determine the effects on an enterprise's electrical bills of adjusting operations so as to keep the maximum demand below a given limit. To solve the problem properly, a candidate would have to understand the ordinary provisions of demand charges and how a commercial electric bill is calculated (not reviewed in this book).

2.2 Management Systems

Industrial engineers frequently help design, plan, or operate management systems— organizational structures, incentive plans, productivity programs such as total quality management (TQM), staffing plans, training programs, arbitration programs, and the like— that directly deal with management and control of the behavior of people in an enterprise. The NCEES analysis of industrial engineering requirements (NCEES 1989) implies that about 15 percent of the exam (1.2 questions on an eight-question exam) should consist of management-systems problems concerning areas identified as organization design, staffing plans, productivity, human resources, and payment systems. Questions should cover planning of management systems, detailed design of management systems, operation of management systems, or a combination. The actual current exam specifications list two questions in which management principles are likely to be emphasized (see section 1.2): an essay question (#173) on work and safety, and a multiple-choice question (#473) on either or both of management systems and computer information systems. In chapter 8, examples E85 and E88 are typical of complete essay problems concerning management per se, and example E95a and E95b are typical of complete essay problems concerning safety.

E3.   You have been invited by Gary Ball, owner of Gary Ball Ford, an automobile dealership in a suburb of Wheeling, West Virginia, to meet with him concerning the possibility of helping him start a TQM program for his dealership, especially the parts and service operations. You were recommended to him as a TQM facilitator by one of your clients. In preparation for the meeting, you have visited the dealership several times and have noted the following things concerning parts and service operations:

1. Most operating procedures seem to be those taught or imposed by Ford and are appropriate for an extremely reliable system.

2. The actual systems at the dealership appear to be unreliable; a high percentage of work is not completed by the time the service writer promised it to the customer, a high percentage of parts orders supposedly made are not made, and a high percentage of parts received are gone by the time the customer brings in the vehicle for them to be installed. Of 20 incoming service customers observed, five were bringing the vehicle back for at least a second visit on the same problem within the past month. Of 27 total customers incoming and outgoing, seven voiced vigorous verbal complaints at some point.

3. A large sign in the service area reads, "Current customer satisfaction index: 94%."

4. Case: A customer asked for a customer-satisfaction rating form. The service writer said he was out of them and referred the customer to the cashier, who said she was out of them. Then the service writer said, "But you will get a phone call from a Ford representative asking whether you were satisfied." The call never came.

5. Case: A customer brought in a car for a recall catalytic converter replacement according to an appointment made when the part came in (although there were about 70 identical converters replaced under the recall program that month, none were stocked in advance). The customer waited for the repair. After 2.0 hours it was found that the part had apparently been used on another job. The customer was sent home with a promise to reorder the part and notify the customer upon receipt. After a week, the customer called back and there was no record of the order. The part was ordered again. After another week, the part came in and was installed.

6. Case: Early in the morning as a female employee arrived, a male employee stated, "You and your husband must have made love last night, because you look radiant—positively radiant." No reply was made.

At your meeting with Gary Ball you hope to get his commitment to launch a TQM program at the dealership, and to use you as consultant and facilitator. Write an agenda that will outline everything that you intend to tell him and ask him at the meeting.

Before giving the agenda, I will review the implications of the above observations and review my aims for the meeting.

The observations show that there is a quality problem and that there does exist hypocrisy and concealment about it. An obvious cause is evident: Procedures seem to be spelled out and perhaps enforced, so that employees tend to substitute following the prescribed procedures for taking the initiative. For example, in the ideal world contemplated by the procedures, the mechanic lets the car cool down, opens the exhaust system, sends the helper to bring the new converter, and installs it. That works fine in the ideal world because the new converter is there. But apparently at Gary Ball Ford the new converter is often not there; hence a well motivated employee will send for the converter before the car is cool, or at least check that it is there—even though this takes extra time. Designate this hypothesis, and the example that goes with it, as *Story 1*. "I" appear not to have observed anything about employees' work attitudes; too bad, because normally I would be armed with a good understanding of them at the first meeting if I had observed the service of 27 customers. I do not place any significant organizational interpretation on observation 6 (the sexist remark); it does not indicate anything unusual or revealing.

This first meeting will involve only Gary and me (as is appropriate), and not the service manager, parts manager, or other employees. It is not appropriate to go for full closure at this meeting, since many more people than just Gary and me must be fully committed for the TQM program to have a chance of success. Thus my ambition at the meeting will be to get Gary to commit to hire me to observe and study the dealership, educate Gary and several others about TQM, set TQM objectives, and build a consensus for starting the program. My agenda for this meeting:

1. Introduce myself and my credentials only to the extent necessary to establish my credibility with Gary. Once he believes I am someone he should be talking to about TQM, proceed to the next item.

2. Listen. With patience for digressions and with as little prompting and leading questions from me as possible, try to find out:

   • What is Gary's motive in investigating TQM? What things does he think could be improved? How does he hope TQM would change his dealership?

   • What qualities or behaviors of his dealership does he appear to be defensive about?

   • Does he value his employees? His customers? Ford? Does he appear to be willing to give consideration to changes that may diminish his personal power?

3. Only if invited, and only if necessary, give an introductory TQM speil.

4. I will almost certainly *not* have occasion to recite the observations listed above. If Gary challenges my general understanding of his operation, I may recite *Story 1*. If Gary denies all specific problems while admitting general ones, I may select an observation or two so that a concrete example is at hand.

5. Try to determine, and to get Gary's agreement about, who besides him and me should be in on the beginnings of the possible TQM project.

6. If Gary shows a willingness to proceed and an understanding of the level of commitment needed, discuss fee and set up the next meeting, to include the service manager, parts manager, chief service writer, and key others.

2.3 Manufacturing Systems

Current IE PE Exam specifications call for two manufacturing problems. The manufacturing essay problem given in the morning can cover these application areas: products, manufacturing processes, maintenance procedures, operations sequencing, machine grouping, robotics, automation, and value engineering. The multiple-choice manufacturing problem given in the afternoon can cover the same application areas. Skills expected to be tested include probability and statistics, measurement and instrumentation, operations research, manufacturing materials, manufacturing processes, systems design and analysis, and cost engineering or engineering economics. These specifications are very general, and in practice the problems usually turn out to be ones that could also be classified as problems in facilities, production, work and safety, or quality control, except that they cannot be in a non-manufacturing environment.

E4.   **Forfitters, Inc. specializes in stainless steel macrofittings such as seamless flanged nipples that allow pipe fabricators to avoid butt welds. Forfitters also fabricates various rotating assemblies in stainless steel. One such assembly, forged of parts A, B, C, D, and E as shown below, requires a tight overall length tolerance on the dimension from the left face of A to the right face of E. This length must be 23±0.03 cm. If the standard deviation of length is 0.01 cm, the process will be considered to be in control. The ±0.03-cm tolerance, like all tolerances in the Forfitters shop, is a ±3σ tolerance.**

Due to the precision of Forfitters' forge-welding process, the final assembled lengths of all parts can each meet a tolerance of ±0.021 cm. The design lengths of parts A, B, C, D, and E are 2, 5, 6, 7, and 3 cm, respectively.

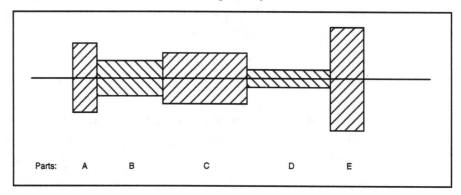

QUESTIONS 1-10:

1.   **The proportion of assemblies that will fail to meet the overall length tolerance is most nearly**

    (A)   0.02
    (B)   0.04
    (C)   0.06
    (D)   0.08

2. What proportion of assemblies would have to meet the overall length tolerance in order for the process to be considered to be conforming and in control?

    (A) 1
    (B) 0.9997
    (C) 0.997
    (D) 0.97

3. With the process centered at 23 cm, an $\bar{x}$-chart is prepared. If its lower and upper control limits are 22.97 cm and 23.03 cm, and are based on the specifications rather than on current process capabilities, what is the apparent sample lot size?

    (A) 1
    (B) 2
    (C) 3
    (D) 4

4. With the process centered at 23 cm, an $\bar{x}$-chart is prepared. If its lower and upper control limits are 22.977 cm and 23.023 cm, and are based on process capabilities, what is the apparent sample lot size?

    (A) 1
    (B) 2
    (C) 3
    (D) 4

5. An $\bar{x}$-chart having LCL = 22.980 and UCL = 23.020 is being monitored. Five successive lots give readings 23.005, 22.985, 22.984, 22.996, 22.978. An out-of-control condition is first detected upon receipt of which reading?

    (A) The second
    (B) The third
    (C) The fourth
    (D) The fifth

6. Assume that the process ordinarily has a scrap rate of 5%. If a p-chart is being designed for monitoring the scrap proportion in lots of size 20, a reasonable LCL, center, and UCL would be

    (A) 0.015, 0.05, 0.085
    (B) 0, 0.05, 0.115
    (C) −0.0962, 0.05, 0.1962
    (D) 0, 0.05, 0.1962

7. The proportion of assemblies that does not meet the overall length tolerance but could be adjusted to do so by milling not more than 0.001 cm off the right end is most nearly

    (A) 0.005
    (B) 0.025
    (C) 0.045
    (D) 0.065

8. The cost of a completed assembly is considered to be $84, or $98 if milling is performed. Forfitters considers nonconforming products to have no scrap value, and considers "cost per conforming piece" to include cost of nonconforming pieces, allocated over conforming pieces only. The cost per conforming assembly is most nearly

    (A) $85
    (B) $87
    (C) $89
    (D) $93

9. If *all* assemblies that were too long could be milled to conform, what would be the answer to the foregoing question?

    (A) $85
    (B) $87
    (C) $89
    (D) $93

10. Of the following choices, assuming that all too-long assemblies can be milled to conform and that the previously cited costs apply, which is the best length on which to center the process of producing the assemblies? (The expected lengths of the five parts would increase proportionately.)

    (A) 23 cm
    (B) 23.01 cm
    (C) 23.02 cm
    (D) 23.03 cm

ANSWERS:

1. The variance of overall length is the sum of the variances of the lengths of the five parts (the lengths are assumed to be statistically independent). Given a 3σ tolerance of ± 0.021 cm, the standard deviation for each part is $0.021/3 = 0.007$ cm. The sum of the variances for the five parts is $\sigma^2 = 5\times(0.007)^2 = 0.000245$, so the standard deviation is $\sigma = 0.015652476$. It is reasonable to assume that the length is normally

distributed. The z statistic for conformance is $z = \pm 0.03/\sigma = \pm 1.91663$. From table 4-3 there is a probability $\alpha \approx 0.028$ that the length is too long, and there is the same probability that it is too short. $0.028 + 0.028 = 0.056$; answer (C) is correct.

2. A convention of quality control (see section 4.3.1) is that a process is considered to be conforming if it consistently produces to specifications—"consistently" meaning that the proportion of instances outside $\pm 3\sigma$ limits is no more than the normal probability associated with being outside $z = \pm 3$. This probability is about 0.0026—0.0013 for being below the lower limit, and 0.0013 for being above the upper limit. Thus a conforming process produces conforming product at least $1 - 0.0026 = 99.74\%$ of the time. It is "in control" if current evidence (such as data monitored on a control chart) indicates it is currently achieving this. Answer (C) is correct.

3. The specifications assume that the assembly-length standard deviation σ is 0.01 cm, so the limits of the $\bar{x}$-chart would be set to the center plus or minus $3\sigma/\sqrt{n}$ where n is the sample lot size. Since the limits are set to the center plus or minus 0.03, n is evidently 1. Answer (A) is correct.

4. Given the length standard deviation $\sigma = 0.015652476$ achieved by the process (see the solution to question 1), if the sample size is n and the upper limit is 23.023, then for $z = 3$ equation 4-14 is $3 = (23.023 - 23)/(\sigma/\sqrt{n})$. Thus $n = (3\sigma/0.023)^2 \approx 4$. Answer (D) is correct. We should note here that the standard deviation of the average length of the n assemblies in the lot is $\sigma/\sqrt{n}$. Three of these, for $n = 4$, is 0.0234787, which would lead (with customary rounding) to setting the upper limit 0.023 above the mean.

5. The process is evidently centered on $(LCL + UCL)/2 = 23$ cm and has sigma of 0.0067 (since 3 sigmas is 0.020). The second and third readings are "below two sigmas" (below $23 - 2 \times 0.0067$). From the rules listed in section 4.3.1, the third reading indicates an out-of-control condition by virtue of being the second in a sequence of three to be outside of two sigmas; answer (B) is correct. The fifth reading, being outside three sigmas, also indicates an out-of-control condition, but it is not the first reading to do so.

6. From the p-chart discussion in section 4.3.1, here $n = 20$, $p = 0.05$, and the average of the $\bar{x}$ statistic (the average number of nonconforming assemblies in a lot) is $np = 1$. The variance of the number of nonconforming assemblies is $np(1-p) = 0.95$; the standard deviation is the square root of this, and three of these standard deviations is 2.924 assemblies, so that for an $\bar{x}$-chart the UCL would be set at $1 + 2.924 = 3.924$ nonconforming assemblies in a lot. Since $p = \bar{x}/n$, the corresponding center and UCL are 0.05 and 0.1962. The LCL for $\bar{x}$ would be zero since $1 - 2.924$ is less than zero, and the corresponding LCL for the p-chart is zero. Answer (D) is correct.

7. From the results already calculated the probability that the assembly is too long is about 0.028. This is the expected proportion of assemblies that can be adjusted by milling. But those assemblies for which the milling would take off more than 0.001 cm cannot be adjusted; these have length at least $0.03 + 0.001 = 0.031$ cm greater than the specification. For these $z = 0.031/\sigma \approx 1.9805$, corresponding to a probability of about 0.024. The difference is about 0.004. Answer (A) is correct.

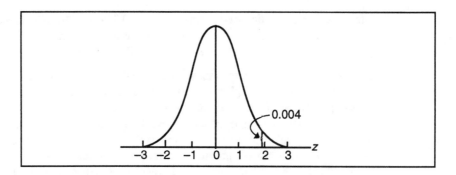

8. The expected cost per assembly (whether or not conforming) can be divided by the probability of conforming.

Class	Proportion	Conforming?	Cost
Too short	0.028	No	84
Milled	0.004	Yes	98
Too long to mill	0.024	No	84
O.K.	0.944	Yes	84

    The expected cost per assembly (whether or not conforming) is $0.028\times84 + 0.004\times98 + 0.024\times84 + 0.944\times84 = \$84.056$. But the proportion conforming is $0.004 + 0.944 = 0.948$. The expected cost per conforming assembly is $84.056/0.948 = \$88.6\overline{6}$. Answer (C) is correct.

9. | Class | Proportion | Conforming? | Cost |
    |---|---|---|---|
    | Too short | 0.028 | No | 84 |
    | Milled | 0.028 | Yes | 98 |
    | O.K. | 0.944 | Yes | 84 |

    The expected cost per assembly (whether or not conforming) would be $0.028\times84 + 0.028\times98 + 0.944\times84 = \$84.392$. But the proportion conforming would be $0.028 + 0.944 = 0.972$. Thus the expected cost per conforming assembly would be $84.392/0.972 \approx \$86.82$. Answer (B) is correct.

10. The criterion would be to minimize the expected cost per conforming assembly. As the centered length increases, the proportion too short will decrease and the proportion too long but reworkable will increase:

Centered length	$z_{too\ short}$	$\alpha_{too\ short}$	$z_{too\ long}$	$\alpha_{too\ long}$	Expected cost per conforming assembly
23	$-0.03/\sigma \approx$ -1.92	0.028	$0.03/\sigma \approx 1.92$	0.028	$(0.028\times84+ 0.028\times98+ 0.944\times84)\div0.972\approx$ $\$86.82$
23.01	$-0.04/\sigma \approx$ -2.56	0.005	$0.02/\sigma \approx$ 1.27775	0.100	$(0.005\times84+ 0.100\times98+ 0.895\times84)\div0.995\approx$ $\$85.83$
23.02	$-0.05/\sigma \approx$ -3.2	0.001	$0.01/\sigma \approx$ 0.639	0.262	$(0.001\times84+ 0.262\times98+ 0.737\times84)\div0.999\approx$ $\$87.76$

Obviously the costs will continue to increase with greater off-centering. Answer (B) is correct.

2.4 Production Planning and Control

Industrial engineers are often responsible for planning and control of production-making operational decisions. In production planning and control, the facilities are fixed and all resources except those acquired specifically for operations are given; the task is to plan and control the direct responses of a system to demands for it to produce.

In a manufacturing environment, for instance, production planning often starts with *demand forecasting*— estimating how much product is needed and when. Given materials and resources on hand and scheduled to be acquired, along with a demand forecast, *production planning* can be performed. A production plan determines, for an immediate future time span, how much product will be produced and when. Given the production plan, engineers can proceed with *material requirements planning*, *line balancing*, and *scheduling and sequencing*. In material requirements planning, it is decided which materials and work-in-progress precursors to the product must be acquired or produced, in what quantities, and when, in order for the production plan to be met. In line balancing, it is decided which resources should be devoted to which parts of the production plan. In scheduling and sequencing, it is decided how parallel and series operations can be arranged for smooth and economical production. From demand forecasting to scheduling and sequencing, all the major activities of production planning and control also occur in non-manufacturing environments (e.g., commercial fishing, printing, grocery check-out, entertainment production, dental practice—any situation in which there is a need to coordinate resources and materials carefully to meet forecasted demand).

E5.   Science Atlantis fabricates its own circuit boards for its cable TV products. Production is based on forecasted demand. For the XA-7 board, recent demand for the months of January, February,..., September was 541, 634, 419, 827, 800, 600, 712, 649, 912. On the basis of this time series and a forecast of 491 for January, the forecast for October is 618.

There is a $5200 cost of setting up for a run, and the monthly holding cost per finished board is considered to be $2.61. Part of the holding cost is due to 5% risk each month that the boards on hand will become obsolete as minor design changes occur.

The minimal attractive rate of return for Science Atlantis is considered to be 1.5% monthly compound interest. A board in inventory has a value of $38.02; if obsolete, $17.00.

A month has 320 operating hours. Each XA-7 board requires 1.065 manhours of operating labor, 8.85 inserter hours, 1.75 washer hours, and 0.71 tester hours. No more than 5 operators, 28 inserters, 6 washers and 4 test stations can be made available for XA-7 fabrication.

QUESTIONS 1-10:

1. The method used for forecasting demand is apparently
    (A) A six-month moving average
    (B) Exponential smoothing with a 0.05 smoothing constant
    (C) Exponential smoothing with a 0.10 smoothing constant
    (D) A method that incorporates trend or seasonality

2. If the forecasting method had been a nine-month moving average (in which case the forecast for October would not have been 618), what probability would be estimated for a demand of at least 1000 in a month?
    (A) Less than 1%
    (B) At least 1% and less than 5%
    (C) At least 5% and less than 10%
    (D) At least 10%

3. With a forecasted demand of 618 boards per month and a production rate of 1000 boards per month, the total monthly setup and holding cost would be minimized by a lot size of most nearly
    (A) 700
    (B) 1600
    (C) 2500
    (D) 3400

4. To minimize monthly setup and holding costs and meet a demand of 618 boards per month, what would be the optimal production rate?
    (A) 600
    (B) 618
    (C) 731
    (D) 900

5. How much of the unit monthly holding cost represents obsolescence?
    (A) none
    (B) $1.00
    (C) $1.05
    (D) $1.90

6. How much of the unit monthly holding cost represents the opportunity cost of capital tied up in inventory?
    (A) none
    (B) $0.32
    (C) $0.57
    (D) $1.90

7. The 30,000-ft^2 "old" warehouse is always full, because its unit monthly operating cost, C_{old}, is lower than that, C_{new}, of the 10,000-ft^2 "new" warehouse, which stays about half full. For any one item, such as the XA-7 board, the contribution of warehouse operating cost to the unit monthly holding cost should be
    (A) C_{new}
    (B) $0.667C_{old} + 0.333C_{new}$
    (C) $0.750C_{old} + 0.250C_{new}$
    (D) $0.857C_{old} + 0.143C_{new}$

8. For a production rate of 1000 boards per month, how many operators, inserters, washers, and testers are required?
    (A) (2, 17, 3, 1)
    (B) (3, 18, 4, 2)
    (C) (3, 25, 5, 2)
    (D) (4, 28, 6, 3)

9. If costs of idle capacity during a run were considered to outweigh all costs associated with inventory, which of the following production rates would be chosen?
    (A) 618
    (B) 750
    (C) 900
    (D) 1200

10. With currently available resources, the maximum possible monthly production rate is most nearly
    (A) 1000
    (B) 1050
    (C) 1100
    (D) unlimited

ANSWERS:

It is probably wise to sketch the demand history to make sure you understand its past behavior.

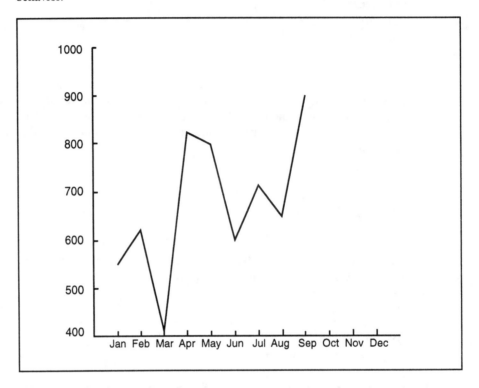

Question 1 requires skill in forecasting, which is reviewed in section 6.1.3.2. The six-month moving average is 750 (equation 6-13). The exponential-smoothing forecast with $\alpha=0.05$ can be calculated by repeated application of equation 6-11; the result is 563.789, or 564 if rounding is done either at the end or at each step. The exponential-smoothing forecast with $\alpha=0.10$ is 618.447 (or 618, 619, or 620, depending on the rounding procedure). A forecast that included trend would presumably respond to the evident upward trend in demand and would produce a forecast somewhere in the neighborhood of 700 to 900. Since the forecast is given as 618, answer (C) is correct.

Question 2 requires skill in basic statistics (see section 4.1). The nine-month moving average is 677.111. Using this method implies an assumption that the nine demands were drawn at random from a single population. The sample standard deviation can be calculated (equation 4-11 or the s routine on a scientific hand calculator) as 153.175, so a demand of 1000 would be (see equation 4-12) $z = (1000 - 677.111)/153.175 = 2.1$ standard deviations greater than the sample mean. From Table 4.4 for the t statistic (page 108), the probability for t = 2.1 with sample size 9 is between 2.5% and 5%. Answer (B) is correct.

Questions 3, 4, 5, and 6 require skill in *economic lot size* (or EOQ—economic order quantity) optimization, which is reviewed in section 6.1.3.1. Question 3 can be answered by applying equation 6-6. Here the demand is $D = 618$ units per month, the setup cost per lot of size Q is $C_p = 5200$, the holding cost per unit per month is $h = 2.61$, and the production rate is $P = 1000$ units per month. Equation 6-6 gives $Q^* = 2538.9782$, so that answer (C) is correct. (Candidates having only a nodding acquaintance with EOQ models will tend to ignore the production rate, use the simplified version of equation 6-6 that omits the quantity $1 - D/P$, obtain the result 1569.2446, and choose incorrect answer (B).)

Question 4 asks whether the current production rate of $P = 1000$ boards per month can be improved upon, considering only setup and holding costs. Equation 6-5 gives the total monthly cost:

$$C_T = \frac{hQ}{2}\left(1 - \frac{D}{P}\right) + CD + C_P\frac{D}{Q}$$

Ignoring any change in the production cost C with production rate P, we see that for any Q an increase in P simply increases the holding-cost term. Thus P should be as small as possible, and since it must be at least 618 boards per month to keep up with the forecasted demand, the optimal is 618; answer (<u>B</u>) is correct. At this production rate there is no inventory, and the optimal lot size Q is infinite—a standing order—so that both the holding-cost and setup-cost terms in equation 6-5 disappear.

Question 5 can be answered by determining the expected value of the monthly loss due to obsolescence. If a board becomes obsolete its value declines from $38.02 to $17.00, and there is a 5% risk of this: $0.05\times(38.02 - 17.00) \approx \$1.05$. Answer (<u>C</u>) is correct. (For a review of expected value, see section 4.1.)

Question 6 requires insight that the interest rate measures the opportunity cost of capital (see section 3.3). A board put into inventory has a value of $38.02. The monthly interest that would otherwise be earned by this amount of capital but is lost by the capital's being tied up in inventory is $0.015\times38.02 \approx \$0.57$. Answer (<u>C</u>) is correct.

Question 7 concerns treatment of marginal costs, reviewed in section 3.1.1.4. The marginal operating cost is C_{new}, because every unit of space used or saved in either warehouse directly or indirectly causes a unit of space to be used or saved in the "new" warehouse as adjustments are made to keep the cheaper warehouse full. Answer (A) is correct; answers (B), (C), and (D) correspond to allocating the costs by fullness, capacity, and usage, none of which reflect the marginal (out-of-pocket) operating cost.

Questions 8, 9, and 10 concern production planning and line balancing methods reviewed in section 6.1. To answer question 8, consider that if a resource is used at a rate U resource-hr per board, and there are $N\times320$ resource-hr available per month, where N is the number of units of the resource available, then the production rate is at most P boards per month: $P \le N\times320\div U$. This implies $N \ge P\times U\div320$. For the various resources, with $P = 1000$:

Operators:	$1000\times1.065\div320 = 3.328 \to 4$
Inserters:	$1000\times8.85\div320 = 27.66 \to 28$
Washers:	$1000\times1.75\div320 = 5.469 \to 6$
Testers:	$1000\times0.71\div320 = 2.219 \to 3$

Answer (D) is correct.

Question 9 requires determining the production rate that has the best balance. Idle capacity occurs when the process is not perfectly balanced, that is, when the integer number of units of a resource assigned, N, exceeds its minimum requirement $P\times U\div320$. For various production rates, we have the following balances:

Resource	U	$P \times U \div 320$ vs. N for monthly production rates P.:				
		618	750	900	1000	1200
Operators	1.065	2.06 → 3	2.50 → 3	3.00 → 3	3.33 → 4	4.00 → 4
Inserters	8.85	17.1 → 18	20.7 → 21	24.9 → 25	27.7 → 28	33.2 → 34
Washers	1.75	3.38 → 4	4.10 → 5	4.92 → 5	5.47 → 6	6.57 → 7
Testers	0.71	1.37 → 2	1.66 → 2	2.00 → 2	2.22 → 3	2.66 → 3

All the production rates except 1200 are feasible (1200 boards per month requires too many inserters and washers). Of the feasible production rates, the rate 900 boards per month is remarkably well balanced. In fact, it has less idle time than the two lower rates do for every resource. Answer (C) is correct.

Question 10 asks for the maximum feasible production rate. From the solution for question 9, we see that 1000 is feasible and 1200 is infeasible. For $P = 1000$, the maximum number of inserters and washers is used, with inserters nearer critical. For 28 inserters, $P \leq 28 \times 320 \div 8.85 \approx 1012$. This is the maximum feasible production rate; answer (A) is correct. A direct way of determining the maximum feasible production rate is to identify the minimum of the resource-limited rates $P \leq N_{avail} \times 320 \div U$. This is $5 \times 320 \div 1.065 \approx 1502$ as limited by operators, $28 \times 320 \div 8.85 \approx 1012$ as limited by inserters, $6 \times 320 \div 1.75 \approx 1097$ as limited by washers, and $4 \times 320 \div 0.71 \approx 1803$ as limited by testers; 1012 is the minimum.

2.5 Inventory Planning and Control

According to exam specifications, inventory planning and control problems will appear on the IE PE Exam primarily as essay problem #172 on production and inventory systems. The application areas listed for this problem are forecasting, production scheduling, project scheduling, production control, inventory control, resource planning, logistics, and distribution. The methodologies listed for this problem are probability and statistics (e.g., analysis of demand distributions, reviewed in section 4.1), computer software (e.g., MRP software, reviewed in section 6.1.3.3.3), operations research (e.g., lot-sizing or EOQ models, reviewed in section 6.1.3.1), work methods and measurement techniques (e.g., time studies, reviewed in section 7.4, as applied to warehousing tasks such as picking, placement, or receiving), manufacturing processes (e.g., line balancing, reviewed in section 6.1.2), systems design and analysis, cost analysis, and engineering economy.

Example E55 in chapter 6 is typical of the kind of straightforward lot-size problem that often appears on the IE PE Exam. Example E56 in chapter 6 is a problem, again typical for the exam, in several aspects of demand forecasting. The practice problem given here as Example E6 is representative of problems that test the candidate's depth of understanding of the basic principles that underlie the methodology—in this case, the probabilistic and cost-analysis principles that underlie lot-size formulas.

E6. A weekly-review inventory information system can be replaced by a continuous-review system at an annual cost of $25,000. The annual benefits of continuous review would be $11,000 plus whatever savings could be realized by reducing safety stock. Annual holding costs are $15,000 plus the cost of capital tied up in inventory, at 15% annual compound interest. The average inventory has a total value of $1,000,000, including $100,000 of safety stock. The inventory turns over 7.8 times annually. Estimate the net annual benefits, if any, of switching to the continuous-review system. Would it be economically worthwhile to switch?

Let a "unit" of inventory be $1. The annual holding cost per unit is $h = 0.015 + 0.15 = 0.165$ $/unit/yr; the total holding cost is $hQ/2 + hs$ (see equation 6.5 and sequel), where $Q/2 = 900,000$ is the average inventory exclusive of safety stock, and $s = 100,000$ is the number of units of safety stock. Thus the total holding cost is $165,000 and the aggregate lot size is $Q = 1,800,000$.

Inventory turnover is defined as average annual demand divided by average inventory. Let the average annual demand be D units per year; then since the turnover is 7.8 times per year, the average annual demand is $D = 7,800,000$ units, or about 150,000 units per week. (The average time between orders for typical classes of items in the inventory is $Q/D = 0.23077$ years or about 12 weeks.)

The 100,000-unit safety stock represents $100,000/150,000 = 0.66\overline{6}$ weeks of demand. The safety stock exists because we order items an average of $0.66\overline{6}$ weeks early.

Now consider the effects of a weekly review cycle. With a weekly review, the reorder point for a typical SKU (class of items) will be detected, on the average, 0.5 weeks after it actually occurs, so to prevent stockouts on the average, we must keep 0.5 weeks of safety stock on hand. But we usually do not want to prevent stockouts merely on the average; we want to reduce the probability of stockout to some small probability p. Obviously if p is small enough it could cause us to keep up to a full week of safety stock (because the reorder point, depending on where in the week it fell, could occur up to a week before the review). Since the actual safety stock is $0.66\overline{6}$ weeks of demand, and weekly review causes a need for safety stock of at least 0.5 weeks of demand and at most one week of demand, we can infer that the holding-cost savings from switching to continuous review would be the holding costs for at least $0.5 \times 150,000 = 75,000$ units, and probably the full 100,000 units. The holding-cost savings would be at least $0.165 \times 75,000 = \$12,375$ per year, and probably the full $0.165 \times 100,000 = \$16,500$ per year.

Since the switch involves a cost of $25,000 per year and has other benefits of $11,000 per year, the net annual benefits would be at least $12,375 - 25,000 + 11,000 = -\$1625$, and probably the full $16,500 - 25,000 + 11,000 = \underline{\$2500}$. <u>Yes</u>, it would be (slightly) economically worthwhile to switch.

2.6 Quality Assurance and Safety

Current specifications for the IE PE Exam provide for a multiple-choice quality-assurance problem (#472) that can test the possible application areas of quality assurance plans (reviewed in section 4.3), reliability analysis (reviewed in section 4.2), control procedures, capability analysis, and quality aspects of design. The work and safety essay problem (#173) can test industrial hygiene and safety, although it often tests other applications instead. Examples E95a and E95b in chapter 8 are typical of IE PE Exam problems where safety is the tested application area.

E7.   A plastic extrusion plant has 25 machines that make wiring harnesses, clips, and other small parts for the automotive industry by receiving a feedstock of plastic chips fed into a hopper, melting the feedstock, and extruding the melt through molds. The feedstock arrives in 800-lb drums. One ounce of feedstock can be tested for metal contamination at a cost of $2. If at least two ounces in the drum have metal contamination, there is a 40% probability that metal will gouge and thereby ruin a $1500 mold. The hoppers at the machines hold 16 lb of feedstock and can become contaminated with other color plastic stock in several ways: filling the hopper using a scoop that has other color plastic dust or chips clinging to it, filling the hopper while hands or clothing are contaminated with other color plastic, picking up trimmings from the floor and putting them into the hopper (trimmings from the extruding head are automatically dropped into the hopper about 30 times per minute, but sometimes they cling and get knocked off the head as it returns for the next operation), doing anything—such as wiping off the top of the machine—that puts plastic dust into the air near the hopper mouth, or failing to follow prescribed procedures in changing colors. Each instance of other-color contamination is assumed to cost $25. An other-color detector that costs $4000 can be mounted at the point where melt enters the extruding head. A stoppage caused by the detector is assumed to cost $14. The company uses a 5-year horizon and a 15% compound interest rate.

QUESTIONS 1-10:

1.   In designing a sampling plan for acceptance sampling of incoming feedstock drums for metal contamination, a natural lot size would be

(A)   4000 ounces
(B)   12,800 ounces
(C)   2 drums
(D)   4 drums

2.   If the incoming drums of feedstock are said to be 4% nonconforming, it is implied that

(A)   4% of two-ounce samples are metal contaminated
(B)   4% of drums contain at least one metal-contaminated ounce
(C)   4% of drums contain at least two metal-contaminated ounces
(D)   4% of drums will ruin a mold

3. If a lot were one drum, and general inspection level II were to be used for a single-sampling plan, the number of one-ounce samples that would be tested for metal contamination would be most nearly

    (A) 80
    (B) 125
    (C) 200
    (D) 315

4. The Acceptable Quality Level (AQL) that appears to be implied by the situation statement is most nearly

    (A) 0.02%
    (B) 0.10%
    (C) 1%
    (D) 2%

5. Let p be the probability that an ounce of feedstock is metal contaminated. Ignoring the sensitivity of the cost of feedstock to quality demands, what is most nearly the sample size necessary to bring p to 0.40%, and would it be economically feasible to test a sample of that size from every drum?

    (A) 1; no
    (B) 5; yes
    (C) 50; no
    (D) 200; yes

6. If a hopper contains 256 ounces of feedstock and the expected number of metal-contaminated ounces is 1.0, the probability that the feedstock in the hopper will ruin a mold is most nearly

    (A) 5%
    (B) 10%
    (C) 15%
    (D) 20%

7. If there have been 4240 instances of color contamination in the 25-machine plant per year, and if it is assumed that *all* instances would be detected and converted to stoppages, the present worth of fitting all machines with other-color detectors is most nearly

    (A) $150,000
    (B) $50,000
    (C) $0
    (D) −$50,000

8. If detectors have the effectiveness assumed in the previous question, the most effective and economical way to reduce the instances of color contamination is probably

    (A) Training of employees
    (B) Fining employees $12.50 for each instance
    (C) Offering a bonus for reduction of instances
    (D) Instituting a recognition award for reduction of instances

9. Now let us examine detector performance more closely. Out of 1,500,000 extrusion cycles in a year, 4240 of them have color contamination. The detectors detect 99.6% of actual contamination instances and falsely detect contamination in 0.4% of non-contamination instances. The probability of an actual instance of contamination when one is detected is most nearly

    (A) 0.00287
    (B) 0.00680
    (C) 0.08461
    (D) 0.41378

10. Accept the data from the previous question, only let the false detection probability be x rather than 0.4%. The manufacturer has offered a free trial of a detector that can be mounted on a machine and used for several months. In order for the detector to do more good than harm, x should be at most approximately

    (A) 0.03%
    (B) 0.2%
    (C) 0.4%
    (D) 0.46%

ANSWERS:

1. A drum is a natural lot. Since testing is done one ounce at a time, the number of observations that would constitute 100% inspection of a lot is 800 lb × 16 oz/lb = 12,800. Answer (B) is correct.

2. Answer (A) is inappropriate, since it implies unreasonably poor quality (virtually every drum would ruin a mold). Answer (D) is reasonable, except that the statement that presumably defines conformance mentions a 40%, not 100%, probability of ruining a mold. Answer (C) is correct; it matches the statement better than answer (D), since it mentions 2 ounces.

3. Z1.4 standard tables (see tables 4-7 and 4-8 in chapter 4) specify sample-size code M for level-II inspection of a lot of size $N = 12,800$. Answer (D) is correct.

4. The situation statement mentions only one quality level: the level such that 2 ounces out of 12,800 have metal contamination. This is 2 nonconformances per 12,800 units, or 0.015625 per 100 units, or 0.015625% nonconforming. Answer (A) is correct.

5. From table 4-8, a sample size of 80 is the smallest that provides enough discrimination to allow at least one nonconformance in a sample. The next-lower size, 50, or the one below that, 32, can achieve $p = 1\%$ while allowing at least one nonconformance, so a good guess at the smallest sample size able to achieve $p = 0.40\%$ would be 32 or 50. As to economic feasibility, $p = 0.40\%$ implies an expected 51.2 metal-contaminated ounces in a drum, so at this quality level virtually every drum would cause the expected $0.40 \times 1500 = \$600$ cost of ruining a mold to be incurred. Thus virtually no benefit would be gained by spending $32 \times 2 = \$64$ or $50 \times 2 = \$100$ on inspection to achieve $p = 0.40\%$. It is not economically feasible to inspect at this level. Answer (C) is correct.

6. Here $p = 1.0/256 = 0.00390625$. By the binomial distribution (see table 4-1 in chapter 4), with $n = 256$, the probability of $x = 0$ ounces being contaminated is $p(0) = (1 - p)^{256} = 0.367159755$. The probability of $x = 1$ ounces being contaminated is $p(1) = 256p(1-p)^{255} = 0.368599597$. Thus the probability of two or more ounces being contaminated is $1 - p(0) - p(1) = 0.264240648$. The probability that a mold is ruined is 40% of this, or 0.105696259. Answer (B) is correct.

7. Assuming that each instance is converted to a stoppage, the detectors would earn a net benefit of $4240 \times (25 - 14) = \$46,640$ per year. An investment of $4000 \times 25 = \$100,000$ is required. At 15% interest the present worth is $-\$100,000 + 46,640(P/A \ 15\%,5) = \$56,344.51$. Answer (B) is correct.

8. The causes of other-color contamination given in the situation statement are recognizable to a qualified quality engineer as stemming more from ignorance or unawareness than from carelessness or bad will. Answers (B), (C), and (D) are incentives—using them would imply a belief that the causes stem from carelessness or bad will. Training of the 50 or so employees who work directly around the machines would clearly cost less than $100,000 initially and incur less annual cost than the $59,360 annual cost of stoppages associated with detectors. Answer (A) is correct.

9. This question can be answered by using Bayes' Theorem (equation 4-33 in section 4.2.2). Let C be the event that an extrusion cycle is other-color contaminated; C' is the event that it is not. Let D be the event that the detector (truly or falsely) detects a contamination; D' is the event that it does not. The probability of contamination is $P(C) = 4240/1,500,000 = 0.002866\overline{6}$, and of course $P(C') = 1 - P(C)$. The probability of detection given contamination is $P(D|C) = 0.996$. The probability of false detection is $P(D|C') = 0.004$. The required answer, the probability of contamination given detection, can be computed directly by Bayes' Theorem:

$$P(C|D) = \frac{P(D|C)P(C)}{P(D|C)P(C)+P(D|C')P(C')} = 0.413776886$$

Answer (**D**) is correct.

10.   This is a *breakeven* question of the type reviewed in section 3.3.3. It is valid and convenient to analyze the situation as if 25 detectors were tried for a year. There are 4240 instances of color contamination. Without detectors, the cost of color contamination would be $4240\times25 = \$106,000$. With detectors, $0.996\times4240 \approx 4223$ actual instances would be converted to stoppages to incur a cost of $4223\times14 \approx \$59,122$, and $x\times(1,500,000-4240)$ unnecessary stoppages would be generated to incur a cost of $x\times1,495,760\times14 = \$20,940,640x$. In order for the total cost with detectors to be less than the total cost without detectors, we require

$$59,122 + 20,940,640x < 106,000$$
$$\text{or}$$
$$x < 0.0022386 \approx 0.22\%$$

Answer (C) is correct.

2.7 Work Methods and Measurement

Essay problem #173 in the current IE PE Exam specifications concerns either work or safety or both. When it concerns work rather than safety, it often treats applications such as measuring work, methods analysis, incentive plans, workplace design, and human-machine interfacing; when it concerns safety, the challenge is often to redesign work to make it safer. Many of the applicable methodologies are reviewed in chapter 7. Ergonomics and human engineering are listed as knowledge areas that can be tested in multiple-choice problem #473; when the main stress of this problem is on management, the challenge is often to measure and design work in a way that is equitable and fair, and when the main stress is on computers, the challenge is often to design suitable human-machine interfaces. Work methods or measurements also frequently show up as major side issues in manufacturing, production, or facilities problems, even though the exam specifications do not mention this. For instance, the production rate in a manufacturing problem may depend on standard times for tasks, where the standard times must be determined from data. A facility layout may depend on the footprint of individual workstations, where the footprint must be determined from ergonomics considerations.

    This review book refers to, but does not contain, the major charts and tables needed to solve problems in work methods and measurement. The candidate should bring to the IE PE Exam a table of human-body dimensions, metabolism tables, speech intelligibility data (articulation index tables), tables of threshold limit values for toxins, tables of point-system plans for job evaluation, tables for predetermined time systems, and the like, rather than rely on this review book for data. The material in this review book on metabolism (section 7.1.2), pushing and pulling (section 7.1.3), lighting (section 7.2.1), lifting (section 7.1.4), and noise protection (section 7.2.1 and section 8.3.1), while seemingly complete enough to solve certain types of problems, is sketchy and not intended to be complete enough to allow exam problems to be solved without use of the proper references.

E8.   **You are the industrial engineer at a 250-employee plant in Phoenix, AZ. Give your answers to the following questions that may arise in the course of your work.**

QUESTIONS 1-9:

1.   **The lab purchases supplies in cartons typically 16" long, 12" wide, and 10" high. Occasionally lab employees must lift a carton from the floor to a 31"-high tabletop. The maximum that a carton should weigh is most nearly**

    (A)   10 lb
    (B)   20 lb
    (C)   40 lb
    (D)   50 lb

2.   **Suppose it were decided on the basis of multiple considerations that 10 kg was the greatest appropriate carton weight for the cartons in the foregoing problem. The lab receives mainly cartons of glassware and cartons of liquid chemicals. Lab employees could appropriately handle cartons containing**

    (A)   Neither glassware nor liquids
    (B)   Liquids but not glassware
    (C)   Glassware but not liquids
    (D)   Both glassware and liquids

3.   **A three-person team is systematically revising the plant's operating procedure manuals. Each manual is a 30-page document. They appear to be on a 90 percent learning curve, and the 50th manual took 10 manhours to prepare. For the total manhours to prepare the 20 remaining manuals, the accepted methodology gives an estimate of most nearly**

    (A)   189 manhours
    (B)   190 manhours
    (C)   194 manhours
    (D)   195 manhours

4. Assuming that the data for the foregoing question represent standard times after 15 percent shift allowances, the standard and normal times for preparation of the 51st document are, respectively,

    (A) 9.97 and 8.47 hours
    (B) 10 and 8.5 hours
    (C) 9.97 and 8.67 hours
    (D) 3.3 and 2.9 hours

5. Outdoor plant workers wait for personnel carriers in sun/rain shelters having 18"-high benches. The shelters are to have horizontal slits to allow seated workers to see the carrier coming. The top and bottom dimensions appropriate for the slit, measured from the floor of the shelter, are most nearly

    (A) 130 and 112 cm
    (B) 135 and 117 cm
    (C) 138 and 109 cm
    (D) 145 and 120 cm

6. Your harsh-environment workers work two 16-hr days per week and are off the rest of the week. Female workers complain of weight gain on the site diet. The nutritionist says they are receiving 3000 kcal daily. If their average level of activity during the 16-hr double shift is enough to burn 0.8 watts per kilogram of body weight over basal metabolism, and they eat and exercise similarly on their off days, the equilibrium body weight of female workers should be most nearly

    (A) 50 kg
    (B) 60 kg
    (C) 70 kg
    (D) 80 kg

7. You must specify the letter height for all-caps warning signs intended for crane operators to read from 500 ft away. The applicable code merely says "easily legible." The 10-point type you are reading now, with capital letters about 0.10" high, is easily legible from 12" away. On this basis, the letter height for the warning signs should be most nearly

    (A) 20"
    (B) 30"
    (C) 40"
    (D) 50"

8. An envelope-stuffing task consists of picking up an envelope with the nonfavored hand, picking up a pre-folded piece of paper with the favored hand, lifting the flap of the envelope with the thumb of the hand that holds it, slipping the paper into the envelope, swiping the flap across a moist sponge, closing the flap, sealing it by passing it between thumb and fingers while applying pressure, and putting it on the completed-work stack. All elements except closing the flap require hand or hand-eye adjustment. The layout is very convenient; all movements are within 6 inches of the center of work. The normal time for this task should be most nearly

    (A) 5 sec
    (B) 6.5 sec
    (C) 11 sec
    (D) 14.5 sec

9. Aluminum edging stock used as trim in a finishing operation easily loses its new look. A winnowing operation for this stock has a standard production quota of 5 lineal ft per sec, or 144,000 lineal ft per shift. Actual average production has been only slightly greater than standard, although there is an incentive plan that offers a bonus for every 100 lineal ft above 110% of standard in a shift. The shift allowance has been changed from 12% to 16%, so the bonus threshold rate must be revised from its current 158,400 lineal ft per shift. For best results, the new bonus threshold rate (in lineal ft per shift) should be set most nearly to

    (A) 137,000
    (B) 139,000
    (C) 151,000
    (D) 153,000

ANSWERS:

1. For compliance to NIOSH lifting standards (see section 7.1.4), the recommended weight limit in kilograms would be $RWL = LC \times HM \times VM \times DM \times FM \times AM \times CM$, where $HM = 25/(25 - 0 + 15.24) = 0.6213$ (since 15.24 is half the 12" dimension, in cm), $VM = 0.775$ (the lift starts at the floor), $DM = 0.82 + 1.8/31 = 0.878$, $AM = 1$ (no turning), $FM = 1$ (infrequent lifting), and $CM = 0.95$ (fair grip). These values give $RWL = 23 \times 0.6213 \times 0.775 \times 0.878 \times 1 \times 1 \times 0.95 = 9.24$ kg or 20 lb. Answer (B) is correct.

2. A box of the specified size filled with empty glassware certainly weighs less than 10 kg (22 lb). A typical liquid weighs at least $0.7 g/cm^3$. The whole volume of the box is $16 \times 12 \times 10(2.54)^3 = 31,463$ cm^3. The amount of liquid that would weigh 10 kg is no more than $10,000 + 0.7 = 14,285$ cm^3. Thus the carton would be too heavy if it contained more than about 50% liquid. But, including padding, liquid is typically packed more densely than that, so the carton would weigh too much. Answer (C) is correct.

3. From equation 3-5 in section 3.1.2, the 90% slope parameter converts to $b = -0.152003094$. From equation 3-3, $a = 10/50^b = 18.123776$. Putting these values into either equation 3-6 or its close approximation equation 3-7, with $n = 50$ and $k = 20$, the result is 194.44 manhours. A linear approximation, which is not acceptable for immature learning curves although it introduces little error here, gives the result 194.71 manhours. Answer (C) is correct.

4. The standard time for the 51st document is $a(51)^b = 9.9699$ hours. Since the 15% allowance is a shift allowance fraction A/S rather than a work allowance fraction A/N (see section 7.4.4 and equation 7-3), the normal time is $N = 9.9699 \times (1 - 0.15) = 8.47$ hours (not $9.9699 + 1.15 = 8.67$ hours). Answer (A) is correct. Answer (D) might trap a candidate who was unaware that standard and normal times are measures of effort, not of elapsed time (if the three people in the crew were to work on the document in parallel, they might require 3.3 hours of elapsed time).

5. Lacking more specific information, the engineer must assume that the workers are both male and female American adults, and that the requirement is the customary one of accomodating people from 5th-percentile females to 95th-percentile males. One popular table of American adult dimensions places the 5th-percentile female's eye at seat height plus 67.5 cm and the 95th-percentile male's eye at seat height plus 84.4 cm. Seat height is 45.72 cm, so the slit would extend from 113.22 cm to 130.12 cm in height from the floor. Answer (A) is correct.

6. Let a female worker's weight be M, let her basal metabolism be the standard 1.16 W/kg for adult females, let the standard 10% be added to basal-plus-activity metabolism for digestion, recall the conversion factor from watt-hours to kcal as 0.86, and let her daily caloric intake be 3000 kcal. By the method reviewed in section 7.1.2,

$$(1.16 \times 24 + 0.8 \times 16) \times M \times 0.86 = 3000 \implies M = 78.03 \text{ kg or about 172 lb}$$

Answer (D) is correct.

7. The type subtends an angle of 0.10/12 radians. Where x is the letter height of the sign 500×12 inches away, the sign's letters subtend an angle of $x/(500 \times 12)$ radians. For equal legibility let the two angles be equal:

$$0.10/12 = x/(500 \times 12) \implies x = 50" \text{ or } 4'2"$$

Answer (D) is correct.

8. Using MTM-3 (reviewed in section 7.4.3; any predetermined time system will give similar results):

Task	Range	Code	TMU
1. Get envelope (and transport to center)	–6	HB	34
2. Get paper (and transport to center)	–6	HB	34
3. Lift flap	–6	TB	21
4. Stuff envelope	–6	TB	21
5. Moisten flap	–6	TB	21
6. Close flap	–6	TA	7
7. Seal envelope	–6	TB	21
8. Stack envelope	–6	TB	21
			180 TMU

180 TMU $\times$ 0.036 sec/TMU = 6.48 sec normal time. Answer (B) is correct.

9.   It is convenient to express the standard time S and normal time N in units of shifts per 1000 lineal ft. S is given as $1/144 = 0.006944444$. For $A/S = 0.12$, equation 7-3 gives $N = (1 - 0.12) \times S = 0.00611111$, and for the new $A/S = 0.16$, the same equation gives, for the same N, a new standard time of $S = N/(1 - 0.16) = 0.00727513$ shifts per lineal ft, which means the new standard production quota is 137,454.545 lineal ft per shift. (More simply, the standard production quota could be corrected by the ratio 0.84/0.88.) The bonus threshold should be set *at* this new standard, not 10% above it (see the first paragraph of section 8.2.1.1). Answer (A) is correct.

2.8 Human Factors

See the introduction to the foregoing section (section 2.7) for a discussion of where human-factors applications are likely to appear in the IE PE Exam. In addition to their importance in work design and measurement problems, human-factors issues are sometimes the main or only focus of a problem. Examples: a problem in which the requirement is to determine the directions and magnitudes of stresses on lower-back vertebrae, a problem in which the requirement is to evaluate alternative computer/human interfaces, or—as in Example E9 below—a problem in which the requirement is to select, evaluate, or devise display systems or control systems.

E9.   SITUATION:

You have agreed to consult for an industrial design firm that is designing a wide but coordinated variety of products, from VCRs to microwave ovens to commercial ovens to elevators. To give the same distinctive look and feel to every product, the firm has decreed that controls will be limited where possible to two devices: a circular backlit button (the button itself is not marked but has variable-color backlighting) with a nearby four-character (or graphic icon) rectangular label, and a slide control that can have either a three-position or continuous slide, with three nearby labels like those near the buttons. Two possible examples are shown below—on the left, a possible control panel for an elevator, and on the right a possible control panel for a pizza oven.

Elevator controls (inside front, to right of door)

Pizza oven controls (right side, around corner from front face)

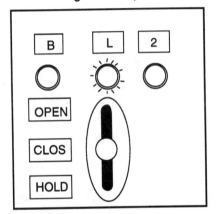 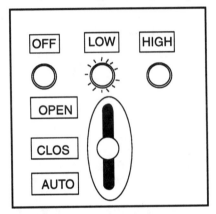

The control-panel functions of the elevator are these: There are three door command states; if HOLD is active, the door will open at the next opportunity and stay open; if OPEN is active, the door will operate normally except that it will wait longer to close; if CLOSE is active, the door will operate normally except that it will wait the minimum time to close. There are four floor commands; if NULL is active, there is no effect from the floor controls in this elevator; if Y is active, a 'go to level Y' command has been added to the command stack (here $Y \in \{0, 1, 2\}$). In the illustration, the CLOSE door command and '1' floor command are active. The panel is immediately to the right of the elevator opening. The elevator has double doors that meet in the center of the opening.

The pizza oven control functions are these: There are three temperature commands, one of which is active; they are OFF, LOW, and HIGH. There are three door command states; if OPEN is active, the top latch on the bottom-hinged oven door is in the release state, leaving the door ajar at the top; if AUTO is active, OPEN will become active when an 'end of cooking' message is received from the timer or thermostat, but otherwise CLOSE is active; if CLOSE is active, the latch is in the secured state unless overridden. The oven door can manually be opened and closed while the latch is in the secured state. The illustration shows a design that had been suggested for an oven whose controls would be on the oven door, but your design must be for an oven where the operator stands facing the oven with the door handle at waist height when closed and at knee height when opened, and the control panel is mounted on the *side*, so that the operator will reach around with the right hand to operate the controls by feel (although craning the neck would allow labels to be viewed). The panel is insulated. Buttons and slide handles protrude 0.25 inches.

REQUIREMENTS:

You are to design and lay out control panels, using all buttons or all slides or a combination. Place buttons, slides, and labels in the most appropriate locations and orientations on the panel, and specify the most appropriate one to four characters for each label. Buttons can be backlit but cannot carry text or graphics. Assume that any disability-access requirements such as Braille or raised graphics will be addressed *after* your basic design is complete.

(a) **Propose an improved design and layout for the elevator controls. Sketch your proposal neatly in the solutions booklet and justify your proposal's features.**

(b) **Propose an improved design and layout for the pizza oven control panel. Sketch your proposal neatly in the solutions booklet and justify your proposal's features.**

SOLUTIONS:

(a) For door-function control, a horizontal (parallel to actual motion) slide is better than a vertical slide or buttons, but the functions must be in order from the most "closish" one—CLOS—on the left to the most "openish" one—HOLD—on the right. The slide should be at the left of the panel, near the doors it controls. The door-function labels are already appropriate. The floor controls should be oriented vertically (parallel to actual motion). Buttons are better than a slide for floor control, because they are the established metaphor, and because the floor-control function is a discrete selection (a slide would be better if the controls actually moved the elevator). The lobby floor should be labeled *LOB* or *LOBY* or *1*, although *L* is acceptable. The dock should be labeled *DOCK*, not *B*. The appropriate label for the second floor is *2*. This design is shown on the left. An alternative layout with the floor buttons to the right of the slide, having labels above each button or below each button, would be acceptable.

Solution (a). Elevator controls.   Solution (b). Pizza oven controls.

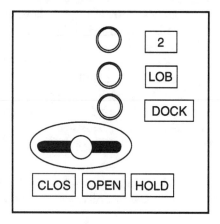 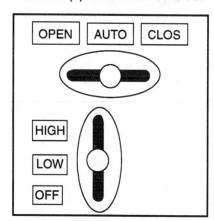

(b) A vertical slide makes more sense than buttons for temperature control, especially since labels are difficult to view. OFF would be the bottom position, HIGH the top; pulling up would be a metaphor for raising the temperature. This control should be at the left of the panel to minimize the necessary reach; the labels can be to the left of the slide (as shown) if viewing them is considered important, or to the right if reach is considered more important than viewing. The door controls should be a horizontal slide; pulling forward (left on the side-mounted panel) would be a metaphor for pulling the door open. This slide should be as high and as far left on the panel as possible, so as to be near the actual door handle (assumed to be mounted at the center of the top of the door). This design is shown on the right.

2.9 Computer Information Systems

In the IE PE Exam specifications, the application areas for multiple-choice problem #473 are computer and information systems, or management principles, or both. Computer systems analysis and design, specification of computer equipment, and computer communication protocols are listed as computer-related application areas for that problem. Computer software is listed as a knowledge area for essay problem #172 (production and inventory systems), because industrial engineers are expected to be conversant with MRP-II software and principles (reviewed in section 6.1.3.3.3), and for multiple-choice problem #472 (quality assurance).

E10.   SITUATION:

Elzy's Database

L. Z. ("Elzy") Echols is in charge of equipment purchasing for a midwestern steel plant. He keeps a database. Each piece or grouping of equipment that he buys is assigned a specification number (e.g., S436). He keeps this, a brief description, the predicted cost, the requested delivery date, and the financial charge number in his database. The specification itself, its originator's name, and many details that he does not keep in his database are kept in hardcopy form in a folder bearing the specification number. He often seeks bids, which are formal price and delivery quotations, from three to five (sometimes one or two) vendors before issuing an order. To obtain these, there is an RFQ (request for quotation) that he sends to vendors; the database tracks its specification number, issue date, vendors to whom sent, and bid due date. The database tracks vendors' replies to RFQs, their cost (price quotation), and delivery (promised delivery timespan in months after the order date). For each specification number, there almost always is eventually an order, and the database tracks its vendor, order date, adjusted cost, and actual delivery date (the adjusted cost is the amount actually paid, which may vary from the price quote due to shipping charges, penalties, or discounts).

Elzy deals with the same vendors repeatedly and has built up a vendor "file" in his database to keep the necessary information so that RFQs and orders can be produced as database applications.

Data on the latest batch of RFQs issued 06–13–93 (June 13, 1993) to vendors C1, C2,..., C6 for five specifications is tabulated below. The vendors who responded all did so on 07–13–93. "NB" indicates no bid; "NR" indicates no RFQ.

Price ($000) / delivery (mo from order date)

	C1	C2	C3	C4	C5	C6
S101	81 / 4	NB	85 / 6	82 / 6	NR	NR
S102	22 / 3	NB	19 / 3	20 / 3	NR	21 / 3
S103	45 / 4	46 / 4	40 / 5	39 / 4	NR	NB
S104	NB	92 / 9	NR	97 / 8	94 / 6	95 / 6
S105	61 / 2	NR	NR	NR	68 / 2	NR

Bids are to be analyzed and acted upon on the following basis: For each specification, issue an order to the vendor who bids the lowest price among those whose delivery is 6 months or less. The orders are to be dated 07–13–93; the expected delivery date is not kept, because it is imputed from the delivery bid and order date.

QUESTIONS 1–10:

1. An appropriate list of entities that would appear in an entity-relationship (E-R) diagram for Elzy's database would be most nearly

   (A) Equipment, specification, order, RFQ, bid, vendor
   (B) Specification, RFQ, order, vendor, account (identified by charge number)
   (C) Order, vendor, specification, equipment
   (D) Specification number, predicted cost, requested delivery date, charge number
   (E) Specification, RFQ, bid, vendor, adjusted cost

2. The relationships between equipment and specifications, and between specifications and orders, respectively, are

   (A) One-to-many, many-to-one
   (B) Many-to-one, one-to-many
   (C) One-to-one, one-to-many
   (D) Many-to-one, one-to-one
   (E) One-to-one, one-to-one

3. Some possible one-to-one relationships in this database would be
   - (A) Equipment to specification, specification to RFQ, and RFQ to bid
   - (B) Specification to RFQ, RFQ to bid, bid to order, and order to specification
   - (C) Specification to order, order to vendor, vendor to RFQ
   - (D) Specification to order, order to RFQ, and RFQ to specification
   - (E) Vendor to bid, bid to order, and order to specification

4. In a relational database design for Elzy's database, the table for specifications and the table for orders
   - (A) Must be separate tables
   - (B) Must be combined into one table
   - (C) Can either be separate or combined
   - (D) Can be combined only if the tables for RFQs and specifications are also combined
   - (E) Should be combined if the tables for RFQs and specifications are not combined

5. Assuming that there exist an RFQ table and a vendor table, data showing which vendors were invited to bid on a given specification would
   - (A) Be kept in the RFQ table
   - (B) Be kept in the vendor table
   - (C) Not be kept, but implied from data in the bid table
   - (D) Be kept in a table having a double key—the specification number and the vendor identifier
   - (E) Be kept in both the RFQ table and the vendor table

6. To express the information given in the situation statement on bids from six vendors on five specifications, how many data words would be required in the bid table?
   - (A) 17
   - (B) 28
   - (C) 30
   - (D) 34
   - (E) 68

7. What would be the key of the bid table?
   - (A) Specification number
   - (B) Vendor identifier
   - (C) Both specification number and vendor identifier
   - (D) Order date
   - (E) Cost and delivery

8. If a single table having a row for each specification were designed to keep all non-vendor information on specifications, RFQs, and orders, how many columns would it have?

    (A) 5
    (B) 8
    (C) 11
    (D) 14
    (E) 17

9. When the adjusted cost becomes known, into how many places in the database must its value be entered?

    (A) Nowhere
    (B) One place
    (C) Two places
    (D) Three places
    (E) Four places

10. If Elzy wishes to query the database to list all the equipment for which bids were requested before today but none have yet been received, the query could most easily be handled by

    (A) An ad-hoc SQL query
    (B) An ad-hoc query by example
    (C) An application function already designed to handle such a query
    (D) Any of the above methods
    (E) None of the above methods

ANSWERS:

The required methods for solving this problem's 10 questons are reviewed in chapter 5.

In order to answer the questions we must perform at least a partial data design. Since one or more pieces of equipment constitute a specification, there is an EQUIPMENT entity having a many-to-one relationship with a SPECIFICATION entity. The SPECIFICATION entity has as characteristics the specification number, the brief description, the predicted cost, the requested delivery data, and the charge number. We can also posit an ORDER entity, in a one-to-one relationship with SPECIFICATION, having as characteristics the vendor, order date, adjusted cost, and actual delivery date. Since almost all specifications become orders, and there is evidently no provision for ordering part of the equipment in a specification from one vendor and part from another, the SPECIFICATION and ORDER entities could possibly be combined; we could call the combination SPECIFICATION (it could as well be called ORDER instead, and a specification could be viewed as an immature order). Also in a one-to-one relationship with SPECIFICATION is RFQ. "He often seeks bids" implies that Elzy also often does *not* seek bids, so it is best not to combine RFQ with SPECIFICATION. RFQ has as characteristics the issue date and bid due date; many specification/orders would fail to have these characteristics. There is obviously a VENDOR entity. An RFQ goes to many vendors, and a vendor responds to many RFQs, so there is a many-to-many relationship between RFQ and VENDOR. This relationship could be given the name BID if we choose to interpret a vendor's non-response a null bid or an infinite-cost bid; alternatively, to keep data only on real bids, we can let the many-to-many relationship between RFQ and VENDOR be called simply RFQ_VENDOR, representing the information of which RFQs are sent to which vendors, and a separate entity called BID would have as characteristics the cost and delivery quotations (an instance of BID would be a particular vendor's response to a particular RFQ). If EQUIPMENT, SPECIFICATION, RFQ, BID, and VENDOR are the entities, a final refinement to the entity-relationship design would be to let BID have a many-to-one relationship with SPECIFICATION instead of with RFQ; informal bids (those not in response to an issued RFQ) could be kept in the database. Here is an E-R diagram:

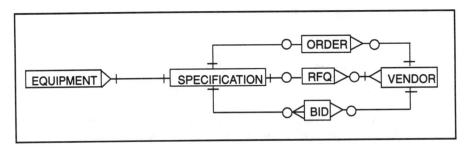

1. The correct answer is (A). Answer (B) treats SPECIFICATION and ORDER as separate entities and includes an ACCOUNT entity which is not represented in the database; answer (C) treats SPECIFICATION and ORDER as separate entities and ignores bids and RFQs; answer (D) lists characteristics, not entities; and answer (E) includes adjusted cost, which is a characteristic, not an entity.

2. The correct answer is (D). There can be many pieces of equipment in a specification but only one specification for a piece of equipment, and there can be only one specification for an order and one order for a specification.

3. The correct answer is (D). (A) is wrong because there can be many instances of EQUIPMENT to one of SPECIFICATION; (B) is wrong because an RFQ can elicit many bids; (C) is wrong because many orders can go to a vendor; (E) is wrong because many vendors can bid on an order.

    To answer further questions we need a relational design. The following design follows straightforwardly from the E-R diagram and the data mentioned in the situation statement; the SPECIFICATION and ORDER entities have been represented in a single SPECIFICATION table, and the many-to-many relationship between RFQ and VENDOR has been represented in an RFQ_VEND table:

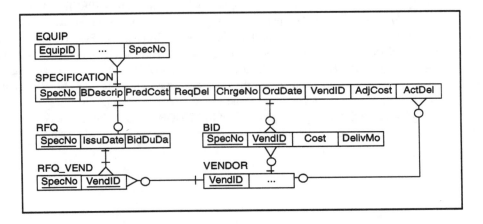

4.   The correct answer is _(C)_. Good practice does not forbid either separating or combining the specification and order tables. Here they are combined, but the combined table has two distinct themes.

5.   The correct answer is _(D)_; see the RFQ_VEND table.

6.   The correct answer is _(E)_. There would be 17 rows in the 4-column BID table.

7.   The correct answer is _(C)_.

8.   The correct answer is _(C)_. The SPECIFICATION table has 9 attributes; 2 more would be added if the RFQ table were combined with it.

9.   The correct answer is _(B)_. In a well-designed relational database, a datum is kept in only one place. Updating the AdjCost value in a row of the SPECIFICATION table is all that is needed.

10.   The correct answer is _(D)_. The mentioned query is not complex and could easily be handled by any of the three mentioned methods. The SQL command, for example, is **select EquipID from EQUIP where SpecNo in (select RFQ.SpecNo from RFQ, BID where RFQ.SpecNo = BID.SpecNo and cost is null and BidDuDa < SYSDATE).**

Chapter 3
Cost Analysis Techniques

Cost analysis skills are the most important (see section 1.3) and most heavily tested (see section 1.2) industrial engineering skills. They include not only engineering economy, but knowledge of cost accounting principles and the ability to estimate costs and benefits. Section 3.1 reviews cost accounting and cost estimating, including learning curves. Section 3.2 reviews benefit estimating. Section 3.3 reviews engineering economy from a modern viewpoint, including compound interest calculations without dependence on tabulated factors, routine handling of inflation and escalation, sensitivity, risk, depreciation, and after-tax analysis. The industrial engineer is expected to have special skills in labor estimation. These are reviewed in section 7.4 (Work Measurement and Standards), section 8.2 (Wage and Salary Administration), and section 3.1.2 (Learning Curves).

3.1 Cost Accounting and Estimating

3.1.1 Cost Treatments and Use of Cost Accounting Data

Cost estimating is performed by industrial engineers both for projects and for ongoing activities. A recommended general reference for cost estimation techniques is *Engineering Cost Estimating*, Third Edition (Ostwald 1992).

3.1.1.1 Detail Estimating

There are two broad approaches to cost estimating: detail estimating and analogy estimating. In detail estimating a project or activity is first broken down into tasks or sub-activities. For a project, this requires work breakdown—the analysis that results in a PERT or CPM project network. The accepted structure for work breakdown, called the work breakdown structure (WBS), is a tree of tasks or elements organized in levels. The WBS is required for many projects done for the U.S. Department of Defense and is also used in general practice. Level 1 is the entire project; its WBS element identifier is 1. Level 2 includes the major elements such as Land, Engineering, Management, and the work itself; for example, in a transmission-line project undertaken by a power company, the elements and their identifiers might be 11 Land, 12 Transmission Line, 13 Engineering, and 14 Management. Level 3 might be 111 Land Acquisition and 112 Environmental Impact Study under 11 Land; and 121 Infrastructure, 122 Substation, 123 Structure, and 124 Conductor under 12 Transmission Line. The WBS continues usually to level 5 or 6. To facilitate detail estimating, any WBS element can be broken down into elements at the next level.

Separate detail estimates are prepared for each task or lowest-level WBS, and their sum (including overall management and engineering tasks not included in estimates for tasks) is the overall cost estimate. Each task's detail estimate is then broken down by cost category. Typical cost categories for a task are labor, materials, subcontracts, facilities, equipment, and engineering. A form can be developed for each category; for example, a labor estimate form may have the following column headings: WBS, description, craft, manhours in period 1, manhours in period 2,... , total manhours (a pseudo-column that sums the manhours columns), gross wage, and cost (a pseudo-column that multiplies total manhours by gross wage). Gross wage is pay plus benefits (FICA, workman's compensation insurance, etc.).

Added to the detail estimates at the appropriate WBS levels are overhead (including costs not tied to tasks such as office expenses, employees' salaries and benefits, and materials and services not charged to any WBS element below Level 1), contingency (a budgeted amount to allow for unexpected problems), and interest on money borrowed for the project.

3.1.1.2 Analogy Estimating

Complementing the detail-estimating approach is that of analogy estimating, in which the cost for an element is estimated by comparing its cost to standard or historical cost data for other elements. One use of analogy estimating is to check the accuracy of detail estimates. For example, suppose there is a detail estimate of $36,200,000 for a 500-kV transmission-line project. Three similar 500-kV projects were built over the last five years, for varying current capacities and varying distances. If the known cost of each of these is corrected for current capacity, distance, and monetary inflation, it becomes an analog estimate for the new project. If the detail estimate does not fall well within the range of the analog estimates, an explanation for the discrepancy is sought.

A linear model is often an adequate basis for an analog estimate. For example, if two otherwise identical transmission-line projects had distances of 15 km and 25 km, respectively, and their inflation-corrected total costs were $35,000 and $50,000, respectively, it is reasonable to infer an analog estimate of $12,500 plus $1500/km. However, when costs are functions of surface area or volume rather than distance or number of parallel units, a linear model does not apply. A famous capacity-vs.-cost model for fluid processing equipment (pumps, vessels, turbines, reactors, furnaces, etc.), where capacity is measured either in volume or in throughput, is the *six-tenths rule:* cost tends to increase as the 0.6 power of the capacity. For example, if a 300-m^3 pressure vessel was fabricated at a cost of $30,000 two years ago, and inflation has been 4% annually, then the fabrication cost for a 400-m^3 similar pressure vessel can be estimated as $30,000 \times (1.04)^2 \times (400/300)^{0.6} = 38,561.26 \approx \$38,600$.

3.1.1.3 Cost Accounting Data

An enterprise's primary historical record of costs lies in its cost accounting data. But cost accounting data must be used with care. In his *Engineering Cost Estimating* textbook, Ostwald writes, "Although cost accounting data may have been wisely and carefully collected and arranged to suit primary purposes for accounting, raw data are usually incompatible with [engineering cost studies]." In *Modern Engineering Economy* (Young 1993), it is stated that "engineering economy's requirements for estimates of consequences of alternatives are distinct from the historical monitoring and control requirements served by cost accounting procedures. This distinction is so profound that cost accounting quantities can be more misleading than helpful."

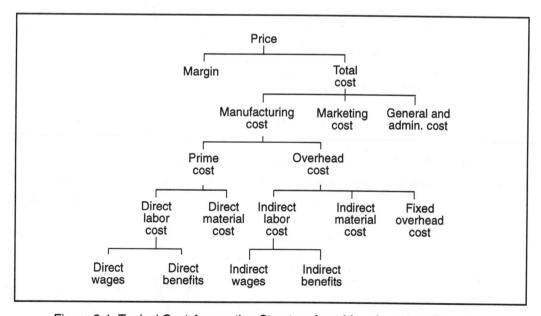

Figure 3-1. Typical Cost Accounting Structure for a Manufacturing Enterprise.

A typical cost accounting structure for a manufacturing enterprise has the structure shown in figure 3-1. Suppose several tens of thousands of units of a communications modem are being manufactured. A unit will sell for a price that is the sum of a margin and a total cost. The total cost is the sum of the manufacturing, marketing, and general and administrative costs. The manufacturing cost is the sum of prime cost and overhead cost. The prime cost is the sum of direct labor cost and direct material cost; the overhead cost is the sum of indirect labor cost, indirect material cost, and fixed overhead cost. Direct and indirect labor each have wage and benefit components.

E11a.   Audio Packaging Service performs packaging of WordStrike, SpreadStrike, DataStrike, StatStrike, and TotalStrike software products. It receives diskettes and books from Strike Corporation at no cost. Classify each of the following cost items:

1.   **Temporary packaging labor under a contract with TempServ, Inc.**
2.   **Wages and employee benefits for the receiving clerk**
3.   **Air conditioning and lighting**
4.   **Packaging materials**
5.   **Separately metered electrical power for shrink-wrap machines**
6.   **Building rent**
7.   **Wages and employee benefits for the president's secretary**
8.   **Wages and employee benefits for the plant engineer**
9.   **Wages, commissions, and employee benefits for sales staff**
10.   **Income taxes**

1.   Direct labor cost (not direct wages and direct benefits, since temporary labor is paid by contract to the temporary labor service)
2.   Indirect wages and indirect benefits (it is not useful or convenient to measure receiving effort per packaging unit)
3.   Fixed overhead cost
4.   Direct material (packaging materials per packaging unit are known)
5.   Direct material (because of the separate meter, shrink-wrap power is a measured input that can be tied to packaging units)
6.   Fixed overhead cost
7.   General and administrative cost
8.   Indirect wages and indirect benefits
9.   Marketing cost
10.   Not in cost accounting

Cost accounting recognizes *fixed and variable costs*. The cost $C(x)$ of producing x units of a good or service is assumed to comprise two terms: f_M is the *fixed cost* when x is in the range denoted M, and $v_M x$ is the *variable cost* for range M, where v_M is the unit variable cost for range M.

$$C(x) = f_M + v_M x \qquad x \in M \qquad (3\text{-}1)$$

The subscript M is not really used in accounting practice; it is included here as a reminder that the values would be different if the level of activity changed very much. The *unit cost* is the unit fixed cost plus the unit variable cost:

$$u(x) = \frac{C(x)}{x} = \frac{f_M}{x} + v_M \qquad\qquad x \in M \qquad\qquad (3\text{-}2)$$

In engineering cost analysis we are concerned not with the fixed and variable costs of cost accounting but with the closely related concepts of marginal and total cost.

3.1.1.4 Cost Treatment
Here we will review several important principles of cost treatment.

A. If a decision alternative causes an increase x in the level of some activity, the decision-relevant unit marginal cost V(x) can be zero and is often greater than the unit variable cost v_M but less than the unit cost u(x). For a particular resource and a particular level of activity x, the unit marginal cost $V(x)$ is defined as the instantaneous slope of the "out-of-pocket" cost curve that relates cost of consuming the resource to the level of activity. Then the additional cost for this resource for an alternative that increases x is approximated as $V(x) \times \Delta x$.

For example, Worth Rubber Company has a maintenance shop to maintain the mills and presses that produce lawnmower tires and similar products. The shop foreman's wages and benefits and the amortization of capitalized tools and equipment come to $30,000 per year and are considered to be fixed costs; the other maintenance workers' wages and benefits and the consumable tools and materials come to $35,000 per year and are considered to be variable costs. The maintained plant currently produces $x = 7000$ units (a unit is a ton of finished product) per year, so the cost accounting system lists the unit fixed cost as $f = \$30,000$ ($f/x = \$4.29$/unit) and the unit variable cost as $v = \$5$/unit.

Now suppose we contemplate a project to market our own house-brand lawnmower using our own tires. Suppose the project will require an additional $\Delta x = 200$ units of lawnmower tires to be produced per year. What is the marginal mill-and-press maintenance cost? The marginal cost might be zero if more than 200 "slightly irregular" units are unsuitable to be sold to customers but are suitable to be used on our own house-brand lawnmowers. The marginal cost might equal the variable cost if the additional level of tire-making activity would use maintenance labor, consumable tools, and maintenance materials in proportion but would have no effect on fixed costs—not even to speed up the time when capitalized maintenance tools and equipment would have to be replaced. In the extreme, the marginal cost might equal the total cost if there were no slack in the fixed-cost maintenance resources, that is, if the shop foreman's time, the capitalized tools, and the equipment were all being used to the hilt.

B. Otherwise-unused resources or materials are free. For example, long before wearing out or becoming obsolete, an air compressor was replaced by a larger one. It could have been sold for $4000, but since its replacement cost was $11,000 it was kept as surplus equipment. When a project that could use the compressor was analyzed, what compressor cost should have been used? Under most cost accounting systems the project account would be charged either $0 or $11,000 for the compressor, but the proper cost is $4000 (because using the compressor prevents selling it for $4000).

In a plant that used 100-psig steam for exact-temperature melting of a plastic, a certain amount of 15-psig exhaust steam and a certain amount of condensate were produced as by-products. Most of the condensate was returned to the boiler as preheated feed water. Some of the 15-psig steam was used for space heating and cleanup, but most of it was simply vented to the atmosphere. The cost accounting data for 15-psig steam listed its fixed cost as $0.31 per unit (reflecting the cost of the boiler plant) and its variable cost as $0.83 per unit (reflecting the cost of fuel, maintenance, and operation of the boiler plant). The allocation of costs among 100-psig steam, 15-psig steam, and condensate was made on the basis of heat content; thus, on a mass basis, 100-psig steam was expensive, 15-psig was cheap, and condensate was very cheap. A project was analyzed that would use some 15-psig steam to preheat liquid stock in a plastic feed tank. What cost should have been ascribed to the steam?

In quantities up to the amount being vented, 15-psig steam should have been treated as free. In higher quantities, if the boiler plant had excess capacity and steam use was not steadily increasing so as to require more boiler-plant capacity in the forseeable future, 15-psig steam should have been treated as being worth $0.83 per unit. (In great quantities, requiring expansion of the boiler plant, $0.83 per unit plus the actual cost of new facilities would be charged, which would probably be close to $0.31 per unit, for an approximate total of $1.14 per unit.)

C. Costs must be exhaustive, unavoidable, and exclusive. All costs that result from acceptance of an alternative should be considered, even if they are *economic externalities* (costs paid by someone else, such as pollution harm). Avoidable costs must be ignored. For example, if the decision is made to beautify a landscape while doing site preparation for a new plant, the cost of beautification should not be considered in analyzing any decisions except that of whether to beautify. Double-counting must be avoided; this principle will be discussed in section 3.2.

Sunk costs form a surprisingly troublesome special category of unavoidable costs. A sunk cost is a cost that will occur regardless of the decision, or that has already occurred. The obvious rule for treatment of sunk costs is to ignore sunk costs, or include them in every alternative.

E11b.   **Elijah purchases an inoperable stove for $100, expecting to sell it for $500 after spending $160 of effort and materials to repair it. But after spending $200 on the repair, he finds it will take yet another $250 to complete the repair, and that it will sell for only $400. What should he do?**

It should be difficult to go wrong here, but Elijah will make the wrong decision if he reasons he should not complete the repair because spending $550 to receive $400 is a bad deal. The decision now is to complete the repair or abandon it. The $100 purchase cost and $200 partial repair cost are sunk. If sunk costs are ignored, the decision is between spending $250 to receive $400, or spending nothing to receive nothing. He should complete the repair, gaining $150. Or, if sunk costs are included in both alternatives, the decision is between having spent $550 to receive $400, or having spent $300 to receive nothing. Again, he should complete the repair, gaining $150 (losing $150 instead of losing $300).

3.1.2 Learning Curves

The earliest and still most widely used model of productivity improvement for repetition of identical or similar tasks or projects is the *learning curve* introduced by Thomas Wright in 1936 to fit the decline in the amount of direct labor needed to build successive aircraft. Let x be the cumulative number of units produced, and let y be the number of hours of direct labor time required to produce the xth unit. Wright's learning-curve model is

$$y = ax^b \qquad (3\text{-}3)$$

where a and b are the parameters of the model. They can be fit to a set of (x, y) data by linear regression using the logarithmic form of equation 3-3 (here we use the natural-logarithm form although Wright used common logarithms):

$$\ln y = \ln a + b\ln x \qquad (3\text{-}4)$$

where $\ln x$ and $\ln y$ are the data, $\ln a$ is the intercept, and b is the slope of the straight line that the model traces in a log-log plot.

As in example 32 in chapter 4, if it took 700, 650, 644, and 637 manhours, respectively, to build the 5th, 6th, 7th, and 8th units, the model would have $a = 939.46$ and $b = -0.1923775$. (In verifying this example by performing linear regression for equation 3-4, do not forget to enter $\ln x$ and $\ln y$ as the data rather than x and y, and do not forget that the regression model gives $\ln a$ rather than a as the intercept and b as the slope; to get a from $\ln a$, take e to the $\ln a$ power.)

We can interpret a as the effort or cost of the first unit (in the fitted curve, not the actual data). We can interpret b in terms of the *slope parameter* $\Phi = 2^b$, which is the fitted ratio of the effort, or cost for the $2n$th unit to the effort, or cost for the nth unit. For example, if the fitted model implies it takes 85% as much time to build the 16th unit as to build the 8th unit, we say the model is an "85% learning curve": $\Phi = 0.85$. Let the fitted model imply that it takes effort or cost y_1 to build the x_1th unit, and y_2 to build the x_2th unit. If $x_2/x_1 = 2$, then from equation 3-3, $y_2/y_1 = 2^b = \Phi$. Thus the learning curve implies that each doubling of production multiplies the unit effort or cost by Φ, and rough estimates can be done in the head: If the 200th unit took 90% of the effort for the 100th unit, the 400th unit should take 90% of the effort for the 200th unit, or 81% of the effort of the 100th unit.

Inverting the definition of the slope parameter, we have

$$b = (\ln \Phi)/\ln 2 \qquad (3\text{-}5)$$

When applying learning curves for cost estimating, more credence is often placed in b than in a. For instance, in the above numerical example where it took 700, 650, 644, and 637 manhours, respectively, to build the 5th, 6th, 7th, and 8th units, consider the problem of estimating the number of manhours to build the 9th unit. From the fitted model, the answer is $a(9)^b = 615.6$. However, it actually took 637 manhours to build the 8th unit, whereas the model says it should have taken 629.7 manhours; there is an "error" of 7.3 manhours. If this "error" is considered to be in the nature of a statistical observation error—building the 8th unit just happened to take 7.3 manhours more than the expected 629.7, and it would have been equally likely to have taken less time than expected—then using the fitted model is appropriate. On the other hand, if the "error" is considered to indicate a *reset* of the level of effort—the intrinsic effort for the 8th and subsequent units was raised 7.3 manhours over its previous level—then the appropriate procedure for estimating effort for the 9th unit would be as follows: First reset a according to $637 = a(8)^b$, or $a = 637/(8)^b = 950.33$; then, with the new a, compute $a(9)^b = 622.7$ manhours, which is 7.1 manhours more than the estimate of 615.6 manhours when a was not reset. Either approach can be appropriate, depending on the nature of the process. Under both approaches, the numerical example represented an "87.5% learning curve" (because 2^b is 0.87516 for the example). The more accepted procedure is not to reset and simply use equation 3-3.

If n units have been produced, the learning curve is often used to estimate the effort or cost for the next k units. Since the curve $y = ax^b$ has a slope that decreases with x, for a mature learning curve it may be appropriate to approximate the average effort or cost per unit simply by linearly averaging y_{n+1} and y_{n+k}. For example, if a security company has handled 3419 alarm calls and the time in minutes to clear a call has been declining according to the learning curve $y = 27.2x^{-0.1724}$, the average time to clear the next 100 calls might be approximated as the average of the estimated time to clear the 3420th call, which is $27.2(3420)^{-0.1724}$ and the time to clear the 3519th call, which is $27.2(3519)^{-0.1724}$. This approximation gives 6.67283 min. per call, which is not too far from the true average of the times given by the model for the next 100 calls (6.67160 min. per call). But earlier in the life cycle, when the curvature of the learning curve is more pronounced, such an approximation is inaccurate. The true average can be closely approximated by an integral or, in these days of convenient computation, simply summed term-by-term.

The average cost per unit for the next k units after n units have been produced is

$$\hat{y}_{n,k} = \frac{1}{k} \sum_{x=n+1}^{n+k} ax^b \qquad (3\text{-}6)$$

This can be closely approximated by the following continuous approximation:

$$\hat{y}_{n,k} = \frac{1}{k} \int_{n+1/2}^{n+k+1/2} ax^b dx = \frac{a\left[(n+k+1/2)^{b+1} - (n+1/2)^{b+1}\right]}{k(b+1)} \qquad (3\text{-}7)$$

E12.   ESOP Advisors has handled six conversions of companies to employee ownership. The sixth conversion took 714 manhours of principals' professional time, and it appears that ESOP is on a 70% learning curve for this kind of project. Estimate the average professional time per project for the next 10 projects.

$b = (\ln 0.70)/\ln 2 = -0.514573$. $714 = a(6)^b$ implies $a = 1795.2$

$\hat{y}_{6,10} = (a/10)[7^b + 8^b + ... + 16^b] = \underline{524.423}$ manhours per project

The continuous approximation $(a/10)[(16.5)^{b+1} - (6.5)^{b+1}]/(b+1)$ gives 524.593 manhours per project, which is very close. A linear average between the estimated times for the 7th and 16th projects would give an overestimate: $(a/2)[7^b + 16^b] = 545.290$ manhours per project.

3.2 Benefit Estimating

Just as costs must be exhaustive, unavoidable, and exclusive, *benefits must be exhaustive, otherwise unobtainable, and exclusive.* Do not fail to include benefits in esthetics, infrastructure, flexibility, or environmental values. But do not include benefits that are not actually caused by the incurred costs. The most common errors in treatment of benefits are *riders* and *double-counting*. A rider is an unprofitable add-on to a profitable project.

E13.   **A profitable project to automate reloading of plastic for six wrapping machines will allow operators to sit at the machines rather than stand. Six ergonomic chairs are included as part of the project. On a typical day, machines #1, #2, #3, and #5 are in use. Is there anything wrong?**

Assuming that the chairs are moderately worthwhile, and assuming that they can easily be moved, only four chairs should be provided. Providing two more chairs than will typically be used constitutes a *rider*. An alternative way of describing the error is that the cost of the two extra chairs is an *avoidable cost*.

Double-counting of benefits occurs most commonly in analyzing benefits of a resource-consumption savings. There are benefits of diminished resource consumption for existing production, or benefits of augmented production for existing resource consumption, but not both.

E14.   **At a plant that produces audio speakers, the cycle time at an assembly workstation can be reduced from 59 to 56 seconds per speaker. The plant operates 260 days per year, 7.5 hours per day, and adds a value of $1.32 per speaker. Labor at the station is worth $66 per hour. Determine the annual benefit from the cycle-time reduction.**

The existing annual labor cost is 7.5 x 260 x 66 = $128,700. The new annual labor cost for the existing production rate is 56/59 of this, so that the annual savings is $6544.07. Note that the value-added datum does not enter into the calculation.

The existing annual production is $7.5 \times 260 \times 3600 \div 59 = 118,983$ speakers, which at $1.32 value-added per speaker earns $157,057.63 of annual revenue. If the new workstation were to work all day, the revenue would be 59/56 of this, so that the annual increase in revenue would be $8413.80. Note that the labor-cost datum does not enter into the calculation.

Either one but not both of the answers is correct—the first if the production rate is to remain the same, the second if the production rate is to increase. In most similar cases, the first answer is the correct one, because to increase production implies that more product can be sold at the same price and that the infrastructure (receiving dock, raw materials warehouse, material-handling system, packaging system, etc.) can handle the increased production.

3.3 Engineering Economy

3.3.1 Time Value of Money

This section reviews discounted cash flow methods, which incorporate the time value of money into comparisons of the economic worths and economic efficiencies of alternatives. The economic worths of alternatives are evaluated by computing the worths of their cash flow sets.

3.3.1.1 Cash Flow Sets
The cash flow set for an alternative is defined with respect to a *baseline*, the same for all alternatives being compared. The set consists of (amount, timing) pairs, one pair for each *cash*

flow. Cash flow amounts are relative to the baseline and must be direct or indirect consequences of the alternative. Cash flow amounts are positive for inflows (benefits or receipts) and negative for outflows (disbursements).

As an illustration, suppose the alternatives are several laser printers under consideration to purchase for a computer system. Further suppose that all laser printers are of a single type so that the benefits are the same for every alternative, and that the benefits are modeled as an $800 inflow at the end of every year for 6 years starting a year after purchase. Let there be two alternative printers under consideration, A1 and A2. A1 has a first cost of $1000 and will have operating costs that are modeled as a series of $300 outflows on the same schedule as the benefits. A2 has a first cost of $800 and operating costs of $400 per year, on the same schedule.

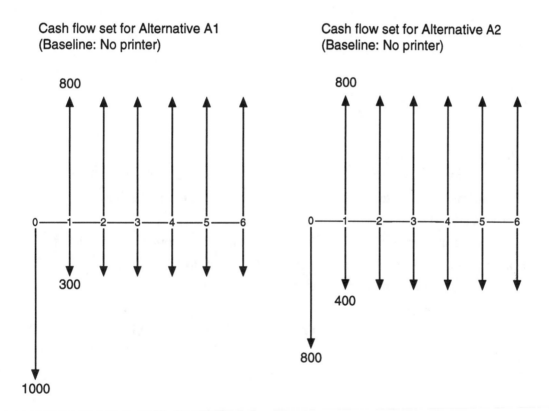

Cash flow set for Alternative A1
(Baseline: No printer)

Cash flow set for Alternative A2
(Baseline: No printer)

The cash flow sets for these alternatives can be composed with respect to any baseline. Let us first illustrate the cash flow sets for the baseline of not having a printer. With this baseline, the benefits are part of each printer's cash flow set. Cash flow sets can be displayed in the form of a *cash flow diagram* that shows positive and negative amounts vertically, positive up and negative down, and shows timings on a horizontal time scale.

All cash flows at a given time may be replaced by a single cash flow whose amount is the net (algebraic sum) of their amounts. The resulting net cash flow set is said to be *indistinguishable* from the original cash flow set.

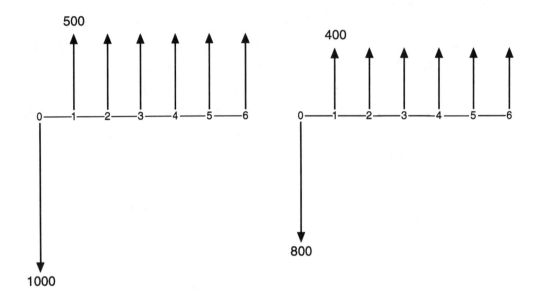

Net cash flow set for Alternative A1
(Baseline: No printer)

Net cash flow set for Alternative A2
(Baseline: No printer)

3.3.1.2 Worth of a Cash Flow Set

Let time be measured in periods of fixed length (one year in the example at hand), and let there be a compound interest rate i for a period of this length (in the example at hand, i is an annual compound interest rate).

Let the net amount of cash flow at time t be A_t. Let there be a *worth evaluation time* denoted m, and a *horizon* denoted n, which is the timing of the final cash flow. Let the timings be 0, 1, ..., n. Then the *worth at time m* of the cash flow set $\{A_t: t=0,1,...,n\}$ is

Worth at evaluation time m of cash flow set $\{A_t: t=0,1,...,n\}$:

$$F_m = \sum_{t=0}^{n} A_t \beta^{t-m} \qquad (3\text{-}8)$$

where $\beta = 1/(1+i)$ is the *single-period discount factor* for interest rate i.

The *present worth*—worth at time $m = 0$—of a cash flow set, denoted P, is consequently

Present worth of cash flow set $\{A_t: t=0,1,...,n\}$:

$$P = \sum_{t=0}^{n} A_t \beta^{t} \qquad (3\text{-}9)$$

The *future worth* of a cash flow set—its worth at time $m=n$—is

Future worth of cash flow set $\{A_i: t=0,1,...,n\}$:

$$F_n = \sum_{t=0}^{n} A_t \beta^{t-n} = \sum_{t=0}^{n} A_t (1+i)^{n-t} \tag{3-10}$$

Note from equation 3-9 that if there is only one cash flow, having amount F and timing n, its present worth is $P = F\beta^n$. Conversely, if the only cash flow is of amount P at time zero, its future worth at time n is $F = P(1+i)^n$.

All these compound interest formulas derive from examining the transactions for a loan. If P dollars were lent at interest rate i for a term of n periods, the borrower would owe $P(1+i)$ dollars at the end of the first period. (By definition i is the additional proportion of a loan amount that its repayment must include as compensation for one period's use of the money.) Continuing the loan for a second period is indistinguishable from having the borrower repay $P(1+i)$ dollars and immediately borrow it again. At the end of the second period the amount owed is $P(1+i)^2$. Continuing the process for n periods gives rise to the formula $F = P(1+i)^n$. Equations 3-8, 3-9, and 3-10 follow by combining the transactions for several such loans at various times.

The present worth of a cash flow set at interest rate i is conceptually a "worth" in the following sense: If you enjoyed the services of a surrogate banker freely willing to lend *and* borrow at rate i, then by the appropriate set of transactions you could covert an entire cash flow set to its present worth at time zero. By the same token, surrogate banking transactions could convert a cash flow set to its worth at an arbitrary time m. The worth of a cash flow set is said to be equivalent at interest rate i to the cash flow set itself.

Most individuals and enterprises are chronic borrowers or chronic lenders. To a chronic borrower, cash inflows and outflows diminish or augment debt load, so the debt load serves effectively as a surrogate banker with i as the interest rate on debt—the *cost of capital*. To a chronic lender, cash inflows and outflows effectively augment or diminish savings or investments, so the savings or investments serve effectively as a surrogate banker with interest rate i as the yield rate or *rate of return on ordinary investments*. For most decision makers, there does exist an interest rate at which worth of a cash flow set is meaningful. The interest rate i at which a decision maker computes worth is called minimal attractive rate of return (MARR).

Future cash flow amounts and timings cannot be known with certainty; they are estimates. Estimates, as sections 3.1 and 3.2 have made clear, are subject to error. Because of risk, natural optimism, cost escalation, taxes—things ignored either intentionally or unintentionally in estimating benefits and costs—cash flow sets tend to be optimistic. MARR is hence usually established as somewhat greater than either the cost of capital or the rate of return on ordinary investments. This is a little like setting your watch 10 minutes ahead so as not to be late; i is set a little high because to be truly worthwhile, a prospective investment must look a little better than just worthwhile.

Let us return to the printer alternatives for which cash flow diagrams were shown. Suppose we use $i = 15\%$ as MARR. Then the present worth of Alternative A1 is

$$P^{(A1)} = -1000\beta^0 + 500\beta^1 + 500\beta^2 + \cdots + 500\beta^6 = \$892.24$$

The present worth of Alternative A2 is

$$P^{(A2)} = -800\beta^0 + 400\beta^1 + 400\beta^2 + \cdots + 400\beta^6 = \$713.79$$

From our interpretation of worth, since the present worth of Alternative A1 is greater than that of Alternative A2 by $178.45, then at time zero it is "worth" $178.45 to choose A1 over A2.

A different baseline can be used. Since the benefits are equal for both alternatives, we could ignore benefits and let the baseline be "Printer" instead of "No printer;" that is, we could evaluate the worths of costs only.

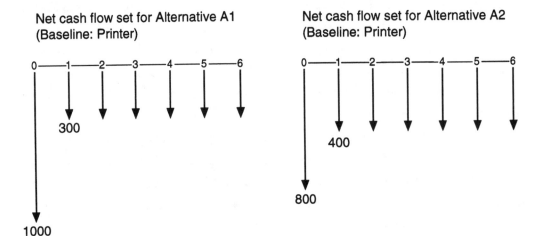

Net cash flow set for Alternative A1 (Baseline: Printer)

Net cash flow set for Alternative A2 (Baseline: Printer)

$P^{(A1)} = -\$2135.34$ and $P^{(A2)} = -\$2313.79$. Again, A1 is better than A2 by $178.45 at time zero.

If the baseline was Printer A1, then the cash flow set for the *incremental alternative* A2 – A1 would be a savings of $200 at time zero with incremental operating costs of $100 per year.

Net cash-flow set for incremental Alternative A2−A1
(Baseline: Printer A1)

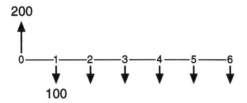

The present worth of the incremental alternative is $P^{(A2-A1)} = -\$178.45$. Choosing A2 when A1 could have been chosen is equivalent to a loss of $178.45 at time zero. The three baselines all yield the same decision; therefore, choice of baseline is a matter of convenience.

Measures of worth can also be chosen. For example, if the future worth had been used instead of present worth, it can be verified that for all three baselines A1 would be better than A2 by $412.76 at time 6—which of course is equivalent (at 15% interest) to $178.45 at time zero. *Note: If by any worth measure the ratio of worths of two alternatives is K, it is also K by any other worth measure.* Thus ($K = 1$), if two alternatives have equal worths by any measure they have equal worths by all measures.

For convenience both in modeling and computing, simple patterns of cash flows are treated as a unit. A single amount or timing pair (e.g., the $200 savings at time zero in the foregoing cash flow diagram) is called a *lump sum*. A pattern of equal cash flows at successive times (e.g., the −$100 cash flows at times {0,1,...,6} in the foregoing cash flow diagram) is called an *equal-payment series*. Other patterns, to be defined below, are the *linear gradient series* and the *geometric gradient series*.

3.3.1.3 Equal-payment Series

An equal-payment series consists of n successive cash flows, one per period, each of the identical amount A. On the series' own time scale, the cash flows occur at times {1, 2,..., n}. Its present worth can be computed not only by summing the terms $A\beta$, $A\beta^2$, and so forth, but also by multiplying A by a closed-form formula denoted $(P/A\,i,n)$ and sometimes called the "pain" factor.

Present worth of equal-payment series {$A: t=1,...,n$}:

$$P = A\beta + A\beta^2 + \cdots + A\beta^n \;=\; A\frac{1-\beta^n}{i} \;=\; A(P/A\,i,n) \tag{3-11}$$

For example, the present worth of −$100 per year for six years can be computed by multiplying −100 by the pain factor. For $i = 0.15$ and $n = 6$, form $\beta = 1/(1+i)$, take β to the n power, subtract

β^n from 1, and divide by i. This yields the pain-factor value 3.78448269. Multiply this by -100 to obtain $-\$378.45$, the present worth of the equal-payment series.

For computers or programmable hand calculators, a convenient form of the pain factor is (for $I \leftarrow i$ and $N \leftarrow n$)

$$\text{PAIN formula: } (1-(1+I)^\wedge-N)/I$$

For spreadsheet computation, there is no advantage to a closed-form formula; simply form a row containing the successive powers of β: $\beta, \beta^2, ..., \beta^n$. Multiply the row by A and sum the row to obtain the present worth of an equal-payment series.

3.3.1.4 Periodic Equivalent

In addition to the present worth, future worth, and worth at an arbitrary time m, there is one additional commonly-used worth measure: the periodic equivalent (called annual equivalent or annual worth if periods represent years). The periodic equivalent of a cash flow set is the amount for an equal-payment series with a given n (not necessarily equal to the horizon for the cash flow set) that is equivalent at i to the cash flow set. We can compute the periodic equivalent of a cash flow set by first computing the set's present worth at i, then dividing by the pain factor. Recall the cash flow set for the incremental alternative A2 – A1, having $200 at time zero and $-\$100$ per year for six years. The present worth at 15% interest was found to be $-\$178.45$. Let us determine the five-year annual equivalent at 15% interest. This is $-178.45/(P/A\ 15\%,5) = -\$53.23$.

3.3.1.5 Linear Gradient Series

A linear gradient series consists of n successive cash flows, one per period, increasing linearly from amount A_1 at time 1 to amount $A_n = A_1 + (n-1)G$ at time n. For example, if annual revenues from an asset with a five-year economic life are estimated to have the amounts {1200, 1100, 1000, 900, 800}, we have a linear gradient series with $A_1 = 1200$, $G = -100$, $n = 5$. The present worth is given by the closed-form formula

Linear gradient present-worth formula for series $\{A_1 + (t-1)G: t=1,...,n\}$:

$$P = \frac{A_1}{i} + \frac{G}{i^2} - \beta^n\left(\frac{A_1}{i} + \frac{nG}{i} + \frac{G}{i^2}\right) \tag{3-12}$$

At $i = 0.15$, the cash flow set at hand has present worth $3445.07. When A_1 is positive and G is negative, as in this cash flow set, the final positive cash flow occurs at L (the positive life) or the next integer time after L, where $L = -A_1/G$. The cash flow set at hand has a positive life of 12 years.

A geometric gradient series consists of n successive cash flows, one per period, increasing geometrically from amount A_1 at time 1 to amount $A_n = A_1(1+g)^{n-1}$ at time n. Each cash flow amount is $(1+g)$ times the previous amount, where g is the geometric growth rate.

For example, if the first cash flow is 990 and the geometric growth rate is 10%, the cash flows are 990, 1089, 1197.90, and so forth. The present worth of a geometric gradient series is given by a variation of the pain factor. Define the *zero projection* of the series as $a_0 = A_1/(1+g)$. (It is the amount projected for time zero.) This example has zero projection $a_0 = 990/(1.10) = 900$. Also, define a *substitute discount factor* α and the corresponding *substitute interest rate* s:

$$\alpha = (1+g)\beta$$

$$s = (1/\alpha) - 1 = (i - g)/(1+g)$$

With these definitions the present worth of a geometric series is computed by multiplying the zero projection by the pain factor that has α instead of β and s instead of i.

Present worth of geometric gradient series $\{a_0(1+g)^t: t=1,...,n\}$:

$$P = a_0 \frac{1-\alpha^n}{s} \qquad \alpha \neq 1 \Leftrightarrow s \neq 0 \qquad (3\text{-}13)$$

For the case $\alpha = 1 \Leftrightarrow s = 0$, where growth exactly offsets discounting, $P = na_0$.

Note that all of the series have their first cash flow at time 1 on the series' own time scale, and that the present worth is one period earlier, at time 0 on the series' own time scale. If time 0 on this time scale is time m on the actual time scale, multiply P (as computed by a series formula) by β^m to determine the series' contribution to present worth of the entire cash flow set.

E15.   An agency has offered Burstyn-Bonds, Inc. an exclusive contract to build replacement engines for H-14 helicopters. The marketing department at Burstyn-Bonds is leery of the deal, having noted that there is no guaranteed minimum demand, and having estimated that the demand will decline 8.5% per year from the 33 units demanded in the year just ended. However, the production and engineering departments have estimated that the immediate cost to accept the contract will be only $400,000 and that a $5000 profit will be earned per unit produced. If the contract is accepted, Burstyn-Bonds is obligated to supply the demand for 10 years. There is no salvage value at the end of the contract. A further consideration is that the existing production facilities are wearing out. The maintenance department has estimated that maintenance expenditures beyond those contemplated in the estimated profits will begin during the third year of the contract and will grow linearly: $30,000 in the third year, $40,000 in the fourth, and so forth. Accepting all estimates, determine the present worth of the proposed contract at a 15% interest rate.

The present worth of the entire cash flow set is (in thousands of dollars) $-400 + P\{$ geometric series of declining profits $\} - \beta^2 P\{$ linear series of increasing maintenance expenditures $\}$.

The geometric series has $a_0 = 165$ ($5000 per unit, 33 units), $g = -0.085$, $n = 10$. The substitute discount factor, for $\beta = 1/1.15$, is $\alpha = (1+g)\beta = 0.795652$, and the corresponding substitute interest rate is $s = 25.68306\%$. From equation 3-13, the present worth of profits is 577.1233 (in thousands).

The linear series has (on its own time scale) $A_1 = -30$, $G = -10$, and $n = 8$. From equation 3-12 the present worth of additional maintenance is -259.4268. The present worth of the proposed contract is $-400 + 577.1233 - \beta^2 259.4268 = -19.0406$ or about $-\$19,000$. The contract is unprofitable.

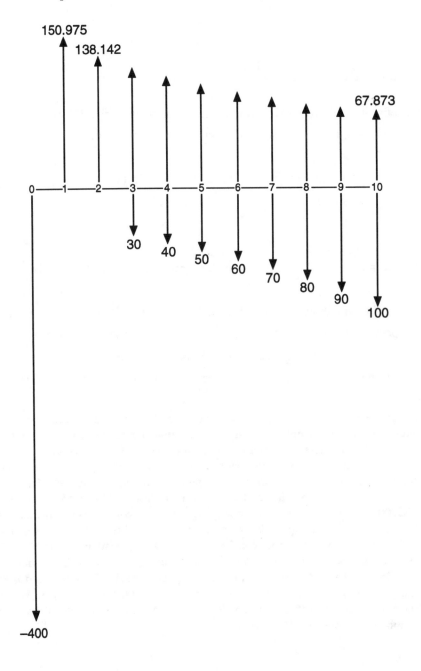

3.3.1.6 Effective and Nominal Interest Rates

When time is measured in years and interest is compounded annually, the interest rate can be denoted i_{eff} and called the effective interest rate to distinguish it from i, the interest rate per period. If there are m periods per year and interest is compounded once per period or m times per year, the relationships between i_{eff} and i are

$$i_{eff} = (1 + i)^m - 1 \tag{3-14}$$

and

$$i = (1 + i_{eff})^{1/m} - 1 \tag{3-15}$$

Thus, for example, a consumer-loan interest rate of 1.5% monthly is an effective interest rate of about 19.56%. The same interest rate can be called a *nominal* rate of 18%. The nominal rate (r) is the ANNUAL PERCENTAGE RATE (APR) required to be clearly stated on loan contracts, and is defined as

$$r = mi \tag{3-16}$$

where, as before, m is the number of periods per year and i is the interest rate per period. Nominal interest rates are cited informally as, for example, "18% compounded monthly" for "1.5% per month." The relationship between the nominal interest rate r and the effective interest rate i_{eff} is

$$i_{eff} = (1 + r/m)^m - 1 \tag{3-17}$$

The nominal continuous interest rate, also denoted r, is defined by letting m increase without bound in equation 3-17, so that i_{eff} goes to the limit $e^r - 1$, where $e = 2.7182818$ is the natural logarithm base. The nominal continuous interest rate has these relationships with i_{eff}: $r = \ln(1 + i_{eff})$, and $\beta = e^{-r}$ where $\beta = 1/(1 + i_{eff})$.

3.3.1.7 Timing Conventions

Timing conventions are used in engineering economy to avoid unnecessary complications. The most commonly used timing convention is the end-of-period (eop) convention. Under the eop convention all cash flows that occur within a period are treated as if they occurred at the end of the period. When there is one period per year, the eop convention is called the end-of-year (eoy) convention. The eop convention is not used for periods longer than a year. For periods of a year or less, however, the eop convention is used in preference to the continuous timing convention even when it introduces some distortion. For example, a labor savings of $3300 per year is probably realized 26 times during the year, once per pay period, but an engineering economic analysis of a labor-saving project with a life of several years would treat the savings as $3300 at the end of each year. Energy savings may be continuous, but can be treated by the eoy convention. The eoy convention, in general, underestimates continuous cash flows by the factor $[\ln(1+i_{eff})]/i_{eff}$.

The following example problem illustrates both the eop timing convention and the periodic equivalent (the worth measure introduced in section 3.3.1.4). One of the uses of the periodic equivalent is to compare alternatives having unequal economic lives when repeatability—the opportunity or necessity to repeat the cash flow set an indefinite number of times—is assumed.

E16. **The tube bundle for a shell-and-tube heat exchanger will last 12 months if the bundle is fabricated of 316 stainless steel, or 18 months if fabricated of Monel metal. The cost of replacing a tube bundle, including lost processing profit, hydrostatic testing, and everything except tube material, is $4000. The material cost is $5000 for stainless, $10,000 for Monel. For an enterprise that uses a MARR of $i_{eff} = 15\%$, which material is better?**

Let us measure time in months and use the eop timing convention. The monthly interest rate is $i = (1.15)^{1/12} - 1 = 0.0117149$. We assume the bundle will be replaced an indefinite number of times, each replacement having the same costs and prospective life. Let $-A^{(316)}$ be the equivalent monthly cost of a stainless steel bundle for its service life of 12 months, and let $-A^{(Monel)}$ be the equivalent monthly cost of a Monel metal bundle for its service life of 18 months.

$$-A^{(316)} = 9000/(P/A\ i,12) = \underline{\$808.33}$$

$$-A^{(Monel)} = 14,000/(P/A\ i,18) = \underline{\$867.19}$$

The <u>316 stainless</u> material is more economical; the equivalent monthly cost for Monel metal is about 7.28% greater than for stainless steel.

Mathematically equivalent to the periodic-equivalent approach is the common-life approach, in which the artificial assumption is made that the horizon is a common multiple of the alternative lives, so that a whole number of replacements will occur for each alternative. For example, if the lives had been 11 and 17 months respectively, a 187-month horizon would be used, but since the lives are 12 and 18 months respectively, a 36-month horizon can be used. Let $-P^{(316)}$ be the present worth of the cost of providing 36 months of service by installing a 316-stainless bundle at times 0, 12, and 24. Let $-P^{(Monel)}$ be the present worth of the cost of providing 36 months of service by installing a Monel metal bundle at times 0 and 18. Let $\beta = 1/(1+i)$.

$$-P^{(316)} = 9000 + 9000\beta^{12} + 9000\beta^{24} = \$23,631.38$$

$$-P^{(Monel)} = 14,000 + 14,000\beta^{18} = \$25,352.23$$

The present worth of the cost of providing 36 months of service using Monel metal is about 7.28% greater than that using stainless steel. By either method, the worths of the two alternatives are in the same ratio.

Note that since a series of replacements is an equal-payment series with time measured in lifetimes, we could have computed, for example, $-P^{(316)} = 9000 + 9000(P/A\ 15\%,2)$ or $-P^{(316)} = 1.15 \times 9000(P/A\ 15\%,3)$. In the corresponding calculation for the Monel alternative, the interest rate for 18-month intervals would be $i_{18} = (1.15)^{1.5} - 1$.

A third mathematically equivalent approach is the infinite-horizon approach, in which an infinite series of replacements is assumed. Since the pain factor for infinite n is $(P/A\ i,\infty) = 1/i$, then if we let $-P_{\infty}^{(316)}$ and $-P_{\infty}^{(Monel)}$ be the respective present worths of the costs of providing bundles forever, we have

$$-P_{\infty}^{(316)} = 9000 + 9000/0.15 = \$69,000$$

$$-P_{\infty}^{(Monel)} = 14,000 + 14,000/i_{18} = \$74,024.62$$

Again the same relative relationship appears: the cost for Monel is 7.28% greater than that for stainless steel.

3.3.1.8 Efficiency Measures

Efficiency measures of investments include rate of return (ROR), benefit/cost ratio (B/C), net present value (worth) index (NPVI), and payback time. Rate of return (ROR) of a cash flow set is defined as the interest rate that makes worth zero. If any worth measure is zero, all worth measures are zero, so future worth, present worth, or even periodic equivalent can be set to zero to determine the rate of return. Rate of return is a measure of how fast returns recover an investment. To see this, consider the present worth of an investment of I dollars at time zero, followed by a perpetual series of A dollars per year. Recalling that the pain factor is $1/i$ when n is infinite, the present worth is $P = -I + A/i$. Solving for i given $P = 0$ yields the ROR, which is denoted i^*: $i^* = A/I$. Thus, for an investment project with this simple structure, the rate of return is the fraction of the investment that each period's returns recover. The relation $i^* = A/I$ would also hold for a finite-horizon investment project if it had a salvage value at time n exactly equal to I, but in the general case i^* must be determined by direct search.

To compute the rate of return i^* for an arbitrary investment alternative, equate zero to the formula for its present (or future) worth with i^* substituted for the interest rate. You cannot solve algebraically for i^* except in certain very special cases. If you try two interest rates i_1 and i_2, and compute the two corresponding worths P_1 and P_2, then you can use the *linear regression* feature of a programmable scientific hand calculator to determine an interest rate normally much closer to i^* than the two interest rates tried. It generally takes only three or four iterations to accurately home in on the ROR. Treat the P values as the independent variable x in the linear regression, and the i values as the dependent variable y; then the x-intercept given by the linear regression routine is the new guess for i.

As an example of an ROR determination using linear regression, determine the rate of return of a project that has an investment of 40 followed by returns of 5 per period for 20 periods. The formula for present worth is $P = -40 + 5(P/A\ i,20)$. Try interest rates of 5% and 20%, yielding present worths of 22.3110517 and -15.6521013. Linear regression gives an intercept of 13.8155%. Try interest rates of 13% and 14%, yielding present worths of -4.87624211 and -6.88434724. Linear regression gives an intercept of 10.57172%. Try interest rates of 10% and 11%, yielding present worths of 2.5678186 and -0.1833594. Linear regression gives an intercept of <u>10.93%</u>, which is accurate to the accuracy shown as could be verified by a fourth iteration, for example using 10.93% and 10.94%. The present worth at exactly 10.93% is about -0.0004, which is very close to zero.

Other methods to compute ROR include successive bracketing (compute P for 10 interest rates in a do-loop, then for 10 more that are between the two rates where P changes sign—this is easy to do on a calculator that programs in Basic language, even if it is not set up in advance), using the zeros-of-a-function feature of a calculator that manipulates user-defined formulas, or using the ROR function of a financial calculator that manipulates user-defined cash flow sets.

To understand the distinction between an efficiency measure such as ROR and a worth measure, consider the "project" whereby someone borrows a nickel from you and pays back a dime a few hours later. The ROR is nearly infinite, but the present worth is only about $0.05. Thus, if the project is *unique* (cannot be repeated at will) and is not *scalable* (able to be sized at will, such as lending $5000 instead of a nickel), ROR is meaningless. But when there exist other similar opportunities or a project can be scaled up in size, ROR may have meaning. ROR can fail to have meaning if it is greater than MARR, for it will often be found that to realize the ROR you would have to reinvest returns at ROR, whereas in reality returns are reinvested at MARR.

Payback time is a measure of liquidity; capital tied up in a project, whether already spent or only obligated, is illiquid. Payback time is defined simply as the number of years (or periods) that it takes for the returns (ignoring interest) to exceed the investment. Note that for the infinite-horizon project in the foregoing discussion, where $i^* = A/I$, the payback time is I/A. An enterprise may choose not to undertake a profitable investment if it ties up funds for too long. For example, if you *knew* that a $40,000 sports car bought today would be worth $550,000 in today's dollars (indexed dollars as defined in the next section) 10 years from now if it were kept untouched, would you be willing to make the investment? (By the way, the rate of return of this investment as a real interest rate d^*, defined in the next section, can be easily calculated algebraically and is very close to 30%.)

Net present value (worth) index or NPVI of a cash flow set is defined as its present worth divided by its investment (considered as positive). For example, if a $40,000 sports car were bought today and were to be sold 10 years from now for $814,000 (*current* dollars as defined in the next section, corresponding to $550,000 *indexed* dollars if there were 4% annual inflation), the present worth at $i = 15\%$ would be $-40,000 + 814,000\beta^{10} = \$161,208.35$. The NPVI for the investment would be $161,208.35 \div 40,000 = 4.03$. NPVI is a measure of *capital efficiency*, useful in budgeting of scarce investment funds. An enterprise should (when other considerations such as liquidity do not dictate otherwise) put its limited investment money where it will gain the greatest present worth per dollar invested.

Benefit/cost ratio or *B/C* is a measure of *cost efficiency*. It is defined as *the ratio of the worth of benefits to the worth of costs*. It is very useful where the size or scope of projects is uncertain or the benefits are difficult to measure in money terms. For example, a $940,000 public health project that can protect 40,000 citizens can be compared to a $75,000 project that can protect 10,000 citizens. The two projects have *B/C* ratios of 42.55 and 133.33 in the arbitrary units of citizens protected per $1000. If the number of citizens to be protected will be determined by available budgets and comparison with other public health problems, the benefit/cost ratio is meaningful; in the long run, a public health agency that chooses programs on a *B/C* basis will have a greater impact on public health per dollar of its funding than one that does not consider cost efficiency.

3.3.2 Inflation and Escalation

Monetary inflation is a general rise in prices, wages, and other cash flows. Although actual inflation occurs in spurts, inflation for future estimated cash flows is considered to be geometric at a constant rate j. If the price of a given package of goods and services is L_0 at time zero, then under inflation rate j it is assumed that the price L_t of the same package at time t will be

$$L_t = L_0(1 + j)^t \tag{3-18}$$

A cash flow is either subject to inflation or it is not. Suppose there is an estimated cash flow amount of $1000 for a cash flow that will occur at time t. Under inflation rate j, if the sense of this estimate is that a check will be written for $1000 at time t, such as for a lease payment or a loan repayment contracted to be $1000 or a payment for a fixed-cost maintenance contract, then the estimate is in *current dollars* (also called inflated, nominal, or after-inflation) and can be denoted $A_t = 1000$. On the other hand, if the sense of the estimate is that a check will be written for an amount $1000(1+j)^t$ dollars, such as for something whose price now would be $1000, then the estimate is in *indexed dollars* (also called real or before-inflation) and can be denoted $W_t = 1000$.

The relationship between current and indexed cash flows is

$$A_t = W_t(1+j)^t \qquad (3\text{-}19a)$$

and

$$W_t = A_t(1+j)^{-t} \qquad (3\text{-}19b)$$

For example, if a repair cost to be paid three years from now is estimated as $2155 on the basis that it would cost $2155 to do the same amount of work today, then at 4% annual inflation the estimate is an *indexed-dollar* estimate, $W_3 = 2155$, and the corresponding *current-dollar* estimate would be $A_3 = 2155(1.04)^3 = \$2424.08$.

Inflation can be ignored or it can be considered. There are two conditions under which inflation can be ignored:

1. If all cash flows are given in current dollars, inflation may be ignored and discounting may be done at the market interest rate i. This is valid when amounts are fixed by law or by contract, or are already inflated.
2. If all cash flows are given in indexed dollars, inflation may be ignored and discounting may be done at the real interest rate d (defined below). In such cases it is customary in casual usage to employ the symbol i for d.

When inflation is *considered*, which it must be when a problem includes both current-dollar and indexed-dollar amounts, we must distinguish between the market interest rate i and the real interest rate d. Given inflation rate j, the real interest rate is defined as follows:

$$d = \frac{1+i}{1+j} - 1 = \frac{i-j}{1+j} \quad \text{real interest rate} \qquad (3\text{-}20)$$

The rule for treatment of current and indexed cash flows is simple:

- Discount current-dollar cash flows at the market interest rate i
- Discount indexed-dollar cash flows at the real interest rate d

E17.   A reactor was recharged with a fresh catalyst today at a cost of $18,150. It must be recharged again at the end of each of the next three years. The catalyst vendor offers a piece of equipment called a catalyst saver. It can be purchased by paying $6000 now and agreeing to pay $6000 at the end of each of the next three years. There are no further relevant consequences after three years. If we purchase the catalyst saver, the vendor guarantees that the amount of fresh catalyst needed will be cut in half. Assume that the recharge costs would correspondingly be cut in half (from what they otherwise would be), and that there will be 6% annual inflation that applies to all components of recharge cost but not to the catalyst-saver purchase contract. At an interest rate of $i = 15\%$, determine the present worth of the catalyst-saver opportunity.

The current cash flows are to be discounted at $i = 15\%$, and the indexed cash flows are to be discounted at $d = (0.15 - 0.06)/1.06 = 8.490566\%$. The same answer will be obtained whether or not the cash flows are all converted to current cash flows. The annual savings in indexed dollars are half today's recharge cost, or $9075; in current dollars the savings for year t will be $9075(1.06)^t$, as given by equation 3-19a with $j = 0.06$.

Current and indexed cash flows:

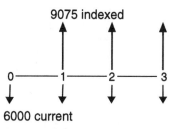

$P = -6000 + 9075(P/A \ d,3) - 6000(P/A \ 15\%, 3)$
$\quad = \$3482.32$

All current cash flows:

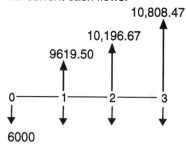

$P = -6000 + [9619.50\beta + 10,196.67\beta^2$
$\quad\quad + 10,808.47\beta^3] - 6000(P/A \ 15\%, 3)$
$\quad = \$3482.32$

The foregoing example demonstrates that it is *not* necessary or desirable to convert all cash flows to a common basis before discounting. Simply discount current-dollar amounts at i and discount indexed-dollar amounts at d.

Geometric escalation in cash flow amounts can be handled similarly to inflation—by a change in the interest rate. A cash flow or set of cash flows is subject to geometric escalation at composite escalation rate g if its current-dollar measure grows geometrically at rate g.

For example, suppose that during a period of 4% annual inflation, the cost of computers fell 3% per year. Then $g = -0.03$ (e.g., a computer that cost $1000 in year 0 would cost $1000(1 - 0.03)^t$ dollars in year t). The real escalation rate v is the geometric rate of growth in the indexed-dollar measure. The composite escalation rate includes inflation, whereas the real escalation rate does not. The relationship among g, v, and j is

$$1 + g = (1 + v)(1 + j) \tag{3-21}$$

Solving for v, for instance, we can see that if the cost of computers fell at a composite escalation rate of $g = -0.03$ during a period of $j = 0.04$ inflation, the real cost of computers fell at a real escalation rate of about 6.73%.

A cash flow or set of cash flows that escalates at composite rate g or real rate v can be discounted at a substitute interest rate s determined as shown in equation 3-22.

$$s = \frac{i-g}{1+g} = \frac{1+i}{(1+v)(1+j)} - 1 = \frac{d-v}{1+v} \qquad (3\text{-}22)$$

E18.   **The cost of maintenance for a plant was \$3759 in the year just ended. General inflation is expected to occur at a 4.5% annual rate, but maintenance costs are expected to undergo real growth at a 1.5% annual rate. At $i = 20\%$, determine the present worth of the next 5 years' costs for maintenance.**

From equation 3-22, with $i = 0.20$, $v = 0.015$, and $j = 0.045$, determine $s = 0.13135503$. (This value for the substitute interest rate can be determined directly from the middle expression in equation 3-22, or from the leftmost expression after determining $g = 0.0606750$, or from the rightmost expression after determining $d = 0.14832536$.) Then the present worth for 5 years is $-3759(P/A\ s,5) = \underline{-\$13,177.68.}$

3.3.3 Sensitivity Analysis and Risk

Future cash flow amounts and timings are estimates. Given estimates of parameters, a worth calculation produces a point estimate of worth. If the point estimate of worth is too inaccurate, a decision based on it may be wrong.

Sensitivity analysis or "what-iffing" is to vary one or more parameters over reasonable ranges of their variation, noting whether a reasonable combination of parameter values can affect the worth sufficiently to cause a change in the decision. If no, then sensitivity analysis will have established confidence in the correctness of the decision. Otherwise, what is gained by sensitivity analysis is an indication of how much more accurately the parameters must be estimated in order to establish such confidence.

A variation of sensitivity analysis is breakeven analysis, in which one directly calculates how great or small a particular parameter's value must be in order for the decision to change.

E19a.   **The present worth of alternative A1 is $P^{(A1)} = -I + R(P/A\ 15\%,4)$, where I is the investment, estimated as \$40,000, and R is the net annual returns, estimated as \$16,000 per year. Another alternative, A2, is estimated to have a present worth of $P^{(A2)} = \$20,000$. There is a reasonable chance that I could be as small as \$30,000, and there is a reasonable chance that R could be as great as \$20,000 per year. What conclusion can be drawn from sensitivity analysis?**

The point estimate of $P^{(A1)}$ is $-40,000 + 16,000(P/A\ 15\%,4) = \$5679.65$. Since this is less than $20,000, the decision in question is to choose alternative A2.

If I were as small as $30,000, then $P^{(A1)}$ would be as great as $15,679.65—an improvement not great enough to change the decision.

If R were as great as $20,000, then $P^{(A1)}$ would be as great as $17,099.57—again, an improvement not great enough to change the decision.

There is nothing in the situation to suggest that there would be a reasonable chance of *both* events $I \le \$30,000$ and $R \ge \$20,000$. (For instance, if these events independently each had a 10% probability, the probability of their combination would be 1%.) Therefore we conclude from sensitivity analysis that <u>confidence has been established in the correctness of the decision</u>.

A breakeven question has a form such as, "How great (or small) must X be in order for Y not to exceed (or not to be less than) Z?" It is answered by replacing X, the *breakeven parameter*, with a symbol, rewriting Y and Z in terms of the symbol to form the inequality that is the *breakeven assertion* ($Y \le Z$), and solving for (or searching for) the value of X that satisfies the assertion.

For example, suppose you have calculated the cost of producing a rush order by using temporary labor; call this cost Y. One of the parameters in the calculation of Y is the wage rate for temporary labor; call this parameter X. Suppose also that you have calculated the cost of producing the order by using overtime; call this cost Z. Now suppose that this breakeven question is asked: What wage rate for temporary labor would be so high that it would be cheaper to use overtime? Substituting a symbol, say x, for the wage rate, write the formula for the cost Y. The breakeven assertion is written by putting ">" after the Y formula and before the value of Z. This assertion says the cost producing the order by using temporary labor exceeds the cost of producing the order by using overtime, and it has one unknown, x. Solve the inequality for x, which is the answer to the breakeven question. In practice, many engineers form an *equality* rather than an inequality, and use their judgment to recognize whether they have found an upper limit or a lower limit. But if it is done with an inequality the result ($x > 14.75$ for example) contains this information as well.

E19b. **In the previous example, it has been suggested that the economic life of alternative A1 may be greater than 4 years. If returns were to continue at $16,000 per year, how long a life would be required for A1 not to be worse than A2?**

Substituting n for 4, we rewrite the present worth of alternative A1 as $P^{(A1)} = -40,000 + 16,000(P/A\ 15\%,n)$. For A1 not to be worse than A2, the value of this expression must equal or exceed $20,000.

$$-40,000 + 16,000(P/A\ 15\%,n) \ge 20,000, \quad \text{or} \quad (P/A\ 15\%,n) \ge 3.75$$

Often where the parameter is a timing or duration (and always when it is an interest rate) it is not fruitful to try to solve algebraically. If we search for the appropriate value of n, we quickly find that 6 years is the shortest life in whole years that makes A1 not worse than A2.

In this case an algebraic solution is also possible. Recalling that the pain factor is $(1 - \beta^n)/i$, where $\beta = 1/(1+i)$, we have

$$(1 - \beta^n)/i \geq 3.75 \quad \Rightarrow \quad 1 - 3.75i \geq \beta^n$$

Take the natural logarithm of both sides, and then divide both sides by $\ln\beta$ (which reverses the sense of the inequality because $\ln\beta$ is negative):

$$\ln(1 - 3.75i) \geq n\ln\beta \quad \Rightarrow \quad n \geq [\ln(1 - 3.75i)]/\ln\beta$$

Since $i = 0.15$ and $\beta = 1/1.15$, the answer is $n \geq 5.9149$ years.

If enough probabilistic information is known or estimated about uncertainty in parameters, one can calculate expected worth. Recall the formula for the expected value of a function, say G, of a random variable X that takes on possible values $\{x_j\}$ with probabilities $\{p_j\}$ that sum to 1:

Expected value of a function of a random variable:

$$E[G(X)] = G(x_1)p_1 + G(x_2)p_2 + \ldots \tag{3-23}$$

If we know the probability distribution of a parameter that is the only random variable in a worth formula, the expected value of the worth can be calculated.

E20.   An enterprise that uses $i = 20\%$ wants to evaluate an investment alternative that requires an investment of 32, brings annual returns of 10 for an uncertain number of years n, and has a negative salvage value (because of site restoration costs) of –5. The present worth of the alternative is $P = -32 + 10(P/A\ 20\%, n) - 5\beta^n$, where $\beta = 1/1.20$. If the chances are $\{20\%, 30\%, 30\%, 20\%\}$ that n will be $\{5, 6, 7, 8\}$, determine the expected present worth of the alternative.

Computing P at the various times, multiplying by the probabilities, and summing, we have

$$E(P) = -4.10326645 \times 0.20 - 0.41938861 \times 0.30 + 2.65050940 \times 0.30 + 5.20875784 \times 0.20$$
$$= 0.890434$$

Note that $E(P)$ is *not* equal to the present worth for the expected life (which for the expected life of 6.5 years would be 1.1854755), because P is not linear in n.

When a cash flow amount is a random variable, the expected worth *is* equal to the worth for the expected amount, because worth is linear in cash flow amounts. It is important to realize that the estimates of parameters used in ordinary deterministic cost calculations should be expected values, not medians or modes (the mode of a random variable is its most likely value). Thus, for example, if a profit had a 90% chance of being $80,000 and a 10% chance of being $50,000, and a single profit estimate was to be used in a deterministic calculation, the correct estimate is $80,000 \times 0.90 + 50,000 \times 0.10 = \$77,000$. The rule for using expected values instead of other central measures should be followed even for estimates of timings and interest rates. Even though expected values of these parameters do not exactly give expected values of worth, less error is introduced than by using any competing measure.

Two types of risk in engineering economy calculations are very easy to account for without needing to deal with probability distributions: ordinary risk and geometric cessation risk.

Ordinary risk: When there is a probability p that a cash flow amount will be the hoped-for cash flow amount H and a probability $q = 1 - p$ that the amount will be zero, use pH instead of H in all calculations.

Geometric cessation risk: When at the end of every period there is a probability p that the estimated cash flows will continue at least for one period and a probability $q = 1 - p$ that no further cash flows will occur, replace the interest rate i with $f = (i + q)/(1 - q)$. Here f is the risk-cognizant substitute interest rate. Geometric cessation risk can be handled in combination with inflation or escalation. If the cash flows subject to geometric cessation risk are indexed amounts discounted at d, replace d with $f = (d + q)/(1 - q)$. Similarly, if the cash flows are escalating and are discounted at a substitute interest rate s, replace s with $f = (s + q)/(1 - q)$.

E21. A $1000 investment is intended to bring in a $200 return at time 2 and a series of five $300 returns at times {3, 4, 5, 6, 7} (nothing at time 1). Determine the intended present worth at $i = 12\%$. Then determine the expected present worth if there is a 10% risk that the series of $300 returns will not occur. Finally (without the 10% risk), determine the expected present worth if there is a 5% risk every period that no further cash flows will occur.

Let $\beta = 1/1.12$.

$$P = -1000 + 200\beta^2 + \beta^2 300(P/A\ 12\%,5) = \underline{\$21.55}$$

To account for a 10% ordinary risk for the series of $300 cash flows, replace $300 with $0.90 \times 300 = \$270$:

$$E(P) = -1000 + 200\beta^2 + \beta^2 270(P/A\ 12\%,5) = \underline{-\$64.66}$$

To account for a 5% geometric cessation risk each period, replace $i = 0.12$ with $f = (i + 0.05)/0.95 = 0.178947368$, and correspondingly replace β with $\alpha = 1/(1+f)$:

$$E(P) = -1000 + 200\,\alpha^2 + \alpha^2 300(P/A\ f,5) = \underline{-\$179.52}$$

3.3.4 Depreciation and Incentives

Governments collect direct fees for services and levy direct taxes on property, sales, and on levels of various kinds of activity. Direct taxes and fees cause no special difficulty in cost analysis, because their effects on an enterprise are the same as those of any other kind of cost of doing business. Income taxes, however, are a different matter. In the United States, federal and state governments also levy taxes on income, which is defined according to complex rules that somewhat distort its basic definition as receipts less disbursements.

One difficulty is that many incentives—financial provisions having the intent of encouraging or discouraging specific behavior—are implemented indirectly through adjusting the rules by which income is defined. The most troublesome such rules are those of depreciation accounting.

Depreciation charges are fictitious expenditures, spread out over time, that total the cost of an asset and are used instead of that cost in tax accounting to determine income. The standard set of depreciation schedules in the U.S. is the Modified Accelerated Cost Recovery System (MACRS) (see table 3-1). As an example, if you spent $1000 on a loading device that could be depreciated on the standard MACRS depreciation schedule for a three-year life class, you would not pay income taxes as if you spent $1000 in the year in which you acquired the device. Instead, you would pay income taxes as if you had spent $333 that year and $444, $148, and $75, respectively, in the next three years.

Table 3-1. Depreciation Fractions for Standard MACRS Depreciation D_t/B_0.

Life class, n	$t = 1$	$t = 2$	$t = 3$	$t = 4$	$t = 5$	$t = 6$	$t = 7$	$t = 8$	$t = 9$	...	$t = n+1$
$n = 3$	0.3333	0.444	0.1481	0.0742							
$n = 5$	0.2	0.32	0.192	0.1152	0.1152	0.0576					
$n = 7$	0.1429	0.2449	0.1749	0.1249	0.0892	0.0892	0.0892	0.0448			
$n = 10$	0.1	0.18	0.144	0.1152	0.0922	0.0737	0.0655	0.0655	0.0655	...	0.0329
$n = 15$	0.05	0.095	0.085	0.0769	0.0693	0.0623	0.0590	0.0590	0.0590	...	0.0299
$n = 20$	0.0375	0.0722	0.0668	0.0618	0.0571	0.0528	0.0489	0.0452	0.0446	...	0.0255

If an enterprise pays income taxes at a marginal tax rate T, then an expenditure of B dollars that is not depreciated but instead is expensed generates a tax relief equal to $B \times T$ dollars at the time of the next taxation deadline. This tax relief is so-called because it is an amount by which the enterprise's tax bill is diminished below what it would be if the expenditure were not allowed to be counted against profit. Such an expenditure is called an expense, as contrasted with a capital expenditure. The depreciation charges for a capital expenditure eventually provide the same total amount of tax relief, but after a delay.

Besides the MACRS family of schedules, two other depreciation schedules are of sufficient importance to review here. *Straight-line (SL) depreciation* with a recovery period of n years has n depreciation charges, each equal to $1/n$ of the depreciable cost of the asset.

The MACRS schedules are actually part of a family called *declining-balance* schedules in which each depreciation charge is a fraction α of an asset's remaining book value. (Book value is the amount not yet depreciated; it starts as the depreciable cost and ends as zero.) The fraction α is commonly $2/n$ (double declining balance) or $1.5/n$, where n is the recovery period in years. When declining balance depreciation was standard (up to 1987), the schedule would continue until the depreciation charge would be less than $1/n$ of the original depreciable cost, whereupon the remaining charges would each be $1/n$ of the original depreciable cost (this was called a switch to straight-line depreciation). The MACRS schedules have this structure, with the modification that they also cut the first-year depreciation charge in half to account for the fact that, on the average, a new asset is acquired one-half year before the end of the taxable year.

Besides the MACRS schedules, the remaining descendant of declining balance depreciation schedules is declining class account (DCA) depreciation, which is a perpetual version of declining balance depreciation. It applies to all the assets of a given life class (a class account) as a group. DCA depreciation is used by large corporations that negotiate permission to use it. Tax authorities grant permission only when the fraction α is not too large. Generally α is considered too large if it causes the depreciation schedule to have a smaller dwell time than that of the MACRS schedule for the same class of asset, where dwell time is the average delay before realization of tax relief for an asset acquired at the beginning of a tax year. Under DCA accounting, when an asset is acquired, its cost is added to the appropriate class account, and each year the depreciation charge for the entire class account is αB, where B is the current value of the account and α is specific to the account; the new value of the account is $(1 - \alpha)B$. The successive depreciation charges are αB, $\alpha(1-\alpha)B$, $\alpha(1-\alpha)^2 B$, and so forth. The successive book values are $(1-\alpha)B$, $(1-\alpha)^2 B$, $(1-\alpha)^3 B$, and so forth.

Table 3-2 gives the MACRS life class and the allowable α for DCA depreciation of various assets.

Table 3-2. MACRS Recovery Periods and Allowable DCA Multipliers.

Asset type	MACRS standard recovery period, n	Maximum allowable DCA multiplier, α
Tooling, loading devices, taxis, racehorses	3	0.5094
Copiers, computers, printers, light motor vehicles, cargo containers, solar energy devices	5	0.3574
Heavy trucks, pumps, generators, manufacturing equipment, office furniture, barns, railroad track	7	0.2762
Casting molds, chemical reactors, refinery equipment	10	0.2064
Sewage plants, ships, telephone lines, power switchgear	15	0.1282
Power plants, sewer line, pipelines, long-lived equipment	20	0.0984

E22.   **A \$5000 heavy-duty laser printer is acquired at time zero, which is six months before the next tax anniversary. Determine the depreciation charges at times 0.5, 1.5, 2.5, and 3.5 if it is depreciated according to each of the following schedules: (a) straight-line depreciation with a 4-year recovery period, (b) the applicable MACRS schedule, and (c) the DCA schedule with the maximum allowable multiplier.**

(a) Straight-line depreciation charges will each be 5000/4 = $\underline{\$1250}$ and will completely depreciate the asset.

(b) The applicable MACRS schedule for a laser printer is that for the 5-year life class, so that from table 3-1 the charges will be $5000 \times \{0.20, 0.32, 0.192, 0.1152\} = \underline{\{\$1000, \$1600, \$960, \$576\}}$, leaving \$864 to be depreciated at times 4.5 and 5.5.

(c) The applicable DCA multiplier is $\alpha = 0.3574$. The charges ascribed to this asset will be $5000\alpha \times \{1, 1-\alpha, (1-\alpha)^2, (1-\alpha)^3\} = \underline{\{\$1787, \$1148, \$738, \$474\}}$, leaving \$853 to be depreciated in future years.

The schedule of depreciation charges is denoted $\{D_\tau\}$ where $\tau = 1, 2, ...$ is the relative time in years after the acquisition of the asset. Note that the schedule itself, cited in this manner, has the built-in assumption that the first depreciation charge occurs one year after acquisition of the asset, whereas in reality it is usually true that, on the average, the first depreciation charge occurs about one-half year after acquisition of the asset, as in the foregoing example.

3.3.5 After-tax Analysis

Income taxation is not decision-neutral. It favors alternatives in which expenditures can be depreciated quickly. If alternative A1 has a greater before-tax present worth than alternative A2, but the expenditures in alternative A2 can be depreciated more quickly, then A2 may have the greater after-tax present worth. Choosing A2 rather than A1 is beneficial to the enterprise according to the difference in after-tax present worth, because taxes are just another expenditure for the enterprise. If A1 has the greater before-tax present worths choosing A2 is detrimental to society as a whole according to the difference in before-tax present worths; this is a cost to society of the economic distortion caused by taxation.

To determine the after-tax present worth of an alternative, we first define the *tax lag* λ, which is the average time from an expenditure to the realization of its tax consequences. This is usually taken as $\lambda = 0.5$ yr. Given the before-tax cash flow set for an alternative, we supplement it with the tax consequences—tax paid at tax rate T on the positive cash flows and tax relief gained by the negative cash flows—to obtain the after-tax cash flow set:

Supplemental cash flows for after-tax analysis:

- For each positive cash flow having current-dollar amount A and timing t, add to the cash flow set a negative current-dollar cash flow of amount $-T \times A$ at time $t + \lambda$.
- For each expenditure that can be expensed having current-dollar amount $-A$ and timing t, add to the cash flow set a positive current-dollar cash flow of amount $T \times A$ at time $t + \lambda$.
- For each expenditure at time t that must be depreciated having schedule $\{D_\tau\}$ of depreciation charges, add a schedule of positive current dollar cash flows of amounts $T \times \{D_\tau\}$ at times $t + \lambda + \{\tau - 1\}$.

E23.   An enterprise that uses i = 15% for after-tax analysis can purchase and install a rolling mill for $5000. For 7 years it will bring benefits that in today's dollars would be $2000 per year. Inflation is expected at 4% annually. The enterprise pays taxes at rate T = 40%. The machine will be depreciated according to the appropriate MACRS schedule. Determine the after-tax present worth of acquiring it, assuming a tax lag of six months.

For clarity, although it involves unnecessary calculations, let us convert benefits and taxes to current dollars. The current-dollar benefit amounts at times $\{t=1,...,7\}$ are $\{2000 \times (1.04)^t\}$, and the taxes are -0.40 times these occurring 0.5 year later.

Time of benefit	Current-dollar benefit	Time of tax	Current-dollar tax
1	2080	1.5	−832
2	2163.20	2.5	−865.28
3	2249.73	3.5	−899.89
4	2339.72	4.5	−935.89
5	2433.31	5.5	−973.32
6	2530.63	6.5	−1012.26
7	2631.86	7.5	−1052.75

A rolling mill belongs to MACRS life class 7, so its depreciation fractions are given in the $n=7$ row of table 3-1. The depreciation charges are these fractions multiplied by 5000, and the tax relief amounts are 40% of these.

Relative time, τ	Time of charge and relief, t	MACRS-7 depreciation fraction	Depreciation charge	Tax relief amount
1	0.5	0.1429	714.50	285.80
2	1.5	0.2449	1224.50	489.80
3	2.5	0.1749	874.50	349.80
4	3.5	0.1249	624.50	249.80
5	4.5	0.0892	446.00	178.40
6	5.5	0.0892	446.00	178.40
7	6.5	0.0892	446.00	178.40
8	7.5	0.0448	224.00	89.60

The after-tax cash flow diagram is shown in figure 3-2. The present worth at 15% interest is $2335.37.

The enterprise does have some control over its taxes by "playing the tax game." Such incentives as investment tax credits, depletion allowances, and accelerated depreciation schedules for certain kinds of investments are intended to cause enterprises to adjust their investment decisions in desired ways as they attempt to maximize after-tax worth. Within the rules laid down by tax authorities, the enterprise's most effective general way of minimizing the effects of taxes

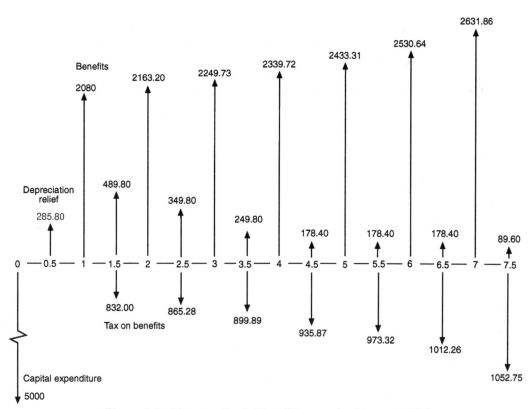

Figure 3-2. After-tax Cash Flow Diagram for Example E23.

is to maximize the proportion of expenditures that can be *expensed* (in effect, depreciated immediately) rather than capitalized. This is what occurs, for example, when you repair old equipment even though it would be cheaper before taxes to purchase new equipment; repairs can be expensed, whereas replacements must be capitalized. Several strategies exist for maximizing the non-capital portions of expenditures: negotiating the highest possible spending limit below which no expenditures are capitalized; isolating portions of large projects that can be treated as expense and managing them separately; substituting repairs for replacements, and "disguising" (within the rules) replacements as repairs; manipulating descriptions (within the rules) to classify capital expenditures in the fastest-depreciating life class allowable; and delaying the actual realization of income or capital gains (Young 1993).

E24.   An enterprise uses $i = 15\%$ for after-tax analysis and will acquire a \$90,000 asset as part of a project. It will be depreciated in the MACRS 5-year life class. The marginal tax rate (federal, state, and local combined) is 48%. In present-worth terms, how much will be saved if \$10,000 of the expenditure can be reclassified as noncapital expense?

The savings is the difference in the present worth of tax relief for a $10,000 expenditure treated in the two alternative manners. Under MACRS 5-year depreciation, the charges $10,000 \times \{0.20, 0.32, 0.192, 0.1152, 0.1152, 0.0576\}$ will occur at times $\{0.5, 1.5, 2.5, 3.5, 4.5, 5.5\}$; the reliefs at these times will be 48% of the amounts, having a present worth at 15% interest of $3552.57.

Under expensing, the relief $0.48 \times 10,000$ will occur at time 0.5, having a present worth at 15% interest of $4476.02. The savings is the difference, or $923.45.

Chapter 4
Probabilistic and
Statistical Techniques

Of the knowledge areas tested in the IE PE Exam, probability and statistics is second in importance only to cost analysis and is the only knowledge area listed for every application area. A typical exam will test probability and statistics in at least three out of eight problems.

4.1 Basic Statistics

4.1.1 Definitions

A random variable X is a variable that can take on various values x. If X is discrete, its sample space is a set of n possible values $\{x_i: i = 1,2,...,n\}$, where n can be finite or infinite. In this finite or countably infinite discrete sample space $\{x_1, x_2,...\}$, the values are listed in ascending order: $x_i \leq x_{i+1}$. If X is continuous, the sample space is an interval such as $x \geq 0$ for nonnegative continuous X.

Associated with random variables are *events*, such as the event that a discrete random variable has the value 5 (denoted $X = 5$) or the event that a discrete or continuous random variable is greater than 4 but not greater than 5 (denoted $4 < X \leq 5$). Associated with events are probabilities. The probability of an event is zero if it did not occur, cannot occur, or will not occur. The probability of an event is 1 if it did occur, must occur, or will occur. The probability of an event is 1/2 if it is equally likely to have occurred or not to have occurred. For a set of mutually exclusive and exhaustive events, the sum of probabilities is one.

4.1.1.1 Cumulative Distribution and Probability Density Functions

The probability of the event that X does not exceed a particular value x is written $P(X \leq x)$. A formula, table, or rule for determining $P(X \leq x)$ for any x in the sample space is called the cumulative distribution function (CDF) for X and is written $F(x)$. As an example of a CDF, if X is the outcome of the roll of a gambling die, where the sample space is $\{1, 2, 3, 4, 5, 6\}$ and each outcome has probability 1/6, then $F(x) = x/6$. That is, the probability that X does not exceed 1 is 1/6, the probability it does not exceed 2 is 2/6, and so forth. The CDF of every random variable goes from zero to one: $F(x_1) \geq 0$ (strictly greater than zero unless the probability of x_1 is zero) and $F(x_n) = 1$ (in the limit if n is infinite).

The probability that a discrete random variable X takes on a particular value x is written $P(X=x)$. A formula, table, or rule for determining $P(X=x_i)$ for any x_i is called the probability function for X and is written $p(x_i)$. The sum of $p(x_i)$ for all i is one, since the random variable must take on some value. As an example of a probability function, if X is the outcome of the roll of a gambling die, then $p(x) = 1/6$ for every x in the sample space. This is the discrete uniform probability function, which is a constant because all the outcomes are equally likely. It is the only probability function where $p(x)$ does not depend on x. The cumulative distribution function and probability distribution function for the discrete uniform distribution that represents a roll of a gambling die can be diagrammed as in figure 4-1.

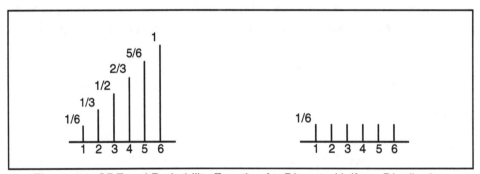

Figure 4-1. CDF and Probability Function for Discrete Uniform Distribution.

For any discrete distribution, given a particular value b, the probability that the random variable does not exceed b is given by the sum of $p(x_i)$ for all x_i that do not exceed b.

Relationship between $F(x)$ and $p(x)$ for a discrete random variable:

$$F(b) = P(x \leq b) = \sum_{x_i \leq b} p(x_i) \qquad (4\text{-}1)$$

Since the probability that a continuous random variable takes on any particular exact value is zero, continuous random variables have probability density functions rather than probability functions. The probability density function of a continuous random variable X is a continuous function $f(x)$ such that the probability that the random variable takes on a value in the range b to $b+db$ is $f(x)dx$. Thus, the probability of an outcome between a and b is the integral of $f(x)dx$ from a to b, and the integral of $f(x)dx$ over the entire sample space is 1 (the probability density is 0 outside the sample space).

Probability density function for a continuous random variable:

$$P(a \leq x \leq b) \; = \; \int_{a}^{b} f(x)dx \tag{4-2a}$$

$$\int_{-\infty}^{\infty} f(x)dx \; = \; 1 \tag{4-2b}$$

The relationship between the CDF and the probability density function for continuous variables is given in equation 4-3.

$$F(b) \; = \; P(x \leq b) \; = \; \int_{-\infty}^{b} f(x)dx \tag{4-3}$$

4.1.1.2 Expected Value, Variance, and Standard Deviation

The expected value (mean) of a random variable is the preferred measure of central tendency. Other measures are the median and the mode. The median is the value such that the variable is equally likely to be smaller or greater; it is the value such that $F(x) = 0.5$ or is closest to 0.5. The mode is the value that is most likely; that is, the value for which $p(x_i)$ or $f(x)$ is maximum. However, the expected value is the best central measure of the variable in this sense: If you must use a central measure in deterministic point-estimate calculations as if the variable could take on only one value, the expected value is the best one value to use. The expected value of a discrete random variable is determined by multiplying each possible value x_i in the sample space $\{x_i:i=1,2,...,n\}$ by its probability, and summing the results.

Expected value (mean) of a discrete random variable:

$$E(X) \; = \; \sum_{i=1}^{n} p_i x_i \; = \; p_1 x_1 + p_2 x_2 + \cdots + p_n x_n \tag{4-4}$$

The expected value of a continuous random variable is determined the analogous way: multiply each possible value x by its probability $f(x)dx$ and sum (integrate) over the entire sample space.

Expected value (mean) of a continuous random variable:

$$E(x) = \int_{-\infty}^{\infty} xf(x)dx \tag{4-5}$$

The expected value of a function $g(X)$ of a discrete random variable X is of course itself a discrete random variable (even if it is a continuous function). By the expected value theorem, its expected value is the sum of the possible values multiplied by their probabilities.

Expected value of a function of a discrete random variable:

$$E(X) = \sum_{i=1}^{n} p_i g(x_i) = p_1 g(x_1) + p_2 g(x_2) + \cdots + p_n g(x_n) \tag{4-6}$$

The expected value of a function $g(X)$ of a continuous random variable X is itself a continuous function and its expected value is given by the continuous version of the expected-value theorem.

Expected value of a function of a continuous random variable:

$$E(x) = \int_{-\infty}^{\infty} g(x)f(x)dx \tag{4-7}$$

E25.   **A German contractor has completed construction of a steel furnace in Indiana and will receive the final payment of 6.2 million German marks at the end of the month in which the specified production rate and quality is first achieved. At an interest rate of 1% monthly, the present worth of the final payment in millions of German marks is 6.2 β^t, where β is 1/1.01 and t is the number of months until payment. If t is equally likely to be any number of months from 1 to 6, determine the expected present worth of the final payment.**

The probabilities of the six t values {1, 2, 3, 4, 5, 6} are {1/6, 1/6, 1/6, 1/6, 1/6, 1/6}. By equation 4-6, with $g(t) = 6.2\beta^t$, the expected present worth is $(1/6) \times 6.2\beta^1 + (1/6) \times 6.2\beta^2 + (1/6) \times 6.2\beta^3 + (1/6) \times 6.2\beta^4 + (1/6) \times 6.2\beta^5 + (1/6) \times 6.2\beta^6 = 1.0333333(\beta^1 + \beta^2 + \beta^3 + \beta^4 + \beta^5 + \beta^6) = \underline{5.988659}$ million German marks. *Note:* The series of powers of β happens to equal the pain factor (*P/A* 1%,6) for 6 payments at 1% interest (see equation 3-11 in chapter 3), which means that spreading out the probability of the payment equally over six months has the same effect mathematically as paying the payment in six equal installments.

The variance of a random variable is the expected value of the square of its deviation from its expected value. The expected value of a random variable is often denoted μ, and the variance is often denoted σ^2. If we let $\mu = E(X)$ and let σ^2 represent the variance of X, then the variance is defined by equations 4-8 and 4-9 for discrete and continuous random variables respectively.

Variance of a discrete random variable:

$$\sigma^2 = E((x-\mu)^2) = \sum_{i=1}^{n} (x_i - \mu)^2 p(x_i) \qquad (4\text{-}8)$$

Variance of a continuous random variable:

$$\sigma^2 = E((x-\mu)^2) = \int_{-\infty}^{\infty} (x-\mu)^2 f(x)dx \qquad (4\text{-}9)$$

The standard deviation of a random variable is σ, the square root of the variance σ^2.

4.1.1.3 Sample Mean, Variance, and Standard Deviation

When a sample is taken, consisting of n observations of an outcome value of a random variable X, let x_i represent the ith observed value. *Note:* Here n and i represent quantities unrelated to the quantities represented by the same symbols in the foregoing discussion. The sample mean is the ordinary average of the observed values—their sum divided by the number of them—and constitutes a sample estimate of the expected value of the random variable whose outcomes were sampled.

Sample mean for n observations $\{x_1, x_2, \ldots, x_n\}$:

$$\bar{x} = \frac{1}{n}\sum_{i=1}^{n} x_i \qquad (4\text{-}10)$$

Please note that the set $\{x_i : i=1,2,\ldots,n\}$ is the set of observations, whereas in the foregoing section the same notation denoted the set of possible values.

The sample variance is the average squared error, where a squared error is the square of the difference (error) between an observed value and the sample mean. Only $n-1$ of the errors are independent (since their sum is zero by the definition of the sample mean, one of the errors could be computed if $n-1$ of them and the sample mean were given).

Sample variance for n observations $\{x_1, x_2 \ldots, x_n\}$:

$$s^2 = \frac{1}{n-1}\sum_{i=1}^{n} (x_i - \bar{x})^2 \qquad (4\text{-}11)$$

The sample variance is a sample estimate of the variance of the random variable whose outcomes were sampled. The sample standard deviation from n observations of a random variable is s, the square root of the sample variance s^2.

4.1.1.4 Chebyshev's Theorem: The Rarity of Outliers

It is rare for an observation to be many standard deviations away from the mean. Chebyshev's Theorem states: *If a probability distribution has mean μ and standard deviation σ, the probability that an observation will have a value that deviates from the mean by more than k standard deviations is less than $1/k^2$.* That is, $P(|x - \mu| > k\sigma) < 1/k^2$. Thus, fewer than one out of nine observations in a sample should be more than three standard deviations away from the mean.

Let us define the z statistic as the number of standard deviations by which an observed value exceeds the expected value:

General definition of the z statistic:

$$z = \frac{x - \mu}{\sigma} \qquad (4\text{-}12)$$

With this definition, Chebyshev's Theorem is $P(|z| > k) < 1/k^2$.

E26.   Ten observations were made of the time to install a cola dispenser. The observed times, in minutes, were 104, 132, 115, 180, 95, 96, 100, 73, 82, 113. The observation of 180 minutes is suspected to be a mistake. Determine the sample mean and sample variance for the nine observations that exclude the suspected one. Then apply Chebyshev's Theorem to determine the maximum probability of observing a time so great as 180 if the random variable actually had the expected value and variance estimated by the sample of nine observations. Does the 180 observation seem extraordinary according to Chebyshev's Theorem?

The sample mean for the restricted sample is 101.1111 and the sample variance is 314.6111; the sample standard deviation is 17.73728. (For the full sample of 10 observations the mean would be 109 and the standard deviation 30.0333.)

If $\mu = 101.1111$ and $\sigma = 17.73728$, then an observation $x = 180$ gives $|x - \mu| > k\sigma$ or $k < 4.44763$, which corresponds to a probability $1/(4.44763)^2 \approx 0.05$. There is at most about a 5% chance of an installation time as great as 180, and in a sample size of 20 you would expect to see about one such event. But it turned up in a sample size of 10, which does seem extraordinary.

Chebyshev's Theorem is quite conservative. For instance, in the foregoing example it assigns at most a 0.05 probability to deviations as great as 4.44763 standard deviations. But with most probability distributions, the chance of a z statistic whose absolute value is more than three is very small. To get tighter bounds on probabilities of rare values, we must assume specific distributions.

4.1.2 Distributions

Table 4-1 gives a summary of some of the more important discrete probability distributions.

Table 4-1. Discrete Probability Distributions.

Discrete distribution	Probability function $p(x_i)$	Expected value	Variance	Remarks
Binomial	$\binom{n}{x} p^x (1-p)^{n-x}$	np	$np(1-p)$	x = the number of occurrences in a sample of size n. p = the probability of an occurrence.
Discrete uniform	$\dfrac{1}{b-a+1}$	$\dfrac{a+b}{2}$	$\dfrac{(b-a+1)^2 - 1}{12}$	x = an integer in the set a to b.
Poisson	$\dfrac{e^{-\lambda t}(\lambda t)^x}{x!}$	λt	λt	$x \in \{0, 1, ...\}$. x = the number of occurrences in time t.
Geometric	$p(1-p)^{x-1}$	$1/p$	$(1-p)/p^2$	$x \in \{1, 2, ...\}$. x = the number of trials to an occurrence. p = the probability of occurrence in a trial.

E27.   **Unscheduled shutdowns occur at an average rate of 15 per year in a large plant that operates in eight-hour shifts 2000 hours per year. It takes negligible time but lots of money to restart after an unscheduled shutdown. Determine the probability of more than one shutdown in a single shift. Also determine the expected number of shifts that will pass before such an event.**

The Poisson distribution applies to this situation. Measuring t in years, $\lambda t = 15/250 = 0.06$ since 15 is the expected number of occurrences per 250 shifts and the time interval is $t = 1/250 = 0.04$ years. The probability of 0 occurrences in a shift is $p(0) = e^{-0.06}(0.06)^0/0! = e^{-0.06} = 0.9417645$, and the probability of 1 occurrence in a shift is $p(1) = e^{-0.06}(0.06)^1/1! = e^{-0.06} \times 0.06 = 0.0565059$. Since all the probabilities $p(0), p(1), p(2),...$ sum to 1, the probability of more than one unscheduled shutdown in a shift is $1 - p(0) - p(1) = \underline{0.0017296}$.

Given the probability of more than one shutdown in a shift, each shift can be considered a trial in which the event has that probability of occurring. The geometric distribution gives the number of trials to an occurrence, and the expected number is $1/p$ where p is the probability of occurrence in a single trial. Thus the expected number of shifts until more than one shutdown occurs in a single shift is $1/0.0017296$ shifts, or $1/(250 \times 0.0017296) = \underline{2.3127}$ _years_.

Table 4-2 gives a summary of some of the more important continuous probability distributions.

Table 4-2. Continuous Probability Distributions.

Continuous distribution	Density function $f(x)$	Expected value	Variance	Remarks
Uniform	$1/(b-a)$ for $a \le x \le b$, 0 otherwise	$\dfrac{a+b}{2}$	$\dfrac{(b-a)^2}{12}$	a = the lower limit, b = the upper limit
Exponential	$\lambda e^{-\lambda x}$ for $x \ge 0$, 0 otherwise CDF is $F(x) = 1 - e^{-\lambda x}$	$1/\lambda$	$1/\lambda^2$	$\lambda > 0$
Gamma with $n > 0$ or Erlang with $n \in \{1, 2, ...\}$	$\dfrac{\lambda e^{-\lambda x}(\lambda x)^{n-1}}{\Gamma(n)}$ for $x \ge 0$, 0 otherwise If n is a positive integer, $\Gamma(n)$ is $(n-1)!$	n/λ	n/λ^2	If n is a positive integer, x is the sum of n exponentially distributed random variables each having expected value $1/\lambda$
Normal	$\dfrac{1}{\sigma\sqrt{2\pi}} e^{-\frac{1}{2}\left(\frac{x-\mu}{\sigma}\right)^2}$	μ	σ^2	$-\infty < x < \infty$ Symmetric: μ is the mode and median
PERT beta	undefined	$\dfrac{a+4m+b}{6}$	$\dfrac{(b-a)^2}{36}$	a = the 1-percentile value; b = the 99-percentile value; m = the most likely value

The uniform distribution is the distribution of choice if all that is known is upper and lower limits. An example would be the diameter of a finished part after all parts having diameters less than a or greater than b had been discarded.

The exponential distribution is the distribution of choice if all that is known is the expected value and the fact that the variable is nonnegative. An example would be a delay given the average delay. For instance, if you were told that the average lateness of delivery of a certain class of part was 3.0 months, an estimate of the probability of a lateness of more than 6.0 months would be $1 - F(x) = e^{-(1/3.0)6.0} = 0.1353$.

The gamma or Erlang distribution is the distribution of choice if what is known is both the expected value and the variance, along with nonnegativity. If the *coefficient of variation* (ratio of expected value to standard deviation), which for the gamma or Erlang distribution is $\sqrt{n}$, is greater than about 3, the normal distribution is more convenient, since it is tabulated. The gamma or Erlang distribution is also the distribution of choice for a random variable that is considered to be a sum of exponentially distributed random variables.

The PERT beta "distribution" is used for activity durations where what is known is the 1-percentile value a (the duration such that there is a 1% probability of a smaller duration), the 99-percentile value b (the duration such that there is a 99% probability of a smaller duration), and the most likely (modal) duration m. For probability inferences the actual beta distribution (not reviewed here) can be used.

E28.   **A tool crib clerk must perform 10 tasks, each considered exponentially distributed with a mean of 0.1 minutes, to serve a worker. Determine the probability that a service will take more than a minute.**

One minute is the expected duration. The distribution is Erlang with $n = 10$ and $\lambda = 10$. The Erlang density function could be integrated to obtain the probability, but the normal approximation applies since the coefficient of variation is $\sqrt{n} = 3.162278 > 3$. The probability that a normal variable exceeds its mean is 0.5.

The Poisson distribution and the exponential distributions are both called Markovian distributions and really represent the same situation—that of pure randomness. If the number of events in a fixed time interval has the Poisson distribution, then the time between two successive events has the exponential distribution. The continuous uniform distribution is also related to the Markovian process in the sense that if a fixed number of Markovian events occur in a fixed time interval, then if one of the events is picked at random, its exact timing within the interval is uniformly distributed.

4.1.3 Hypothesis Testing

A statistical hypothesis is a statement about the distribution of a random variable—a statement that will be supported if a test rejects its alternative decisively. To establish statistical support for a hypothesis H_1 we must reject a null hypothesis H_0. The null hypothesis should be the obvious alternative to H_1, and data will either reject or fail to reject it.

4.1.3.1 Type-I and Type-II Error

As a measure of the decisiveness required to reject the null hypothesis, we select a small probability, often 0.05, of committing the type-I error: rejecting the null hypothesis when it is actually true. This can be interpreted as the probability that we could be mistaken in allowing H_1

to stand by rejecting H_0. For instance, an engineer might hope to establish that a new portland cement formulation is stronger than the usual formulation. If μ_1 is the mean strength of the new formulation and μ_2 is the mean strength of the usual formulation, one would test the hypothesis $H_1: \mu_1 > \mu_2$ against the null hypothesis $H_0: \mu_1 \le \mu_2$. Suppose $\alpha = 0.05$ was chosen, data was taken, and the null hypothesis was rejected. The rejection would occur because statistical calculations had shown that if H_0 were true, there would have been at least a $1 - \alpha = 95\%$ chance that data would be more consistent with H_0 than was the actual data. To say the same thing, if H_0 were true, there would have been at most a 5% chance that data so inconsistent with it would have been obtained.

Think of a type-I error in connection with claims in a medical journal. If you read 100 articles claiming that this or that treatment is effective, and all the authors used $\alpha = 0.05$, then perhaps about five of the claims will be wrong. In one such case, for example, a drug was administered and 14 out of 17 patients improved, whereas under the null hypothesis of ineffectiveness only eight would have been expected to improve. The article was published. In a follow-on study, 51 out of 100 patients improved whereas 47 would have been expected to improve, and the null hypothesis of ineffectiveness was not rejected. Luck had fooled the original author.

A type-II error occurs in the opposite way: the null hypothesis is not rejected although it is actually false. Statistically, the cure for both types of errors is to take more data.

Why is hypothesis testing so indirect? Why must we marshal support for a hypothesis by shooting down its alternative? The answer is that if there is uncertainty, data can only on rare occasions directly verify any hypothesis; data can only be inconsistent with a hypothesis to a greater or lesser degree.

Consider, for example, the hypothesis that a coin is "fair" in the sense that, when flipped, it will fall heads (H) with probability 0.5 and tails (T) with probability 0.5. A truly fair coin might give the data HTTHTHHHT. This is very consistent with $P(H)=0.5$, but it is even more consistent with $P(H)=5/9$. The only way to get convincing support for a hypothesis is to define an alternative (null) hypothesis in advance and obtain data very inconsistent with the alternative hypothesis.

4.1.3.2 Sampling Distributions

In order to determine probabilities that data are consistent with hypotheses, we need sampling distributions. The most important one is the normal distribution of a sample sum of size n. By the central limit theorem, if a sample $\{x_1, x_2, ..., x_n\}$ consists of n independent observations of a random variable that has mean μ and variance σ^2 (regardless of its distribution), then the sample sum Σx tends to be distributed normally with mean $n\mu$ and variance $n\sigma^2$. By inserting this mean and variance into the general z-statistic definition (equation 4-12) the sample-sum test statistic z_n is defined in equation 4-13.

Sample sum test statistic:

$$z_n = \frac{\Sigma x - n\mu}{\sigma\sqrt{n}} \qquad (4\text{-}13)$$

E29.   **Under a hypothesis, a gamma-distributed random variable has mean 3.75 and standard deviation 0.181. A sample of 20 observations gives a sample mean of 4.01. By how many standard deviations does this result differ from the hypothesis?**

Under the hypothesis, $\mu = 3.75$ and $\sigma = 0.181$. The sample sum is $x = 20 \times 4.01 = 80.2$. With these values, equation 4-13 gives sample sum test statistic $z_n = \underline{6.424063}$.

Let us define the *sample mean* as

$$\bar{x} = (x_1 + x_2 + \cdots + x_n)/n = \Sigma x/n$$

Equation 4-13 can be expressed in terms of the sample mean by dividing both numerator and denominator by n.

Sample-mean test statistic z (known variance):

$$z_n = \frac{\bar{x} - \mu}{\sigma/\sqrt{n}} \qquad (4\text{-}14)$$

Table 4-3 is a special form of the normal probability table, made convenient for hypothesis testing.

Another important sampling distribution is the *t distribution*, formerly known as Student's *t* distribution. When a hypothesized distribution has no *a priori* variance σ^2 that can be assumed, so that the available estimate of variance is a sample variance s^2 based on n observations, then the probabilities of being *t* sample standard deviations away from the sample mean $\bar{x}$ follow the *t* distribution with $k = n - 1$ degrees of freedom. (The number of degrees of freedom is the number of independent quantities that go into a calculation. When the sample standard deviation is used, one of the observations could be inferred from the sample standard deviation and the other $n - 1$ observations. Therefore, only $n - 1$ independent observations exist in the calculation of a *t* statistic.)

Table 4-3. Normal Probability Table (One-Tailed).

Probability α that a normal random variable is at least z_α standard deviations away from its mean			
z_α	α	α	z_α
1.0	0.159	0.20	0.84
1.1	0.136	0.19	0.88
1.2	0.115	0.18	0.92
1.3	0.097	0.17	0.95
1.4	0.081	0.16	0.99
1.5	0.067	0.15	1.04
1.6	0.055	0.14	1.08
1.7	0.045	0.13	1.13
1.8	0.036	0.12	1.18
1.9	0.029	0.11	1.23
2.0	0.023	0.10	1.28
2.1	0.018	0.09	1.34
2.2	0.014	0.08	1.41
2.3	0.011	0.075	1.44
2.4	0.008	0.07	1.48
2.5	0.006	0.06	1.55
2.6	0.005	0.05	1.64
2.7	0.003	0.04	1.75
2.8	0.003	0.03	1.88
2.9	0.002	0.025	1.96
3.0	0.001	0.02	2.05
3.1	0.001	0.01	2.33
3.2	0.001	0.001	3.10
3.3	0.000	0.0001	3.73

The *t statistic* for a sample mean $\bar{x}$ (the number of *sample* standard deviations by which the sample mean exceeds the hypothesized mean μ) is given by equation 4-15, where s is the sample standard deviation and n is the number of observations in the sample.

Sample-mean test statistic t (unknown variance):

$$t = \frac{\bar{x} - \mu}{s/\sqrt{n}}$$ (4-15)

Table 4-4 gives the *t*-statistic values for various sample sizes for which there are various probabilities α that a sample mean is more than t sample standard deviations away from a hypothesized mean.

Both the normal distribution and the t distribution are symmetric about the mean. Because of this, the absolute values $|z|$ and $|t|$ can be used, or $-z$ can be substituted for z and $-t$ for t.

E30a. **A lift truck is warranted to operate at least 6 hours on a fully charged battery. In trial runs the truck has operated 5.4, 5.9, 6.3, 5.1, and 5.5 hours. At the $\alpha = 0.05$ level, can we reject the hypothesis that its average operating time is at least 6 hours?**

The sample is of size $n = 5$, its sample mean (equation 4-10) is $\bar{x} = 5.64$ hours, and its sample standard deviation (equation 4-11) is $s = 0.4669047$ hours. For a hypothesized mean of $\mu = 6$ hours, the t statistic (equation 4-15) is -1.724; the sample mean is 1.724 sample standard deviations below the hypothesized mean. From table 4-4, a sample of size 5 would have to be 2.132 standard deviations from the hypothesized mean for there to be only a 5% chance of falsely rejecting the hypothesis. Thus we <u>cannot reject</u> the hypothesis.

Note that if the risk of false rejection had been set at $\alpha = 0.10$ instead of 0.05, the critical t would have been 1.533, and the sample results *would* have been sufficient to reject the 6-hour claim.

A common error committed by engineers is to use the z test where the t test applies. Note that if s had been treated as σ, table 4-2 shows that a z statistic 1.64 standard deviations away from the mean is enough to reject at $\alpha = 0.05$. Thus if the standard deviation were known or hypothesized, a sample of five observations averaging 5.64 would be enough to reject the hypothesis of 6 with a doubt of only 0.05; but since the standard deviation is estimated from the sample, the t test shows that rejection cannot be done with such small doubt.

E30b. **Estimate the smallest number of observations that would allow rejection of the hypothesis in the foregoing example.**

Assuming that the same sample mean and sample standard deviation were obtained in a sample of size n as were obtained in the foregoing sample of size five, we need to find the smallest n such that $|t|$ would be greater than the critical t in the t-statistic table in the $\alpha = 0.05$ column for the row for that n. This occurs for <u>$n = 7$</u>. (For $n = 7$, with a sample mean of 5.64 and a sample standard deviation of 0.4669047, the t statistic is -2.040, or $|t| = 2.040$,

Table 4-4. Table for the *t* Statistic.

The $t_{\alpha,k}$ statistic such that with probability α a sample mean is $t_{\alpha,k}$ sample standard deviations away from the hypothesized mean, for various sample sizes					
Sample size, n	Degrees of freedom, k	Probability, α			
		$\alpha = 0.10$	$\alpha = 0.05$	$\alpha = 0.025$	$\alpha = 0.01$
2	1	3.078	6.314	12.706	31.821
3	2	1.886	2.920	4.303	6.965
4	3	1.638	2.353	3.182	4.541
5	4	1.533	2.132	2.776	3.747
6	5	1.476	2.015	2.571	3.365
7	6	1.440	1.943	2.447	3.143
8	7	1.415	1.895	2.365	2.998
9	8	1.397	1.860	2.306	2.896
10	9	1.383	1.833	2.262	2.821
11	10	1.372	1.812	2.228	2.764
12	11	1.363	1.796	2.201	2.718
13	12	1.356	1.782	2.179	2.681
14	13	1.350	1.771	2.160	2.650
15	14	1.345	1.761	2.145	2.624
16	15	1.341	1.753	2.131	2.602
17	16	1.337	1.746	2.120	2.583
18	17	1.333	1.740	2.110	2.567
19	18	1.330	1.734	2.101	2.552
20	19	1.328	1.729	2.093	2.539
30	29	1.311	1.699	2.045	2.492
∞	∞	1.282	1.645	1.960	2.326

and the critical t for $n = 7$ and $\alpha = 0.05$ is 1.943.) If the results so far are typical, two further observations ought to be enough to reject the hypothesis that the battery lasts for at least 6 hours.

4.1.3.3 Summary of Hypothesis Tests on Means

The following is a summary of the most important tests for means of populations. When the variances of sampled populations are known or hypothesized, a z statistic is used; when the variances of sampled populations are estimated from the sample data, a t statistic is used. When the hypothesis states that a sampled population has a mean greater (or less) than either a standard or the mean of another population, a *one-tail* test is used; when the hypothesis states that a sampled population has a mean that differs significantly from either a standard or the mean of another population, a *two-tail* test is used. Rejection can occur in either direction, so for type-I errors of 5%, for example, the critical z or t statistic in a two-tail test would be one that has a 2.5% probability.

In the following discussion let μ be the unknown mean of the sampled population (if there is a second sampled population let μ_1 and μ_2 be the unknown means); let μ_0 be a standard value or hypothesized value of a mean under the null hypothesis; let σ^2 be the known or hypothesized variance of a population (subscripted if there are two populations); let s^2 be the sample variance of a population (subscripted if there are two); let $\bar{x}$ be the sample mean of a population (subscripted if there are two); and let n be the sample size (subscripted if there are two).

4.1.3.3.1 Known Variance Means Tests

Test that a mean is greater than a given value μ_0: The tested hypothesis is $H_1: \mu > \mu_0$, and the null hypothesis is $H_0: \mu = \mu_0$. Compute the z statistic for mean comparison to μ_0 and reject H_0 if $z_0 > z_\alpha$. Here z_0 is the computed statistic and z_α is from table 4-3.

z statistic for mean comparison to μ_0:

$$z_0 = \frac{\bar{x} - \mu_0}{\sigma/\sqrt{n}} \tag{4-16}$$

Test that a mean is less than a given value μ_0: The tested hypothesis is $H_1: \mu < \mu_0$, and the null hypothesis is $H_0: \mu = \mu_0$. Compute the z statistic for mean comparison to μ_0 and reject H_0 if $z_0 < -z_\alpha$.

Test that a mean differs significantly from a given value μ_0: The tested hypothesis is $H_1: \mu \neq \mu_0$, and the null hypothesis is $H_0: \mu = \mu_0$. Compute the z statistic for mean comparison to μ_0 and reject H_0 if $|z_0| > z_{\alpha/2}$. Here $z_{\alpha/2}$ is the normal statistic from table 4-3 for half the selected probability; this is a two-tailed test in which the null hypothesis can be rejected if the sample mean is either too large or too small, so the probability of false rejection in one direction is half the total probability of false rejection.

Test that the mean of population 1 is greater than that of population 2: There are two separate samples, not necessarily of the same size, and the two populations do not necessarily have the same variance. The tested hypothesis is H_1: $\mu_1 > \mu_2$, and the null hypothesis is H_0: $\mu_1 = \mu_2$. Compute the z statistic for comparison of two means and reject H_0 if $z_0 > z_\alpha$. Here z_0 is from equation 4-17 (below) and z_α is from table 4-3.

z statistic for comparison of two means:

$$z_0 = \frac{\bar{x}_1 - \bar{x}_2}{\sqrt{\dfrac{\sigma_1^2}{n_1} + \dfrac{\sigma_2^2}{n_2}}} \qquad (4\text{-}17)$$

Test that the mean of population 1 differs significantly from that of population 2: The tested hypothesis is H_1: $\mu_1 \neq \mu_2$, and the null hypothesis is H_0: $\mu_1 = \mu_2$. Compute the z statistic for comparison of two means and reject H_0 if $|z_0| > z_{\alpha/2}$.

4.1.3.3.2 Unknown Variance Means Tests

Test that a mean is greater than a given value μ_0: The tested hypothesis is H_1: $\mu > \mu_0$, and the null hypothesis is H_0: $\mu = \mu_0$. Compute the t statistic for mean comparison to μ_0 and reject H_0 if $t_0 > t_{\alpha, n-1}$. Here t_0 is the computed statistic and $t_{\alpha, n-1}$ is from table 4-4.

t statistic for mean comparison to μ_0:

$$t_0 = \frac{\bar{x} - \mu_0}{s/\sqrt{n}} \qquad (4\text{-}18)$$

Test that a mean is less than a given value μ_0: The tested hypothesis is H_1: $\mu < \mu_0$, and the null hypothesis is H_0: $\mu = \mu_0$. Compute the t statistic for mean comparison to μ_0 and reject H_0 if $t_0 < -t_{\alpha, n-1}$.

Test that a mean differs significantly from a given value μ_0: The tested hypothesis is H_1: $\mu \neq \mu_0$, and the null hypothesis is H_0: $\mu = \mu_0$. Compute the t statistic for mean comparison to μ_0 and reject H_0 if $|t_0| > t_{\alpha/2, n-1}$. Here $t_{\alpha/2, n-1}$ is the $t_{\alpha,k}$ statistic from table 4-4 for half the selected probability α; this is a two-tailed test in which the null hypothesis can be rejected if the sample mean is either too large or too small, so the probability of false rejection in one direction is half the total probability of false rejection.

Test that the mean of population 1 is greater than that of population 2: There are two separate samples, not necessarily of the same size, and the two populations do not necessarily have the same variance. The tested hypothesis is H_1: $\mu_1 > \mu_2$, and the null hypothesis is H_0: $\mu_1 = \mu_2$. Compute the t statistic for comparison of two means and reject H_0 if $t_0 > t_{\alpha,k}$. Here t_0 and the number of degrees of freedom k are from equations 4-19 and 4-20 (below) and $t_{\alpha,k}$ is from table 4-4 (using the k column and disregarding the n column).

t statistic for comparison of two means:

$$t_0 = \frac{\bar{x}_1 - \bar{x}_2}{\sqrt{\dfrac{s_1^2}{n_1} + \dfrac{s_2^2}{n_2}}} \tag{4-19}$$

Degrees of freedom for t-test with two samples:

$$k = \frac{\left(\dfrac{s_1^2}{n_1} + \dfrac{s_2^2}{n_2}\right)^2}{\dfrac{\left(s_1^2/n_1\right)^2}{n_1 - 1} + \dfrac{\left(s_2^2/n_2\right)^2}{n_2 - 1}} \tag{4-20}$$

Test that the mean of population 1 differs significantly from that of population 2: The tested hypothesis is H_1: $\mu_1 \neq \mu_2$, and the null hypothesis is H_0: $\mu_1 = \mu_2$. Compute the t statistic for comparison of two means and reject H_0 if $|t_0| > t_{\alpha/2,k}$.

4.1.4 Curve Fitting

4.1.4.1 Chi-square Goodness of Fit

The chi-square or χ^2 *distribution* with v degrees of freedom is the distribution of the sum of the squares of v independent z statistics. It is an important sampling distribution for many reasons (for example, the sum of squares of a sample of size n follows the chi-square distribution with $n - 1$

degrees of freedom), but the most versatile application of the chi-square distribution is to test whether two populations differ significantly by comparing predicted and observed distributions of outcomes.

Let H_1 be a sampled distribution that differs significantly from an assumed distribution, and let H_0 be that they are the same. We have great latitude in what to observe. Typically the observations will be of a random variable, and its outcome values will be classified into *cells* of a histogram. Boundaries of the cells are set so that the number of observations predicted to fall in each cell if the null hypothesis is true is at least five and is approximately the same for every cell. There are at least three cells; let the number of cells be k. The number of degrees of freedom for the chi-square distribution of the numbers of observations that fall into various cells is $v = k - 1$.

Let O_j be the observed number of outcomes in cell j from a sample of n outcomes. Let E_j be the expected number of outcomes in cell j according to the assumed distribution under the null hypothesis. The *chi-square statistic* is given by equation 4-21.

The chi-square sample statistic:

$$\chi^2 = \sum_{j=1}^{k} \frac{\left(O_j - E_j\right)^2}{E_j} \tag{4-21}$$

Note that the sample size is

$$n = \sum_{j=1}^{k} O_j = \sum_{j=1}^{k} E_j$$

Table 4-5 gives the critical values of the chi-square statistic for various numbers of degrees of freedom $v = k - 1$ and various error probabilities α. Call the critical values $\chi^2_{k-1,1-\alpha}$. We follow the rule: reject H_0 when $\chi^2 > \chi^2_{k-1,1-\alpha}$. To reject is to conclude that the discrepancy between predicted and observed outcomes is too large to be due to chance, with at least a $1 - \alpha$ probability.

E31.   According to your design of an automatic warehouse picking system, in its benchmark test it should require 20, 30, or 38 seconds to reach picking positions, with probabilities 0.30, 0.35, and 0.35, respectively. In the first benchmark tests, there were 21, 17, and 12 observations of the three values of picking time. At the $\alpha = 0.10$ level of significance, can you conclude that something is wrong?

Table 4-5. Table for the χ^2 Statistic.

The $\chi^2_{k-1,1-\alpha}$ statistic such that with probability $1-\alpha$ a set of observed cell populations differs from the hypothesized set too much to be due to chance					
No. of cells, k	Degrees of freedom, ν	Probability, $1-\alpha$			
		$1-\alpha = 0.90$	$1-\alpha = 0.95$	$1-\alpha = 0.975$	$1-\alpha = 0.99$
2	1	2.706	3.841	5.024	6.635
3	2	4.605	5.991	7.378	9.210
4	3	6.251	7.815	9.348	11.345
5	4	7.779	9.488	11.143	13.277
6	5	9.236	11.070	12.833	15.086
7	6	10.645	12.592	14.449	16.812
8	7	12.017	14.067	16.013	18.475
9	8	13.362	15.507	17.535	20.090
10	9	14.684	16.919	19.023	21.666
11	10	15.987	18.307	20.483	23.209
12	11	17.275	19.675	21.920	24.725
13	12	18.549	21.026	23.337	26.217
14	13	19.812	22.362	24.736	27.688
15	14	21.064	23.685	26.119	29.141
16	15	22.307	24.996	27.488	30.578
17	16	23.542	26.296	28.845	32.000
18	17	24.769	27.587	30.191	33.409
19	18	25.989	28.869	31.526	34.805
20	19	27.204	30.144	32.852	36.191
21	20	28.412	31.410	34.170	37.566
22	21	29.615	32.671	35.479	38.932
23	22	30.813	33.924	36.781	40.289
24	23	32.007	35.172	38.076	41.638
25	24	33.196	36.415	39.364	42.980
26	25	34.382	37.652	40.646	44.314
27	26	35.563	38.885	41.923	45.642
28	27	36.741	40.113	43.195	46.963
29	28	37.916	41.337	44.461	48.278
30	29	30.087	42.557	45.722	49.588

There are $k = 3$ cells. The observed cell frequencies are $\{O_j\} = \{21, 17, 12\}$. The sample size is $n = 21 + 17 + 12 = 50$. The expected cell frequencies are $\{E_j\} = \{15, 17.5, 17.5\}$. From equation 4-21, the chi-square statistic for the sample is

$$\chi^2 = \sum_{j=1}^{3} \frac{(O_j - E_j)^2}{E_j} = \frac{(21-15)^2}{15} + \frac{(17-17.5)^2}{17.5} + \frac{(12-17.5)^2}{17.5} = 4.142857$$

From table 4-5, the critical chi-square value for $v = k - 1 = 2$ degrees of freedom and a probability $1 - \alpha = 0.90$ of avoiding type-I error, is 4.605. Since χ^2 does not exceed $\chi^2_{k-1,1-\alpha}$, we cannot reject the hypothesis that nothing is wrong. The benchmark test indicates that the picking system may not perform according to the design, but more data would be required to establish this with desired confidence.

4.1.4.2 Linear Regression

If we have n data pairs $\{x_i, y_i: i=1,2,...,n\}$, where Y is considered to be a linear function of X with a slope b, an intercept a, and a random error ε (the error being independent for each data pair and having mean zero and constant variance σ^2), then the parameters of the straight-line relationship can be estimated by linear regression. The linear regression procedure determines the parameters $\hat{a}$ and $\hat{b}$ of a linear regression line $y = \hat{a} + \hat{b}x$ so as to minimize the sum of the squares of the distances between y_i and y at $x = x_i$.

Most scientific hand calculators have a linear regression function. When that is not available, the following procedure can be followed.

Compute $\bar{x}$, the sample mean of the x_i values (equation 4-10); similarly, compute $\bar{y}$, the sample mean of the y_i values. Compute the estimated slope by equation 4-22:

$$\hat{b} = \frac{\sum_{i=1}^{n} y_i (x_i - \bar{x})}{\sum_{i=1}^{n} (x_i - \bar{x})^2} \tag{4-22}$$

Compute the estimated intercept as $\hat{a} = \bar{y} - \hat{b}\bar{x}$.

Linear regression can be used not only to fit straight-line relationships, but to fit power functions and exponential functions by changing the variable. For example, consider the first illustration in chapter 3, section 3.1.2:

E32.　According to a learning-curve model, if it took 700, 650, 644, and 637 manhours, respectively, to build the 5th, 6th, 7th, and 8th units of a product, how many manhours would be estimated to build the 20th unit?

Making explicit changes of variables to avoid confusion, let the learning-curve model of section 3.1.2 be $w = \alpha z^{\beta}$, where w is the direct labor hours to build the zth unit and α and β are the learning-curve parameters. If we take the natural logarithm of both sides of the model equation, we get $\ln w = \ln \alpha + \beta \ln z$. Let $y = \ln w$, $a = \ln \alpha$, $b = \beta$, and $x = \ln z$. Then the logarithm form of the model equation becomes $y = a + bx$.

The data for this model are $\{y_i\} = \{\ln w_i\} = \{\ln 700, \ln 650, \ln 644, \ln 637\}$ and $\{x_i\} = \{\ln z_i\}$ $= \{\ln 5, \ln 6, \ln 7, \ln 8\}$. Supposing no linear regression program is available, we compute $\bar{x}$ $= 1.85663727$, $\bar{y} = 6.48813$, $\hat{b} = -0.192377$, and $\hat{a} = 6.8453$. In the model $w = \alpha z^{\beta}$, we have $\alpha = e^{6.8453} = 939.46$ and $\beta = -0.192377$. Finally, for $z = 20$, the model gives $w = 939.46$ $\times (20)^{-0.192377} \approx \underline{528}$ estimated manhours to build the 20th unit.

Linear regression with a zero intercept determines the best line through the origin. It has $\hat{a}$ $= 0$ and has $\hat{b}$ calculated from equation 4-22 with $\bar{x} = 0$.

4.2 Reliability and Failure Analysis

4.2.1 Life Distributions

Let Y be the failure age of a component. The reliability function for the component is the probability that the component survives to age y. Recalling the cumulative distribution function $F(y)$ (defined in section 4.1.1 as the probability that Y does not exceed the given value y), we see

$$R(y) = 1 - F(y) \tag{4-23}$$

The expected value of the failure age of a component, $E(Y)$, is called the mean time to failure and is often denoted θ.

Let Y have a density function $f(y)$. Then the hazard function, which is the instantaneous failure rate at age y, is defined as

$$h(y) = f(y)/R(y) \tag{4-24}$$

Recalling that $f(y)dy$ is the probability of failure in the interval y to $y + dy$, and that $R(y)$ is the probability of having survived to y, we see that $h(y)dy$ is the probability of failure in the interval y to $y + dy$ for a unit that has survived to y.

The exponential distribution is the only life distribution that has a constant hazard function. If the mean time to failure is $\theta = 1/\lambda$, the reliability function for an exponentially distributed life is $R(y) = e^{-\lambda y} = e^{-y/\theta}$, and the hazard function is $h(y) = f(y)/R(y) = \lambda e^{-\lambda y} / e^{-\lambda y} = \lambda = 1/\theta$. Note

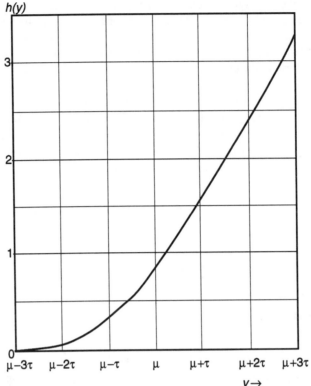

Figure 4-2. Hazard Function for the Normal Distribution.

that the probability of surviving the mean failure age is only $R(\theta) = e^{-1} = 0.36787944$. Most of the failures occur early. This life distribution is appropriate for components that do not deteriorate or wear out, but simply run a constant risk, like that of being struck by lightning.

The normal distribution has the increasing hazard function plotted in figure 4-2. It is appropriate for a component whose failures are due to a fairly predictable wearing-out process. The coefficient of variation—ratio of the mean age at failure μ to the standard deviation σ— should be great enough, say $\mu/\sigma > 2.5$, so that the normal distribution's inclusion of negative variates can be ignored.

The Weibull distribution is the most flexible life distribution because one of its parameters, β, directly sets the shape of the hazard function. When $\beta = 1$, the hazard function is constant and the Weibull distribution is identical to the exponential distribution; when $\beta = 2$, the hazard function is linear; when $\beta = 3$, the hazard function is quadratic. Many components have a hazard function that grows with age more than linearly but less than quadratically, so β is commonly between 2 and 3.

The density function of the Weibull distribution is

$$f(y) = \frac{\beta}{\alpha}\left(\frac{y}{\alpha}\right)^{\beta-1} e^{-(y/\alpha)^{\beta}} \qquad (4\text{-}25)$$

The CDF of the Weibull distribution is

$$F(y) = 1 - e^{-(y/\alpha)^\beta}$$

(4-26)

The reliability function for the Weibull distribution is

$$R(y) = 1 - F(y) = e^{-(y/\alpha)^\beta}$$

(4-27)

The hazard function for the Weibull distribution is

$$h(y) = \frac{\beta}{\alpha}\left(\frac{y}{\alpha}\right)^{\beta-1}$$

(4-28)

The sample mean is a good estimate of the expected life, but the proportion of observations exceeding y is a poor estimate of $R(y)$. Estimates of $R(y)$ for the Weibull distribution should be based on fitting α and β from the sample and using equation 4-27.

Where $\Gamma(\cdot)$ is the tabulated *gamma function* (for integer h, $\Gamma(h+1) = h!$) the best estimates of the mean life and standard deviation of life are those from the Weibull mean and variance formulas given in equations 4-29 and 4-30.

$$E(y) = \alpha\Gamma(1 + 1/\beta)$$

(4-29)

$$\sigma^2 = \alpha^2\left(\Gamma(1 + 2/\beta) - \Gamma^2(1 + 1/\beta)\right)$$

(4-30)

Equation 4-31 gives the percentage points of the Weibull distribution—the value y_p such that P (or $100P$ percent) is the probability that $y \leq y_p$. In other words, y_p is the value such that $F(y) = 1 - R(y) = P$. The $100P$th Weibull percentile is

$$y_P = \alpha\left[-\ln(1 - P)\right]^{1/\beta}$$

(4-31)

To fit the Weibull parameter from a sample, it is necessary first to estimate $R(y)$ from the sample. For estimating $F(x)$ for any continuous distribution from a small sample, there is a better method than simply estimating i/n as the CDF value for the ith-smallest observation in a sample of size n. The recommended procedure is to use the *median rank plotting formula* given in equation 4-32, where n observations are ranked in increasing order $x_1, x_2,..., x_i,..., x_n$ so that x_i is the ith-smallest observation:

$$\hat{F}(x_i) = 1 - \hat{R}(x_i) = \frac{i - 0.3}{n + 0.4} \qquad (4\text{-}32)$$

Thus for a Weibull sample, where the ordered observations are $\{y_i\}$, we can estimate $R(y_i)$ as $1 - (i - 0.3)/(n + 0.4) = (n - i + 0.7)/(n + 0.4)$.

Given the $R(y)$ estimates, α can be estimated according to the implication of equation 4-27 that $R(\alpha) = e^{-1} = 0.367879441$. From the two observations whose estimated R values bracket this value, linearly interpolate between them to estimate α.

To estimate β, equation 4-27 can be rearranged to allow estimation of β by linear regression with a zero intercept. Taking the natural logarithm of both sides of equation 4-27, we have $-\ln R(y) = (y/\alpha)^\beta$; taking logarithms again, we have $\ln\ln(1/R(y)) = \beta\ln(y/\alpha)$. This is a straight line through the origin having the form $y = bx$ where $b = \beta$ is the slope, $x = \ln(y/\alpha)$ is the independent variable, and $y = \ln\ln(1/R(y))$ is the dependent variable.

Given a set of data pairs $\{x_i, y_i\}$, the estimate of β is

$$\beta \approx \frac{\sum_{i=1}^{n} (y_i/\alpha)\ln\ln(1/R(y_i))}{\sum_{i=1}^{n} (y_i/\alpha)^2}$$

E33.   All parts in the drive train of the Carmody P50 sports coupe should have an expected life of at least 100,000 miles and should have at least an 85% probability of surviving at least 50,000 miles. Twelve exemplars of a spline shaft have been tested with the following results, sorted by age to failure:

Replication, i	Age to failure, y_i
1	33,480
2	52,920
3	69,120
4	77,040
5	93,600
6	100,080
7	106,920
8	114,840
9	125,640
10	139,680
11	165,600
12	183,600

Determine whether the spline shaft appears to meet the requirements, assuming a Weibull distribution.

The sample mean life is 105,210 miles, the median life is 100,080 miles, and 83.33% of the shafts in the sample lasted at least 50,000 miles. Thus the answer is not clear from the sample without fitting the parameters of the distribution.

Replication, i	Age to failure, y_i	$R(y_i)$	y_i/α
1	33,480	0.943548	0.287793
2	52,920	0.862903	0.454899
3	69,120	0.782258	0.594153
4	77,040	0.701618	0.662234
5	93,600	0.629068	0.804583
6	100,080	0.540323	0.860285
7	106,920	0.459677	0.919081
8	114,840	0.379032	0.987161
9	125,640	0.298387	1.079998
10	139,680	0.217742	1.200685
11	165,600	0.137097	1.423493
12	183,600	0.056452	1.578220

Using the median rank formula to estimate $R(y)$, we can compute the values shown in the third column. From $R(\alpha) = e^{-1} = 0.367879441$, we can interpolate between replications 8 and 9 to estimate $\alpha = 116,333.5852$, the critical age. Dividing by α, we can compute the y/α values shown in the fourth column.

We can estimate β by linear regression with a zero intercept:

$$\beta \approx \frac{\sum_{i=1}^{12} (y_i/\alpha) \ln \ln(1/R(y_i))}{\sum_{i=1}^{12} (y_i/\alpha)^2} = 2.3781886$$

Now we can compute $R(y)$ for $y = 50,000$:

$$R(y) = e^{(y/\alpha)^\beta} = e^{-0.134225412} = \underline{0.8743929}$$

Having an estimated expected life of 105,210 miles (more accurately, it is 103,112 miles by equation 4-29) and an estimated 87.43929% probability of surviving at least 50,000 miles, the spline shaft does appear to meet the requirements. (Fewer than 85% of the sampled splines survived 50,000 miles, but if the hazard of failure increases smoothly with age according to the Weibull distribution, a reliability *more* than 85% at 50,000 miles is implied by the sample as a whole.)

4.2.2 Bayesian Analysis

The conditional probability of event A given event B, denoted $P(A|B)$, can be multiplied by the probability of event A, denoted $P(A)$, to determine the joint probability of events A and B, denoted $P(A, B)$: we write the formula $P(A, B) = P(A|B)P(B)$. By the symmetry of definitions of events, we can also write the similar formula $P(A, B) = P(B|A)P(A)$.

We denote as A' the event that A does not occur. Of course $P(A) + P(A') = 1$. Now the sum of the joint probabilities of B with both possibilities A and A' is $P(B)$. We can write $P(B) = P(B|A)P(A) + P(B|A')P(A')$, the law of addition.

For example, if a parking lot contains 10 cars, four of which are American-made, and three of the cars are dark-colored, let A = "A car is American-made," let A' = "A car is not American-made," let B = "A car is dark-colored," and let B' = "A car is not dark-colored." To express the given facts we can write $P(A) = 0.4$ hence $P(A') = 0.6$, and $P(B) = 0.3$ hence $P(B') = 0.7$. Now suppose none of the non-American-made cars in the lot are dark-colored; we can write $P(B|A') = 0$ hence $P(B'|A') = 1$. What is the probability that a car is American-made and dark-colored? This probability is $P(A, B)$, and it can be computed either by the formula $P(A, B) = P(A|B)P(B)$ or by the formula $P(A, B) = P(B|A)P(A)$. But we have not yet obtained either of the needed conditional probabilities. However, we can determine $P(B|A)$ by solving for it in the law of addition: $P(B) = P(B|A)P(A) + P(B|A')P(A')$ implies $0.3 = P(B|A) \times 0.4 + 0 \times 0.6$, which implies $P(B|A) = 0.75$. Thus $P(A, B) = P(B|A)P(A) = 0.75 \times 0.4 = 0.3$; of the 10 cars, three are American-made and dark-colored.

It often happens that conditional probabilities are known in one direction (e.g., the likelihood that a murderer or an innocent person would be in possession of a smoking gun) and the requirement is to compute conditional probabilities in the opposite direction (e.g., the likelihood that a person in possession of a smoking gun is a murderer or an innocent person). To solve such problems, the law of addition can be rearranged in the form known as Bayes' Theorem.

$$P(A|B) = \frac{P(B|A)P(A)}{P(B)} = \frac{P(B|A)P(A)}{P(B|A)P(A) + P(B|A')P(A')} \qquad (4\text{-}33)$$

Often there are more than two mutually exclusive possibilities in a family of events. For example, a random variable X might take on any value in a sample space $\{x_i : i = 1, ..., n\}$. For such a case we have the general form of the law of addition.

$$P(B) = \sum_{i=1}^{n} P(B|x_i)P(x_i) \tag{4-34}$$

The right-hand side of equation 4-34 can replace $P(B)$ in the denominator of Bayes' Theorem.

As an example of the use of Bayes' Theorem, consider a cancer test that when applied to 500 patients known to have the targeted cancer gave a positive result for 497 of them, and when applied to 300 patients known not to have cancer gave a positive result for 8 of them. If about 5% of the population has the targeted cancer, how likely is it that a positive test result indicates the targeted cancer for a person selected at random?

We can define A = "the person has the targeted cancer" and B = "the test result is positive." We have the estimates $P(A) = 0.05$, $P(B|A) = 497/500$, and $P(B|A') = 8/300$.

$$P(A|B) = \frac{P(B|A)P(A)}{P(B)} = \frac{P(B|A)P(A)}{P(B|A)P(A) + P(B|A')P(A')}$$

$$= \frac{(497/500) \times 0.05}{(497/500) \times 0.05 \ + \ (8/300) \times 0.95} = \underline{0.66237}$$

E34a. A missile fuel system has had a reliability of 95% in the past; historically it has failed in 5% of engine activations. After a modification there is a suspicion—call it a 30% subjective probability—that the reliability has been reduced to 90%. If 40 new test runs are made and the system has no failures, what would be the revised level of suspicion that the reliability had been reduced?

A = "the reliability is 90%"; A' = "the reliability remains 95%"; B = "the system passes all 40 tests." By the binomial distribution, the probability of passing all 40 tests is p^{40}, where p is the reliability. Thus $P(B|A) = (0.90)^{40}$ and $P(B|A') = (0.95)^{40}$. With these values and $P(A) = 0.30$, Bayes' Theorem gives $P(A|B) = \underline{0.04697674}$.

E34b. For the fuel system of the foregoing example, suppose that instead of the 40 test runs mentioned above, n test runs are made and the results are typical of 95% reliability (e.g., 2 failures in 40 trials or 5 failures in 100 trials). How many trials would be required to reduce the suspicion to 5% or less?

Supposing n to be a multiple of 20, the binomial distribution gives

$$P(B|A) = \frac{n!}{(0.95n)!(0.05n)!}(0.90)^{0.95n}(0.10)^{0.05n}$$

$$P(B|A') = \frac{n!}{(0.95n)!(0.05n)!}(0.95)^{0.95n}(0.05)^{0.05n}$$

Inserting quantities into Bayes' Theorem, dividing both numerator and denominator by the numerator, and simplifying, we obtain

$$P(A|B) = \cfrac{1}{1 + \left(\cfrac{0.95}{0.90}\right)^{0.95n} \left(\cfrac{0.05}{0.10}\right)^{0.05n} \cfrac{0.70}{0.30}}$$

Now for $P(A|B) = 0.05$, further simplifying yields

$$\left(\frac{0.95}{0.90}\right)^{0.95n} \left(\frac{0.05}{0.10}\right)^{0.05n} = \left(\frac{1}{0.05} - 1\right)\left(\frac{0.30}{0.70}\right)$$

$$(1.016846836)^n = 8.14285714$$

$$n = \frac{\ln 8.14285714}{\ln 1.016846836} = \underline{125.528}$$

It would take about 125 or 126 test runs with typical 95% results to achieve the required confidence. For example, if 119 of 125 runs were successful, $P(A|B)$ would be about 0.04219.

4.2.3 Stress-strength Interference

Let X be a *stress* variable (a variable that measures a challenge to a system) whose value is normally distributed with mean μ_X and variance σ_X^2. Let Y be a *strength* variable (a variable that measures resistance to stress) whose value is normally distributed with mean μ_Y and variance σ_Y^2. Failure will occur if $X \geq Y$ (see the shaded area in figure 4-3). Let the reliability be the probability that strength is greater than stress: $R = P(Y>X)$. Equation 4-35 gives the relationships between the density functions $f(x)$ for stress and $g(y)$ for strength and the cumulative distribution functions $F(x)$ for stress and $G(y)$ for strength.

The reliability R is the probability $1 - \alpha$ for a normally distributed random variable that has mean $\mu_Y - \mu_X$ and variance $\sigma_Y^2 + \sigma_X^2$. For example, if a walkway is designed to withstand 200 ± 70 lb/ft^2 loading and the actual loading is 100 ± 50 lb/ft^2, the reliability is $1 - \alpha$ for the z-statistic $(200 - 100)/(70^2 + 50^2)^{1/2} = 1.162476$; thus from table 4-3, R is approximately 0.88. (The $\pm$ notation for a normally distributed random variable indicates the standard deviation.)

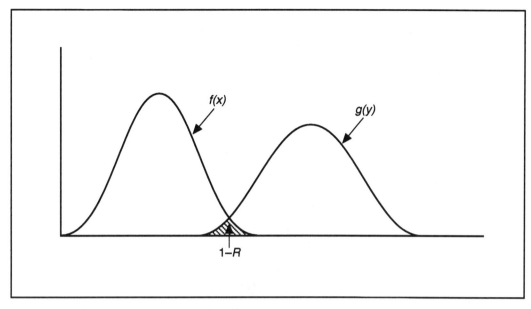

Figure 4-3. Stress-strength Interference.

$$R = P(Y > X) = \int_{-\infty}^{\infty} g(y) \left(\int_{-\infty}^{y} f(x)dx \right) dy = \int_{-\infty}^{\infty} g(y)F(y)dy \qquad (4\text{-}35)$$

$$= \int_{-\infty}^{\infty} f(x) \left(\int_{x}^{\infty} g(y)dy \right) dx = \int_{-\infty}^{\infty} f(x)[1 - G(x)]dx$$

Let k denote the *safety factor*: $k = \mu_Y / \mu_X$; let $c_Y = \sigma_Y / \mu_Y$ denote the *coefficient of variation* for strength, and let $c_X = \sigma_X / \mu_X$ denote the coefficient of variation for stress. In terms of these quantities, the reliability is $1 - \alpha$ for the normal z-statistic

$$\frac{k - 1}{\sqrt{c_Y^2 k^2 + c_X^2}}$$

4.2.4 Fault Trees

A fault tree is a graphical representation of the Boolean logic of a system failure. It starts with a top event—a broad consequence such as release of radioactive water—and ends with the primary events—basic failures such as failure of valve to respond to "close" command that can set off a chain of intermediate events to cause the top event. Figure 4-4 summarizes the most important elements of a fault tree.

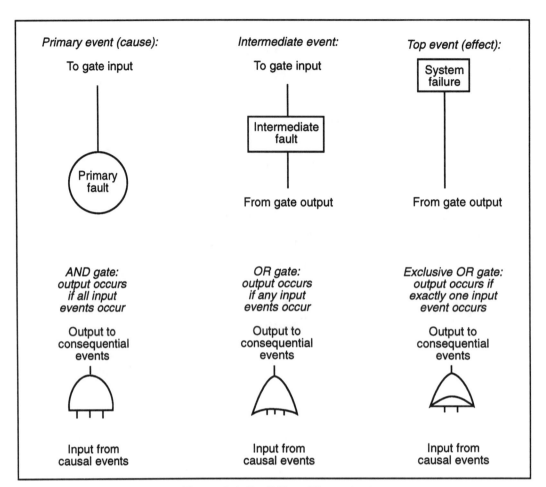

Figure 4-4. Fault Tree Elements.

E35.   **The motor that is the driver to pump 17C may fail to start. This may occur because the motor itself has failed, or its thermal overload switch is stuck open (depriving the motor of current), or the motor's starter has failed (also depriving the motor of current), or for lack of power to the system. Lack of power can occur only if both the main and emergency power supplies are down. Express these failure scenarios in a fault tree.**

Figure 4-5 gives a solution as a candidate might sketch it in the solution booklet. Note that there are three ways to deprive the motor of current so that the intermediate event, "lack of current to motor," is defined.

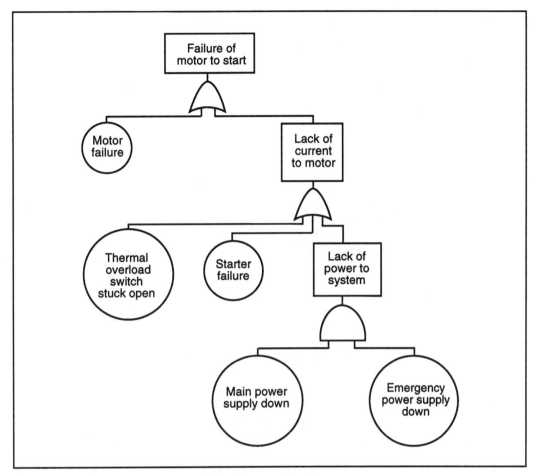

Figure 4-5. Fault-tree Solution to Example E35.

If probabilities are known for the primary events in a fault tree, the consequential probabilities for intermediate events and the top event can be computed. The first step is to adopt a basis for the probabilistic analysis, such as "one hour of operation" or "one cycle" or "one attempt to operate." Next, assuming mutual independence of all primary events, assign their probabilities of occurring.

Let Q_i represent the probability of the ith fault event on the input side of a gate. If the fault event is failure of subsystem i, and if reliability R_i of the subsystem is on the same basis as that of the fault tree, then $Q_i = 1 - R_i$. Let Q_{AND} represent the probability of the fault event on the output side of an AND gate. Then, assuming mutual independence, we have the *AND-gate probability relationship:*

$$Q_{AND} = Q_1 \times Q_2 \times \cdots$$

For example, if the basis for example E35 was "one start attempt" and the reliabilities of the main power supply and the emergency power supply were 0.994 and 0.900 respectively, then the fault probability Q for the event "lack of power to system" would be $(1 - 0.994) \times (1 - 0.900) = 0.0006$.

Let Q_{OR} represent the probability of the fault event on the output side on an OR gate. Then, assuming mutual independence, we have the *OR-gate probability relationship:*

$$Q_{OR} = 1 - [(1 - Q_1) \times (1 - Q_2) \times \cdots] = 1 - R_1 \times R_2 \times \cdots$$

For example, if in example E35 the reliability of the thermal overload switch is 0.930, the reliability of the starter is 0.990, and the fault probability for "lack of power to system" is as calculated above, then the fault probability Q for the event "lack of current to motor" would be $1 - [0.930 \times 0.990 \times (1 - 0.0006)] = 0.07985242$. To complete the example, if there is a 0.003 risk of motor failure, the probability of the top event, "failure of motor to start," would be 0.08261286.

4.3 Statistical Quality Control

4.3.1 Control Charts

A control chart is a time-series plot of values of a process variable or of an attribute (an attribute is a count, a proportion, or presence or absence of a characteristic). A control chart serves to detect changes in an ongoing process as successive *lots* of a product or service are produced by the process. From every lot consisting of N successive units, a sample of n units is selected at random. Each sample of n units is tested, yielding a value that is plotted on the control chart. As time goes on, if the process undergoes a significant change, the chart will show sample values wandering too far away from their established or intended mean. In the U.S., the practice is to establish an upper control limit (UCL) three sigmas (standard deviations) above the mean value and a lower control limit (LCL) three sigmas below the mean. If three sigmas above the mean is greater than the maximum possible value, UCL is set to the maximum possible value; if three sigmas below the mean is less than the minimum possible value (often zero), LCL is set to the minimum possible value.

A process is considered to be out of control if a control chart shows any of the conditions listed below:

- One point outside three sigmas
- Of three successive points, two outside two sigmas
- Of five successive points, four outside one sigma
- Eight successive points on the same side of the mean

The usual policy for reacting to an out-of-control indication is to take immediate action to investigate the cause. The type-I error (risk of investigating unnecessarily) is approximately α = 0.003 when the foregoing rules are followed unless the distribution of the charted quantity is not reasonably close to normal.

Three kinds of control charts are used the most: the $\bar{x}$-chart (average), the p-chart (proportion), and the R-chart (range). We will review these and also the s-chart (standard deviation), which is more flexible and efficient than the R-chart and is supplanting the R-chart now that calculation of the sample standard deviation need never be done by hand.

The $\bar{x}$-chart allows detection of changes in the level of a process, as measured by sample averages. A succession of samples, each of size n, is taken. If the variable has a mean μ_0 and a variance σ_0^2, regardless of whether it is normally distributed, then its sample mean $\bar{x}$ should be approximately normally distributed and should have a sample mean $\mu = \mu_0$ and a sample standard deviation $\sigma = \sigma_0 / \sqrt{n}$ if the process is in control. We center the $\bar{x}$-chart on the mean μ, establish UCL at $\mu + 3\sigma$, and establish LCL at $\mu - 3\sigma$. The limits are modified if they are beyond the possible range of the variable; a common case is that the random variable X is the number of defects or the number of nonconforming units so that $\bar{x}$ is small, say 2.5, and with a moderate standard deviation, say 1.0, LCL is set to zero rather than to the impossible value –0.5.

The p-chart tracks a proportion or percentage and has an understandability advantage over the corresponding $\bar{x}$-chart when the variable being tracked is a per-unit variable. For instance, suppose a process for extruding plastic wiring harness clips ordinarily has a scrap rate of $p = 5\%$, and that a sample of size $n = 100$ is taken every hour. We assume that the number of nonconforming clips $\bar{x}$ in a sample follows the binomial distribution (see table 4-1) and thus has an expected value of $np = 5$ and a variance of $\sigma^2 = np(1 - p) = 4.75$ or a standard deviation of $\sigma = 2.179449$. Using the three-sigma convention, an $\bar{x}$-chart for X (the number of nonconforming clips in the sample) would be centered on $\mu = 5$, would have an upper control limit $5 + 3\sigma$ = 11.538348 $\rightarrow$ 11.5 (it is customary to round off the limits), and would have a lower limit of zero (because $5 - 3\sigma$ is less than zero and a negative number of nonconforming clips is impossible). Note that if the sample size were changed to 50 or 200, it would be centered on 2.5 or 10 rather than on 5.

The corresponding p-chart would be centered on 0.05 or 5% regardless of sample size. The proportion nonconforming is $1/n$ times the number nonconforming. UCL would be 0.115 or 11.5%, and LCL would be zero. These would change with sample size, but not so drastically as the limits for the $\bar{x}$-chart.

To illustrate a p-chart, let us suppose that at time zero the process under discussion is in control and producing at a 5% scrap rate, but that at time 12 the process suddenly goes out of control and begins producing at a 10% scrap rate. The p-chart might appear as in figure 4-6. Under the rules for detection, action would be taken in this particular case at time 14 because:

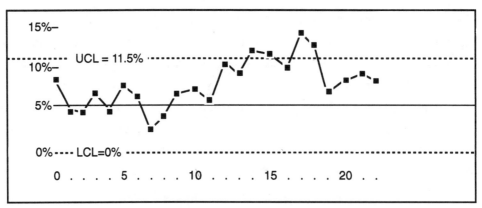

Figure 4-6. A *p*-chart for a Process That Goes Out of Control.

- One point outside three sigmas occurs at time 14
- Of three successive points, two outside two sigmas occur at time 14
- Of five successive points, four outside one sigma occur at time 15
- Eight successive points on the same side of the mean occur at time 16

The *R*-chart and *s*-chart track dispersion of a process. When a control device starts chattering or overshooting, or a sorting system stops functioning, the variability of a process may increase without necessarily being accompanied by a change in the level. The man with one foot in an ice bucket and the other on hot coals knows that being comfortable on the average is not enough. Consistency is itself a quality virtue: a customer can better use thinner gold plating, thinner electrical insulation, lighter chain links, weaker dyes, and so forth, if they are dependably consistent. Restaurant patrons prefer a vegetable soup that is the same each time to one that is tastier on the average but varies.

When samples of size n are taken of a process variable that has standard deviation σ_0, the sample range R has an expected value $d_2\sigma_0$ and the standard deviation of the sample range, σ_R, has an expected value $d_3\sigma_0$. The quantities d_2 and d_3 depend on n and are tabulated in table 4-6. For example, if the standard salinity of a snack food is 16.1 ± 3.8 (the $\pm$ notation indicates $\sigma_0 = 3.8$) and 6 specimens are tested from each lot, then the expected value of the sample range is $2.534 \times 3.8 = 9.6292$, and the expected value of the standard deviation of the sample range is $0.848 \times 3.8 = 3.2224$.

Table 4-6. Factors for Dispersion Control Charts.

Number of observations, n	R-chart factors		s-chart factors	
	$d_2 = E(R/\sigma_0)$	$d_3 = E(\sigma_R/\sigma_0)$	$c_4 = E(s/\sigma_0)$	$c_5 = E(\sigma_s/\sigma_0)$
2	1.128	0.853	0.798	0.603
3	1.693	0.888	0.886	0.463
4	2.059	0.880	0.921	0.389
5	2.326	0.864	0.940	0.341
6	2.534	0.848	0.952	0.308
7	2.704	0.833	0.959	0.282
8	2.847	0.820	0.965	0.262
9	2.970	0.808	0.969	0.246
10	3.078	0.797	0.973	0.232
11	3.137	0.787	0.975	0.220
12	3.258	0.778	0.978	0.210
13	3.336	0.770	0.979	0.202
14	3.407	0.762	0.981	0.194
15	3.472	0.755	0.982	0.187
16	3.532	0.749	0.984	0.181
17	3.588	0.743	0.985	0.175
18	3.640	0.738	0.985	0.170
19	3.689	0.733	0.986	0.166
20	3.735	0.729	0.987	0.161
21	3.778	0.724	0.988	0.157
22	3.819	0.720	0.988	0.153
23	3.858	0.716	0.989	0.150
24	3.895	0.712	0.989	0.147
25	3.931	0.709	0.990	0.144

R-chart construction proceeds as follows:

1. Center the R-chart at $d_2\sigma_0$
2. Place UCL at $d_2\sigma_0 + 3 d_3\sigma_0$
3. Place LCL at $d_2\sigma_0 - 3 d_3\sigma_0$, but not less than 0

For example, with $\sigma_0 = 3.8$ and $n = 6$, we center the R-chart at 9.6292, establish UCL at 9.6292 $+ 3 \times 3.2224 = 19.2964$, and establish LCL at 0, since $9.6292 - 3 \times 3.2224$ is less than 0.

s-chart construction proceeds as follows:

1. Center the s-chart at $c_4\sigma_0$
2. Place UCL at $c_4\sigma_0 + 3c_5\sigma_0$
3. Place LCL at $c_4\sigma_0 - 3c_5\sigma_0$, but not less than 0

For example, with $\sigma_0 = 3.8$ and $n = 6$, we center the s-chart at $3.8 \times 0.952 = 3.6176$, establish UCL at $3.6176 + 3 \times 0.308 \times 3.8 = 7.1288$, and establish LCL at $3.6176 - 3 \times 0.308 \times 3.8 = 0.1064$.

Suppose that moisture got into the salt feeder in the process at hand so that it began feeding salt in clumps (but at the same average rate because the rate into the feeder remained unchanged so that the $\bar{x}$-chart tracking the salinity might not pick up anything wrong). A sample of 6 observations might be {16.9, 15.9, 28.0, 20.3, 9.01, 8.95}. This sample would have the quite ordinary sample mean 16.51, but a high sample range $R = 19.05$ and a high sample standard deviation $s = 7.2154$. Compared to the UCL's 19.2964 for the R-chart and 7.1288 for the s-chart, note that this sample would *not* be outside the upper limit for the R-chart but *would* be outside the upper limit for the s-chart. The s-chart is more sensitive because the R statistic responds to only part of the information in the sample.

E36.   **At an airport, the takeoff wait time, W, starts when the ground controller clears an aircraft to begin to taxi and ends when the ground controller clears the aircraft to seize a runway for takeoff. The established practice does not attempt solely to minimize W, because that would discriminate too much according to hangar location and would too often violate the FIFO (first in, first out) ideal and make W too variable. Both W and its dispersion are to be tracked using control charts. When the established practice is being properly followed, the mean may drift anywhere within the range from 5 to 9 minutes, but the standard deviation stays approximately at 2.12 minutes.**

From each half-hour of operation, a sample of three observations of W is automatically retained from operations data to the nearest minute. Thirteen successive samples are as follows: (5 8 6), (6 3 5), (1 4 7), (3 2 5), (6 5 9), (8 4 2), (5 6 4), (7 3 8), (11 10

3), (13 9 11), (8 6 5), (8 1 10), (14 9 6). **Determine whether the process goes out of control during the 13 half-hours.**

First let us compute the sample means and sample standard deviations (also sample ranges for using the R-chart as an alternative to the s-chart).

The w-chart (that is the $\bar{x}$-chart for W) would be centered on the band from 5 to 9, with UCL $= 9 + 3 \times 2.12 = 15.36$ and LCL $= 0$ (since $5 - 3 \times 2.12$ is less than zero). The mean is well within control.

If dispersion is tracked with an s-chart, the chart would be centered at $c_4\sigma_0 = 0.886 \times 2.12 = 1.87832$, with UCL $= 1.87832 + 3c_5\sigma_0 = 1.87832 + 3 \times 0.463 \times 2.12 = 4.823$ and LCL $= 0$. Figure 4-7 shows the s-chart as a candidate might draw it in the solutions booklet. With respect to dispersion, the process is identified as <u>out of control at sample 13</u> (two successive points outside two sigmas).

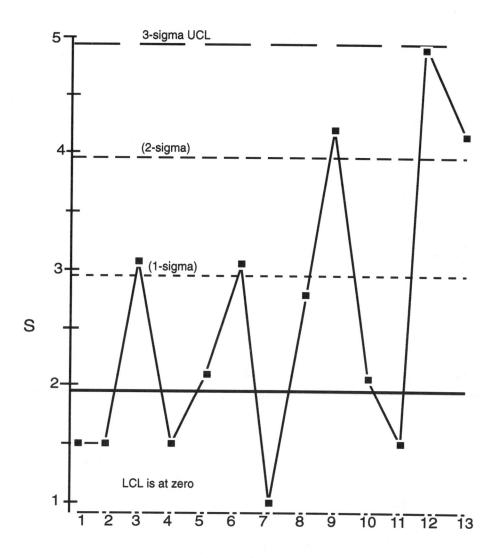

Figure 4-7. *s*-chart Solution to Example E36.

If dispersion is tracked with an R-chart, the chart would be centered at $d_2\sigma_0 = 1.693 \times 2.12$ $= 3.58916$, with UCL $= 3.58916 + 3d_3\sigma_0 = 3.58916 + 3 \times 0.888 \times 2.12 = 9.23684$ and LCL $= 0$. The same conclusion is reached as with the s-chart, since samples 12 and 13 are both beyond the two-sigma level of $3.58916 + 2 \times 0.888 \times 2.12 = 7.35428$; the process is identified as out of control at sample 13.

4.3.2 Acceptance Sampling

When a consumer receives units of a good or service as a sequence of successive lots of size N from a producer, the process of deciding whether to accept or reject each lot on the basis of sampling from the lot is called acceptance sampling. Various standard plans for acceptance sampling have been published. We will review in detail the most commonly used single sampling plan published by the American National Standards Institute (ANSI) and will touch briefly on various double sampling plans.

In a single sampling plan, a single sample of n observations is chosen randomly from the lot of size N and a decision is made to accept or reject the lot. The Z1.4 standard published by ANSI and the virtually identical MIL-STD-105 standard published by military procurement agencies provide a set of single sampling plans that control the producer's risk α (the risk of type-I error—rejecting an acceptable lot) and the consumer's risk β (the risk of type-II error—accepting an unacceptable lot). Acceptability in the Z1.4 (MIL-STD-105) plans is based on a predetermined acceptable quality level (AQL), which is the minimally acceptable proportion of nonconforming units such that the probability of acceptance is near 95%.

To design a single sampling plan from the Z1.4 standards, follow these steps:

1. Choose AQL.
2. Choose a lot size N.
3. Choose an inspection level.
4. Determine a sample size code from Z1.4 table I (here, table 4-7).
5. Determine the sample size n and the acceptance number c for *normal inspection* from Z1.4 table II-A (here, table 4-8). Z1.4 provides a switch from normal inspection to tightened inspection whenever two or more lots out of five are rejected.
6. Determine the sample size and acceptance number for tightened inspection from Z1.4 table II-B (here, included in table 4-8).

Z1.4 provides a switch from tightened inspection back to normal inspection whenever five consecutive lots are accepted. (There is also an optional switch to reduced inspection from normal inspection whenever 10 consecutive lots are accepted, but we will not review reduced inspection here.)

The acceptable quality level is chosen on the basis of process requirements and cost. It is the greatest proportion of nonconforming units that the consumer is willing to accept. The single sampling plan will encourage the producer to meet AQL but will give the producer little or no incentive to do better than AQL. Rejection of a lot will be rare if the producer consistently provides at least AQL.

The lot size N is chosen on a natural basis—a shipment, a carton, a roll, a shift's production. It should be small enough so that the quality within a lot is relatively homogeneous. For example, if it is generally true that a container of 1000 clips in bulk tends to be either perfect or not, the container is a natural lot; no smaller lot would make sense, since bulk packaging jumbles the clips. On the other hand, a roll of tape or wire may reasonably be divided into several lots, since packaging preserves the order of production. If the producer's process tends to be subject to upsets that span an average of K units, a lot size of approximately $2K$ units is reasonable.

The inspection level is chosen to control the consumer's risk. Smaller risk is achieved by inspecting greater fractions of lots. The inspection levels available are denoted from smaller to greater fractions, *S-1, S-2, S-3, S-4, I, II,* and *III*. Level *II* is the most commonly used inspection level. If the product is of critical importance and inspection is not too costly, level *III* is used. If inspection is so costly that very small sample sizes are required, and the sampling risks are not great (e.g., for crash testing of automobiles), the special levels *S-4* to *S-1* can be used.

For each combination of lot size N and inspection level, there is a sample-size code—an uppercase letter from *A* to *R*, omitting *I* and *O*. These codes express the approximate proportion of the lot to be sampled and are listed in table 4-7.

Table 4-7. Sample-size Codes for Various Lot Sizes and Inspection Levels.

Lot size, N	Special inspection levels			General inspection levels		
	S-1	*S-2*	*S-3*	*I*	*II*	*III*
2 to 8	A	A	A	A	A	B
9 to 15	A	A	A	A	B	C
16 to 25	A	A	B	B	C	D
26 to 50	A	B	B	C	D	E
51 to 90	B	B	C	C	E	F
91 to 150	B	B	C	D	F	G
151 to 280	B	C	D	E	G	H
281 to 500	B	C	D	F	H	J
501 to 1200	C	C	E	G	J	K
1201 to 3200	C	D	E	H	K	L
3201 to 10,000	C	D	F	J	L	M
10,001 to 35,000	C	D	F	K	M	N
35,001 to 150,000	D	E	G	L	N	P
150,001 to 500,000	D	E	G	M	P	Q
500,001 and over	D	E	H	N	Q	R

Table 4-8 gives the sample sizes n and acceptance numbers c_N for normal and c_T for tightened single sampling for various AQL. Sample sizes are the same for normal and tightened inspection. The acceptance numbers for normal and tightened inspection are separated by a slash. The corresponding rejection numbers are greater by one; for example, for sample size code letter H and AQL = 10%, under normal inspection a lot would be accepted if there were at most 10 nonconforming units in the sample (and rejected if there were 11 or more), and under tightened inspection a lot would be accepted if there were at most 8 nonconforming units in the sample (and rejected if there were 9 or more).

Table 4-8. Acceptance Numbers for Single Sampling: c_N Normal, c_T Tightened.

Sample size code letter	Sample size	Acceptable Quality Level (AQL) (Table gives acceptance numbers for normal/tightened inspection.)										
		Percentage nonconforming							Nonconformances per 100 units			
		0.01%	0.04%	0.10%	0.40%	1%	4%	10%	40	100	250	1000
		c_N/c_T	c_N/c_T	c_N/c_T	c_N/c_T	c_N/c_T	c_N/c_T	c_N/c_T	c_N/c_T	c_N/c_T	c_N/c_T	c_N/c_T
A	2	0/0	0/0	0/0	0/0	0/0	0/0	1/1	2/1	5/3	10/8	30/27
B	3	0/0	0/0	0/0	0/0	0/0	0/0	1/1	3/2	7/5	14/12	44/41
C	5	0/0	0/0	0/0	0/0	0/0	0/0	1/1	5/3	10/8	21/18	44/41
D	8	0/0	0/0	0/0	0/0	0/0	1/1	2/1	7/5	14/12	30/27	44/41
E	13	0/0	0/0	0/0	0/0	0/0	1/1	3/2	10/8	21/18	44/41	44/41
F	20	0/0	0/0	0/0	0/0	0/0	2/1	5/3	14/12	21/18	44/41	44/41
G	32	0/0	0/0	0/0	0/0	1/1	3/2	7/5	21/18	21/18	44/41	44/41
H	50	0/0	0/0	0/0	0/0	1/1	5/3	10/8	21/18	21/18	44/41	44/41
J	80	0/0	0/0	0/0	1/1	2/1	7/5	14/12	21/18	21/18	44/41	44/41
K	125	0/0	0/0	0/0	1/1	3/2	10/8	21/18	21/18	21/18	44/41	44/41
L	200	0/0	0/0	0/0	2/1	5/3	14/12	21/18	21/18	21/18	44/41	44/41
M	315	0/0	0/0	1/1	3/2	7/5	21/18	21/18	21/18	21/18	44/41	44/41
N	500	0/0	0/0	1/1	5/3	10/8	21/18	21/18	21/18	21/18	44/41	44/41
P	800	0/0	1/1	2/1	7/5	14/12	21/18	21/18	21/18	21/18	44/41	44/41
Q	1250	0/0	1/1	3/2	10/8	21/18	21/18	21/18	21/18	21/18	44/41	44/41
R	2000	0/0	2/1	5/3	14/12	21/18	21/18	21/18	21/18	21/18	44/41	44/41

E37.   Circuit chips arrive in lots of 300 and we want to perform single sampling at level II to achieve a quality level of 1% nonconforming. A chip is nonconforming if it fails to function. How many chips should we test from each lot, and how many nonconforming chips would be acceptable in a sample? If samples from 14 successive lots are found to contain {0, 0, 1, 2, 1, 0, 2, 0, 1, 0, 0, 0, 1, 1} nonconforming chips, which lots are rejected, what switching is done, and when?

From table 4-7 with a lot size of 300 (281 to 500) and level II, the sample size code letter is H. From table 4-8 the sample size for normal or tightened inspection given code H is <u>50</u>, and the acceptance number for AQL = 1% is $c_N = \underline{1}$ for normal inspection (for tightened inspection $c_T = 1$, also). Lots 4 and 7 are rejected; the rejection of lot 7 is the second within five lots, so there is a switch to <u>tightened inspection beginning with lot 8</u> (in the actual Z1.4 tables, there would be an arrow pointing to a different plan). The acceptance of lot 12 is the fifth consecutive acceptance, so there is a resumption of <u>normal inspection beginning with lot 13</u>.

The acceptable quality limit is not the only basis for designing sampling plans. No set of sampling plans can exactly control the producer's risk α or the consumer's risk β, because for small samples a change of ±1 in the sample size or acceptance number can greatly change the acceptance probability. However, the Z1.4 (MIL-STD-105) plans are those that come as close as possible to setting the producer's risk to $\alpha = 0.05$. If a sampling plan is based on AQL = 1%, for example, and the producer is barely meeting the requirement, roughly 95% of the lots will be accepted. (In actual capital Z1.4 tables, there would be an arrow pointing to a different plan.)

An alternative basis for sampling plans is the limiting quality level (LQL), formerly known as the lot tolerance percent defective. The Z1.4 plans that rarely reject a 1% nonconforming lot (AQL = 1%, α roughly 0.05) will rarely accept a 9% nonconforming lot (LQL = 9%, β roughly 0.05). If the consumer's main intent is to guard against a given dangerous or costly percentage of defectives, that percentage can be set as LQL and the consumer can go to the operating characteristic curves in the Z1.4 standard to determine the equivalent AQL-based plan.

Another possible basis is the indifference quality level (IQL), which is the level of nonconformity such that the lot acceptance probability is 0.5. The Z1.4 plans that rarely reject a 1% nonconforming lot and rarely accept a 9% nonconforming lot will have an equal probability of accepting or rejecting a 3.5% nonconforming lot, according to the operating characteristic curves published in the Z1.4 standard. See figure 4-8 for the general nature of the relationships among α, β, AQL, LQL, and IQL.

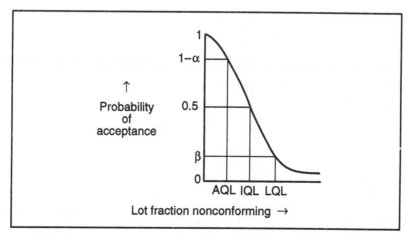

Figure 4-8. General Operating Characteristics of Sampling Plans.

Closely related to the IQL is the average outgoing quality limit (AOQL), which is the average fraction nonconforming. The Z1.4 standard contains tables that list AOQL for each sampling plan. Thus, if the concern is to achieve a given average quality, the design can start by setting AOQL.

Double sampling plans are more difficult to administer than single sampling plans but require less testing for the same α or β. In a double sampling plan a small sample of size n_1 is taken and its number of nonconforming units or nonconformities, x, is compared to the first acceptance number c_1 and the second acceptance number c_2. Three outcomes are possible: if $x \leq c_1$, the lot is accepted; if $c_1 < x \leq c_2$, a second sample of size n_2 is taken; and if $x > c_2$, the lot is rejected. If a second sample is taken, let its number of nonconforming units or nonconformities be y, so that the total of nonconforming units or nonconformities is $x + y$. Then if $x + y \leq c_2$, the lot is accepted; otherwise it is rejected. Extensive tables for both single and double sampling plans, indexed by AOQL, are available in *Sampling Inspection Tables* (Dodge and Romig).

4.4 Queueing Models

Queueing theory is an important subject for industrial engineers. The IE PE Exam covers only the relatively few basic queueing models reviewed here because simulation is the most practical way to handle problems that go beyond these basic models.

4.4.1 Basic Queueing Definitions

A queue is a waiting line, such as people waiting to be served by a sales clerk, incoming calls waiting to be processed by a telephone switchboard, or a backlog of repair orders waiting to be executed. In a queueing model, permanent entities are called servers and transient entities are called customers. Customers enter the system, await their turn for service, seize a server, and, when service is completed, release the server and leave. Customers arrive according to a probability distribution with an average arrival rate λ. At any given time, each server is either *idle* (not serving a customer) or *busy*. If an arrival occurs and any server is idle, the arriving customer does not wait but immediately seizes an idle server and begins service. If a server becomes idle and any customer is waiting in the queue, the eldest (by arrival time) customer immediately seizes the server and begins service. Service times (durations) are independent variates from a probability distribution with mean $1/\mu$, where μ is the average service rate.

Let the number of servers be c. Let the maximum number of customers or system capacity be M. This is a limit on n, the total number of customers in the system which includes both the number waiting (n_q) and the number being served. If a customer arrives while $n = M$, the arrival is refused, and the customer turns away without being counted or affecting the future arrival rate.

Thus, for queueing models in which M is not infinite, an effective arrival rate λ_{eff} exists that is less than λ, and λ in such models is called the offered load.

Queueing theory treats both long-run and transient statistics, but here we are interested in long-run averages, the most important ones of which are listed below:

L the long-run expected number of customers in the system

L_q the long-run expected number of customers in the queue (in the system but not yet being served)

W the long-run expected duration of a customer's stay in the system

W_q the long-run expected duration of a customer's stay in the queue before being served

For these quantities to exist, the arrival and service processes must be stationary (λ and μ may not vary with time), and the service process must be able to keep up with the arrival process; that is, if $M=\infty$, so that $\lambda_{eff}=\lambda$, then we require $\lambda < c\mu$, since otherwise the number of customers would grow without bound. We define $\rho = \lambda/\mu$, and we also define the traffic factor ρ/c. Of course, the traffic factor for a single-server ($c=1$) system is ρ.

It should be emphasized that the average *throughput rate* or production rate of a system is not μ or λ; it is λ_{eff}. If a barber in a single-barber haircutting shop can perform $\mu = 3$ haircuts per hour, and $\lambda = 2.5$ haircut customers arrive per hour, and 10% of the potential customers are turned away because the shop is full 10% of the time, then the throughput is $\lambda_{eff}=2.5\times(1-0.10)$ $= 2.25$.

The quantities L, L_q, W, and W_q depend on the long-run probability distribution of n, the number of customers in the system. Let these probabilities be $\{ \pi_n : n=0,1,...,M \} = \{ \pi_0, \pi_1,..., \pi_M \}$. Since π_M is the long-run probability that the system is full, and customers are turned away when the system is full, it is also the long-run proportion of customers turned away. Hence, we have the following relationship between the effective and offered arrival rates:

$$\lambda_{eff} = \lambda(1-\pi_M) \tag{4-36}$$

Since the average wait in the queue is W_q and the average service time is $1/\mu$, and the customer's stay in the system is made up of waiting and service, an immediate consequence of the definitions of W, W_q, and μ is the *waiting-time law*:

$$W = W_q + 1/\mu \tag{4-37}$$

Since L is the long-run expected value of n, it can be computed from the definition of expected value:

$$L = \sum_{n=0}^{M} n\pi_n = \pi_1 + 2\pi_2 + \cdots + n\pi_n + \cdots + M\pi_M \qquad (4\text{-}38)$$

A similar definition exists for L_q. Since the number of customers waiting in the queue is $n_q = 0$ when $n \leq c$, and is $n - c$ otherwise, we have

$$L_q = \sum_{n=c+1}^{M} (n-c)\pi_n = \pi_{c+1} + 2\pi_{c+2} + \cdots + (n-c)\pi_n + \cdots + (M-c)\pi_M \qquad (4\text{-}39)$$

As a consequence of the foregoing equations, the long-run average number of customers being served is

$$L - L_q = \sum_{n=0}^{c-1} n\pi_n + c\sum_{n=c}^{M} \pi_n \qquad (4\text{-}40)$$

4.4.2 Fundamental Queueing Relationships

Along with the waiting-time law $W = W_q + 1/\mu$, *Little's law* is the most fundamental relationship in queueing theory. Consider a queueing system that operates for a long time T during which time J customers arrive. The number of customers in the system increases by one when a customer arrives and decreases by one when a customer departs, as in figure 4-9.

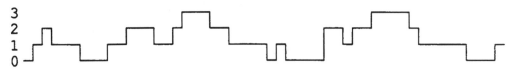

Figure 4-9. Queuing System.

Let the time spent by the successive customers in the system be $\{d_1, d_2, ..., d_J\}$. Figure 4-9 gives the number of customers in the system, so an estimate of L is the average height of the graph, which is the area under the graph divided by T. But the area under the graph is that of a set of rectangles, one for each customer, having widths $\{d_1, d_2, ..., d_J\}$ and height 1. Thus the estimate of L is $(d_1 + d_2 + \cdots + d_J)/T$.

Since W is the average time spent in the system, its estimate is clearly $(d_1 + d_2 + \cdots + d_J)/J$. Of course the estimate of the effective arrival rate λ_{eff} is the sample average arrival rate J/T.

Now the three foregoing estimates can approach the true long run averages L, W, and λ_{eff} as closely as desired by making J and T as large as necessary. Combining the three estimates, we obtain Little's law:

$$L = \lambda_{eff} W \qquad (4\text{-}41)$$

As an example of Little's law, if Georgia has only 50,000 prison beds, so that in the prison system the average population cannot exceed $L = 50,000$, and the average arrival rate is $\lambda_{eff} = 4500$ prisoners per month (of course this is also the number of releases per month), then the average prison stay W cannot be more than $50,000/4500 = 11.11$ months.

Little's law applies to any system or subsystem. In particular, the queue is a subsystem having the same throughput rate λ_{eff} as the whole system, so Little's law for the queue is

$$L_q = \lambda_{eff} W_q \qquad (4\text{-}42)$$

4.4.3 Arrival Distributions

The worst arrival distributions are those for batch arrivals since, for example, if only one server is idle, then all but one customer in the batch must wait. The best arrival distribution is deterministic arrivals, one every $1/\lambda$ time units, as in an appointment system, so that the only waiting is caused by longer-than-average service times.

The arrival process of greatest importance is the Markov process, in which the number of arrivals in a given time interval follows the Poisson distribution and the time between successive arrivals (the interarrival time) follows the exponential distribution. If the average arrival rate is λ, then the probability of zero arrivals by time t is $P[N(t)=0)] = e^{-\lambda t}$ and the probability of exactly n arrivals by time t is given by equation 4-43.

$$P[N(t) = n] = \frac{(\lambda t)^n e^{-\lambda t}}{n!} \qquad (4\text{-}43)$$

The corresponding distribution of the time to the next arrival is the exponential distribution with cumulative distribution function

$$F(t) = 1 - e^{-\lambda t} \qquad (4\text{-}44)$$

The Markov process is memoryless: regardless of whether an arrival has just occurred or if it has been a long time since the last arrival, the probability of n arrivals in the next t time units is given by equation 4-43 and the probability that more than t time units will pass before the next arrival is equal to $e^{-\lambda t}$ (from either equation 4-43 or equation 4-44). The Markov process represents pure randomness and is realistic for many actual arrival processes such as equipment failures or calls arriving at a switchboard.

4.4.4 Service Distributions

The worst service processes would be batch service distributions in which the service time (duration) for the first member of a batch of m customers would be m and the service time for the remaining members would be zero. The best service distribution is deterministic service times, $1/\mu$ for each customer, so that the only waiting is caused by bunched arrivals.

The most widely realistic service time distribution is the gamma or Erlang distribution (see table 4-2). For example, if a service consists of a sequence of four tasks, each exponentially distributed with mean $1/\phi = 0.20$ minutes, the service time follows the Erlang distribution with mean $\mu = 4 \times 1/\phi = 0.80$ minutes and standard deviation $\sigma = \sqrt{n}/\phi = 0.40$ minutes.

For mathematical convenience, the exponential distribution is often used for service times, but it is not realistic for many actual situations. It represents pure randomness and is the distribution that would hold approximately if the service were a series of many stabs at getting rid of the customer, each stab having the same likelihood of succeeding. More often, a service is a series of steps that must all be completed in sequence, so that the gamma or Erlang distribution is more realistic. However, the exponential distribution of service time gives convenient formulas for π_n, L, L_q, W, and W_q, and is widely used even though its variance is too high and it overestimates π_n for large n and hence overestimates L, L_q, W, and W_q.

4.4.5 Single-server Queues

Define $\rho_{eff} = \lambda_{eff}/\mu$. For any single-server queueing system, regardless of the arrival and service distributions, the probability that the server is idle and the system is empty is $\pi_0 = 1 - \rho_{eff}$. As a consequence of equation 4-40, the long-run average number of customers being served in a single server system (which is the same as the long-run probability that the server is busy), is given by equation 4-45.

$$L - L_q = \sum_{n=1}^{M} \pi_n = 1 - \pi_0 = \rho_{eff} \qquad (4\text{-}45)$$

4.4.5.1 M/M/1/∞ Queues

Few queueing models are convenient for routine use. The most convenient and widely used queueing model is the one designated M/M/1/∞ in standard queueing nomenclature. Deciphered, this means a Markov arrival process (first M), a Markov service process (second M), a single server (1), and an infinite capacity (∞).

For the M/M/1/∞ model we have $c = 1, M = \infty, \lambda_{eff} = \lambda, \rho_{eff} = \rho = \lambda/\mu$. We assume $\lambda < \mu$, that is, $\rho < 1$ (the server can, on the average, keep up with arrivals). The system goes empty from time to time, temporarily builds up when arrivals fall closely together and/or service times are long, but in the long run is empty a proportion $\pi_0 = 1 - \rho$ of the time. The average throughput is λ customers per unit time.

The long-run probability distribution of the number of customers in the system is $\{ \pi_n : n = 0,1,...\} = \rho^n(1 - \rho)$. That is,

$$
\begin{aligned}
\pi_0 &= 1-\rho \\
\pi_1 &= \rho(1-\rho) \\
\pi_2 &= \rho^2(1-\rho) \\
&\vdots \\
\pi_n &= \rho^n(1-\rho) \\
&\vdots
\end{aligned}
\tag{4-46}
$$

From the foregoing equation and equation 4-38, we have the long-run expected number of customers in the M/M/1/∞ queueing system:

$$
L = \frac{\rho}{1-\rho}
\tag{4-47}
$$

The long-run expected number of customers in the queue of the M/M/1/∞ queueing system is

$$
L_q = L-\rho = \frac{\rho^2}{1-\rho}
\tag{4-48}
$$

For example, if the arrival rate to an M/M/1/∞ system is 90% of the service rate, then the long-run average contents of the system is $L = 0.90/0.10 = 9$ customers, and the long-run average number of customers waiting in the queue is $L_q = L - \rho = 9 - 0.90 = 8.1$ customers. Let the arrival rate be $\lambda = 100$ customers per hour (so that the service rate is $\mu = 111.111$ customers per hour). Then the long-run average time spent by a customer in the system is $W = L/\lambda = 9/100$

= 0.09 hours. The average service time is $1/\mu = 0.009$ hours, so the long-run average time in the queue is $W_q = W - 1/\mu = 0.081$ hours. To verify this from L_q, note that $W_q = L_q/\lambda = 8.1/100 = 0.081$ hours.

E38a.   During the busy period of work on a maintenance shutdown, workers arrive at the safety engineer's trailer at an average rate of 8 per hour, seeking welding permits. The safety engineer can issue a welding permit in an average of 6 minutes. Assuming the arrivals and services are Markovian, determine the average number of workers at the trailer (including the one whose permit is being worked on).

$\lambda = 8/\text{hr}$. $\mu = 1/(6 \div 60) = 10/\text{hr}$. $\rho = 0.8$. $L = \rho/(1-\rho) = 0.8/0.2 = \underline{4}$ workers.

4.4.5.2 M/G/1/∞ Queues

The M/G/1/∞ system is like the M/M/1/∞ system except that the service time distribution is not Markovian. The G in M/G/1/∞ indicates a *general* distribution of service time. Given the mean $1/\mu$ and standard deviation σ of service time, but not its entire distribution, we cannot determine the long-run probabilities $\{\pi_n\}$ (although we can determine the empty probability π_0 from equation 4-45), but the *Pollaczek-Khintchine formula* allows us to determine L, L_q, W, and W_q.

For the M/G/1/∞ model we have $c = 1$, $M = \infty$, $\lambda_{\text{eff}} = \lambda$, $\rho_{\text{eff}} = \rho = \lambda/\mu$. We assume $\lambda < \mu$, that is, $\rho < 1$ (the server can, on the average, keep up with arrivals). The system goes empty from time to time, temporarily builds up when arrivals fall closely together and/or service times are long, but in the long run is empty a proportion $\pi_0 = 1 - \rho$ of the time. The average throughput is λ customers per unit time. The Pollaczek-Khintchine formula is

$$L = L_q + \rho = \frac{\rho^2 + \lambda^2\sigma^2}{2(1-\rho)} + \rho \qquad (4\text{-}49)$$

E38b.   In the foregoing example, the service time had an average of 6 minutes but was assumed to be exponentially distributed. However, the standard deviation of the safety engineer's service time to issue a permit is actually 4 minutes, whereas from Table 4-2 it would equal the mean of 6 minutes if the service time were Markovian. Revise the estimate of the average number of workers at the trailer accordingly.

$\lambda = 8/\text{hr}$. $\mu = 1/(6 \div 60) = 10/\text{hr}$. $\sigma = 0.06\overline{6}$ hr. $\rho = 0.8$. $L = [0.8^2 + 8^2 \times 0.06\overline{6}^2]/[2 \times 0.2] + 0.8 = \underline{3.111}$ workers. Note that if the standard deviation of service time implied by the exponential distribution (0.10 hr) were put into the Pollaczek-Khintchine formula, the answer would match that of the earlier example.

E38c.   OSHA provides a computerized welding permit application procedure in which the worker steps up to a terminal and interacts with a computer program. OSHA claims this process takes exactly 6 minutes every time (practically zero standard deviation).

If this procedure were installed in the safety engineer's trailer under the conditions of the foregoing example, what would be the effect on the average number of permit-seeking workers at the trailer?

$\lambda = 8/\text{hr}$. $\mu = 1/(6+60) = 10/\text{hr}$. $\sigma = 0$ hr. $\rho = 0.8$. $L = [0.8^2 + 8^2 \times 0^2]/[2 \times 0.2] + 0.8 = \underline{2.4}$ workers. Compared to a manual system having $\sigma = 0.06\overline{6}$ hr, the procedure would provide a decrease of 0.711 in the average number of workers at the trailer.

4.4.6 Multiple-server Queues

The M/M/c/M queueing model is the only multiple-server model that is reasonably convenient and flexible for routine work. It overestimates the long-run populations and waiting times because of its Markovian service process, but offers direct estimation of the effects of variation in number of servers and system capacity.

In the M/M/c/M model the arrivals are Markovian at an average rate of λ customers per unit time. The service process is Markovian with an average service time of $1/\mu$ time units. Because the service time distribution is exponential, the standard deviation of service time is $1/\mu$ time units—an unrealistic but mathematically necessary aspect of the model. The number of servers is c. (The system can hold a maximum of M customers, including those being served.)

The system is not necessarily constrained to keep up with the offered load when the capacity M is finite. It turns away a proportion π_M of the potential customers and processes customers at an average rate of $\lambda_{\text{eff}} = \lambda(1 - \pi_M)$ customers per unit time.

Formulas for the probabilities $\{ \pi_n \}$ are based on Markovian analysis using the fact that the departure rate from the system increases as the number of customers increases until it reaches a maximum when all servers are busy. The departure rate is 0, μ, 2μ,..., $(c-1)\mu$, $c\mu$, $c\mu$ and so forth. We define a quantity D which will be the denominator in all the π_n formulas. D has $M + 1$ terms, one for each value of n from 0 to M. It is a sum in which each term is ρ/n times the previous term until $n = c$, after which each term is ρ/c times the previous term (as before, $\rho = \lambda/\mu$). Equation 4-50 shows D in term-by-term form as well as in standard notation.

$$D = \sum_{n=0}^{c-1} \frac{\rho^n}{n!} + \frac{\rho^c}{c!} \left[\frac{1-(\rho/c)^{M-c+1}}{1-\rho/c} \right]$$

(4-50)

$$= 1 + \rho + \frac{\rho^2}{2!} + \frac{\rho^3}{3!} + \cdots + \frac{\rho^c}{c!} + \left(\frac{\rho^c}{c!}\right)\left(\frac{\rho}{c}\right) + \left(\frac{\rho^c}{c!}\right)\left(\frac{\rho}{c}\right)^2 + \cdots + \left(\frac{\rho^c}{c!}\right)\left(\frac{\rho^c}{c}\right)^{M-c}$$

Of course the $\rho^3/3!$ term in D does not exist if $c < 3$, and the ρ^2 term does not exist if $c < 2$. Also, the closed form does not exist if $\rho = c$. When $\rho = c$ the quantity in brackets in equation 4-50 becomes simply $[M - c + 1]$. Now the nth probability π_n is the nth term of D divided by the whole of D. That is, $\pi_0 = 1/D$, $\pi_1 = \rho/D$, and so forth. That is,

$$\pi_0 = \frac{1}{D}$$

$$\pi_n = \begin{cases} \dfrac{\rho^n}{n!}\pi_0 & \text{for } n < c \\[2mm] \dfrac{\rho^n}{c!\,c^{n-c}}\pi_0 & \text{for } n \geq c \end{cases} \qquad\qquad (4\text{-}51)$$

These formulas cover all cases of M/M queues. After computing the long-run probabilities π_n for $n = 0$ to M, if M is not too large it is possible, term-by-term, to determine the long-run populations and times from their definitions:

$$L = 0\pi_0 + 1\pi_1 + 2\pi_2 + \cdots + M\pi_M$$

$$L_q = 0\pi_0 + \cdots + 0\pi_c + 1\pi_{c+1} + 2\pi_{c+2} + \cdots + (M - c)\pi_M$$

$$W = \frac{L}{\lambda_{\text{eff}}} \quad \text{where } \lambda_{\text{eff}} = \lambda\left(1 - \pi_M\right)$$

$$W_q = \frac{L_q}{\lambda_{\text{eff}}}$$

For large M it may be more convenient to use the closed-form formula for L_q, given in equation 4-52a for $\rho \neq c$ and in equation 4-52b for $\rho = c$.

$$L_q = \pi_0\left(\frac{\rho^{c+1}}{(c-1)!(c-\rho)^2}\right)\left[1 - \left(\frac{\rho}{c}\right)^{M-c} - (M-c)\left(\frac{\rho}{c}\right)^{M-c}\left(1 - \frac{\rho}{c}\right)\right], \quad \rho \neq c \qquad (4\text{-}52\text{a})$$

When $M = \infty$, the factor in brackets in equation 4-52a is simply 1.

$$L_q = \pi_0\left(\frac{\rho^c(M-c)(M-c+1)}{2c!}\right), \quad \rho = c \qquad (4\text{-}52b)$$

Given L_q, recall $\lambda_{\text{eff}} = \lambda(1 - \pi_M)$. L can be computed simply as

$$L = L_q + \lambda_{\text{eff}}/\mu = L_q + \rho_{\text{eff}} \qquad (4\text{-}53)$$

4.4.7 Queueing Costs

The principal design relevant cost tradeoffs for queueing systems are between customer costs—waiting, service duration, and turnaways—and the costs of providing service. As more servers (or less variable servers) are added, customer waiting diminishes; as faster servers are added, the waiting and service time both diminish. In either case, if the system has a finite capacity, turnaways also diminish.

The customer cost of waiting is generally proportional to L_q. The combined customer cost of waiting and service is generally proportional to L. In example E38c, for instance, a computerized procedure was estimated to reduce L by 0.711 workers. If the workers' average hourly wage plus benefits was \$14.21, then $0.711 \times 14.21 = \$10.10$ would be the hourly savings in customer waiting and service that would help justify the cost of installing and operating the computerized procedure. The customer cost of turnaways is generally proportional to the average number of customers turned away per unit time, which is $\lambda - \lambda_{\text{eff}}$.

The cost of providing service usually includes an initial capital cost per server and a continuing cost per server per unit time. This makes the cost generally proportional to c unless there is also a fixed cost for changing the system. Costs for increasing the service rate or decreasing the variance of service time may also be involved.

E38d. The Switchco shop in Topeka fabricates made-to-order telephone switches. It operates 40 hours per week and completes switches at a Poisson rate of 2.4 per 8-hour working day. At a capitalized cost of \$180 per working day, Switchco could operate a two-station test facility that could test up to two completed switches at a time at a Markovian rate of 1.6 switches per day at each station. Alternatively, at a capitalized cost of \$150 per working day, Switchco could operate a fast one-station test facility that could test an average of $2.6\overline{6}$ switches per day with a service time standard deviation of 0.14 days. The cost of having a completed switch delayed while waiting for testing or being tested is \$20 per working day. Which alternative is best?

Under either alternative, Poisson arrivals are at $\lambda = 2.4$/day and there are no turnaways ($M = \infty$). The first alternative is an M/M/2/∞ system; $c = 2$, $\mu = 1.6$/day, and $\rho = 2.4/1.6 = 1.5$. From equation 4-50,

$$D = \sum_{n=0}^{1} \frac{\rho^n}{n!} + \frac{\rho^2}{2!}\left[\frac{1}{1-\rho/2}\right] = 1 + \rho + \frac{\rho^2}{2!}\left[\frac{1}{1-\rho/2}\right] = 1 + 1.5 + 4.5 = 7$$

Thus $\pi_0 = 1/7$, and from equation 4-52a with $M = \infty$,

$$L_q = (1/7)\left(\frac{(1.5)^3}{1! \times (0.5)^2}\right) = 1.92857$$

Since $M = \infty$, λ_{eff} is simply λ, so that equation 4-53 gives $L = L_q + \rho = 3.42857$. The corresponding cost of delay is $L \times 20 = \$68.57$ per day, so that the total cost including the capitalization cost of $180 is $\underline{\$248.57}$ per day.

The second alternative is an M/G/1/∞ system with $1/\mu = 1/2.6\overline{6} = 0.375$ days, $\sigma = 0.14$ days, $\rho = 2.4 \times 0.375 = 0.9$. From equation 4-49,

$$L = \frac{\rho^2 + \lambda^2 \sigma^2}{2(1-\rho)} + \rho = 4.61448 + 0.9 = 5.51448$$

The corresponding cost of delay is $L \times 20 + \$110.29$ per day, so that the total cost including the capitalization cost of $150 is $\underline{\$263.29 \text{ per day}}$. Since this is more expensive, the <u>first alternative</u> is best.

Chapter 5
Computers and
Information Systems

Qualified industrial engineers are not expected to have computer programming skills, but they are required to be knowledgeable about computer software, hardware, and systems design. In the report, *Analysis of Professional Activities and Requirements of the Engineering Profession* (NCEES 1989), practicing industrial engineers reported computer and information system skills as either necessary or helpful in 12 of their 20 most important work activities. Software skills are about the fifth most important of all IE-specific job tools; hardware and systems design skills rank fifteenth and sixteenth. Skills in all three computer-related areas—software, hardware, and systems design—are considered necessary not only for design and operation of computer information systems, but for design of manufacturing systems as well. To lesser degrees, these skills are needed for facilities design and engineering, management systems design and operations, manufacturing systems operations, design and operation of production planning and control systems, and operation of inventory and quality assurance systems.

Computers and information systems are evolving faster than any other part of the technological environment. Industrial engineers have a special role with regard to rapidly changing technologies: making new technology fit gracefully into an enterprise. The industrial engineer is the engineer expected to perform or supervise the overall systems design when operations are automated or computerized. For example, an industrial engineer would not do the technical design of a robotics system, but would design the tasks to be performed by the robotics, along with the tasks to be performed by the non-robotics elements of the system and the interfaces between these two parts of the overall system.

This chapter reviews the unchanging fundamentals that every industrial engineer should grasp in order to deal with the technical aspects of computers and information systems. (The important human factors issues concerning interfaces of people with computers are reviewed in chapter 7.)

In each of the following parts of this chapter, we will also review basic vocabulary and important computer ephemera (things subject to change). Had you lived a century ago, you might have been expected to be familiar with 200 or so words concerning horses and horse-drawn transportation. Today, a qualified engineer is expected to be familiar with hundreds of new words and concepts concerning computers and information systems. How new? Well, you could have gone to a bookstore the day this book was published and been unable to find any dictionary in which you could look up *meg* (megabyte, as in eight megabytes of memory) or *mip* (millions of operations per second). Yet millions of people started speaking of megs (and recognizing the abbreviation mb for megabyte) in the early 1990s, as soon as personal computers moved from having kilobytes of memory (no one spoke of 640kb as 0.64 mb) to having megs of it.

The appendix at the back of this book is a glossary of computer and information terms with which industrial engineers should be familiar. Most of its entries are described more fully in the body of this chapter.

5.1 Information and Data Economy

A *datum*, or single item of *data*, is a number or a string of characters. A datum fits in a *field* of a *record*. On a disk or other storage medium outside the computer's central memory, a collection of records is a *file*, viewed as a rectangular data object having a row for each record and a column for each field. Inside the computer, the records can be viewed as rows of a *matrix* or *array* (a matrix is a two-dimensional array). Each field occupies one or more *words* of central memory. The smallest word in common use is the *byte*, which is eight binary digits or *bits*. (In communication between the computer and the outside, a byte commonly carries seven bits; the eighth bit is used for parity checking. For example, if a sending device sends out the seven bits 0110111, it also sends out the eighth bit 1 because the seven bits total 5, an odd number. The receiving device performs a parity check by testing whether the oddness or evenness of the sum of the first seven received bits matches that of the eighth received bit.) Other word lengths, such as 16-bit, 32-bit, and so forth, are in common use. In a file, fields have different lengths (number of words in the field), but the same field has the same length in each record. In an array, every field has the same field length.

5.1.1 Information

The word "information" comes from the Latin *informare*, which means to give form or structure. Modern definitions of information, in line with communication theory and the entropy function in thermodynamics, define information as *reduction of uncertainty*. The definition can be quantified; in simple situations we can actually measure the amount of information.

5.1.1.1 Information in File Searching

Let a file contain N records. For simplicity, let N be one less than an integer power of 2: 1, 3, 7, 15, 31, 63, 127, etc., where the powers are 1, 2, 3, 4, 5, 6, 7, etc. Thus if n is a positive integer, we have $N = 2^n-1$, and conversely $n = \log_2(N+1)$. (For other file sizes, the formulas developed here will be approximately correct.)

Now consider the task of retrieving a particular record from the file when that record is equally likely to be in any position. Let our measure of retrieval effort be *number of accesses* of the file. For example, let the file contain customer records. If we want to retrieve the record for "Jones1749" to see how much money customer Jones1749 owes us, we first assume the file is in random order and no index exists, so Jones1749 could be anywhere from record 1 to record N. We start at the top and access every record until we find the Jones1749 record. With probability $1/N$, Jones1749 is the first record and it takes one access; with probability $1/N$, Jones1749 is the second record and it takes two accesses, etc., so that the expected number of accesses is $(1/N)(1+2+...+N) = (N+1)/2$ accesses.

For example, if 1023 records are in random order, it takes an average of 512 accesses to find a particular one. This gives a quantified notion of information: the expected value of the uncertainty inherent in having the Jones1749 record lost among 1023 records, as measured by number of accesses as the unit of information, is 512. Conversely, we can say that the act of performing the accesses has created 512 units of information.

Now suppose the file is sorted by customer, or an index is prepared that points to the file by customer. This effort, which can be done in advance to support thousands or millions of customer retrievals, will create a great amount of uncertainty reduction or information. Now when a record is accessed, we ascertain whether or not it is the Jones1749 record; if it is not the Jones1749 record, we also ascertain whether the Jones1749 record comes earlier or later than the one accessed. This allows the efficient binary search procedure to be performed as follows: (1) Access the middle record among those under consideration; (2) If the record being sought is the accessed one, stop; (3) If the record being sought is above the accessed one, eliminate the accessed one and all below it from consideration; (4) If the record being sought is below the accessed one, eliminate the accessed one and all above it from consideration; (5) Go to step 1. This is the most efficient possible procedure if the record is equally likely to be anywhere in the file.

As an example of binary search, let us find Jones1749 in the following alphabetically sorted file of 15 records.

Ahmed1100	Access Ignat2007; keep those below
Ahmed1166	it under consideration; access
Andre4430	Jones2447; keep those above it
Bravo0089	under consideration; access Jerbi1092;
Elems4682	keep the one below it under consideration;
Hemno2223	Finally, access Jones1749.
Ivens1000	
Ignat2007	Four accesses are required to find
Janke8963	Jones1749 in the sorted file. (An
Jerbi1092	average of (15+1)/2 = 8 accesses would
Jones1749	have been required if the file had not
Jones2447	been sorted or indexed.)
Lumti9069	
Royer3542	If Jones1749 had been located elsewhere
Sales5516	the number of accesses could have been smaller:
	3, 2, or even 1.

The expected number of accesses in binary search of a sorted file having $N = 2^n - 1$ records is

$$A = \frac{(n-1)2^n + 1}{2^n - 1} = \left(\frac{N+1}{N}\right)\log_2(N+1) - 1 \qquad (5\text{-}1)$$

For large N this approaches $\log_2 N - 1$.

For the 15-record example, the formula gives an expected number of accesses $A = 49/15 \approx 3.2667$. To verify this, note that if the record being sought were in position 8, there would be 1 access; if in position 4 or 12, 2 accesses; if in position 2, 6, 10, or 14, 3 accesses; and if in one of the eight odd-numbered positions, 4 accesses. Since it is equally likely to be in any of the 15 positions, the expected number of accesses is given by $(1/15)[1 + 2\times2 + 3\times4 + 4\times8] = 49/15 \approx 3.2667$.

Note that the large-N approximation gives about 2.9069 accesses, which is inaccurate because 15 records is not very many.

As a more practical example, for a file with 1023 records, the formula gives about 9.0098 accesses and the large-N approximation gives about 8.9986 accesses. For a file with 32,767 records, the average number of accesses is about 14 (the exact formula gives about 14.00003).

5.1.1.2 Definitions of Information

Obviously it would be wasteful not to sort or index large files before using them. On the assumption that files would always be sorted or indexed, the large-N approximation could be used as a definition of information. We could propose $\log_2 N - 1$ as a measure of the amount of information gained when a definite value of a variable is determined out of N equally likely possible values. As we will see below, the unit of this measure is *bits*; the familiar binary digit, known as the bit, is the natural unit of information.

Such a definition can be useful conceptually in top-level design of information systems. For example, suppose two approaches are being investigated for handling data in a robot vision system. Let approach A involve manipulating data in 16 tables having 3940 rows each; let approach B accomplish the same job by manipulating data in five small tables and one large table having 70,000 rows. A typical set of operations under approach A would create roughly $16 \times (\log_2 3940 - 1) \approx 175.1$ bits of information, while a typical set of operations under approach B would create roughly $\log_2 70000 - 1 \approx 15.1$ bits of information. Thus, other considerations being equal for the two approaches, approach A will require about 11.6 times as much processing as B.

The standard definition of information gained by eliminating uncertainty among N equally likely possibilities is $\log_2 N$, that is, the large-N approximation without subtracting 1. This comes from a process slightly more simple than binary search of a file—a numerical version of the "twenty questions" game. A number x, unknown to the questioner but known to a source, can be any integer from 0 to 4095, and the questioner can identify it by asking a series of yes-or-no questions. The optimal strategy for asking the questions is to form each question so as to reduce the number of possibilities by one-half. This can always be done if the number of possibilities N is an integer power of 2 (not, as above, one less than that); let $N = 2^n$ where n is an integer. Here the number of equally likely possibilities is 4096, which is 2^{12}. (For other N, the number of remaining possibilities eventually becomes an odd number, so that the two "halves" differ in size by 1.) In the present example, the questioner can ask, "Is it not more than 2047?" or, "Is it not less than 2048?" or "Is it even?"—any question for which a yes or no answer will reduce the number of possibilities by one-half. It will always take exactly $\log_2 4096 = 12$ questions, no matter what the actual number is. (If the questioner uses a sub-optimal strategy, such as asking "Is it 341?" the *expected* number of questions will be more than $\log_2 N$ even though there is a possibility of luckily hitting it in fewer questions).

The standard definition of information is very closely related to binary numbers and to digital communication design. The binary representation of the decimal integer 4095 is 111111111111, so a string of 12 bits is adequate to transmit a number between 0 (transmitted as 000000000000) and 4095. Thus the amount of information transmitted is a direct measure of the load on a communication system.

When the possibilities are not all equally likely, there is less uncertainty. The general definition of information for N possibilities, numbered $i = 1, 2, ..., N$, having probabilities $\{p_i\}$ which sum to 1, is

$$H = -\sum_i p_i \log_2 p_i = \sum_{i=1}^{N} p_i \log_2 \frac{1}{p_i} \qquad (5\text{-}2)$$

This is the definition of the amount of information that would be gained by going to certainty; that is, H is the number of bits of existing uncertainty. The minimum possible value of H, corresponding to already having certainty, is zero: When there is certainty, so that $p_i = 1$ for $i = k$ and $p_i = 0$ for $i \neq k$, every term of H vanishes, so that $H = 0$; that is, if the alternative sought is known to be in the kth position, the amount of information to be gained is at its minimum of zero.

The amount of information to be gained by achieving certainty is maximized (maximal existing uncertainty) when the alternative sought is equally likely to be any one of the N possibilities, so that we have the uniform probability distribution $p_i = 1/N$, $i = 1, 2, ..., N$. We can compute H for this case:

$$H = -\sum_{i=1}^{N} \frac{1}{N} \log_2 \frac{1}{N} = \frac{1}{N} N \log_2 N = \log_2 N = \frac{\ln N}{\ln 2} \qquad (5\text{-}3)$$

Thus the amount of information to be gained by achieving certainty, starting from N equally likely possibilities, is $\log_2 N$, as before.

Let us return to the 15-record list from which we were seeking Jones1749. If this list is a selection (say of customers whose bills are past due) from a large customer file, the distribution of names in the file makes it unlikely, although not impossible, for Jones1749 to be far away from the typical zone for names starting with "J." Let the probability distribution for the location of Jones1749 in the 15 record list, determined by statistical methods, be as follows:

position	1	2	3	4	5	6	7	8
probability	0.01	0.02	0.04	0.12	0.18	0.28	0.16	0.07

	9	10	11	12	13	14	15
	0.04	0.03	0.01	0.01	0.01	0.01	0.01

For these probabilities we can compute $H \approx 3.053$. This can be compared with $\log_2 15 \approx 3.907$ to conclude that a method able to exploit the probability distribution in retrieving names from a list like this could save up to roughly 22% of the effort compared to a method that did not exploit the probability distribution. Of course, this ignores the effort in the statistical exploitation itself and assumes complete exploitation.

This illustrates the nature of the information concept and the intuitive meaning of H: given a sorted list of 15 names and the characteristics of a sought name among them, the name being sought is about four bits of information (or four questions or four retrievals) away from identification, or only about three bits away if a probability distribution of similar sharpness to the one in the example is used. Put another way, if the information inherent in the probability distribution is available and usable, only about three bits of information are needed to find the data for a sought customer. But if the distribution is not available and usable, about four bits need to be created.

The concept of information gives us a rough, overall measure of how much work a computer system needs to do to perform a given job. This measure is independent of *how* the computer system does the job; it indicates the work intrinsic to the job itself.

E39.   **Users of a set of four inventory systems have been getting 2.5-second response times from queries and transactions, of which the retrieval of data accounts for 0.6 seconds. It takes 0.5 seconds for the user to specify which system is involved, so the total elapsed time has been 3.0 seconds for a typical query or transaction. If the wrong system is specified, an error message is received and the user selects another system and tries again; but users almost never make this kind of mistake. It has been proposed to combine the four inventory systems into one. Users would not need to specify which system is involved. Would the proposed change be beneficial to users, or would it be detrimental?**

Assuming that the four systems are of roughly equal sizes, combining the four systems will make the file size go from N to $4N$, where N is the file size for one system. Assuming that queries and transactions take advantage of indexed files (it would be wasteful if they did not), the retrieval effort is proportional to $\log_2 N$. Since $\log_2 4N = \log_2 4 + \log_2 N = 2 + \log_2 N$, we see that the quadrupling of file size adds 2 accesses. The same result follows from reasoning that each access roughly halves the size of the searched file, so 2 accesses of the $4N$ file gives us a file of size N.

Compared to the 0.5 seconds saved by combining the files, are the extra 2 accesses significant? Since we are not given N, let us use a breakeven approach to seek N such that the 2 extra accesses would add as much as 0.5 seconds to the expected retrieval time. This would mean that they nearly doubled the present 0.6-second retrieval time. For that to happen, N would have to be small enough to require only 2 or 3 accesses in the first place, which is unreasonably small (for example, $N = 7$ gives $A = 2.42857$ expected accesses). Obviously the file size is much larger than 7 records, so we can conclude that the proposed change is beneficial to users. Users would save time, and they would no longer need to bother with knowing which inventory system applies to a given query or transaction.

5.1.1.3 Information Computation

Alternatives with zero probability do not contribute to H and should be excluded from computation since most computer and calculator routines will balk at ln0 even though 0ln0 is zero. In equation 5-2, include in the sum only those values of i for which $p_i \neq 0$. H can be calculated using natural logarithms $\ln p_i$ and converted to bits by dividing the result by $\ln 2 = 0.693147181$.

In calculating information for a sample distribution, the data actually available are counts or *frequencies* rather than probabilities. If we have a set of frequencies $\{f_i\}$, they provide estimates $\{f_i/T\}$ of the probabilities $\{p_i\}$, where T is the sum of the frequencies: $T = \sum_i f_i$. To compute H in the most natural way on a hand calculator, first compute the sum of the frequencies multiplied by their natural logarithms: let $V = \sum_i f_i \ln f_i$. Then subtract V from $T\ln T$ and divide the result by $T\ln 2$. That is, use the following *frequency version of the general information equation*:

$$H = \frac{1}{T \ln 2}\left\{ T \ln T - \sum_{i \neq 0} f_i \ln f_i \right\} \qquad T = \sum_i f_i \qquad (5\text{-}4)$$

Equation 5-4 follows from equation 5-2 by substituting f_i/T for p_i and simplifying. Note that since H is a function of the proportions $\{f_i/T\}$, information is not scaled to experiment size. That is, if 10 experiments or 1000 experiments gave the same sample proportions, they would give the same estimate of information.

As an example of equation 5-4 in a human performance experiment, a group of people could choose among five buttons to press according to instructions, and they actually pushed the buttons the following numbers of times respectively: (5, 0, 5, 6, 4). The information in this response set is $H = [1/(20\ln 2)][(20\ln 20) - (5\ln 5 + 5\ln 5 + 6\ln 6 + 4\ln 4)] = 1.9854753$ bits.

In estimating the difficulty of mental tasks such as recognition and recall, as for performing work measurement or setting time standards (reviewed in section 7.4), H can be used as a measure of mental or perceptual difficulty. Also, H can be used in testing alternative designs of controls (reviewed in section 7.3.2) or documentation. Suppose, for example, a comparison is to be made between two labeling schemes for a control panel. A user is presented with a *stimulus set*, which is a set of items. Each item has a probability of being correct, so substituting these probabilities into equation 5-2 yields the number of bits of *information in the stimulus set*. If the items are equally likely, and there are N of them, the information in the stimulus set is $\log_2 N$ bits; if they are not equally likely the information in the stimulus set is less than $\log_2 N$ bits. For each stimulus, the user chooses a response. Each item has a probability of being chosen (in an experiment, the observed proportion of times a response is chosen is interpreted as this probability). Substituting these probabilities (or proportions) into equation 5-2 yields the number of bits of information in the response set. Since the same N possibilities exist as for the stimulus set, the maximum information in the response set is $\log_2 N$ bits. The N^2 possible stimulus-response pairs form the *stimulus-response set*, having maximum information $\log_2 N^2 = 2\log_2 N$. Substituting the probabilities (or proportions) for each response for each stimulus into equation 5-2 gives the number of bits of information in the stimulus-response set.

To illustrate these concepts, suppose a baseball coach tried 10 times to signal batters to bunt or swing; of the five times he signalled to bunt, the batters bunted four times and swung one time; of the five times he signalled to swing, the batters bunted two times and swung three times. Let the data be arrayed in a *stimulus-response matrix* like that in figure 5-1.

Response	Stimulus		Row totals	Response proportions
	Bunt	Swing		
Bunt	4	2	6	0.6
Swing	1	3	4	0.4
Column totals	5	5		
Stimulus proportions	0.5	0.5		

Figure 5-1. Stimulus-response Matrix.

The stimulus set has one bit of information (the answer to one yes-no question would tell the batter exactly what the coach wanted). The response set has 0.97095 bits of information. The stimulus-response set has 1.84644 bits of information.

Some simple sums and differences of information indicate how well the system performs. Let $H(S)$, $H(R)$, and $H(SR)$ represent the information in the stimulus set, response set, and stimulus-response set, respectively. Then we define the *throughput*, T, as the amount by which the uncertainty is reduced by the responses, where the initial uncertainty is the sum of information in the stimulus and response sets and the final uncertainty is the information in the stimulus-response set.

$$T = H(S) + H(R) - H(SR) \qquad\qquad \textit{throughput} \quad (5\text{-}5)$$

The greater the throughput, the better the system performs. If batters had always done what the coach tried to signal, the throughput would have been all of $H(S)$; that is, if the elements in the stimulus-response matrix had been 5, 0, 0, 5, then T would have been $1 + 1 - 1 = 1$. But with the actual mistakes that were made, the throughput is only 0.12451 bits. Throughput is zero if responses are random, and it is the full $H(S)$ if responses are perfect.

The *noise, Z,* is the measure of how badly the system failed to reduce uncertainty or how badly the stimuli failed to predict the responses. It is the amount of information in the response set that is not throughput, or the amount of information in the stimulus-response set that was not in the stimulus set. In the bunt-swing example the noise is 0.84644 bits.

$$Z = H(R) - T \;=\; H(SR) - H(S) \qquad\qquad noise \quad (5\text{-}6)$$

Finally, the *equivocation, E,* is the measure of how badly the responses failed to postdict the stimuli. It is the amount of information in the stimulus set that is not throughput. In the bunt-swing example the equivocation is 0.87549 bits.

$$E = H(S) - T \;=\; H(SR) - H(R) \qquad\qquad equivocation \quad (5\text{-}7)$$

E40.   **Air traffic controllers were tested in situations where they had five different actions to choose from: actions A, B, C, D, E. The actions they should have taken were recorded as stimuli, and the actions they actually took were recorded as responses. New display scopes were installed in an effort to improve their performance. They were rated on 63 instances of the actions before the new scopes were installed; after the new scopes were installed, they were rated on 125 instances of the actions. The data, shown as stimulus-response matrices, follows:**

Performance using old *scopes:*   *Performance using* new *scopes:*

9	3	0	0	2
0	8	1	1	0
0	0	7	4	2
1	2	1	10	0
0	0	2	2	8

21	2	0	0	1
0	16	2	2	1
0	0	14	2	2
1	1	2	21	0
3	6	7	0	21

To what extent do these tests indicate that the new scopes help the air traffic controllers do a better job?

Old scopes: The column sums are 10, 13, 11, 17, 12, giving $H(S) = 2.29656$ bits in the stimulus set. The row sums are 14, 10, 13, 14, 12, giving $H(R) = 2.31140$ bits in the response set. The stimulus-response set (the whole matrix) has 3.56212 bits. From these, the throughput is 1.04584 bits, the noise is 1.26556 bits, and the equivocation is 1.25072 bits.

New scopes: The column sums are 25, 25, 25, 25, 25, giving $H(S) = 2.32193$ bits in the stimulus set. The row sums are 24, 21, 18, 25, 37, giving $H(R) = 2.27632$ bits in the response set. The stimulus-response set (the whole matrix) has 3.39830 bits. From these, the throughput is 1.19995 bits, the noise is 1.07638 bits, and the equivocation is 1.12198 bits. Since the throughput is greater with the new scopes, they do improve the performance of the controllers.

5.1.2 Data Sources

Probably the most common mistake made in information systems design is underestimating the costs and impacts of gathering, verifying, storing, and maintaining data. Industrial engineers are expected to be particularly good at avoiding data economy pitfalls.

Data sources in decreasing order of desirability:

- Existing data
- Standard sources already established and maintained for other purposes with greater quality than is required for this purpose
- Knowledge bases
- Reusable data
- The user

Given the need for a datum, before seeking a source for it, ask whether it is a consequence of other data. Computational power has become quite inexpensive, and it is often better to recalculate than to save. For instance, in an interactive scheduling application, the schedule might previously have been defined and archived as the start times and durations of all activities, but in more advanced systems it is continually recalculated from more basic data (durations, precedences, and fixed start times). The reason to avoid saving consequences is not to save storage and memory (which have also become quite inexpensive), but to allow consequential data to change automatically when more basic data is changed. For example, normal times and allowances should be archived in a work-standards database, but standard times should not (see section 7.4). If there is a continual work measurement procedure, the data from which normal times are calculated should be archived unless recalculating them when needed would be impractical or invalid.

Sources of reusable data are:

- Data in active memory carried over from one part of a session to the next
- Archival ("restart") files that allow active memory to be restored to a former state
- Persistent-data files from an application designed to allow parts of its data to form the skeleton of data files for future similar applications
- Defaults

As an example of sources of reusable data, consider the U.S. Army program FUELEST, which aids the estimation of how much fuel is needed for an operation, which (in a data sense) is a collection of actions. For each action, fuel consumers, conditions, and requirements exist. For example, in the action type convoy, the consumers are wheeled vehicles; the conditions are such factors as road surface, weather, and time of day (for poor roads in rain at night the fuel consumptions would be multiplied by correction factors) and the requirements are distance, load, and elevation change. FUELEST computes estimates of fuel requirements for convoys by multiplying fuel consumption per kilometer of travel by the distance and summing for all designated vehicles. Two estimates using the same vehicle list can be done easily because the vehicle list stays in active memory during a session. For a convoy similar to a previous one, the user can retrieve its restart file and edit it. If several convoys are to share certain data but not other data, the user can perform persistence designation on a restart file to designate which data (persistent data) will retain the same values and which data (nonpersistent data) will revert to null. In future applications that use the restart file, the nonpersistent data will be given specific values.

FUELEST also uses defaults. For example, the default consumer list for an action involving a set of military units is their combined tables of active equipment. These tables are imported from an existing database that maintains them daily. FUELEST replaces a manual system in which a logistics officer manually put together a list of all equipment and multiplied their travel distances or number of hours of operation by fuel consumption factors printed in manuals. FUELEST requires the user to enter data only when it is unique to the particular operation.

The user is the data source of last resort. Always import data from standard sources if possible. A knowledge base is nonvolatile data (data that rarely changes), such as map and terrain data, roadway data, or standard tables such as vehicle fuel consumption tables. A knowledge base can be kept economically as a local copy to avoid the continuing costs of importing data. Although the user is the data source of last result, manual overrides should be permitted for all data.

5.1.3 Data Volatility

Volatile data is data that changes rapidly. The design of an information system must segregate data by volatility (as well as by authority to change it) and must make it easier to change more volatile data and harder to change less volatile data. For example, in an interactive scheduling system several plans (schedules) can be proposed for a given project. A plan is developed by playing a sort of computer game on a displayed Gantt chart of the project by moving, stretching, and squeezing activity bars until due dates are met and resources are not overused. It must be very easy to manipulate the current schedule; it must be harder to declare and name a plan; and it must be harder still to change requirements such as resource availabilities, precedences, or due dates. If the user can change volatile and nonvolatile data at the same level of action, fundamental things might inadvertently be changed.

As another example, consider a point-of-sale system. The sale transactions (how much of which item is purchased) are volatile, but the prices are nonvolatile, so the cashier should not be easily able to change prices while handling purchase transactions.

5.1.4 Data Structures

Data are kept in memory (locations within the computer, rapidly accessible to the CPU, volatile) or storage (located outside the computer, less rapidly accessible to the CPU, nonvolatile) in the form of words. Words have lengths, the shortest and longest lengths in common use being one byte (8 bits) and 64 bits.

Rectangular data structures, also known as flat data structures, are of the greatest interest to industrial engineers. With the rise of relational databases, nonflat data structures such as trees, variable length records, or nested arrays have declined in importance to the practicing engineer. This review excludes nonflat structures and also excludes such formerly more important topics as linked lists and B-trees.

All rectangular data structures—files, arrays, tables—have the same overall structure. (An exception is that arrays and spreadsheets can alternatively be defined and used in a form that is the transpose of the overall structure described here, that is, with the row and column roles interchanged.) A row of an array (or record of a file or tuple of a relation) contains data for an instance of an entity, object, or relationship that the file, array, or table represents. To represent an entity, object, or relationship is to keep data that consists of values of its attributes. A column of an array (or field of a file or attribute of a relation) contains data for a single attribute for all instances that the file, array, or table represents. A spreadsheet is an array around which utilities are provided to make it easy to enter, delete, edit, or label blocks of data and save, delete, or replace the entire array.

Software utilities designed to handle rectangular data structures include file manipulation commands in operating systems such as DOS or Unix, matrix manipulation features in various computer languages, and database management systems (DBMS). With the exception of spreadsheet utilities, these utilities all assume the following things about a rectangular data structure:

- The most volatile element is a datum or value kept in a single cell or word. The user or application will often change individual values, so this must be done very efficiently and conveniently.

- A row is less volatile than a datum. The user or application will sometimes add or delete entire instances, so insertion or deletion of rows must be done somewhat efficiently and conveniently.

- Columns are nonvolatile. The user or application will seldom or never add or delete attributes, so protection must be provided to prevent this from being done when unintended.

The following distinctions can be made among files, arrays, and relations:

- In a file, the number and order of columns (fields) are defined in advance as part of the *structure* of the file. The structure is kept as *meta-data*—data kept *about* the file but not kept *in* the file. Row order is relevant to manipulations and must be tracked by the user or applications. The number of rows is not part of the structure, but is implicitly defined and kept as meta-data. The values in the fields are data. The operating system makes it easy to save, replace, and delete whole files, but not to work within them.

- In an array, the number and order of both rows and columns are defined in advance as part of the structure and kept as meta-data. The user or application must track them. The values in the elements of the array are data. Ways to define and perform mathematical manipulations on arrays are provided, but (except in the case of spreadsheets) users and applications are left to deal explicitly with row and column counters rather than implicitly with names. To save an array, a file must be defined (spreadsheets and the APL language are exceptions).

- In a relation, the order of columns (attributes) is defined as structure and kept as meta-data but is irrelevant to most manipulations and easily queried or controlled. Column headings are also kept as meta-data and easily changed. Both order and number of rows are irrelevant to most manipulations but are easily queried or controlled if desired. The user and applications deal implicitly with names and can avoid dealing explicitly with structure, even in saving, replacing, and deleting data.

Some practice may be required to design appropriate rectangular structures. It is almost always best when designing a spreadsheet, array, or file to design it according to relational database design principles (reviewed in detail in section 5.4.). Three vignettes and two practice examples of good rectangular design follow. We start with representation of data for an organization chart (example E84 in section 8.1 also treats data representation of an organization chart):

Pfyffe Pfixers generates a report showing its management organization:

Name	Position	Supervisor of
Martin	Pres	Joel, Mary
Joel	VP1	Ellen, Pat
Mary	VP2	John A, John B
Ellen	MgrA	
Pat	MgrB	
John A	MgrC	
John B	MgrD	

For human readers, about the only way to improve this report would be to sort it alphabetically by name or display it as an actual chart. However, it has fundamental faults as a format for archiving the data.

One fundamental fault is that it shows the less basic relationships of which *names* supervise which *names*, rather than the more basic relationships of which *positions* supervise which *positions*. Martin, Joel, and Mary may come and go, but Pres will still supervise VP1 and VP2. To fix that fault, the third column could be altered to contain VP1 and VP2 instead of Joel and Mary.

Another fundamental fault is that whether or not the first fault is fixed, we do not know how many words are needed for the third column. Some people or positions may supervise many people or positions, others none. (Section 5.4 will show that this violates "first normal form.") What can be done? A position supervises a variable number of positions. Yes, but conversely, a position is *supervised by* exactly one position. Thus we can restructure the data as follows:

Name	*Position*	*Supervised by*
Martin	Pres	
Joel	VP1	Pres
Mary	VP2	Pres
Ellen	MgrA	VP1
Pat	MgrB	VP1
John A	MgrC	VP2
John B	MgrD	VP2

Note that this structure wastes not one word of data. Including the null entry for the position that supervises Pres, this table contains 7 rows and 3 columns, or $7 \times 3 = 21$ words (headings are ignored in citing sizes of tables). By contrast, the original table must contain $7 \times 4 = 28$ words if the maximum number of positions supervised by any one position is 2; more typically, if the "span of control" is 6 or more, requiring $7 \times 8 = 56$ words or more. Note that the null values cannot be omitted if the structure is to be rectangular; in the original table, at least 2 and probably 6 columns would have to be provided for *Supervisor of*.

The above vignette illustrates (or at least asserts) four general principles:

1. Always save data on causes, not effects; save basic data rather than consequential data.

2. The structure of saved data should be totally independent of the structure of reports. Data should be saved and manipulated in the most correct way, regardless of reporting requirements, because it is trivial to produce reports structured and formatted in any way desired.

3. The correct design usually is more efficient than other designs in its use of space (unless the other designs store consequential rather than basic data).

4. Null values count. There is no way to avoid setting aside the full amount of space for a rectangular data structure. That is, the fact that some spaces will be filled with null values cannot be exploited to save space.

The next vignette considers the structure of input data for a linear programming solver (see section 6.3).

In what form should data equivalent to the simplex tableau be saved? A possibility is the matrix form, but nearly all linear programs have a sparse (mostly filled with zeros) matrix. For a 2000-constraint, 1000-variable problem, 2000×1000 = 2 million words would be required, and perhaps only 8000 of them would contain a nonzero number. The LINDO form, e.g., 2X1 + 3X2 ≤ 4, is another possibility but this would require parsing and is not a rectangular form. (LINDO is the most widely used solver that uses the form. Actually the form was incorporated into EZLP, an academic solver published by John J. Jarvis circa 1974, and was known in academic circles prior to that.) The best choice is the MPS form, which is the form actually used commercially. (MPS is the designation introduced by IBM in 1975. Control Data had used the same form since the 1950s.) It keeps the data as a list of triplets: column label, row label, value. This form is rectangular (each triplet a row of a table that has three columns) and wastes no space. Obviously the other forms can be reconstructed from it. The MPS form cannot be improved upon and is actually the correct relational manner of archiving the data.

The final vignette considers the representation of a family "tree."

A genealogist collects data on members of a family, including who is whose father, brother, first cousin, aunt—the "blood" relationships. How should the blood-relationship data be kept? One way might be to archive pairwise relationships. Obviously an N×N matrix, or even its upper-triangular half (e.g., putting 'aunt' in the cell for row i and column j if person i was person j's aunt), would be wasteful. Besides, where would we stop? Would we manually derive from explicitly collected data other data, such as the fact that if someone has aunts, that person's siblings also have the same aunts, and put all the results in the matrix? Doing so would violate the principle of archiving only basic data. What is the basic blood-relationship data? It is the parent-child relationship. Should we list the children of each person? No, that scheme has difficulties pointed out earlier. We might try a list of (parent, child) name pairs. That is much better. Let us display this scheme for the example that Walter and his wife, Bertha, have two children, Donald and Bonnie; Donald and his wife, Bobbie, have three children, Connie, Skip, and Dave; Bonnie and her husband, Alfie, have two children, Gwen and Donna. The pairs would be as on the left below. An alternative scheme would be to list child-father-mother triplets, as on the right below.

Parent	Child		Child	Father	Mother
Walter	Donald		Donald	Walter	Bertha
Bertha	Donald		Bonnie	Walter	Bertha
Donald	Connie		Connie	Donald	Bobbie
Bobbie	Connie		Skip	Donald	Bobbie
Donald	Skip		Dave	Donald	Bobbie
Bobbie	Skip		Gwen	Alfie	Bonnie
Donald	Dave		Donna	Alfie	Bonnie
Bobbie	Dave				
Bonnie	Gwen				
Alfie	Gwen				
Bonnie	Donna				
Alfie	Donna				
Walter	Bonnie				
Bertha	Bonnie				

The child-father-mother scheme is best because (1) the parent-child scheme fails to archive which parent is the father or mother, so everyone's gender would need to be archived; (2) the child-father-mother table has fewer words—here 21 words compared to 28—and efficiency is often a sign of elegance; and (3) simple statements can be made about the child-father-mother table, such as "There is a row for each person" and "Every person has a father and a mother," whereas statements of similar simplicity cannot be made for the parent-child table.

E41a.   **The numbers in each node in figure 5-2 are node identifiers; the numbers below each node are throughput limits; the letters below each arc are arc identifiers; and the numbers above each arc are travel distances. Archive all the data, including the structure of the network, in a set of tables.**

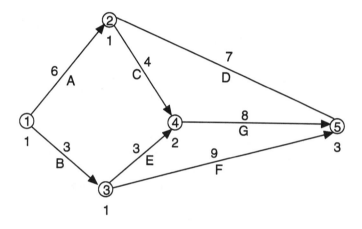

Figure 5-2. Network for Example E41a.

Each arc has an identifier, a travel distance, a "from" node, and a "to" node. Each node has an identifier, a throughput limit, a (possibly empty) set of "entering" nodes, and a set of "leaving" nodes. The structure of the network is completely represented if *either* the "from" and "to" nodes are archived for each arc *or* if all the "entering" arcs and all the "leaving" arcs are archived for each node. Obviously the former option is better because it gives a rectangular table whereas the latter option does not. (How many "entering" arcs would we need to allow for each node?) We will have two tables, one with a row for each node and one with a row for each arc, and put the structure information in the arc table.

Node ID	Throughput limit		Arc ID	"From" node	"To" node	Travel distance
1	1		A	1	2	6
2	1		B	1	3	3
3	1		C	2	4	4
4	2		D	2	5	7
5	3		E	3	4	3
			F	3	5	9
			G	4	5	8

This is the best way to archive the data. An *incidence matrix*, where the structure would be archived in a 5×5 table with one row for each node and one column for each node, with the arc identifier in cell (*i,j*) if the arc goes from node *i* to node *j*, would be inefficient and inelegant compared to this database. And, of course, an incidence matrix could readily be constructed from this database if needed for computation or display.

E41b.   You are preparing to take stopwatch data on congestion at a tool counter. When the server at the counter is busy, workers wait their turn and are served in the order in which they arrived. Your boss has asked for a report on the average total time workers (not to be identified by name) spend in the system (not broken down into time in the queue and time being served), or other data from which average time in the system can be calculated. The notes she gives you from having done an informal dry run indicate the following: the tool counter was idle when she began; she wrote down #1 and 10:44:40 (the time) when a worker arrived; she wrote down #2 and 10:44:58 when another worker arrived; she wrote down 10:45:07 to the right of #1's other data when #1 left; she wrote down #3 and 10:45:21 when another worker arrived; she wrote down 10:50:00 to the right of #2's other data when #2 left; and she wrote down 10:50:07 to the right of #3's other data when #3 left. You are to take data for several hours, starting and stopping, as she did, with the system empty. Determine the best scheme for taking the data, and illustrate your scheme using the data from your boss's dry run.

Note that from Little's Law (section 4.4) the average time is the average population divided by the average throughput rate. Thus you can keep statistics on population rather than time.

A very poor scheme would be to record the elapsed time in the system for each worker. Although this would take only six words to represent the boss's data, observing it directly would require not only keeping track of each worker but having as many stopwatches as the greatest total number of workers in the system. We will analyze three schemes: the boss's scheme, a population-tracking scheme, and an event-tracking scheme.

	Boss's scheme:			Population tracking scheme:		Event tracking scheme:	
Worker	Arrival time	Departure time		Population	From time	Event	Time
#1	10:44:40	10:45:07		1	10:44:40	A	10:44:40
#2	10:44:58	10:50:00		2	10:44:58	A	10:44:58
#3	10:24:21	10:50:07		1	10:45:07	D	10:45:07
				2	10:45:21	A	10:45:21
				1	10:50:00	D	10:50:00
				0	10:50:07	D	10:50:07

The boss's scheme is not best, because it requires the observer to keep track of workers. Doing so is a wasted effort because workers could be reconstructed from data obtained from the other schemes. The other schemes are about equally easy for the observer. The population-tracking scheme (in which the number of workers in the system is recorded) is slightly preferred because the event-tracking scheme (in which each event is identified as an arrival or departure) requires separate recording of the starting system population and leaves room for error if a single incorrect datum is recorded (for instance, if one departure was recorded as an arrival, the data would be as if two extra workers were in the system for the rest of the run).

5.2 Design and Operation of Computer Systems

The IE PE Exam does not test whether a candidate is familiar with the latest hardware and software, and in any case, this review could not cover such ephemeral material. However, industrial engineers are often expected to specify basic computer-system requirements and therefore must be conversant with the major capabilities and limitations of commonly used hardware, software, and communications methods. In communications, for instance, you could be expected to know such things as what a LAN is and perhaps even what CSMA/CD and token passing are, what "baud rate" means and what are some of the common baud rates, and whether or not it is reasonable for users to routinely operate interactively with host computers hundreds of miles away. (The answer to this last question is no, not until long-distance connect time becomes cheaper. The glossary in the appendix will help with the other questions.)

Representation of information in a database, the subject of the preceding vignettes and examples, is perhaps the most important computer-related skill area for industrial engineers. Section 5.4 offers more review and practice of data design for representation.

5.2.1 Hardware

Industrial engineers are expected to be familiar enough with computer hardware to recognize the various hardware components of a system, know which major functions they perform, and know the major size and speed measures by which their overall capabilities are cited.

The information appliance generally appropriate for personal office use by an engineer is a personal computer, available as of this writing in desktop or laptop models. The major components of a desktop model are the main unit, which houses the CPU, power supply, memory, hard disk drive, and diskette drive; a separate monitor; and a separate keyboard unit. All three are combined in one piece in a laptop model. A printer is a separate component, or printing can be done centrally through a local-area network (LAN).

The computer can be connected to a LAN and through a LAN to a larger network, so that the personal computer can act as a terminal. The LAN usually provides file-serving capabilities and central printing facilities. The computer can also have a built-in modem allowing it to communicate over telephone lines.

Three major operating systems within the mainstream of software support are available for engineers to use: DOS, Macintosh, and Unix. DOS-based personal computers, formerly known as IBM-compatible, are available with Windows, an interactive interface utility that allows software to have menu-driven interfaces similar to those available on Apple Macintosh computers. Unix is the operating system used when the personal computer acts as a terminal connected to a host computer.

Actual standards for the components (subject to rapid improvement with time) are a 486-DX (not 486-SX) CPU for DOS machines or the equivalent for Macintosh machines; 4 to 12 mb of memory; at least a 100-mb hard disk drive; a 3.5-inch (1.44-mb) diskette drive; a VGA or super-VGA color monitor; a 105-key keyboard; and a laser printer. One workable arrangement, either for DOS or Macintosh users, is a laptop with a separate VGA monitor and keyboard unit. The laptop can be used anywhere, while at the office, the more readable monitor and easier-to-use keyboard can be plugged in to form the equivalent of a desktop system.

For extensive computer-aided design or heavy computation, the next step up is a workstation-level computer system. The "minicomputer" is no longer relevant.

For process control on the factory floor, the programmable controller is used. Programmable controllers have a real-time operating system. They receive feedback signals from a process (say temperature in a vat). Their program compares the feedback signals to a setpoint (say the desired temperature) and determines and outputs a corrective signal (say a command to open a steam value further) according to the control functions (say proportional and reset control; see section 7.3.2).

Hand-held computer devices are in use especially for inventory work. Wand readers for bar codes have become economical and reliable. A typical unit can read and retain hundreds of bar codes before downloading them. These devices are typically used for counting inventory or processing received shipments.

5.2.2 Software

Industrial engineers are expected to be generally familiar with operating systems and word processing, spreadsheet, and programming languages, but the IE PE Exam does not explicitly test such familiarity. An example of implicit software familiarity testing is that a logical sequence in the situation statement of a problem might be written in pidgin Pascal, which—other than the logic flow diagram (see section 5.5.3)—is the de facto standard way to communicate logic.

5.3 Information System Application Design

Industrial engineers often specify requirements for information systems. Sections 5.3.1, 5.3.2, 5.3.3, and 5.3.4 briefly review the required knowledge for information system development and documentation.

5.3.1 Functional Surveying

An important early step in developing requirements for an information system is to develop a functional survey report—a complete, well-organized list of every function the system will perform. A functional survey assembles a list of functions described at a level that is as specific as possible without inappropriately restricting how the function is to be performed. Without a functional survey, designers tend to omit critical functions, usually those that have to do with unusual conditions, error correction, or unusual but legitimate uses of the system. For example, a designer of an electronic chess set forgot to include castling. The designer of another electronic chess set failed to provide for setting up the board for such things as end-game practice. The set, which failed in the marketplace, could reach an arbitrary setup only by starting with a full board and making legal plays until the position was reached—a very tedious task. Since setting up an end game is something that people can do and sometimes choose to do with an ordinary chess set, a proper functional survey would have avoided this deficiency.

Functional surveying can be contrasted with facility or resource surveying (section 5.3.2). In functional surveying, everything the system will do is listed. In facility or resource surveying, which is appropriate when the system is to replace an existing system, all the facilities or resources in the existing system are listed; the idea is that the new system must have a functional equivalent for each of them. Even when there is an existing system, functional surveying is usually more powerful and effective.

Before a functional survey begins, the engineer must prepare a high-level description of the system. The high-level description must be detailed enough so that, if a function is suggested, the description can be consulted to determine whether or not the function is one that the new system must perform. For example, an electronic chess set—besides choosing good moves, functioning as an opponent, and perhaps functioning as a consultant (suggesting moves to the human player)—is a substitute for a standard chess set. If this last phrase ("substitute for a standard chess set") is not further clarified as part of the high-level description, then *of course* the set must allow setting up an end game.

E42a.   **The Scrabble® crossword game is played on a 15×15-cell board with 100 letter tiles that each fit on a cell. Some of the cells on the board are marked with labels indicating premiums for tiles (double letter, triple letter) played on the cell or for words played across a particular cell (double word, triple word). Each player has a rack that holds seven tiles. Each tile is marked with a letter and value, a number from 1 to 10. You are assumed to already be familiar with the Scrabble crossword game, its apparatus, its rules, and its scoring. Assume you are a consultant. Your client has conceived an electronic Scrabble crossword game set that will not play the game but will keep score and provide the dictionary and timer. With this high-level description, perform a functional survey.**

Implicit in the high-level description is that the electronic set will perform *every* function presently provided by the non-electronic game and by resources and facilities customarily present if they will not be included with the new set. For example, a table and chairs are customarily present with the non-electronic game, so if the new set is to be played, say by airline passengers, the function "being supported so that players can see and manipulate components" must be listed.

Let us discuss some of the issues that illustrate how to perform a functional survey. For example, some Scrabble game sets have a lazy Susan turntable and some do not. When playing with a game that does not have a lazy Susan, players often manually turn the board so they can read the words in the usual left-to-right manner; thus a function "reorient board" exists. But what is *board*? Board means the equivalent of the actual board. The function "display board" means that the players must be presented with a visual display (painted? LED?) equivalent to the board. In the same vein, other game objects—tiles, racks, dictionary, timer—must have their functions defined. For example, "tiles must be displayed on the board and in the rack."

With the non-electronic set, tiles are drawn ("draw tiles") from a sack, from being face down on the table, or from inside the lid of the box that stores the set. Is there an object "sack"? Yes, that name is fine for the reservoir of yet unused tiles. We will use such names as board, tile, cell, sack, and so forth, to mean objects that will perform the equivalent functions as these entities do. We are now ready to perform the functional survey—to list all the things that the players and the set will do:

Functional Survey for Electronic Scrabble Crossword Game Set

Prerequisite functions:

* Provide board, four racks, sack, and aside area (the aside area is for drawing tiles before replacing turned-in tiles in a pass)
* View board and tiles on board
* Reorient board for four view directions
* View tiles in player's own rack
* Hide one's rack from other players but let them see "backs" of tiles
* Heft sack (estimate number of remaining tiles)
* Populate sack initially with 100 tiles in standard letter distribution
* Maintain sack population as tiles are moved to and from it
* Generate drawn tile randomly from population
* View "backs" of tiles in aside area
* Perform dictionary lookup
* Disallow or allow secrecy of dictionary use and/or its results
* Allow or prevent the addition and deletion of words to and from the dictionary
* Consult rules and frequency distribution
* Save/load board, rack, sack states
* Provide timer that displays remaining time and can be set, reset, and disabled

Manipulation functions:

* Draw tiles (from sack to rack)
* Move tiles within rack (9 positions, 7 tiles)
* Play tiles (from rack to board)
* Remove tiles (from board to rack, as when successfully challenged or when better play is seen before end of turn)
* Return tiles to sack or to aside area (as when turning in tiles or correcting errors)

Play functions:

* Allow player declaration (which racks are active)
* Decide which player plays first
* Keep track of whose turn it is
* Establish start of a player's turn
* Establish end of a player's turn
* Manage scoring:
    * Compute score of a turn
    * Announce score of a turn
    * Record score of a turn or increment player's total score
    * View all players' total scores or play score history

- Allow for correction or alteration of scores
- Manage challenges:
  - Establish challenge and identify player and challenger
  - Look up challenged word (announce existence or nonexistence)
  - Establish result of challenge
  - Revise total scores or play score history for successful challenge
  - Delete/do not delete challenger's next turn for unsuccessful challenge
- Manage passing:
  - Establish player's passing of a turn
  - Allow 0 to 7 tiles to be returned to sack or to aside area by passing player (this allows drawing before replacement)
  - Allow passing player to draw tiles to replace returned ones
  - Allow replacement drawing to exclude returned tiles
- Manage end of game:
  - Establish end of game
  - Revise total scores for rack contents at end of game
  - Announce final scores at end of game
- Manage timing of plays:
  - Allow timing to be activated or disabled
  - Allow player-specific time limits
  - Announce a turn's time-limit arrival and/or approach

If your list is less complete than the foregoing, try to review how you could organize your work better to prevent omissions. Scrabble crossword game players do heft the sack; they do look at the scoresheet to see the score histories; they do make corrections or arbitrary changes to the score, as for allowing a handicap; they do sometimes allow players to look up a word other than to determine the outcome of a challenge; they do play in an environment where it is easy to see if someone tries to sneak a peek at the dictionary; they do sometimes allow plays to be rescinded and replaced with better ones. They would not view a system kindly if it failed to provide for these things. It is much better to face all the issues at functional-survey time than later. A qualified industrial engineer can systematically determine *all* of the requirements of a system before undue investment is made in a deficient system.

It should be noted that a functional survey lists what the system and user will do, not what the system will do. For instance, players of a game can easily keep track of whose turn it is, and it would be poor design to have a game program take over this function unless the designer were sure of being able to let players handle *all* exceptions conveniently. Yet a functional survey should list even the functions that already are handled outside the system and will continue to be handled outside the system; otherwise, there is the risk that the system will fail to allow those functions to be performed. Consequently, designers must be aware that the functional survey is not a list of system requirements.

5.3.2 Facility and Resource Surveying

Facility surveys or resource surveys are sometimes substituted for functional surveys. The following example shows that the functional survey is more powerful.

E42b.   **As in the preceding example, assume that your client has conceived an *electronic Scrabble crossword game set* that will not *play* the game but will keep score and will provide the dictionary and timer. With this high-level description, perform a resource survey. That is, list all resources now in use whose functional equivalents must be provided in the electronic set or its environment.**

Resource Survey for Electronic Scrabble Crossword Game Set

Environment:
- Table, chairs, lighting
- Set of written rules and tile frequency distribution
- Scoresheet and writing implement
- Dictionary
- Timer

Set:
- Board
- Tiles
- Racks
- Sack

Obviously, compared to the functional survey, this achieves far less progress toward the design.

5.3.3 Logic Flow Diagramming

Procedures in an application exist at several levels. At the program design level each element of a procedure is typically performed by one or a few lines of source code in a procedural language. Logic flow diagramming, or flowcharting, was once the primary tool for documenting logic at the program-design level, but pseudocode—pidgin C—is the usual tool today. Engineers typically use flowcharting at the next higher routine level, where each element of the procedure is typically performed by a subroutine or a user act.

There are many standard flowchart node symbols inherited from the days when programs were full of "goto" statements and a logic flow diagram was the most readable way to document the behavior of a program. The military specification MIL-STD-806 standardized many of these symbols, and some of the more important ones are shown in figure 5-3.

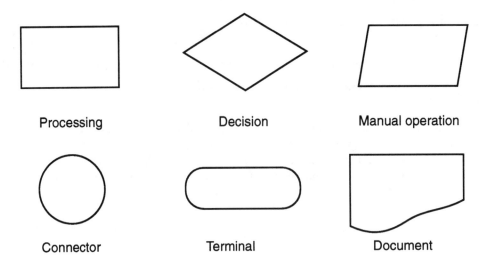

Figure 5-3. Standardized Symbols.

Most flowchart logic is built from three basic components: the sequence, the selection, and the repetition. These components are shown in figure 5-4.

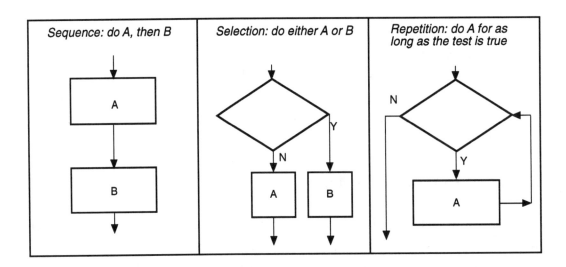

Figure 5-4. Basic Components of Flowchart Logic.

The thing that flows in a logic flow diagram is called logic or control. Control passes from one location in the flowchart to another. In a procedure, one task is done at a time, so the flowchart shows the sequence in which tasks are done. The flowchart is constructed so that logic flows generally downward. Along with the passing of control goes the passing of data. Many of the nodes receive data, create new data, and pass the new data to the next node. If there is a name for a data stream, it can be placed next to the arc that shows it going from one node to the next. Each node has a name or description, which is placed inside or beside it.

E43.   **A computer lab has computers and other equipment available for use by appointment. A database and application program maintains property and maintenance records on the equipment; validates authorized users of two types—ordinary and administrator; creates and maintains user appointments; and schedules maintenance, backups, and upgrades without disrupting appointments. An application program is to be designed to delete a piece of equipment removed from the database. Write a logic flow diagram for this application.**

Before writing the logic flow diagram, it is necessary to decide specifically what the application should do, if anything, besides merely deleting records in the database pertaining to the removed equipment. Obviously, not all users should be validated to delete equipment. Also, the identity of the user who deletes equipment should be captured and stored (not only because deleting could be a way to cover theft, but also as part of maintaining an audit trail for major equipment transactions). It is also necessary to avoid deleting equipment for which appointments exist. The qualified engineer will recognize that it is inappropriate to attempt to automatically reschedule appointments, and will conclude that the application should display a list of affected appointments, give the user the opportunity to delete them, and require at least an override or confirmation by the user before deleting equipment while any affected appointments still exist. Users must also confirm the deletion even if no affected appointments exist. Let us assume that the program will flatly refuse (be unable) to delete equipment for which appointments exist.

Let the logic start with entry by a user of an EQUIP_DELETE command with an effective DELETION_DATE. A possible flowchart is shown in figure 5-5.

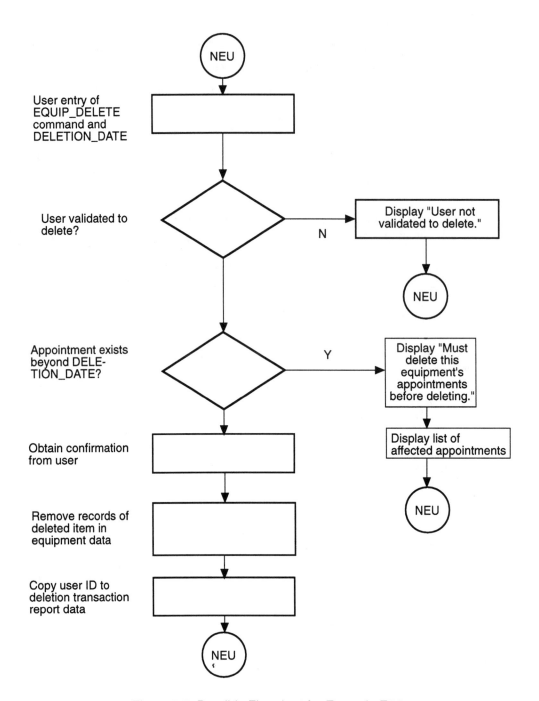

Figure 5-5. Possible Flowchart for Example E34.

As a further exercise, reconsider whether copying of the user identity is in the best place (the answer appears at the end of this subsection).

Figure 5-6 shows two logic flow diagrams for creating an appointment for a student to use a station in a computer lab. As an industrial engineer, compare the two procedures and decide which one is better.

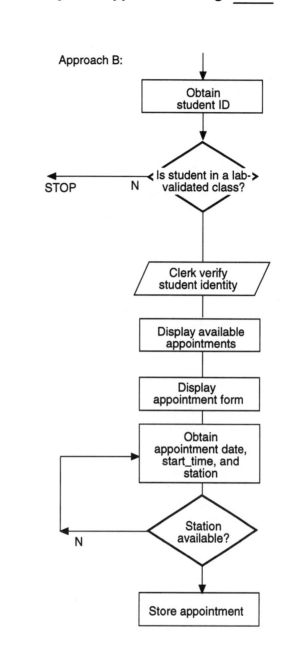

Figure 5-6. Two Approaches to Creating a
Student Appointment in a Computer Lab.

The two main themes of the application are to validate the student's right to use the lab and to specify the date, time, and station of the appointment. Approach A has the disadvantages of obtaining the appointment date at least twice, of obtaining the class name and section, and of mixing the two themes. (It first addresses the appointment requirements, then the student's validation, and then again the appointment requirements.) Note that "Display available appointments" means two different things: In approach A, the display would presumably show the hours the lab is open with at least one station free on the requested date. In approach B, the display would presumably show the same things for *all* dates (or "Obtain appointment date. . ." could be moved to come before "Display available appointments"). Approach A makes the clerk ask the student for the class name and section; since the database under both approaches obviously contains enrollment data, the only possible benefit of bothering with these two entries would be to tie the appointment to the class and section. In this way, an instructor, for example, could recover the fact that Fred had claimed he was using the lab for his chemistry class rather than for his physics class. Approach B is the better approach.

The answer to the "further exercise" after example E43 is no, the copying of the user identity is not in the best place. It should be moved to become the first step after entry of the delete command. Not only would the move consolidate the user-validity logic into one area of the procedure, but it would collect the identity of users who attempt to delete equipment, which is better for the crime detection purpose of this feature than merely collecting the identity of those who succeed.

5.3.4 Systems Development

Industrial engineers are often called upon to manage development of information systems. Many frameworks for systems development have been published. All of them involve basically the following phases:

A. Definition development
B. Requirements development
C. Software design
    1. Data design
    2. Application design
        a) Functional design
        b) Program design
D. Implementation
    1. Prototyping
    2. Coding
    3. Level 1 testing (checking)
    4. Level 2 testing (validating)
    5. Beta testing (user testing)

The major milestones of a system development effort are usually the adoption (approval) of major documents. The definition-development phase ends with acceptance or rejection of a proposal. If funding is obtained and a project team is formed, the requirements-development phase begins. It includes preliminary data design, preliminary application design, and selection of the hardware and software platform. It ends with a requirements document, and the software-design phase begins. Most of what an industrial engineer would consider "design" will have already been done during the requirements-development phase. It is good practice to produce a preliminary version of the user manual as part of the requirements document. Software designers should be given a valid relational database design and logic flow diagrams for the major applications in the requirements document.

Program specifications culminate the software design phase. The project is turned over to programmers for implementation. Acceptance of system documentation ends the implementation phase. System documentation consists both of internal documentation (within the software) and external system documentation.

The major documentation that is not a development milestone is the user documentation. The user manual, a preliminary version of which should have been developed during the requirements documentation phase, is revised during testing to conform to the as-built system and is delivered along with the system documentation. In addition to a user manual, a reference manual is also prepared.

The distinction between a reference manual and a user manual is analogous to the distinction between a table of contents and an index. The user manual is organized according to functions that system developers predict users will want to perform. If the user wants to perform a certain task, he or she looks in the user manual to see how to do it. By contrast, the reference manual is organized according to features or capabilities. Several features or capabilities are used in performing what the user perceives as a given function.

As examples of reference manuals and user manuals, consider how a word processing program user might use each. Suppose the user wants to put the same small table into several places in a report. In the user manual, the user may find the recommended way to do this. In the reference manual, the user may find many features that in the right combination can do the job efficiently. Suppose the user investigates the "move" feature, for example, whose reference documentation refers to the "block" feature. By gaining enough understanding of both features, the user may come to realize that one of the intents was to enable exactly what he wants to do. On the other hand, suppose the user investigates the "macro" feature. By gaining enough understanding, the user may come to realize that its capabilities also enable exactly what he wants to do (he can define the table as a macro and invoke it in many places). As another alternative, suppose the user investigates file manipulation features. He may come to realize that the table can be saved and retrieved to many places in the report, providing another method of doing what he wants to do. Finally, inspection of the "delete" and "undo" features may reveal that it is possible to delete the table to make it the last deleted item and then use "undo" to restore it in many places. These examples show that both types of user documentation are needed.

Rapid prototyping is a variation on the system development process. In rapid prototyping, early development is performed to the point where a demonstration can be made of some of the most pivotal features and functions. This allows users to see and "feel" how the system will work. Rapid prototyping builds user support for the project and provides diagnostic feedback to redirect the further design.

To illustrate rapid prototyping, consider a group of linked spreadsheet applications that was rapidly developed for a videotape duplicating studio. The prototype system proved capable of computing and displaying the appropriate prices to charge for various custom services, computing and displaying the optimal way to decide how much of a given duplicating job to do in parallel and how much to do serially, and computing and displaying a "hot list" of jobs that should be done next in order to meet due dates and leave an appropriate mix of resources to perform other jobs. The prototype system computed very slowly and required the entire current backlog of jobs to be keyed in, but these deficiencies did not interfere with user evaluation of its basic capabilities. Approval was gained for development of a production-level version of the same system which would compute rapidly, import its data automatically from the database that already supported sales and billing, and have a much more convenient user interface than was provided by the spreadsheets. Here, the key to rapid prototyping was that the spreadsheet applications were easy to build, and that their deficiencies, while unacceptable for a production system, did not cloud the issues that were the principal concerns of the potential users.

One of the most important considerations in system design is to maintain close user involvement in all phases of development. Nearly all authorities on system development emphasize this point. In the days when only the company computer guru or the IBM representative knew anything about computers, it was common for users to develop some very tentative preliminary requirements (being ignorant of what would or would not be possible). They would turn the project over to computer professionals, wait, and finally receive a system that was far from being what they needed. Those days are gone. The modern way to maintain close user involvement is to put the potential users in direct managerial and technical control of the project itself.

5.4 Relational Database Design

Representation is the most important information-system skill for industrial engineers. The best techniques for designing workable data representations are those of relational database design.

The representation problem is this: Given a set of applications that are to be supported in a given environment, design a database to support them. This entails developing the quantities and descriptors—data—that will formalize information for computer processing. Information—not number of bits of uncertainty as in section 5.1, but rich, flexible perceptions about entities and their characteristics—must be converted to sterile, inflexible data suitable for automated handling.

If we talk about an application (e.g., a point-of-sale system) we use nouns, modifiers, verbs, and other parts of speech. If the application is to be computerized, some of the *nouns and modifiers* (e.g., price, 15 cans of corn) will be converted into *data*, and some of the *verbs* (e.g., determine, scan) will be converted into *logic*.

Three design techniques break the representation problem into manageable steps that achieve progress toward a data design by focusing on certain aspects while ignoring others. To simplify the job of developing a valid relational design, use these techniques first: genus graphs (reviewed in section 5.4.1), entity-relationship design (reviewed in section 5.4.2), and object design (reviewed in section 5.4.3). These techniques will be discussed below. Section 5.4.4 will review relational database theory, database management systems (DBMS), and the structured query language (SQL).

5.4.1 Genus Graphs

The structured modeling technique developed by Art Geoffrion (May 1987) includes a very useful conceptual tool: the *genus graph*. A genus graph can organize the important parts of a data representation without requiring difficult decisions about which parts of the model are entities, relationships, characteristics, objects, properties, attributes, constraints, or objectives.

Call all parts of the model *elements* regardless of their meaning or structure. For example, the standard Hitchcock transportation model has sources, sinks, links, supplies, demands, flows, upper and lower flow limits, costs per unit flow, supply constraints, demand constraints, flow constraints, and an objective function. It does not matter that some of these things are very different from others. Each group of like elements is a genus (plural *genera*): source genus, sink genus, link genus, supply genus, and so forth. To create a genus graph, we arrange genera into a graph showing which ones are defined by (in Geoffrion's terminology, call) which others. We can speak either concretely or abstractly by saying "defined." Concretely, the objective function is "defined" when we know its value, which requires the flows and costs-per-unit flow. Therefore, the objective function genus *calls* both the flow genus and the cost-per-unit flow genus. Abstractly, the same conclusion follows from the mathematical definition of the objective function: a sum of flows multiplied by costs-per-unit flow.

Similarly, each supply constraint is defined on flows and supplies. (Concretely, satisfaction or violation of the constraint depends on the flows and supplies. Abstractly, the mathematical definition of a supply constraint is that a sum of flows does not exceed a supply.) Hence, the supply-constraint genus calls the flow genus and the supply genus. Each demand constraint is defined on flows and a demand, so the demand-constraint genus calls the flow genus and the demand genus. Each flow constraint is defined on a flow and an upper or lower flow limit, so the flow-constraint genus calls the flow genus and the upper-and-lower-flow-limit genus.

The flow genus and the cost-per-unit flow genus do not call each other; they both call the link genus. Although "flow" appears in the name of the cost-per-unit flow genus, each one of these costs is a number independent of the corresponding amount of flow. Each link has a cost and a flow, so the cost genus and the flow genus each call the link genus.

To verify this abstractly, recall the usual symbols x_{ij} and c_{ij} for the flows and costs; they include the link name, so each is defined on a link. The links themselves are defined on the sources and sinks since each is defined as the path from a given source to a given sink. Note that their usual symbols are (i,j), where i and j are source and sink names, respectively. Thus, the link genus calls the source genus and sink genus.

Finally, the supply genus calls the source genus, and the demand genus calls the sink genus. We are now ready to draw the genus graph. The most primitive genera—the ones that do not call any others—go at the bottom. When a genus calls another genus, the calling genus (the less primitive genus) is placed higher than any genus it calls, and lines are drawn between calling and called genera. The resulting genus graph for the transportation problem is shown in figure 5-7.

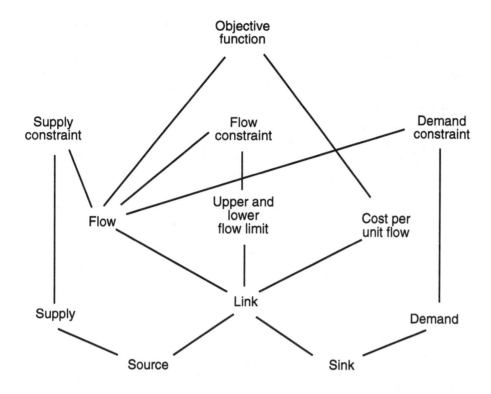

Figure 5-7. Genus Graph for Transportation Problem.

An entire constraint, such as "The sum of the flows from a source shall not exceed the source's supply," is not shown as a single element, even though doing so would make a single genus of them instead of the two genera supply constraint and supply. This is because condensing the model would destroy some of its structure. The constraint really has three parts: a left-hand side ("the sum of the flows from a source"), a comparison ("shall not exceed"), and a right-hand side ("the source's supply"). The right-hand side calls only the source genus (each source has a supply), whereas the left-hand side and the comparison have meaning only when supplies and flows are known. Hence the constraints are represented by a supply-constraint genus that contains left-hand sides and comparisons and calls both the flow genus and the supply genus, and by a supply genus that calls only the source genus.

E44a.   In a project-scheduling database for a single project, the project is broken down into tasks. Precedence relationships among the tasks require that some tasks must be completed before others begin. The project's schedule is the scheduled start times and durations of all tasks. The planned completion date depends on the schedule. Time-feasibility constraints in the project require the schedule to satisfy all precedence relationships and meet an established due date.

Resources have availabilities and are consumed by tasks. Resource-feasibility constraints are time-specific scheduled consumptions of a resource (the sum of its consumptions by individual tasks for a time interval) and are not to exceed availability of the resource in that time interval. Construct a genus graph for this situation.

Since there is only one project, no project genus exists. The most primitive genera are due date, task, and resource. The precedence genus calls the task genus.

Now if we straightforwardly translate the problem statement, we assert start time and duration genera that call the task genus, a schedule genus that calls them, and a planned completion-date genus that calls the schedule genus. Although it would make sense to combine them all into a single schedule genus, we will carry the genera separately.

The availability genus calls the resource genus. Since there are tasks that consume resources, a consumption genus calls the task and resource genera. The total resource consumption genus calls the schedule and consumption genera. (The fact that this genus does not depend on the planned completion date is a slight justification for not condensing the completion date into the schedule.) Finally, the resource-feasibility-constraint genus calls the total-resource-consumption genus and the availability genus.

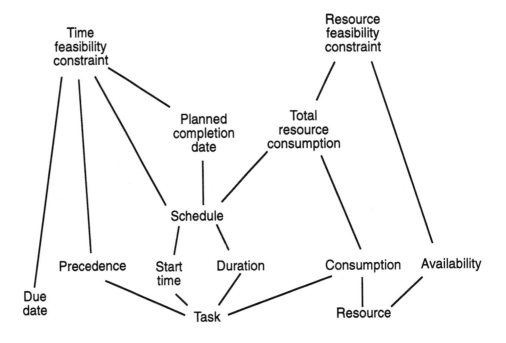

Figure 5-8. Genus Graph for Example E44a.

E44b.   Revise the project scheduling genus graph to allow consumption of resources by activities to depend on task durations but not on task start times.

The revision is done by moving the consumption genus higher and letting it call the duration genus.

The fact that consumption depends on only part of the schedule is a strong justification for not condensing the start time and duration genera into a single genus. The necessity of the schedule genus is questionable since any genera that call it could simply call one or both of start time and duration. But since "schedule" is something that is fixed in people's minds as a single concept and often referenced as a unit, it should be retained.

To engineers accustomed to dealing with scheduling algorithms rather than interactive scheduling software, it may seem counterintuitive not to have start time and duration call precedence. In most project-scheduling algorithms, precedences are used to calculate the schedule in such a way that violation of precedences would be impossible. If this is to be the case, start time and duration should call precedence, which should not be called by the time feasibility constraint genus. On the other hand, in most interactive scheduling software the user is free to try schedules that violate time feasibility constraints. The system complains about the violations but does not prevent them. The genus graph is correct for this case.

Actually, it is rare for an application procedure to have much effect on a genus graph. For instance, some scheduling models use complicated precedence modeling allowing up to X% of a task to be done before the last Y% of a predecessor is finished. That complication would not affect the genus graph.

5.4.2 Entity-relationship Design

An *entity* is something in the real world that has *characteristics*. In an entity-relationship design, entities are represented by keeping data that represent their characteristics. The word *entity* can mean either *entity class* or *entity instance*. For example, if data is being kept on engineers, then Delal Buyukakten, an industrial engineer, may be an instance of the entity ENGINEER. Entity-relationship design (E-R design) does not focus on entity characteristics nor on entity instances. E-R design concerns only entity classes and the relationships among them.

Entities have several kinds of *relationships* with each other, approximately described in English as "has a" or "is a" or "has many" or "consists of" or "corresponds to." For example, we may say "An automobile has an engine," meaning that there is an entity class AUTOMOBILE and an entity class ENGINE, and that there is a relationship between them. The semantics of the situation dictate whether this is a one-to-one relationship that says, for example, every automobile in the parking lot has one engine, and every engine in the parking lot is in one automobile, or something else. If the semantics are such that an instance of the class AUTOMOBILE is an automobile *model* (as when discussing the available options offered by the manufacturer), then the same sentence might mean that each model of automobile comes with a given model of engine, and if a given model of engine is used in more than one model of automobile, the relationship would be a many-to-one relationship.

Semantics cannot be represented unambiguously in a database, but a database design can and must be made to be consistent with whatever the semantics happen to be. To achieve this consistency, E-R design is very useful. By eliminating the clutter of characteristics—that is, by eliminating everything that will become the data itself and focusing on the structure of relationships between entities—E-R design enables us to determine exactly the basic structure before investing further effort.

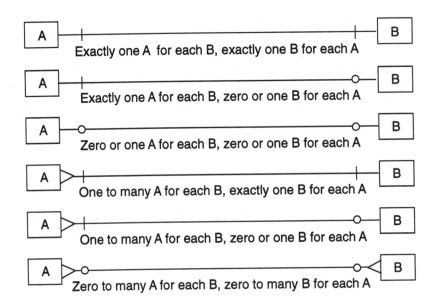

Figure 5-9. Diagramming of Minimum and Maximum Cardinality for Relationships.

The graphical symbol for a relationship between two entities is a line drawn between them with cardinality symbols at each end. Minimum cardinality at the *A* end of a relationship between entities *A* and *B* is either zero or one—zero if there need not necessarily be an instance of entity *A* for each instance of entity *B* and one if there must be an instance of entity *A* for each instance of entity *B*. Minimum cardinality is indicated by a small oval or circle if it is zero and by a small hash mark if it is one. Maximum cardinality at the *A* end of a relationship between entities *A* and *B* is either one or many—one if there can be at most one instance of entity *A* for each instance of entity *B* and many if there can be many instances of entity *A* for each instance of entity *B*. Maximum cardinality is indicated by a crow's foot for *many* and by lack of a crow's foot for *one*.

Suppose that Suzie's Restaurant has dishes such as "hamburger with everything" and "western omelet" and that each dish has ingredients such as "ground beef patty" and "lettuce." From the semantics of the situation, we know that each dish can have several ingredients and must have at least one ingredient, and that the same ingredients can appear in many dishes. Thus, we can say that between the DISH entity and the INGREDIENT entity the relationship is many-to-many:

The hash mark on the left constitutes a design decision that no ingredient should be in the database unless it appears in at least one dish. Otherwise, an oval would be placed near DISH instead of a hash mark.

In E-R design, names are assigned to all many-to-many relationships and also to any relationships that have semantically natural names. In this example, the relationship must be named. What is the semantically natural name for it? Since the relationship is one that specifies what ingredients are in each dish, it will be called the recipe for the dish.

RECIPE
(relationship)

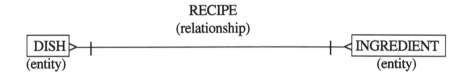

Like entities, relationships have instances. An instance of the relationship RECIPE is the pairing of a dish with an ingredient: a western omelet uses two eggs. The entire ingredient list for western omelet is a set of instances of RECIPE, and the list of dishes that use egg is another set of instances of the same relationship.

The power of E-R design is illustrated by the history of *indexing tools* for assisting book indexers. Until the mid-1980s, no one had built a competent indexing tool. Tools existed that allowed an indexer to tag words or phrases for finding by the tool, which then listed them with page numbers. But this was merely a concordance, not an index. For example, if the author used "SL" in the book as meaning "straight-line depreciation," the tool could easily produce an entry showing all the page numbers for "SL" and one showing all the page numbers for "straight-line depreciation," but they would be separate. Tools offered no automation to make an entry showing all the page numbers for the concept straight-line depreciation which would combine the page list for both "SL" and "straight-line depreciation."

Finally, it was realized that an entry is not the same thing as a concept nor an indicator (a word or phrase that indicates a concept). Let the entities be ENTRY, CONCEPT, INDICATOR, and PAGE (see figure 5-10). A concept has many indicators, but each indicator (e.g., "SL") indicates only one concept. A concept also has many entries (e.g., "straight-line depreciation" and "depreciation, straight-line"), but an entry is for only one concept. An indicator appears on many pages and can be found automatically. Hence, a concept appears on many pages, which are merely the combined pages for all the concept's indicators. Since these are what should be listed for each one of the concept's entries, the automation of indexing is thus achieved.

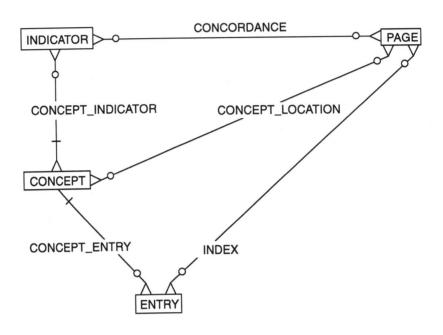

Figure 5-10. E-R Diagram for Indexing.

E45.   A grocery store stocks SKUs (stock-keeping units), each of which has a price to be kept in the store's point-of-sale database. When a customer checks out, there is a group of items sold, each of which is reported as one line on the receipt. Let "bill" be a name for the combination of item sales in an instance of the customer's checking out; the bill is what is reported as the whole receipt. The database will not track customers, but it will track cashiers (for each bill, there is a cashier who handled it). The database will track inventory continuously, decrementing the on-hand count of the SKU for each item sold, and producing inventory replenishment orders, for which purpose it will track vendors and which SKUs each vendor can provide. The same SKU can be ordered from more than one vendor. Every SKU must have at least one vendor, but a vendor is not immediately removed from the database if no SKUs of that vendor are currently in the database. Old bills are often purged, so when a cashier reports to work there may be no bills in the database that were handled by the cashier. Draw the E-R diagram for this situation.

SKU is an entity. The CUSTOMER entity will not be tracked; ignore it. ITEM SALE is an entity; there is one instance of SKU for each instance of ITEM SALE; there are many instances of ITEM SALE for each instance of SKU; there must be an SKU for each ITEM SALE, but an SKU can have zero ITEM SALEs. There is one BILL for many ITEM SALEs, and each ITEM SALE is on one BILL; there can be no instance of either without the other. One CASHIER exists for each BILL, and zero to many BILLS exist for each CASHIER. A VENDOR is an entity; there are one to many VENDORs for each SKU and zero to many SKUs for each VENDOR.

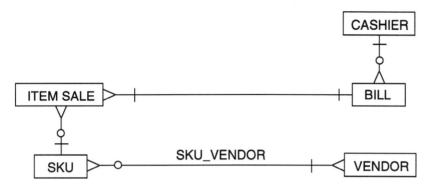

Figure 5-11. E-R Diagram for Example E45.

Since the relationship between SKU and VENDOR is many-to-many, it was given a name. Since the relationship tells which vendors sell which items, it could be called "catalog," but that name seems no more natural than the default name that can always be given to a relationship—a compound name consisting of the names of the two entities it links. If the CUSTOMER entity were tracked, it would have a one-to-one relationship with BILL, with a hash mark at the customer end to indicate there can be no bill without a customer and an oval at the bill end.

5.4.3 Object Design

An *object* is a named collection of properties. Objects can represent *entities* and *relationships*. Whereas an entity is a class of things in the real world, and an entity instance is a particular member of the class, an object that represents an entity is a computer representation of it, and an object instance that represents an entity instance is a computer representation of the instance.

Object design is more comprehensive than structured modeling since it classifies genera into objects and properties and assigns properties to the proper objects. Object design is also more comprehensive than E-R design since it handles properties (which are ignored in E-R design). The ideal starting point for object design is to have already completed both structured modeling and E-R design, although many situations may not be too complex to perform object design directly.

At present, object design is chiefly valuable as the ideal starting point for relational design. It is not less comprehensive than relational design; in fact, the object design of a database expresses nearly all of the information that would be contained in a relational design of the same database. The *structure* of an object design is easier for people to understand and create than that of a relational design, but no one has figured out how to display the *contents* of an object design conveniently except by displaying the data as it would appear in the equivalent relational design. Since object design is easier to perform than relational design, and since the conversion of object design to relational design is almost unambiguous, an objective DBMS would be welcome in which the user could work with object diagrams rather than with relations. No such thing yet exists, but as late as 1985 no true relational DBMS existed either.

Recall from section 5.4.2 the following E-R diagram for Suzie's Restaurant in which there are two entities and a many-to-many relationship:

To see how object design treats entities, relationships, and properties, let us look at the entire relational database, including data:

Suzie's Database

DISH	(DCODE	DNAME	DPRICE)
	HE	Hamb w/every	1.75
	HB	Hamburger	1.30
	CB	Cheeseburger	1.65
	WO	Western Omel	1.30

RECIPE	(DCODE	ICODE	IQUAN)
	HE	GB	1
	HE	BU	1
	HE	LE	1
	HE	TO	2
	HE	ON	1
	HB	BU	1
	HB	GB	1
	HB	LE	1
	CB	BU	1
	CB	GB	1
	CB	LE	1
	CB	CH	1
	WO	EG	1
	WO	TO	2
	WO	ON	2
	WO	HM	1

INGRED	(ICODE	INAME	ICOST	ONHAND)
	GB	G Beef Pat	0.40	30
	BU	Hamb Bun	0.08	14
	LE	Lettuce	0.04	29
	ON	Onion	0.03	81
	TO	Tomato	0.07	3
	CH	Cheese	0.15	29
	EG	Egg	0.06	13
	HM	Ham	0.20	35

The DISH entity of E-R design has been translated to a DISH relation having attributes DCODE, DNAME, DPRICE. The INGREDIENT entity of E-R design has been translated to an INGRED relation having attributes ICODE, INAME, ICOST, and ONHAND. Before discussing the translation of the many-to-many relationship RECIPE, let us show the *object diagrams* for the two objects that represent the DISH and INGREDIENT entities. Let us name the objects, unimaginatively, DISH and INGRED:

DISH: **INGRED:**
DCODE   ICODE
DNAME   INAME
DPRICE   ICOST
IQUAN $\Big\}$ ONHAND
INGRED $\Big\}_{MV}$ **DISH**$_{MV}$

In the list of properties for the object DISH, we see the three properties archived in the relational table of the same name, but we also see a *multivalued set of properties*; the brace gathers IQUAN and **INGRED** into a set, and the MV subscript indicates the set is multivalued. One of the properties in the set, **INGRED**, is an *object property* indicated by its boldface type. What the multivalued set of properties means here is this: one "property" of a DISH is how much (IQUAN) of each ingredient (**INGRED**) is required to make it. In the list of properties of the object INGRED, we see the four properties archived in the relational table of the same name, but we also see a *multivalued object property*, which means that one "property" of an ingredient is that it appears in many dishes. The object properties in the two object diagrams actually express the RECIPE relationship without the object designer's having had to conceive of a RECIPE object.

An object property, indicated by the boldface name of an object, is listed in the diagrams of other objects rather than its identifier (e.g., ICODE for **INGRED**) because this allows the object designer not to worry about which property is the identifier and which other properties, if any, are to be "inherited." For example, by having **INGRED** in its property list, the DISH object "inherits" any necessary properties of an ingredient in its list, such as ICOST, and it is immaterial whether the INGRED object has unique ICODEs or unique INAMEs or both.

If the object designer had conceived of RECIPE as a separate object, a different but also valid object design would have resulted, as follows.

DISH:	**RECIPE:**	**INGRED:**
DCODE	DCODE	ICODE
DNAME	IQUAN	INAME
RECIPE	**INGRED** $\Big\}_{MV}$	ICOST
		RECIPE$_{MV}$

In the object design above, the object property **RECIPE** in the DISH object diagram expresses the idea that every dish has a recipe. The multivalued object property **RECIPE**$_{MV}$ in the INGRED object diagram expresses the idea that an ingredient appears in multiple recipes. This design, and the prior one, are both valid in the sense that they would lead to the same relational design. The advanced reader will note that in the first design, **DISH**$_{MV}$ could have been omitted from the INGRED diagram; in the second design, **RECIPE**$_{MV}$ could have been omitted from the INGRED diagram; and in the second design, the **RECIPE** object is conceived such that one of its instances is a list of all ingredients and quantities for a dish, whereas an instance of the *relationship*, as seen in both the E-R diagram and the relational table RECIPE, is one ingredient and its quantity for one dish.

E46.   **A manufacturing plant produces each product as a sequence of operations. Each operation belongs to a specific product and consists of a sequence of tasks. Sometimes the same task appears in more than one operation. An engineer responsible for setting time standards performs experiments, each consisting of replicated observations of a task, for some of the tasks. The observations are performed by videotape. Technicians analyze the tapes by breaking a task into elements and recording the duration and performance pace for each element. Assume that each product, operation, task, and any other object has a name and a description. Perform an object design, that is, list the objects and give properties for each object.**

There is a PRODUCT object having as one of its properties the set of operations that comprise it. There is an OPERATION object having its parent product as an object property and having a set of tasks that comprise it as one of its properties. There is a TASK object having a set (not just one) of operations in which the task appears, and a set of elements that comprise the task. There is an ELEMENT object. An industrial engineer, being familiar with work analysis, realizes that the same elements can appear in many tasks, so the set of tasks in which the element appears is one of its properties. There is an EXPERIMENT object having many instances for each task. There is an OBSERVATION object having many instances for each element in each experiment.

PRODUCT:	**OPERATION:**	**TASK:**
PNAME	OPNAME	TNAME
PDESCRIP	OPDESCRIP	TDESCRIP
OPERATION$_{MV}$	**PRODUCT**	**OPERATION**$_{MV}$
	TASK$_{MV}$	**ELEMENT**$_{MV}$

ELEMENT:	**EXPERIMENT:**	**OBSERVATION:**
ELNAME	EXNAME	OBNAME
ELDESCRIP	EXDESCRIP	OBDESCRIP
TASK$_{MV}$	**TASK**	**EXPERIMENT**
	OBSERVATION$_{MV}$	**ELEMENT**
		DURATION
		PACE

5.4.4 Relational Design

Relational design is the one best way to structure data in a wide variety of situations. A relational database is more consistent, easier to understand, and more convenient to work with than any other kind of database.

5.4.4.1 Relations: Tuples, Attributes, and Keys

A relation (relational table) is a collection of *tuples* (rows). Each tuple contains values of a fixed set of *attributes*. Each attribute has an attribute name and a domain. Attribute names can be displayed as column headings. The domain consists of three parts: the semantic meaning of the attribute; the type and size of the attribute (e.g., CHAR(4) for an attribute whose values are character stings having up to four characters, NUMBER(9.3) for an attribute whose values are numbers having nine decimal digits, three of which are after the decimal point, or *DATE* for an attribute that is a calendar date); and special restrictions (e.g., cannot be null or must be nonnegative).

Suzie's database, displayed in the previous section, is a small example of a relational database consisting of three relations. Examine the DISH relation, for example. It is displayed as a four-row, three-column table of values, with the heading, DISH (DCODE DNAME DPRICE). The heading indicates that DISH is the name of the relation; that it has three attributes having names DCODE, DNAME, and DPRICE; and that DCODE (the attribute whose name is underlined) is the *key*.

The key of a relation is one or more attributes whose values uniquely identify a tuple. In the DISH table, since DCODE is the key, there can be only one row having 'HE' as the value of DCODE. Note that the RECIPE relation has a dual key, DCODE and ICODE. In the RECIPE table, only one row can have both DCODE = 'HE' and ICODE = 'GB'.

E47.   **Frapdubers come in two types, plain and ridged; in two sizes, large and small; and in two colors, red and blue. The price of a frapduber is $3 for plain and $4 for ridged, plus $2 extra if large and $3 extra if blue. A correct relational database for this situation is three relations: FRAPBASE(Type, BasePrice), FRAPSIZE(Size, SizePrem), FRAPCOLOR(Color, ColorPrem). Display the relations with their keys indicated and fill them with all data.**

FRAPBASE obviously has a row for each type; FRAPSIZE obviously has a row for each size; and FRAPCOLOR obviously has a row for each color. Thus, the keys are Type, Size, and Color, respectively.

FRAPBASE	(Type	BasePrice)
	plain	3
	ridged	4

FRAPSIZE	(Size	SizePrem)
	large	2
	small	0

FRAPCOLOR	(Color	ColorPrem)
	red	0
	blue	3

5.4.4.2 Relational Theory: Dependencies and Normal Forms

A relational database is well *normalized* if its relations are all in domain/key normal form. The ascending series of normal form is described as follows:

A relation is in this normal form...	*...if it is in all more basic normal forms and obeys these constraints:*
First normal form (1NF)	It has atomic (single-valued) attributes.
Second normal form (2NF)	All of its nonkey attributes are functionally dependent on all of its key.
Third normal form (3NF)	It is free of transitive dependencies.
Boyce-Codd normal form (BCNF)	Every one of its determinants is a candidate key.
Fourth normal form (4NF)	It is free of multivalued dependencies.
Domain/key normal form (DKNF)	All logical restrictions on its contents are logical consequences of its key and its attributes' domains.

First normal form requires that every attribute in a table must be single-valued. For example, if each *part* in an assembly has up to three *subparts*, the database cannot have this form:

```
PART(PartNo Descrip Subparts)          SUBPART(SubNo Cost)
    A1   box   31, 72                          31   88
    A2   tap   31, 80                          72   53
                                               80   85
```

The database in this form is not well normalized, because the *Subparts* attribute of the PART table is not atomic.

How is a database fixed that has tables with non-atomic attributes? A wrong but formerly widely-used way to accommodate multiple-valued attributes was to expand them: let there be Subparts1, Subparts2, and Subparts3 "fields" in the PART table. This is wrong not so much because it is inefficient (archiving nulls for parts having fewer than three subparts), but because it artificially separates data structurally. Insofar as subpart 72 is concerned, there is *no real meaning* in the fact that it is the second—not the first or third—subpart listed for part A1. The following aphorism should be stated to help prevent making this kind of mistake: *Never enshrine data as structure.* There is a better way.

Since each part has several subparts, the relationship between PART and SUBPART is either one-to-many or many-to-many. (The data proves it is many-to-many, because subpart 31 is a subpart of two different parts.) Whenever a relationship is one-to-many, the key of the "parent" relation is simply listed in the relation of the "child." Here, if it were true that each SUBPART had a single "parent" part, PartNo could have been made an attribute of the SUBPART table. But a many-to-many relationship exists between parts and subparts. When a relationship is many-to-many, it is expressed in a separate relation having a dual key consisting of the keys of each relation. The corrected database is stated becomes:

PART (PartNo	Descrip)	SUBPART	(SubNo	Cost)	USE	(SubNo	PartNo)
A1	box		31	88		31	A1
A2	tap		72	53		31	A2
			80	85		72	A1
						80	A2

As another example of first normal form failure, consider an Address attribute that includes the zip code. If database applications are to use the zip code in any way (e.g., to sort addresses by zip code), it violates first normal form to have the zip code stored as part of an address. However, if the zip code is merely viewed as the last few characters of the address, not to be used in any logic, there is nothing wrong. As a third example, suppose an astrologer stored people's birthdates. If any applications used only the month and day (e.g., to determine the astrological sign) while ignoring the year, the birthdate would fail to be atomic; the database could be fixed by keeping month and day as one attribute and year as another.

Note that both the *use* to be made of a database and the semantics of the situation determine whether a relation is in first (or any) normal form. We might ask, for example, whether it is wrong to have an equipment number such as M-93-40-0047, where we can tell from the equipment number that this is a machine (M) as opposed to another type of equipment, that it was acquired in 1993 (93), and that it is the 47th machine in the plant area whose code is 40. The answer is that such an equipment number is fine, so long as no database applications are expected to parse the number to find out any of these facts.

E48. **A database for a company cafeteria keeps track of meals given to employees. The following tables are part of the database:**

EMP_MEAL	(SSN	#Br	#Lu	#Su)	MEAL_VAL	(Br	Lu	Su)
	41	4	5	0		3.50	4.80	7.50
	42	0	6	0				
	44	0	0	5				
	47	0	0	4				
	62	0	0	6				
	71	4	4	0				
	72	0	0	4				

Here SSN lists employees' social security numbers (pretend they are two digits); #Br, #Lu, and #Su are the numbers of breakfasts, lunches, and suppers, respectively, fed to an employee during the pay period; Br, Lu, and Su mean the values of a breakfast, lunch, and dinner, respectively. A programmer, trying to write an application to compute pay equivalent to meals for tax purposes, claims the data design is unworkable. She reminds you, "Meal is an object." Identify what is wrong and fix it.

Since "Meal is an object," then breakfast, lunch, and supper are instances of the meal object and should be values of the meal name. This design violates the aphorism "Never enshrine data as structure." The logic of applications would have to deal separately with three kinds of meals as if they were different, when really the only data-relevant difference among them is their value. A correct design would be as follows, where an instance of the object represented by the new EMP_MEAL table is an instance of one employee being fed one meal:

EMP_MEAL	(SSN	Meal	Quan)		MEAL_VAL	(Meal	Value)
	41	Br	4			Br	3.50
	41	Lu	5			Lu	4.80
	42	Lu	6			Su	7.50
	44	Su	5				
	47	Su	4				
	62	Su	6				
	72	Br	4				
	71	Br	4				
	72	Su	4				

Note that this more elegant design is no less efficient than the bad design. No zeros need to be kept.

Second normal form requires that all nonkey attributes be functionally dependent on all of the key. A *functional dependence*, written A → B to indicate that attribute B functionally depends on attribute A, means that for each value of A—the *determinant*—there must be only one value of B. For example, in the final EMP_MEAL table above, there are two key attributes (SSN and Meal) and one nonkey attribute (Quan). Now the semantics of the situation are that Quan is not the quantity of people with a given social security number nor the quantity of meals of a given type, but rather it is the quantity of meals of a given type fed to a person with a given social security number. Thus, Quan depends on all of the compound key, and the table *is* in second normal form.

On the other hand, suppose the EMP_MEAL table had been *joined* with the MEAL_VAL table (see section 5.4.4.6 for the join operation) and was being maintained in the database in the following form:

EMP_MEAL	(SSN	Meal	Value	Quan)
	41	Br	3.50	4
	41	Lu	4.80	5
	42	Lu	4.80	6
	44	Su	7.50	5
	47	Su	7.50	4
	62	Su	7.50	6
	72	Br	3.50	4
	71	Br	3.50	4
	72	Su	7.50	4

Now the table would fail to be in second normal form, because Value, a nonkey attribute, is functionally dependent on Meal, which is only part of the key.

Third normal form requires that a table be free of transitive dependencies. A *transitive dependency*, written $A \rightarrow B \rightarrow C$, is the condition in which attribute C is functionally dependent on attribute B, which in turn is functionally dependent on attribute A. Thus C depends on A, but through B. If A is the key, B belongs in the table, but C should be in a table for which B is the key. If A and B are a compound key, the situation discussed immediately above results in which the table is not in second normal form (because C depends on only part of the key), and again C should be in a table for which B is the key.

Suppose you observed the results of a series of quality inspections and noted the results as follows.

Lot	Weight	Result
334	677	passed
392	684	passed
393	589	failed

Now suppose you subsequently learned that the inspection standards were not lot-specific, but that any lot passes if its weight is 600 or more and fails otherwise. What is wrong with the way the data was recorded, and what would have been a better form in which to have recorded it?

Since one row exists for each lot, Lot is the key. Since Lot is not a compound key, the data cannot fail to be in second normal form. Since each lot has a weight (Lot $\rightarrow$ Weight) and each weight has a result (Weight $\rightarrow$ Result), we have a transitive dependency (Lot $\rightarrow$ Weight $\rightarrow$ Result). Thus the answer to the first part of the question is that this form of data keeping would violate 3NF. A better data-keeping form would be simply to record the first two columns, Lot and

Weight. The Weight → Result dependency, being compactly expressible mathematically, should be kept not in the database but in the application logic. (We would not keep a table saying 589 fails, 590 fails, etc.)

Boyce-Codd normal form is essentially a more stringent form of third normal form. A transitive dependency is the simplest kind of dependency complex that can occur among three or more attributes, and all dependency complexes are bad. Recall the 2NF requirement that every nonkey attribute must depend on all of the key. Third normal form says, further, that a nonkey attribute that depends on the key indirectly, through a transitive dependency, is troublesome. The Boyce-Codd normal form eliminates the qualifier "through a transitive dependency." But all dependency complexes cannot simply be outlawed, because it is allowable to have synonym keys or candidate keys. For example, if an inventory is kept of the frapdubers mentioned in example E47, it is not practical to deal with plain, large, red frapdubers on the one hand and ridged, small, blue frapdubers on the other hand. That is, it would be unwieldy to have a table FRAP(Type, Size, Color, OnHand) with a triple key. A code or name would have to be invented for each one. For example, a relation with key "FrapID" would look like the following.

FRAP	(FrapID,	Type,	Size,	Color,	OnHand)
	PLR	plain	large	red	1674
	PLB	plain	large	blue	88

Now with FrapID being a synonym for it, the triplet (Type, Size, Color) is a *candidate key*. The table is well normalized with either key. In the form shown, all the nonkey attributes depend on the key. (For example, FrapID → Type since for a given value of FrapID there is one value of Type.) In the alternative form FRAP(FrapID, Type, Size, Color, OnHand) all the nonkey attributes depend on the key since for a given value of the triplet (Type, Size, Color) there is one value of FrapID. Thus, synonym or candidate keys cause no trouble.

We do not want to define Boyce-Codd normal form in such a way as to complain about the ease with which we can write, for instance, FrapID → (Type, Size, Color) → OnHand. This is *not* a transitive dependency, because a dependency on both members of a synonymous pair is not indirect. OnHand depends directly on FrapID and also on (Type, Size, Color), since FrapID and (Type, Size, Color) are synonyms, that is, they are the same thing (FrapID ←→ [Type, Size, Color]). There are also cases of candidate keys which are semantically not synonyms. For example, if every employee has a company car and every company car is checked out to an employee, either the car identifier or the employee identifier could be used interchangeably. They could even appear in the same table (in fact they must, once) if its key is either one of them.

To avoid outlawing synonyms and other forms of candidate keys, the definition of Boyce-Codd normal form is that *every determinant in a table must be a candidate key*. The following vignette illustrates that a relation can be in the third normal form and yet fail to be in Boyce-Codd normal form.

> A machine can perform several tasks. A task can use several materials. A material is used in only one task. In keeping track of which material is chosen for each combination of machine and task, it is proposed to keep the data in a table of the form (Machine, Task, Material). Is anything wrong?
>
> Obviously the table is in 1NF. It is in 2NF also, since its only nonkey attribute—Material—is not determined by either Machine or Task alone. It is in 3NF, since it has no transitive dependency.
>
> But the dependency Material → Task ("A material is used in only one task") exists. This is not a candidate key because Material does not determine Machine. Thus, we have a determinant that is not a candidate key, and the table fails to be in Boyce-Codd normal form.
>
> But does this failure cause any anomalies? Yes, there is a deletion anomaly: suppose we delete the only machine that was assigned to use a given material. Then we would lose the only record of which task that material is used on. There is also the corresponding insertion anomaly, that we cannot archive the task that a material uses until a machine is assigned to use that material.
>
> To fix the problem, decompose the table into two tables: (Machine, Material) with a double key would show all the assigned machine/material combinations; (Material, Task) would show the task in which each material is used.
>
> The way to have avoided the problem in the first place would have been to realize that the functional dependency Material → Task implies that there must be a table with Material as its key and Task as a nonkey attribute. The mistake was in structuring the table in the same manner as a *report* that was desired from it. Remember that the format of the desired reports should have no influence on how the data is archived. If the information is in the database, it can be reported in any format.

Fourth normal form requires a table to be free from *multivalued dependencies*. A multivalued dependency (MVD), written A →→ B, occurs when a *set* of values of B must *all* occur for a given value of A, independent of any other attributes.

For example, in a delivery system, suppose there are several *routes*, each of which must be run on certain *days* of the week. For each route there are several *vehicles* from which to choose (the day of the week does not restrict which vehicle can be chosen). The day assignments and vehicle options are to be kept in the following form.

Route	Day	Vehicle
106	Mon	74744
106	Thu	74744
106	Mon	80888
106	Thu	80888
204	Wed	70700
204	Wed	72722

The key could be (Route, Day). Does this table properly archive the facts that route 106 runs on Mondays and Thursdays and can use vehicle 74744 or 80888, and that route 204 runs on Wednesdays and can use vehicle 70700 or 72722?

To see why it does not properly archive these facts, try to add Fridays to route 106. If only the tuple (106 Fri 74744) were added, the table would say route 106 can use vehicle 80888 on Mondays and Thursdays but not on Fridays. Therefore, the tuple (106 Fri 80888) would also have to be added.

This illustrates the definition of a multivalued dependency (MVD). Mathematically, the definition is: Let X and Y be disjoint attributes or sets of attributes in a table, and let Z be the remaining attribute or attributes. Let t_1 and t_2 be two rows with the same X value. The MVD $X \rightarrow\rightarrow Y$ exists if the semantics demand that there *must* exist a row (call it t_3) having t_1's Y value and t_2's Z value. This definition can be diagrammed as follows (where a blank value means the value can be anything):

	X	Y	Z		
t_1	a	b		}	The MVD $X \rightarrow\rightarrow Y$ exists
t_2	a		c		if for two rows like this,
t_3	a	b	c		there must be one like this.

Incidentally, since the attributes Y and Z are symmetric in the definition, a complementary MVD $X \rightarrow\rightarrow Z$ exists for the MVD $X \rightarrow\rightarrow Y$. In this example, the complementary MVD says that if there is a fixed set of days a route runs, independent of the vehicles, there must be a fixed set of vehicles from which to choose, independent of the day. This does not exclude the possibility that the set contains only one member. What it does imply is this: if assigned days for routes are independent of vehicle choices for routes, then vehicle choices are independent of assigned days.

If MVDs are found in a table, it must be decomposed so that each of the multivalued attributes is in a separate table. For this example, the proper tables are (with the key of each table underlined) as follows.

Route	Day		Route	Vehicle
106	Mon		106	74744
106	Thu		106	80888
204	Wed		204	70700
			204	72722

To further illustrate MVDs, recall the frapdubers of example E47. The three tables given in the example are needed to archive what frapduber models exist since the types, sizes, and colors are all independent. A single table of the form FRAP(FrapID, Type, Size, Color) would have MVDs. If, however, certain types came only in certain sizes and colors, so that not all combinations existed and there were no MVDs, the single table would be correct and would show only the combinations that actually existed.

Domain-key normal form, which is the highest normal form, requires that all logical restrictions on a table's contents must follow logically from the table's key and the domains of its attributes. This requirement is so general that, unlike the other normal forms, the domain-key normal form(DKNF) does not offer any specific formal procedures to check a table. However, its philosophy is useful in at least two ways. First, you can generally evaluate whether a table is adequate by trying to identify possible problems and seeing whether the structure prevents them all. Second, since possible logical subtleties are much harder to trace when a table has more than one theme, we have the excellent practical advice that *every table should have only one theme*. There are some exceptions to this—the most notable exception is that an inventory table with a row for each SKU can safely have two themes: 1) nonvolatile information about the SKU, and 2) volatile inventory information such as the on-hand quantity.

5.4.4.3 Relational Design: Synthesis and Analysis

The normal forms reviewed in the previous section have to do with the *analytical* approach to relational design: given a table, does it need to be decomposed? The opposite approach is *synthetic*.

In the synthetic approach, starting with a genus graph (section 5.4.1), an E-R design (section 5.4.2), or an object design (section 5.4.3), the designer builds up tables (synthesis means building up). If a valid table can be built, the whole representation problem diminishes in size, and eventually the conceptually most difficult part of the problem will be left isolated and simplified.

Table 5-3 lists some synthesis recommendations for building relational tables from various starting points.

Table 5-3. Synthesis Recommendations for Relational Design.

To build a table starting from...	...proceed as follows:
An object diagram where the object represents an entity; or an entity in an E-R diagram	Identify the object's name or *object identifier*. Make it into the key attribute of the object's defining relation. Make the simple properties of the object into nonkey attributes. If foreign object *B* is a single-valued object property of the object, first identify *B*'s object identifier (the property that will become the key of *B*'s table); make *B*'s key attribute into a nonkey attribute for this object's table. Reserve all multivalued items for later treatment; none of them will appear in the object's defining relation.
A multivalued property in an object diagram	Define a relation with the object identifer as half of the key. Make the multivalued property the other half of the key.
A reciprocal pair of multivalued object properties in an object diagram (many-to-many relationship)	E.g., BOOK is a multivalued property of AUTHOR and AUTHOR is a multivalued property of BOOK. Define a relation with each object's identifier as half its key.
A primitive genus in a genus graph	Unless the primitive genus is a property of the "grand entity" and will not go in the database (*Due date* in Example E44a) it is an object identifier. Define a relation with the object identifier as its key. Of the genera that call only this genus, make those that are merely properties into nonkey attributes.
An object-genus or entity-genus in a genus graph (i.e., a genus that is not merely a property)	Define a relation with the object or entity identifer (the genus name) as the key. Of the genera that call only this genus, make those that are merely properties into nonkey attributes. Change into nonkey attributes the identifiers of the object- or entity-genera called by this genus.
A many-to-many relationship between entities *A* and *B* in an E-R diagram	Define a relation with *A*'s identifer as its key. Define a relation with *B*'s identifier as its key. Define a relation with *A*'s identifier as half its key and *B*'s identifier as the other half of its key. (Fill the three relations with nonkey attributes that depend on the respective keys.)
A one-to-many relationship between entities *A* and *B* in an E-R diagram	(One *A* to many *B*.) Define a relation with *A*'s identifier as its key. Define a relation with *B*'s identifier as its key. Make *A*'s identifier into a nonkey attribute in *B*'s relation.
A one-to-one relationship between objects or entities *A* and *B*	If the minimum cardinality is zero at *A* and one at *B*, or if there are many fewer instances of *A* than of *B*, consider making *B*'s identifier into a nonkey attribute of *A*'s relation. Otherwise, if *A* is perceived to "belong" to *B*, make *A*'s identifier into a nonkey attribute in *B*'s relation.
A theme	Identify the determinant in the theme. Define a relation with the determinant as the key and with attributes that depend on all of it and only it as the nonkey attributes.

E49.   Starting with the genus graph of figure 5-7, design a set of relational tables for the transportation problem.

First, following the procedure for "a primitive genus in a genus graph," *Source* and *Sink* are objects. Let their identifiers be Source# and Sink#, respectively. Define a SOURCE table with key Source# and nonkey attribute Supply. Define a SINK table with key Sink# and nonkey attribute Demand.

Next, following the procedure for "an object genus in a genus graph," *Link* is an object. Let its identifier be Link#. Define a LINK table with Link# as its key. *Flow, Upper flow limit, Lower flow limit*, and *Cost per unit flow* are genera that call only this genus and are merely properties. Let the LINK table have corresponding nonkey attributes Flow, UpLimit, LoLimit, and Cost. The Link genus calls the object genera Source and Sink. Let the LINK table have Source# and Sink# as nonkey attributes. Everything higher in the genus graph is consequences, not basic data, and should not be archived in the database. Thus the tables in the database are:

SOURCE(Source#, Supply)   SINK(Sink#, Demand)

LINK(Link#, Flow, UpLimit, LoLimit, Cost, Source#, Sink#)

As a more complex example of relational synthesis, let us design the relational tables for the book-indexing tool whose E-R diagram was given in figure 5-10, without producing an object design along the way. Recall from section 5.4.2 that what allowed competent indexing software to be built was the realization that these three things are distinct: an index *entry*, the *concept* that an entry indexes, and the *indicators* of the concept that appear in the text. For example, *Paradiso, Richard A., Jr.* may be an entry for the *"RAP"* (his nickname) concept, one of whose indicators is *"Paradiso."* Any page on which *Paradiso* or any other indicator of *RAP* appears would be one of the pages for the entry (and for other entries for the *RAP* concept, if any).

Entry, concept, and indicator were conceived as entities, having these relationships:

Page was also conceived as an entity. In the E-R design its relationship with *indicator* was discovered to be a *concordance* (a primitive, literal index), and its relationship with *entry* was the *index* itself. These results were diagrammed in figure 5-10.

Now comes the task of designing the relational database that will now be designed to provide the data structure for the indexing tool. From table 5-3, we can infer these points about converting an E-R diagram to a relational design:

- Each entity becomes a relation
- Each many-to-many relationship becomes a relation

This example will illustrate two of the following three points concerning exclusions from a relational design.

- An entity (or object-genus, or object) will not become a relation if it is merely an attribute or if its only characteristics are its identifier and relationships that are expressed elsewhere. (For example, in it-to-many relationships and one-to-one relationships expressed in the other entity's relation.)
- An entity (or object-genus, or object) will not become a relation if it can become a *view*—a structure like a relation but derived entirely from other relations in the database.
- A characteristic or property will not be archived as an attribute if it is derived from other data and reasonably able to be reconstituted whenever needed.

The relational ways of depicting relationships are summarized below:

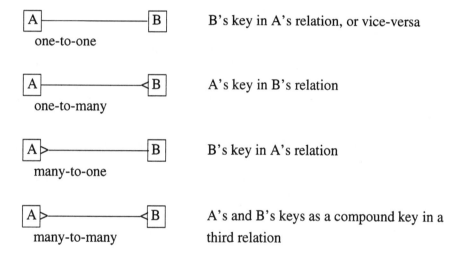

one-to-one	B's key in A's relation, or vice-versa
one-to-many	A's key in B's relation
many-to-one	B's key in A's relation
many-to-many	A's and B's keys as a compound key in a third relation

Note that an "it-to-many" relationship—one or many A to many B—does not require an attribute in A's relation; instead, A's identifier is kept elsewhere to express the relationship.

Let us convert the E-R design of figure 5-10 to a set of relations.

In figure 5-10, the entities INDICATOR, PAGE, CONCEPT, and ENTRY are given. Let the identifier String be the key for the relation INDICATOR. Since INDICATOR has many-to-many relationship with CONCEPT, there must be a CONCEPT_INDICATOR relation:

CONCEPT_INDICATOR (String, ConceptID).

There is no need for the INDICATOR (String) relation, since it has only its identifier. Since INDICATOR has a many-to-*many* relationship with PAGE, no page identifier should be put in the CONCEPT relation.

Let PAGE have the identifier Page#. All its relationships are many-to-*many*, so it has only its identifier. Its relation can be omitted (Page# becomes an attribute in other relations).

CONCEPT has the identifier ConceptID. All its relationships are one-to-*many* or many-to-*many*, so it has only its identifier (its pages, indicators, or entries cannot be listed in its table because in each case there are many). Its relation can be omitted.

Let ENTRY have EntryText, whose value will be the actual text string of the entry, as its identifier. (Sophisticated indexing systems split this into head and subentries with their own structure; let us simply allow such entries as "Depreciation; straight-line" and "Depreciation; declining-balance" to be properly assembled by the application software.) EntryText is the key, and the many-to-*one* relationship with CONCEPT requires ConceptID to be an attribute.

ENTRY(<u>EntryText</u>, ConceptID)

Figure 5-10 shows the many-to-many relationships CONCORDANCE, CONCEPT_LOCATION, and INDEX. To link its entities, CONCORDANCE has the double key String and Page#.

CONCORDANCE(<u>String</u>, <u>Page#</u>)

Similarly CONCEPT_LOCATION would have the structure (<u>ConceptID</u>, <u>Page#</u>). Since the page numbers for each indicator (in CONCORDANCE) and the concept for each indicator (in INDICATOR) imply the page number for each concept, CONCEPT_LOCATION is merely a *view*. Also, it links two entities whose relations are to be omitted, so it may be omitted.

INDEX has the structure (<u>EntryText</u>, <u>Page#</u>). Since the page numbers for each concept (in the view CONCEPT_LOCATION) and the entries for each concept (in ENTRY) imply the page numbers for each entry, INDEX is merely a *view*. Since INDEX is the finished product, it will be shown.

View: INDEX(<u>EntryText</u>, <u>Page#</u>)

5.4.4.4 Relational Diagrams

A relational diagram documents all of a relational design except domains. It shows the names, attribute names, and keys of every relation in a database, and it indicates graphically the relationships among relations. It does not show domains—meanings, formats, and restrictions on relation names, attribute names, and attribute values; nor does it show data contents (values of attributes).

Using the same notation for maximum and minimum cardinality as is used for E-R diagrams, a relational diagram shows relationships in terms of how many rows (tuples) of one relation can or must exist for each row of another relation. The maximum cardinality at relation A for its relationship with relation B is shown by a crow's foot (many) or absence of a crow's foot (one) at A; the minimum cardinality is shown by an oval or circle (zero) or a hash mark (one) at A.

These relationships are nearly always many-to-one or one-to-many, with the key of the "one" relation as an attribute of the "many" relation. One-to-one relationships sometimes occur, and two relations can have the same key (e.g., a MEAL table giving specifications of the meals in a hospital cafeteria and a TODAY_MEAL table giving inventory and delivery information for today's meals). Many-to-many relationships occur only in cases where a relation is omitted for lack of attributes other than an identifier (e.g., a JOB table lists a required certification code for each job available and a CANDIDATE table lists the certification code for each candidate, and there is no need for a certification-code table).

E50. **Draw a relational diagram for the book-indexing tool database developed at the end of section 5.4.4.3.**

Recall that three relations and a view were developed:

CONCEPT_INDICATOR (String, <u>ConceptID</u>)

ENTRY(<u>EntryText</u>, ConceptID)

CONCORDANCE(<u>String</u>, <u>Page#</u>)

INDEX(<u>EntryText</u>, <u>Page#</u>) *(view)*

We must display these items so as to show the relationships among them and provide links with maximum and minimum cardinality indicators. Note that CONCEPT_INDICATOR and ENTRY are linked by the nonkey attribute ConceptID. This is a many-to-many link since the CONCEPT relation is omitted; there are many indicators for each entry and many entries for each indicator. (If CONCEPT were retained, the links would be as in figure 5-10.) We will have minimum cardinality of zero at the INDICATOR end because an entry could be defined without an indicator. (Figure 5-10 shows that although every entry has a concept, not every concept has an indicator.) Minimum cardinality is zero at the ENTRY end also, because not every defined concept necessarily ends up being found in the book. (Figure 5-10 shows that although every indicator has a concept, not every concept has an entry.)

CONCORDANCE and the INDEX view are linked by the Page# attribute. The link is many-to-many because PAGE is omitted. Let the minimum cardinality be zero at the INDEX end since not every concept has an entry. Minimum cardinality is one at the CONCORDANCE end since a row of INDEX (an entry and page number) cannot be generated unless at least one indicator of the entry was found on the page.

CONCEPT_INDICATOR and CONCORDANCE are linked by the String attribute. The relationship is many concept-string instances to many concordance instances. (Those instances give all the pages on which a given indicator string appears.) Each row in CONCORDANCE refers to one or more rows in CONCEPT_INDICATOR that have the same string, and such a string must exist, so the maximum cardinality is one at the CONCEPT_INDICATOR end. Minimum cardinality is zero at the CONCORDANCE end, since it is possible to find that no page in the book contains a given string.

ENTRY and the INDEX view are linked by the EntryText attribute. The link is one-to-many, with minimum cardinality of one at the Entry end and zero at the INDEX end.

We use the standard notation for relational diagrams, which puts each relation in a box. Although the links arise through specific attributes, the links are *not* necessarily drawn to point to the specific attributes; they link boxes (relations as a whole), not specific attribute names.

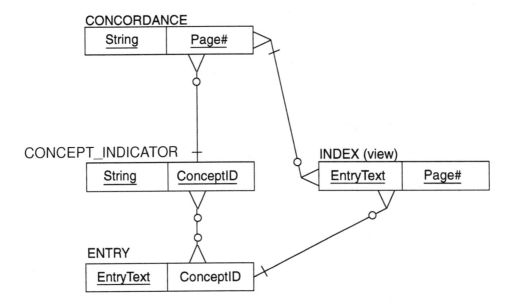

Figure 5-12. Relational Diagram for Indexing-tool Database (E50).

5.4.4.5 Database Management Systems (DBMS)

A database management system (DBMS) is a software product that historically provides the following capabilities:

- To define and modify the structure of a database
- To fill a database with data
- To insert, update, and delete data in a database
- To process logically complicated queries from a database
- To support database application-program development
- To generate reports from a database
- To support database administration and security

However, as of 1992 it became true that any new DBMS also constitutes a complete application programming language.

The heart of a DBMS is its *engine*, which processes logical I/O requests and converts them to physical I/O requests sent by the DBMS to the computer's operating system, which in turn sends I/O commands to the storage devices. Besides the engine, the DBMS consists of various *utilities* that interact with users (interactive application users, system developers, data administrators) and with application programs.

The main benefit of a DBMS is that it allows programmers to deal with data in logical rather than physical terms. Consider, for example, a program written in a third generation (procedural) language (Pascal, C, Fortran, Basic, APL). If the program reads and writes data to files, the programmer must design the structure of the files, keep track of exactly where data is kept within the designed structure, and arrange for the application program to issue physical I/O requests to the operating system at run time. By contrast, with a DBMS the only thing the programmer deals with for file I/O are table names, attribute names, and data values.

For example, from Suzie's database (section 5.4.3), consider the application function of determining the total cost of the ingredients that go into a hamburger dish. With or without a DBMS, the application developer would previously have designed files that could archive the relevant data somehow. A comparison of the development effort to provide the application function without and with a DBMS is shown below.

Without a DBMS:

Declare a subroutine that will be passed a dish code

Write a statement to read the recipe file

Write a statement to read the ingredients file

Write the logic to extract the dish's ingredients and quantities from the local copy of the recipe file, and to count how many there are

Write the logic to extract the resulting ingredients' costs from the local copy of the ingredients file

Write the logic of a loop to multiply each ingredient's quantity by its cost, and to sum the results

Provide for invoking the subroutine and passing the dish code

With a DBMS:

Write the following SQL query:

```
select sum (IQUAN*ICOST)
from RECIPE, INGRED
where RECIPE.ICODE =
INGRED.ICODE and
DCODE = '&dish';
```

Provide for invoking the command and passing the dish code

Software products with the trademarked names Oracle, Informix, Access, Foxbase, and dBaseIV are examples of modern DBMS. They provide linkages with commonly used programming languages either through *precompilers* (e.g., SQL commands are written within Pascal source code, and the precompiler translates the result to pure Pascal source code) or through integration of SQL and other database-manipulating interactive tools within an interactive language (e.g., Microsoft provides as part of its Access DBMS the Access Basic language, which is an extended version of Microsoft Basic that includes database functions).

5.4.4.6 Structured Query Language (SQL)

The universal language for database manipulation is the Structured Query Language (SQL). (The common pronunciation of SQL, originally "sequel," is now "ess-cue-ell.") It handles only database definition and maintenance tasks, I/O tasks (plus minimal mathematics but no procedural logic) for applications, minimal report-generation tasks, and minimal database administration and security tasks.

SQL will be reviewed in terms of the DBMS capabilities listed at the beginning of this section. SQL commands are issued either interactively by the user (typically by running a saved command) or by a running application program.

1.   To define and modify the structure of a database:

The command **describe catalog** returns the structure of the catalog. The catalog is a table (a relation) like any other, but it lists all the tables in the user's database. From the results of this command (a list of all the catalog's attribute names and their data types), suppose you see that the table-name attribute is TABLENAME. Then the command **select tablename from catalog** will return a list of the names of all the tables in the database. To see the structure of a given table, the DISH table in Suzie's database for example, the command **describe dish** will return the structure. Recall that the DISH table has the structure (<u>DCODE</u>, DNAME, DPRICE). The result of the command will be a report saying that the table has the attribute DCODE with values that are of the type CHAR(2), that is, two-character strings (recall the data consists of values such as 'HE' and 'HB'); that DNAME is of the type CHAR(12); that DPRICE is of type NUMBER(5.2), that is, a five-digit number with two digits after the decimal; and that DCODE is identified as having the NOT NULL restriction. This is because DCODE is the key of the table, and the only "awareness" of key status that a DBMS has is that a row cannot exist if the attributes declared as NOT NULL do not have values. As this paragraph has shown, an SQL user is bootstrapped to the task of getting oriented to a strange existing database.

Given a relational design and an empty database (to empty a database of table TOOLS, issue the command **drop table tools**), try to define a table (the RECIPE table in Suzie's database for example). Issue the following command: **create table recipe (dcode char(2) not null, icode char(2) not null, iquan number(3))**. This is the same information that will be reported if you later issue the command **describe recipe** (DCODE has 2 characters and must not be null, and so forth).

Commands for modifying table structures are not reviewed here. A view is just like a table, except that it is retained in the system as a set of rules for reconstituting it from data in other tables. The command **create view inventory as select...** would provide the rules for getting the view's data each time it is used; it can be used just as if it were a table.

2. *To fill a database with data:*

Once a table has been created, it can be filled with data. The "insert" command appends a row to a table. Let it have parameters and issue it repeatedly with various values. For example, if the command **insert into recipe values ('&dishcode', '&ingredcode', '&ingrequan')** is saved under the name FILLREC (**save fillrec** does this in Oracle), then **run fillrec HE GB 1** would put in the first row. ("*Save*," "*run*," and so forth are not SQL but DBMS-specific commands.) SQL does not have commands to import data from spreadsheets, but DBMSs do provide such capabilities. Note that although names and commands are not case sensitive ("INSERT INTO RECIPE" and "insert into recipe" are the same), data is case sensitive (the hamburger code 'HE' is not 'hE' or 'he').

3. *To insert, update, and delete data in a database:*

SQL's command **insert** for inserting rows has already been reviewed. To change a value in the database, the **update** command is used. For example, let us change the cost of an egg (ICODE value EG in the INGRED table) from $0.06 to $0.07. Since we want to put 0.07 in the EG row, the command **update ingred set icost = 0.07 where icode = 'EG'** will do it. More advanced updates (e.g., adding 10% to all prices except that of cheese) can be made by using SQL's ability to accept an *expression* or a *subquery* after the equals signs. Of course, $<, >, \geq$ (usually as >=), etc. can be used instead of = where appropriate.

To delete a row in a table or to delete all rows meeting a condition, use an SQL command such as **delete ingred where icode = 'CH'** to delete the cheese row, or **delete ingred where icost < 0.08 and icode <> 'EG'** to delete all rows for cheap ingredients except eggs. (<> is used for $\neq$ in most systems.)

4. *To process logically complicated queries from a database:*

Logically complicated queries are SQL's strength. The **select** command, which is used for all queries, has the basic syntax

> **select** <attribute list>
> **from** <table or join>
> **where** <condition>

The attribute list is * for all attributes, or a list of attribute names, or a list of expressions (simple mathematical or logical functions of attribute names). The command **select * from dish** will return the whole DISH table. The command **select dcode, dprice from dish** will return only the two listed columns:

DCODE	DPRICE
HE	1.75
HB	1.30
CB	1.65
WO	1.30

To illustrate expressions, from the table PROPERTY(ParcelNum, SellPrice, SqFt) that lists selling prices and floorspace, the command **select parcelnum, sellprice/sqft from property** would return the price per square foot for every property.

Instead of a table name or a view name after **from**, a query can have a list of two or more tables separated by commas. Such a list, and subsequent conditions after **where**, specify a *join* of two or more tables. To review a join, recall the three tables displayed below in the frapdubers database from example E47:

FRAPBASE	(Type	BasePrice)	FRAPSIZE	(Size	SizePrem)
	plain	3		large	2
	ridged	4		small	0

FRAPCOLOR	(Color	ColorPrem)
	red	0
	blue	3

The cartesian product of the three tables, denoted FRAPBASE, FRAPSIZE, and FRAPCOLOR, would have attributes Type, BasePrice, Size, SizePrem, Color, and ColorPrem, and eight rows of data (comprised of every combination of rows) as follows: (plain 3 large 2 red 0), (plain 3 large 2 blue 3), (plain 3 small 0 red 0), (plain 3 small 0 blue 3), (ridged 4 large 2 red 0), (ridged 4 large 2 blue 3), (ridged 4 small 0 red 0), (ridged 4 small 0 blue 3). A join is those rows from a cartesian product that meet conditions. For example, the command **select * from frapbase, frapsize, frapcolor where type = 'ridged' and size = 'large' and color = 'red'** would return only one row:

TYPE	BASEPRICE	SIZE	SIZEPREM	COLOR	COLORPREM
ridged	4	large	2	red	0

Incidentally, if the * in the foregoing command were replaced by **baseprice + sizeprem + colorprem** the result would be the total price (6) of a ridged, large, red frapduber.

Most joins are of tables that share attributes. For example, recall the two tables from the solution to example E48:

EMP_MEAL	(SSN	Meal	Quan)		MEAL_VAL	(Meal	Value)
	41	Br	4			Br	3.50
	41	Lu	5			Lu	4.80
	42	Lu	6			Su	7.50
	44	Su	5				
	47	Su	4				
	62	Su	6				
	72	Br	4				
	71	Br	4				
	72	Su	4				

Suppose we want to determine the total values of meals of each type given to employee 41. The cartesian product (EMP_MEAL, MEAL_VAL) has many meaningless rows—all the rows where the part from EMP_MEAL is for one meal and the part from MEAL_VAL is for another. But these meaningless rows can be eliminated by the condition that the values in the two meal columns for a row are the same: emp_meal.meal = meal_val.meal. (Note the use of the table name before a decimal point to identify which table an attribute comes from if attribute names are identical in two tables.) We will also have the condition that it is employee 41, and we will use the expression **Quan*Value**. The SQL command is

```
select emp_meal.meal, quan*val
from emp_meal, meal_val
where emp_meal.meal = meal_val.meal
and ssn = 41
```

The result will be

MEAL	QUAN*VALUE
Br	14.00
Lu	24.00

SQL has the following group functions which give results that combine rows: sum, avg, max, min, count, stddev, and variance. For example, the total value of meals of all kinds provided to employee 41 is returned by the following command:

select sum(quan*value)
from emp_meal, meal_val
where emp_meal.meal = meal_val.meal
and ssn = 41

The result is 38.00.

An SQL *subquery* is a command, enclosed in parentheses, that returns a result and is treated as if it were the result. For example, the foregoing command, in parentheses, could be imbedded as a subquery in an SQL command (or imbedded as a subquery in a subquery, to any number of levels). A query can use a subquery as part of an expression or part of a condition such as **where mealallowance > (select...)**. This is the same as **where mealallowance > 38.00**. Subqueries are often used after the word "in," as in the SQL phrase "where ssn in (select...)." In this phrase, the subquery would be one that returns social security numbers for the desired group of employees.

The word **distinct** or **unique** can be placed immediately after **select** to prevent returning duplicate rows. After **where**, not only can there be **and** clauses but also **or** clauses. Use parentheses to make the meaning clear in a sequence of **and**'s and **or**'s.

5.   *To support database application-program development:*
SQL supports program development only in the senses of providing a standard way to express query logic and providing commands to replace *read* and *write* logic in programs.

6.   *To generate reports from a database:*
SQL queries have minimal formatting capabilities. Every DBMS has a report-generating utility, but these utilities are not standardized.

7. *To support database administration and security:*

The SQL command **grant select, update on part_inventory to zelda identified by xx447**, for example, grants to a user having username *zelda* and password *xx447* the right to issue **select** commands and **update** commands (that is, both to see and to change data) in the *part_inventory* table.

E51.   The following relational tables store data on parts, on vendors, and on which vendors can supply which parts:

VENDOR(<u>VID</u> Phone)   PART(<u>PID</u> Weight)   VENDOR_PART(<u>VID</u> <u>PID</u> Cost)

VENDOR		PART		VENDOR_PART		
101	5551428	PIN	2	101	PIN	82
102	5558892	BOLT	20	101	BOLT	99
129	5557411	NUT	13	102	PIN	93
				102	NUT	77
				129	NUT	75

Write an SQL command that returns a list of telephone numbers for vendors who can supply pins.

The command can use either a subquery or a join. Using a subquery, the condition would be that VID would be *in* a list of vendors returned by a subquery. This would be simply those vendors in the VENDOR_PART table having 'PIN' as the PID value in their row. To avoid returning a list giving the same vendor more than once, it is good practice to use the *unique* qualifier in the subquery. The main query would be from the VENDOR table, which has a row for each vendor, so *unique* would not be used there.

        select Phone
        from VENDOR
        where VID in
                (select unique VID
                from VENDOR_PART
                where PID = 'PIN')

Using a join:

        select unique Phone
        from VENDOR, VENDOR_PART
        where VENDOR.VID = VENDOR_PART.VID
        and PID = 'PIN'

E52a.   **Refer to Suzie's database from section 5.4.3. Write an SQL command to list the name of every ingredient in a hamburger given the DCODE value 'HB'.**

The ingredients in a hamburger are the ones having ICODE values in the same row of the RECIPE table where DCODE is 'HB'. A subquery can return these ICODE values and a query from the INGRED table can list the corresponding INAME values:

```
select iname
from ingred
where icode in
        (select icode
        from recipe
        where dcode = 'HB')
```

Alternatively, if the INGRED and RECIPE tables are joined, the rows having the same ICODE in both ICODE columns and having 'HB' in the DCODE column would have the desired INAME values:

```
select iname
from ingred, recipe
where ingred.icode = recipe.icode
and dcode = 'HB'
```

E52b. Extending the foregoing example, write a command to list the name of every ingredient in an arbitrary dish, starting not with its code but with its name. Let the name be given as parameter '&dishname'.

Using subqueries, simply substitute a subquery for 'HB' in the command:

```
select iname
from ingred
where icode in
        (select icode
        from recipe
        where dcode =
                (select dcode
                from dish
                where dname = '&dishname'))
```

Using a join, we must bring the DISH table into the join. Now the meaningful rows are those having not only the same ICODEs in the two ICODE columns but also the same DCODES in the two DCODE columns:

```
select iname
from ingred, recipe, dish
where ingred.icode = recipe.icode
and recipe.dcode = dish.dcode
and dname = '&dishname'
```

E52c. Extending the foregoing examples, write a command to return the total cost of all the ingredients in a Western Omelet, starting with the 'WO' dish code.

The cost of a particular ingredient in a dish is its quantity (IQUAN in the RECIPE table) multiplied by its unit cost (ICOST in the INGRED table). The expression **iquan*icost** can be used. Both IQUAN and ICOST must be in the same table, so the two tables should be joined. (Whenever the **select** line of a query refers to attributes from more than one table, a join is required, so the subquery approach will not work here.) The sum over all rows of this column expression is the desired result, so the **sum** group function can be used:

> **select sum(iquan*icost)**
> **from recipe, ingred**
> **where recipe.icode = ingred.icode**
> **and dcode = 'WO'**

Chapter 6
Optimization
and Scheduling

This chapter reviews optimization and scheduling methodologies that industrial engineers use in production planning and design, production scheduling, inventory control, project scheduling and control, layout, and location analysis. Some of the methods are quite general and can be applied to many application areas; dynamic programming, for example, is used in design, production, inventory, scheduling, and other applications. Other methods, such as PERT and lot-size models, are application-specific. An attempt to review such a wide variety of techniques with any completeness or evenness would be foolhardy; instead, the selected techniques constitute an attempt to match what has most often been covered in actual IE PE Exams.

6.1 Production Planning and Scheduling

A *production system* utilizes facilities and labor, and perhaps other resources, to process raw materials and component parts into finished products. Production takes place at production centers that perform operations. The sequence of production centers through which the materials flow in becoming a product is a *routing*.

Material waiting to be processed or being processed constitutes *in-process inventory* or work in progress (WIP). There is also finished-product inventory. Packaging is done either as the last step in production or as the first step in distribution.

6.1.1 Production Planning and Design

Demand drives production, whether the product is produced to inventory or produced to order. Forecasting of demand will be covered in section 6.1.3. Given demand and classes of resources, production-planning problems concern which classes of resources to apply. Given demand and potential facilities, production-design problems concern selection and sizing of facilities to acquire or activate. Production scheduling—the choice of which particular resources to apply and when—will be covered in section 6.1.2.

In a *serial production process*, a product passes through a given sequence of *stages*—either production centers or operations. Let there be N stages, and let them be numbered $n = 1, 2,..., N$ from first to last. Let x_n represent the flow rate *entering* stage n, in units of product per time period. The demand flow rate is x_{N+1} (the flow rate leaving the last stage N and entering the non-stage $N+1$). Let each stage have a *scrap rate* q_n; the stage processes x_n units per time period, but $q_n x_n$ units per time period are scrapped, so that the next stage processes $x_{n+1} = x_n \times (1-q_n)$ units per time period.

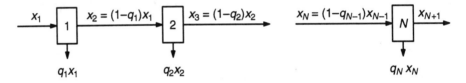

Figure 6-1. An *N*-stage Serial Production Process.

Equation 6-1 gives the number of units (we will stop saying "per time period") that must enter stage n to meet a demand $x_{N+1} \geq D$.

$$x_n = \frac{x_{N+1}}{(1-q_n)(1-q_{n+1}) \ldots (1-q_N)} \geq \frac{D}{(1-q_n)(1-q_{n+1}) \ldots (1-q_N)} \qquad (6-1)$$

For example, suppose a 10-stage production process has a scrap rate of 2% at each stage. How many units per hour must be started in stage 1 to meet a demand of 40 good units per hour? Note that equation 6-1 has $N - n + 1$ factors in its denominator. Here $N = 10$, $D = 40$, $n = 1$, and there are 10 factors, each equal to 0.98, so the answer is $x_1 = 40 / (0.98)^{10} = 48.955 \approx$ <u>49 units per hour</u>.

For $n = 1, 2,..., N$, let u_n represent the capacity of stage n, so that the processing rate at stage n is limited by

$$x_n \leq u_n, \quad n = 1, 2,..., N \qquad (6-2)$$

Production systems can be *continuous* or *intermittent*. A continuous production system produces a large volume of a single product or a family of closely related products. All products (if there is more than one) have the same routing, and the production centers are laid out according to this routing. A continuous production system can be *paced*, in which case there is no WIP inventory and the production rate must continuously be exactly the same at each stage. An *assembly line* is an example of a paced continuous production system. There is a *cycle time* denoted $c = 1/x_{N+1}$, and a paced process strictly requires $x_n = 1/c$ for every stage n. On the other hand, if sufficient WIP inventory is provided between successive stages, a continuous production process requires only the same overall average production rate at each stage. A slow stage can produce makeahead WIP on overtime; during the continuous production hours, the previous stage can produce partly to WIP, and the succeeding stage can produce partly from WIP. The amount of WIP required after a slow stage is simply the deficit in its production rate multiplied by the time between WIP replenishments. WIP also provides a buffer for random variations in production rate. The queueing models reviewed in chapter 4 (section 4.4) provide methods to determine the required additional amounts of WIP for this purpose.

E53a.   **A four-stage serial production process has a 6% scrap rate at each stage. It is fairly well balanced: the production rates are 20, 24, 19, and 18 units per hour at stages 1, 2, 3, and 4, respectively. The process is paced, with no WIP inventory. Determine the maximal production rate.**

Let x_i represent the flow in units per hour entering stage i; x_5 is the flow of finished units out of stage 4.

$$x_1 \le 20 \quad \Rightarrow \quad x_5 \le (0.94)^4 20 \quad \Rightarrow \quad x_5 \le 15.615$$
$$x_2 \le 24 \quad \Rightarrow \quad x_5 \le (0.94)^3 24 \quad \Rightarrow \quad x_5 \le 19.934$$
$$x_3 \le 19 \quad \Rightarrow \quad x_5 \le (0.94)^2 19 \quad \Rightarrow \quad x_5 \le 16.788$$
$$x_4 \le 18 \quad \Rightarrow \quad x_5 \le (0.94)18 \quad \Rightarrow \quad x_5 \le 16.92$$

Limited by stage 1, the maximal production rate is <u>15.615 units per hour</u>.

Some engineers define cycle times for each stage of a process, but "the" cycle time is $c = 1/x_{N+1}$, the average time required to produce one good unit of product out of the last stage N. The *throughput time*, T, is the average time spent by a unit from entering stage 1 to leaving stage N. Let W_n be the long-run average waiting time in the WIP queue waiting to enter stage n (this is W_q from section 4.4). Since the arrival rate to the WIP between stages $n-1$ and n is $1/c$, the average WIP contents is $L_n = W_n/c$; conversely, if an average WIP inventory of L_n units is kept before stage n, the average WIP dwell time is $W_n = cL_n$. There are $N-1$ possible WIP locations before each stage except the first. Thus the throughput time is

$$T = Nc + \sum_{n=2}^{N} W_n = Nc + c\sum_{n=2}^{N} L_n = \left[N + \sum_{n=2}^{N} L_n\right] \times c \qquad (6\text{-}3)$$

E53b.   **For the foregoing example, determine the cycle time and the throughput time at the maximal production rate.**

$$c = 1/x_s = 1/15.615 \approx \underline{0.064 \text{ hr.}} \quad T = 4c \approx \underline{0.256 \text{ hr.}}$$

E53c.   **For the foregoing example, let there be an average WIP inventory of 30 units kept between each pair of stages. With these buffers, recompute the throughput time at the maximal production rate.**

The four-stage process has three buffers with average contents $L_2 = L_3 = L_4 = 30$. From equation 6-3 with $c = 1/15.615$, $T = 4c + c\times(30+30+30) \approx \underline{6.02 \text{ hr.}}$

In contrast to continuous production systems, which are useful for single or related products, there are *intermittent production systems*, which occur when different products must be made, so that a given processing center performs a given set of operations on different products. If most of the products have similar routings, the facility can be laid out as a *flow shop*; for example, if various metal parts are first cut on a lathe and then finished on a grinder, the shop may be laid out to conserve material handling cost by placing lathes and grinders so that incoming material flows first to a lathe, then a grinder, then out. Otherwise the facilities can be laid out functionally; for example, several machines that can be operated by the same machinists may be placed together. This arrangement is called a *job shop*.

When parallel resources can be used at a production center in a continuous production system, or when there is a forecasted demand for resources in a flow shop or job shop, there is a basic design problem called the *capacity balancing* problem. In example E53a, for instance, the production rates were 20, 24, 19, and 18 units per hour, and after correction for scrap rates, the solution showed that the capacities in terms of good finished units were 15.615, 19.934, 16.788, and 16.92 units per hour for stages 1, 2, 3, and 4, respectively. These capacities are not perfectly balanced; stages 2, 3, and 4 have unused capacity compared to stage 1. Given a demand D_n for production center n, either in terms of units it processes or in terms of finished units, and given its capacity m_n on the same basis as D_n, the number of machines needed is determined by rounding up D_n/m_n. But rounding up is usually not done if the ratio is barely greater than an integer, because estimates of capacities and demands are usually not perfectly accurate.

If M_n machines or units of resource are provided at a production center and the number of machines or units needed is D_n/m_n, then the utilization at the production center is $U_n = (D_n/m_n)/M_n$. $1-U_n$ is the idle proportion of machines or resources. Sometimes it is meaningful to define an average utilization for an entire process, but not unless the resources at each center are roughly comparable in cost, because utilization of more expensive machines is more important than utilization of cheaper ones.

E53d. **In the situation of the foregoing three examples, let there be a new forecasted demand for 20 units per hour. Let stage 1 consist of 5 machines in parallel, each with a capacity of 4 units per hour (3.123 finished units per hour); let stage 2 consist of 6 machines in parallel, each with a capacity of 4 units per hour (3.322 finished units per hour); let stage 3 consist of 5 machines in parallel, each with a capacity of 3.8 units per hour (3.358 finished units per hour); and let stage 4 consist of 9 machines, each with a capacity of 2 units per hour (1.880 finished units per hour). Determine how many machines must be added to meet the new forecasted demand, and compare the new machine balance with the existing balance.**

Stage 1: $20 \div 3.123 \approx 6.40 \rightarrow 7$.   Add 2 machines to the existing 5 at stage 1.

Stage 2: $20 \div 3.322 \approx 6.02 \rightarrow 6$.   Do not round up. Keep the existing 6 at stage 2.

Stage 3: $20 \div 3.358 \approx 5.96 \rightarrow 6$.   Add 1 machine to the existing 5 at stage 3.

Stage 4: $20 \div 1.880 \approx 10.64 \rightarrow 11$.   Add 2 to the existing 9 at stage 4.

The utilizations are approximately 91.5%, 100.3%, 99.3%, and 96.7%.

See section 6.3.2 for a dynamic production-planning model.

6.1.2 Line Balancing

An assembly line has rigid movement of a workpiece from one workstation to the next. No scrap is allowed; any appreciable damage or nonperformance causes the whole line to stop. Risky tasks, tasks that have uncertain performance times, and tasks that simply do not fit comfortably into the whole are done off line. At each workstation, the workpiece arrives from the previous station with clockwork regularity, and material to be added to the workpiece is available in bulk or arrives from off line with the workpiece or slightly in advance of need. For example, the assembly line in an automobile assembly plant may consist of 40 equally spaced workstations. At one station, the steering-wheel assembly is fitted into the car. This assembly, built offline, consists of the steering wheel and steering column, with gearshift lever, directional-signal controls, and ignition lock, all included in a one-piece assembly. The cycle time may be 60 seconds. This may be more time than is needed to bring the assembly in position, place it, and make the mechanical connection to the steering mechanism. Accordingly, the engineer may add some tasks that are convenient to do here, such as connecting the electrical leads to a wiring harness that is already in place. Conversely, if the cycle time is too short for the required tasks, the engineer may be able to identify a task that can be done at the previous station, or at the following station, or offline. Such reassignments of tasks to other stations constitute *line balancing*. (The engineer may also go beyond line balancing and redesign tasks or provide new tools or methods to make them easier.)

The approximate number of stations is set by engineering and management considerations. Apportioning the work among k stations will cause idle time resulting in a balance delay if the tasks cannot be grouped such that each station has exactly $1/k$th of the work, but with just one station there is no idle time or balance delay. Volvo has made cars that way, in fact: a crew builds the whole car at one station. However, this means that the crew members must each have many different skills, and the station cannot be set up permanently to do a certain thing; for example, if the best way to add the engine to the assembly is to lower it into the chassis by crane, a station dedicated to that task could have the crane permanently mounted, whereas at a single huge station the crane would have to be moved to and from the car or the car would have to be moved to and from the crane. Otherwise a permanent crane would interfere with facilities needed for other tasks. Thus we see that dividing a process into stations avoids setups and simplifies work.

To handle the more routine aspects of line balancing, computerized mathematical methods are available. Consider the following *single-product line-balancing model*:

There is a set of n tasks, numbered $i = 1, 2,..., n$, to be performed on each workpiece. The ith task has a duration or *processing time p_i*. None of the tasks can be performed in parallel, so if there were only one workstation the cycle time would be the sum of all the processing times. If there are k workstations, and there is a cycle time c, then the throughput time is $T = kc$, and the *idle time* per cycle (that is, per workpiece) is

$$I = kc - \sum_{i=1}^{n} p_i \tag{6-4}$$

There is a minimum number of required stations k_{min}. (Otherwise the trivial answer to the problem would always be to have just one station, since that would give zero idle time; but if there were just one station, it would have greater processing times than the estimated ones.)

There are *precedences*: task r is a *precedessor* of task s if task r must be performed at a workstation that is not downstream of the workstation at which task s is performed. Figure 6-2 displays the precedences and task times for a nine-task line-balancing example problem.

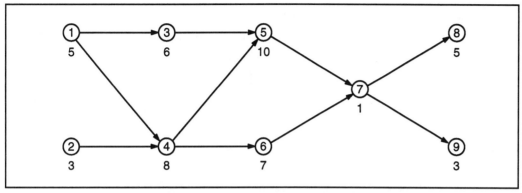

Figure 6-2. Precedence Diagram for Line-balancing Example.

In figure 6-2 the circles represent tasks and the arrows represent precedences. The numbers inside the circles are task identifiers $\{i\}$, and the numbers below the circles are task processing times $\{p_i\}$. (Figure 6-2 is a *precedence diagram*; for line balancing, a precedence diagram is more convenient than the arrow diagram used in project scheduling, in which tasks are represented by arrows and precedences by their relative placement.) In the example problem shown in figure 6-2, the sum of the processing times is $\Sigma_i p_i = 48$.

The single-product line-balancing problem is to assemble the n tasks into $k \geq k_{min}$ stations so as to obey precedences and minimize I.

Since the cycle time c shared by all stations cannot be less than the greatest single processing time $p_{max} = \max\{p_i\}$, there is an *upper bound on k*: the number of stations should be no more than $k_{max} = \Sigma_i p_i / p_{max}$. In the example, the greatest single processing time is 10, so $k \leq 48/10 = 4.8 \approx 5$ stations; a greater number of stations would be unbalanced because the smallest total of task times at a station would necessarily be less than 10.

The recommended procedure is to perform a balance for various feasible numbers of stations k between k_{min} and k_{max}. The sequence of balances can start either with k_{min} or with a k that has the potential to achieve a perfect balance. For each k, the modified Kilbridge and Webster line-balancing heuristic can be used to seek a good balance; this is the only line-balancing method we will review here.

Each use of the modified Kilbridge and Webster line-balancing heuristic starts with a fixed cycle time c. Since equation 6-4 with $I = 0$ implies that a perfect balance has $kc = \Sigma_i p_i$, the upper bound on k translates to a *lower bound on the cycle time*: $c \geq \Sigma_i p_i / k_{max}$. Similarly, an *upper bound on the cycle time* is the sum of the processing times divided by k_{min}: $c \leq \Sigma_i p_i / k_{min}$. Supposing the processing times $\{p_i\}$ to be integer, the only possible numbers of stations that could give a perfect balance (zero idle time) are integer values of $\Sigma_i p_i / c$ where c is between its lower and upper bounds. To find these, express $\Sigma_i p_i$ as a product of prime numbers and divide by its partial products.

In the example, there are 9 tasks having processing times $\{p_i\} = \{5, 3, 6, 8, 10, 7, 1, 5, 3\}$. Let at least $k_{min} = 3$ stations be required to keep facilities from being too crowded and skill requirements too broad. The sum $\Sigma_i p_i = 48$ has prime factors $2 \times 2 \times 2 \times 2 \times 3$. Among these, the partial products are 2, 3, 4, 6, 8, 12, 16, 24. Since c must be at least $p_{max} = 10$ and not greater than $48/3 = 16$, we see that the possible k values of $48/12 = 4$ stations or $48/16 = 3$ stations are the only feasible numbers of stations that could give a perfect balance. The number of stations should be no more than $k \le \Sigma_i p_i / p_{max} = 4.8 \approx 5$, so we must use the modified Kilbridge and Webster procedure only for cycle times corresponding to $k = 3$, 4, and 5; for $k = 3$ and 4 the possibility of a perfect balance is not ruled out.

The modified Kilbridge and Webster line-balancing heuristic for k stations:

1. Draw the precedence diagram so that each task is placed as far left as possible and all the precedence arrows are oriented from left to right.

2. Let the intended cycle time corresponding to k be $c = \Sigma_i p_i / k$. If c is not an integer the possibility of a perfect (zero idle time) balance is ruled out.

3. Form all the trial groupings of tasks into station *S1* that meet these conditions:

    3a. No task not in trial grouping G is a predecessor to any task in it.

    3b. The sum of the processing times in *S1* does not exceed c, but would exceed c if another task were added: $\Sigma_{i \in G} p_i \le c$.

4. Of the trial groupings meeting conditions 3a and 3b, let the group having the greatest sum of processing times constitute station *S1*. *S1* is the grouping G^* such that $\Sigma_{i \in G^*} p_i = \max_G (\Sigma_{i \in G} p_i)$. Draw a boundary around *S1*.

5. Call the next station *SJ*. Form all trial groupings G of unassigned tasks that meet these conditions:

    5a. No *unassigned* task is a predecessor to any task in the trial grouping G.

    5b. The sum of the processing times in *SJ* does not exceed c, but would exceed c if another task were added: $\Sigma_{i \in G} p_i \le c$.

6. Of the trial groupings meeting conditions 5a and 5b, let the group having the greatest sum of processing times constitute station *SJ*. *SJ* is the grouping G^* such that $\Sigma_{i \in G^*} p_i = \max_G (\Sigma_{i \in G} p_i)$. Draw a boundary around *SJ*.

7. If any unassigned tasks remain, go to step 5. Otherwise stop. The final number of stations is either k or $k+1$.

Let us apply the modified Kilbridge and Webster procedure to the example for an intended 4 stations. The intended cycle time is $c = 48/4 = 12$. Since this is an integer, the possibility of a perfect balance is not ruled out. For the first station we can try the grouping $\{1, 2\}$, which has $\Sigma_{i \in \{1,2\}} p_i = 8$; we cannot add further tasks to this trial grouping, since the addition of either task 3 or task 4 would make the sum greater than 12. Another trial grouping is $\{1, 3\}$, which has $\Sigma_{i \in \{1,3\}} p_i = 11$; we cannot add further tasks to this trial grouping, since adding task 2 would make the sum greater than 12, and tasks such as task 4 and task 5 have predecessors not in the existing station and thus cannot be added. Of the two trial groupings, since 11 is greater than 8, we establish $\underline{S1 = \{1, 3\}}$.

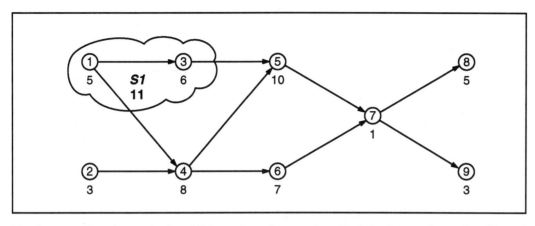

For the second station, tasks 3 and 8 form the only grouping that is both precedence-feasible and cycle-time-feasible. We establish _S2 = {2, 4}_.

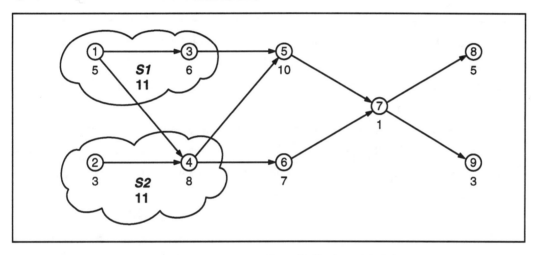

For the third station, the feasible groupings are {5} and {6}, since {5, 6} is not cycle-time-feasible and task 7 cannot be added to either because the other is a predecessor. Since {5} has the larger sum of processing times, establish _S3 = {5}_.

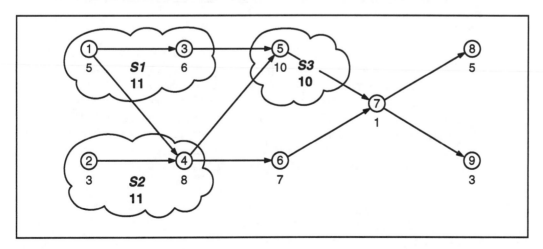

For the fourth station, the only choice is to establish $\underline{S4 = \{6, 7, 9\}}$, and finally {8} is left for the fifth station: $\underline{S5 = \{8\}}$.

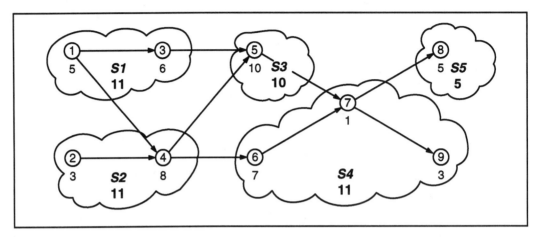

This balance ends with $\underline{5}$ stations, a cycle time of $\underline{11}$ (since 11 is the maximum sum of task times at any station), and, from equation 6-4, an idle time per cycle of $5 \times 11 - 48 = \underline{7}$.

The following variation of the procedure is equivalent to the *original* Kilbridge and Webster heuristic: In steps 3b and 5b, add stations to trial groupings until the task time is *not less* than c, and in steps 4 and 6, select the trial grouping having the *least* sum of processing times. This variation ends in step 7 with either k or $k–1$ stations. In other words, whereas in the modified heuristic tasks were grouped to get at most the intended cycle time, in the original heuristic tasks were grouped to get at least the intended cycle time.

The reader can verify that the original heuristic with an intended number of four stations gives these four stations: $S1 = \{1, 2, 3\}$, $S2 = \{4, 6\}$, $S3 = \{5, 7, 9\}$, and $S4 = \{8\}$. The cycle time for this balance is 15, and the idle time is $4 \times 15 - 48 = 12$.

E54.   The nine tasks having the precedences and processing times shown in figure 6-2 are to be grouped into no fewer than three workstations. Determine the best line balance that can be achieved.

Using the modified Kilbridge and Webster heuristic for $k = 3$ stations, we determine the intended cycle time as 48/3 = 16. For the first station, the feasible groupings are {1, 2, 3} with processing-time sum 14 and {1, 2, 4} with sum 16; thus $S1 = \{1, 2, 4\}$ having a processing-time sum 16. For the second station, the feasible groupings are {3, 5} with sum 16 and {3, 6} with sum 13; thus $S2 = \{3, 5\}$, having a processing-time sum 16. For the third station, the only feasible grouping is $S3 = \{6, 7, 8, 9\}$, having processing-time sum 16. This balance gives 3 stations, a cycle time of 16, and an idle time of $3 \times 16 - 48 = 0$. Since this is a perfect balance, this is the best line balance that can be achieved.

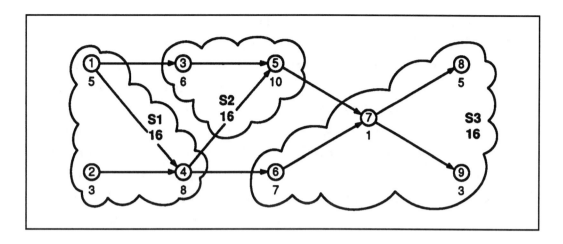

6.1.3 Inventory Control

An *inventory* is a collection of items produced or acquired in advance of demand. Production or acquisition to inventory rather than in direct response to demand yields benefits that include allowing production to occur in runs of economical size, allowing immediate delivery to demand, and avoiding shortages or delays in meeting demand without incurring a need for elaborate prediction of demand and adjustment of production or acquisition. The disbenefits are the costs of keeping and managing inventory. Operating without inventory is called *just-in-time* (JIT) operation, which requires production or acquisition to be very quick and reliable.

Lot-sizing models, which help determine the best size of production runs or acquisitions, are reviewed in section 6.1.3.1. Demand forecasting, which drives several production and inventory models, is reviewed in section 6.1.3.2. Production and inventory planning methods for predictable but dynamic (time-varying) demand are reviewed in section 6.1.3.3. Probabilistic considerations in inventory control are reviewed in section 6.1.3.4.

For each *stockkeeping unit* (SKU) in an inventory system, the number of units currently on hand, x, is also called the *inventory level* of that SKU. There can also be a number of units ordered but not yet on hand, o, and $x+o$ is called the *inventory position* for the SKU (the number of units on hand and soon to be on hand). A unit of an SKU is frequently a carton or case or pallet load. Differently packaged quantities of the same product are different SKUs unless they are interchangable. The age of a unit is very important for food and other perishable products, but will not be treated here. For most products, whether perishable or not, a first in, first out (FIFO) policy is used in managing the individual units of an SKU, but it requires placing in one location and picking from another; an alternative is last in, first out (LIFO), as when items are placed at the front and picked from the front.

The unit of time is the year, or alternatively the month. We will use the year to be specific. For a given SKU the *demand rate* in units per year is denoted D, and the *production rate* in units per year during a production run is denoted P. P is often instantaneous, that is, infinite. The *lot size* or *order quantity*, which is the number of units produced in one run or acquired in one order, is denoted Q. In managing inventory the policy is often expressed in terms of Q and a *reorder point*, r, which is x (or, alternatively, $x+o$) such that when the inventory (or position) is observed to be r or fewer units, a production run is begun or an order is placed for $Q-x+r$ units, which would bring the inventory (or position) up to $Q+r$ units if production were instantaneous and began immediately. For items ordered, there is a *lead time*, which is the time from placement of an order to receipt of the ordered items; for produced units we assume production to begin immediately. Note that if demand and production both occur at steady rates D and P, and production of a lot whose size is Q units is begun when $x = 0$, the maximum inventory will be $Q \times (1 - D/P)$.

6.1.3.1 Lot Sizing (EOQ Models)

Suppose the demand and production rates D and P were known and constant and production runs of Q units each were begun each time the inventory level reached zero. The graph of inventory level as a function of time would appear as in figure 6-3.

Let there be an inventory *holding cost* or carrying cost in dollars per unit per year, denoted h, applied to the average inventory, which is half the maximum inventory, so that the total carrying cost in dollars per year is $(hQ/2)(1 - D/P)$. Note that this cost is proportional to Q. Let there be a *unit production cost* or unit purchase cost in dollars per unit, denoted C, so that the total production or purchase cost in dollars per year is CD. Note that this cost is independent of Q. Let there be a setup cost per production run or a cost of placing and receiving an order, in dollars per run or per order, denoted C_p. Since there are D/Q runs or orders per year, the total setup or order cost in dollars per year is $C_p D/Q$. Note that this cost is inversely proportional to Q.

The problem of choosing Q to minimize the total costs given in this model is the *economic order quantity* (EOQ) or *deterministic lot sizing* problem. Let the *total cost* C_T in dollars per year be defined as the sum of the three costs listed above:

$$C_T \;=\; \frac{hQ}{2}\left(1 - \frac{D}{P}\right) + CD + C_p \frac{D}{Q} \tag{6-5}$$

The C_T is quadratic in Q. Let Q^* be the order quantity or lot size that minimizes this total cost. Q^* is given by equation 6-6.

$$Q^* \;=\; \sqrt{\frac{2C_p D}{h}\left(\frac{1}{1 - D/P}\right)} \tag{6-6}$$

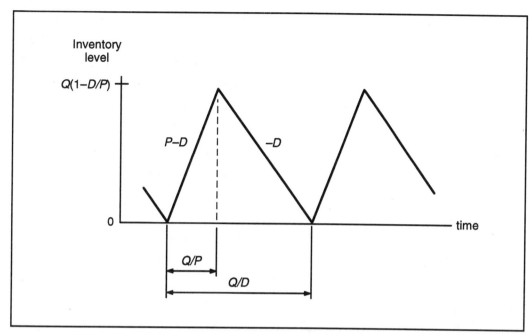

Figure 6-3. Inventory Level Versus Time.

The factor in parentheses is 1 when replenishment is instantaneous. The minimum of C_T is rather shallow; that is, C_T does not increase very much if Q is somewhat greater or smaller than Q^*. The EOQ model is robust; Q^* is a fairly good estimate of the optimal order quantity for real situations that do not exactly fit the assumption of the model, provided that the cost parameters are realistically estimated.

The cost parameters are somewhat challenging to estimate in practical situations. The unit holding cost h should contain the opportunity cost of capital tied up in inventory, iC where i is the annual compound interest rate used in economic decision making (see MARR in chapter 3). It should also contain space rental or building amortization for the portion of space used by a unit. It should contain a share of the costs of lighting, heating, and other utilities for the storage facilities if they are not included in space rental. And it should contain the expected costs of deterioration or pilferage. The setup or ordering cost per run, C_p, should contain those costs of a production run, commonly called setup costs, that are fixed costs of the run (as opposed to variable unit costs, which are contained in C); when the units are being ordered rather than produced, C_p contains all the costs of placing an order, including the fixed part of the costs of receiving the order.

Let T denote the *order period* or time between successive production runs or orders: $T = Q/D$. For example, if $D = 35,000$ units per year and $Q = 15,000$ units per order, then the time between orders is $T = 15/35 = 0.42857$ years. T is often constrained for production-scheduling convenience to be an integer number of months or weeks, or an integer fraction of a year. Thus we would not usually plan to schedule a run every 0.42957 years, but every five months ($T = 0.416$ years) or six months ($T = 0.5$ years). The *period order quantity* (POQ) is determined by first calculating Q^*, then calculating $T^* = Q^*/D$, then rounding T^* to the nearest feasible order period $T_p^* \approx T^*$, and finally determining $[POQ] = T_p^* D$. POQ is a planned quantity; when the actual time comes to place an order or schedule a run, the order or run size will be corrected to subtract the amount actually on hand x and on order o, and also for safety stock or allowable shortage as discussed below.

A shortage occurs when part of the demand cannot be met immediately, and this part is either lost or is *backordered*—scheduled to be met later.

For the case where demand encountering a shortage is lost, we do not allow back orders. We add a *safety stock* of s units of the SKU; s can be set according to probabilistic considerations (section 6.1.3.4). Safety stock incurs a carrying cost hs dollars per year, which is added to C_T. Note that it is not a function of Q, and (like the production or purchase cost CD) does not affect the selection of Q. Safety stock may be viewed as a separate inventory.

For the case where backorders are allowed, let z denote the *unit shortage cost* in dollars per unit per year of delay. For instance, if $z = \$7.41/yr$ and 2300 units per year are backordered for an average of 0.011 year (about four days), the total shortage cost is \$187.473/yr. Let M denote the *allowable number of units back ordered per run*. The inventory level will change with time as shown in figure 6-4, and the total cost C_T will be as given in equation 6-7.

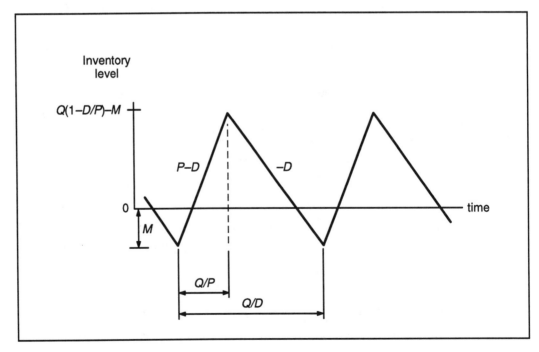

Figure 6-4. Inventory Level Versus Time with Shortages.

$$C_T = \frac{hQ}{2}\left(1 - \frac{D}{P}\right) - hM + CD + C_P\frac{D}{Q} + \frac{M^2}{2Q}\left(\frac{h+z}{1-D/P}\right) \tag{6-7}$$

To verify equation 6-7, note that from the geometry of the graph for each cycle, there is a shortage for the last M/D time units before a production run starts and the first $M/(P-D)$ time units of the production run, and the average shortage while there is one is $M/2$ units; also, there are D/Q cycles per year. As may be verified by setting the derivatives of C_T with respect to both Q and M to zero in equation 6-7, the order quantity or lot size Q^* and the allowed shortage M^* that minimize C_T are given by equation 6-8.

$$Q^* = \sqrt{\frac{2C_PD}{h}\left(\frac{1}{1-D/P}\right)}\sqrt{\frac{h+z}{z}}$$

$$\tag{6-8}$$

$$M^* = \sqrt{\frac{2C_PD(1-D/P)h}{z(h+z)}}$$

E55a. **Valdosta Nut Farm has a shelling machine normally used for pecan shelling. During the walnut season, there is a weekly demand for the shelling of 30,000 lb of walnuts. The machine can shell 90,000 lb of walnuts per week. Every time the shelling machine is diverted to walnuts, the changeover and changeback costs are $4000. Shelled walnuts deteriorate quickly if shelled in advance of demand; let the holding cost be $1.50 per lb per week. If no shortages are allowed, what quantity of walnuts should be shelled per run, what is the total cost per week (ignoring the cost of the walnuts themselves), and what contribution do the holding and setup costs make to the total cost per week? By trying run lengths of 10% less and 10% more than calculated, verify that the minimum total cost is achieved.**

Here we measure time in weeks rather than years, and the unit of quantity is the pound. For $D = 30,000$, $P = 90,000$, $C_p = 4000$, and $h = 1.50$, equation 6-6 gives $Q^* = \underline{15,492\text{ lb}}$. Each run would have a duration of $Q^*/P = 0.1721$ weeks, and the run's production would serve $Q^*/D = 0.5164$ weeks of demand. From equation 6-5 with $C = 0$, the total cost at a lot size of Q^* is $7745.97 + 0 + $7745.97 = \underline{\$15,492}$ per week, exactly half from holding and half from setup. The equality of the lot size in pounds and the weekly cost in dollars is a coincidence, but the even split between holding and setup costs always occurs.

For a lot size 10% below Q^*, or 13,943 lb, the total cost is $6971.37 + 0 + $8606.63 = \underline{\$15,578}$, with more setup cost than holding cost, and for a lot size 10% above Q^*, or 17,041 lb, the total cost is $8520.56 + 0 + $7041.79 = \underline{\$15,562}$ per week, with more holding cost than setup cost. Both total costs are greater than the minimum, but only slightly. In practice, one would probably choose two runs per week, each of lot size $Q = 15,000$ lb, giving a total cost of $15,500 per week.

E55b.   Valdosta Nut Farm's customers can wait two or three days for their orders to be filled. If backorders were allowed and a unit shortage cost of $1/lb. per week of delay were assumed, what would be the revised optimal lot size and allowed shortage?

Note that the previous $Q*$ from equation 6-6 can merely be multiplied by the square root of $(h+z)/z$ to yield $Q*$ in equation 6-8. With $z = 1$, the result is $Q* = \underline{24,495\ lb}$. The second formula in equation 6-8 gives $M* = \underline{9798\ lb}$.

6.1.3.2 Forecasting Methods

Except when an enterprise can successfully market everything it can produce, production and inventory planning is based on forecasts of demand. Industrial engineers distinguish between forecasting and prediction. Forecasting, as such, involves formal mathematical methods of manipulating observable data to estimate future variables. This section reviews three methods of *time-series forecasting*, where the observed data consists of past values of the variable being forecast: *exponential smoothing* (and moving averages) for variables assumed to drift with no long-term trend, *double exponential smoothing* for variables following a trend, and *Winters' method* for variables exhibiting seasonal variation.

A *time series* is a time-ordered sequence of values. Let x_t denote the observed value at time t, and let successive values x_1, x_2,..., x_{T-1} be observed at times $t = 1, 2,...,T-1$. At time $T-1$ a forecast is made for the values at time T and beyond.

All forecasting methods are based on assumptions about the stochastic process that generates the time series. The most commonly useful forecasting method, *exponential smoothing*, is based on the *drifting constant process*. If a variable follows this process, and the process is at some *level* at time t, the observation x_t differs from the level by the amount of an *observation error*, denoted ε_t. The observation error is an independent random variable with mean 0 and variance σ_ε^2. Thus the level cannot be observed directly. The level drifts between observations by an *increment* denoted δ_t. The increment is an independent random variable with mean 0 and variance σ_δ^2. Letting b denote the initial level before time 1, the observation at time t is

$$x_t = b + \sum_{m=1}^{t} \delta_m + \varepsilon_t \tag{6-9}$$

It can be shown that the optimal way to forecast this variable, optimal meaning that the expected forecast error is zero and the variance of forecast error is minimized, is by a *linear filter* forecast

$$\hat{x}_{T-1} = \sum_{t=1}^{T-1} c_t x_t \tag{6-10}$$

where the $\{c_t: t=1,...,T\}$ coefficients that express the forecast as a linear function of past observations converge toward exponential smoothing very quickly after the process starts. For this model, the forecast made *at* time T, denoted $\hat{x}_T$, is *for* time $T+1$ and all future times. The *exponential smoothing forecast* is

$$\hat{x}_T = \alpha x_T + (1-\alpha)\hat{x}_{T-1} \tag{6-11}$$

where α is the smoothing constant.

For example, suppose the demand for a certain kind of hemostat in a hospital was forecasted to be 27 units in July and the actual number demanded in July was 34. If exponential smoothing was being used and the smoothing constant was $\alpha = 0.05$, then the forecast for August would be $34\times0.05 + 27\times0.95 = 27.35$ units.

For the forecast made at time $T-1$ and first "tested" by the observation at time T, the *forecast error* is defined by most authors as $e_T = x_T - \hat{x}_{T-1}$. That is, the forecast is subtracted from the observation, so that a positive error represents a low forecast; other authors subtract the observation from the forecast.

As an example of analysis of forecast errors for exponential smoothing, suppose that with $\alpha = 0.10$ a week's demand had been forecasted as 5.0000 and the actual demand was 2, and then the actual demands for the following weeks were 3, 7, and 9. The first forecast error was $2 - 5.0000 = -3.0000$. The following forecasts were $0.1 \times 2 + 0.9 \times 5 = 4.7$, then 4.53, 4.777, and 5.1993. Hence the second, third, and fourth forecast errors were $3 - 4.7 = -1.7$, then 2.47, and finally 4.223 (note that the final forecast 5.1993 has no observation with which to be compared). The standard deviation of the forecast errors $\{-3.0000, -1.7, 2.47, 4.223\}$ is 3.4074 (section 4.1.1.3 reviews the computation of sample standard deviation).

The variance of forecast error would be minimized if the smoothing constant were set to α^* as given by equation 6-12. Since standard deviations of level increments and observation errors cannot be observed directly, the usual way of setting α given historical data is to search for the value that would have minimized the sum of squares of past forecast errors. To set α from first principles, note that the factor in parentheses in equation 6-12 is near 1 when σ_δ is small compared to σ_ε (that is, when the drift in level is small compared to the observation error), so that $\alpha = \sigma_\delta/\sigma_\varepsilon$. This means the smoothing constant should be the ratio of long-term to short-term variability.

$$\alpha^* = \frac{\sigma_\delta}{\sigma_\varepsilon}\left(\frac{\sqrt{4+\sigma_\delta^2/\sigma_\varepsilon^2} - \sigma_\delta/\sigma_\varepsilon}{2}\right) \tag{6-12}$$

A heuristic consideration that helps provide a basis for choosing α is as follows: let p be the probability that the forecast error is due to a change in level, and let the forecast error otherwise be due to observation error. Then $\alpha^* = p/(1-p)$. In the hemostat example, if it was estimated that there was a 5% probability that the greater-than-forecasted demand was due to a permanent shift in the demand process, α would be set to $0.05/0.95 = 0.05263 \approx 0.05$.

A widely used and intuitively appealing forecasting statistic is the *moving average*, which is the simple arithmetic average of the last N observations:

$$M_T = \frac{x_T + x_{T-1} + \cdots + x_{T-N+1}}{N} = \frac{1}{N} \sum_{t=T-N+1}^{T} x_t \qquad (6\text{-}13)$$

Moving-average and exponential-smoothing forecasts can be compared to each other on the basis of average age of the data used in the forecast. The average age of the last N observations used in a moving-average forecast is $(N-1)/2$. On the other hand, the exponential-smoothing forecast gives a weight α to the age-zero observation, $\alpha(1-\alpha)$ to the age-1 observation, $\alpha(1-\alpha)^2$ to the age-2 observation, and so forth, so that the average age of the observations used in an exponential-smoothing forecast is $(1-\alpha)/\alpha$. Equating the average ages, we obtain the relationship between α and N for age-equivalent exponential-smoothing and moving-average forecasts:

$$N = \frac{2}{\alpha} - 1 \qquad \alpha = \frac{2}{N+1} \qquad (6\text{-}14)$$

For example, a 12-month moving average is age-equivalent to exponential smoothing with a smoothing constant of $\alpha = 0.153846$.

If a process is truly a drifting constant process, moving-average forecasts $\{M_t\}$ will not perform as well as exponential-smoothing forecasts $\{\hat{x}_t\}$; the variance of forecast error will tend to be slightly greater for moving averages. If a process has a steady trend, both kinds of forecast will lag behind the trend by the same amount. If the trend is steep and persistent, neither kind of forecast is appropriate, and a symptom of this will be that the best N will be small or the best a large, but between the two, exponential smoothing will perform better. If a process is cyclic or seasonal, both kinds of forecast will lag behind. However, in the special case that N equals or approximates the cycle length, as in a 12-month moving average for a variable such as natural-gas consumption, the moving average will perform better than exponential smoothing. Neither method, of course, attempts to forecast the cyclic or seasonal variations themselves.

Double exponential smoothing is appropriate for forecasting a trending variable. If there is a linear trend with slope a superimposed on the drifting constant process, then "single" exponential smoothing will produce forecasts that are consistently low (or high, if a is negative) by an expected amount $a(1-\alpha)/\alpha$. To take this into account, double exponential smoothing maintains two smoothing statistics rather than one.

Let S_T be the single exponential-smoothing statistic (the same as $\hat{x}_T$ in equation 6-11). This statistic's expected value lags behind the variable's expected value by the amount $a(1-\alpha)/\alpha$. Also let $S_T^{[2]}$ be the double exponential-smoothing statistic that smooths the single-exponential smoothing statistic. That is, we smooth x_T with the statistic S_T and smooth the statistic S_T with the statistic $S_T^{[2]}$:

$$S_T = \alpha x_T + (1-\alpha)S_{T-1}$$

$$S_T^{[2]} = \alpha S_T + (1-\alpha)S_{T-1}^{[2]}$$

(6-15)

The double-smoothing statistic $S_T^{[2]}$ lags behind its target S_T by the same expected amount $a(1-\alpha)/\alpha$ that S_T lags behind x_T. That is, the expected value of $S_T^{[2]}$ is less (more, if the slope is negative) than the expected value of S_T

$$E\left(S_T^{[2]}\right) = E(S_T) - a\frac{1-\alpha}{\alpha}$$

just as the expected value of S_T differs from the expected value of x_T:

$$E(S_T) = E(x_T) - a\frac{1-\alpha}{\alpha}$$

But since these two equations imply

$$a = \frac{\alpha}{1-\alpha}\left[E(S_T) - E\left(S_T^{[2]}\right)\right]$$

it is natural to estimate the current slope at time T from the current statistics accordingly:

$$\hat{a} = \frac{\alpha}{1-\alpha}\left[S_T - S_T^{[2]}\right]$$

(6-16)

From equation 6-15 the expected current level is $E(S_T) + a(1-\alpha)/\alpha$, so it is natural to estimate the current level from the current estimates S_T and $\hat{a}$:

$$\hat{x}_T = S_T + \hat{a}(1-\alpha)/\alpha = 2S_T - S_T^{[2]} \qquad (6\text{-}17)$$

A forecast for τ periods ahead is, of course, the current level plus τ times the current slope. Thus from the slope in equation 6-16 and the level in equation 6-17, the double-exponential-smoothing forecast made at time T for time $T+\tau$ is

$$\hat{x}_T(T+\tau) = \left(2 + \frac{\alpha\tau}{1-\alpha}\right)S_T - \left(1 + \frac{\alpha\tau}{1-\alpha}\right)S_T^{[2]} \qquad (6\text{-}18)$$

To perform double exponential smoothing, we start with an initial estimated level $\hat{b}$ and estimated slope $\hat{a}$ and compute initial smoothing statistics

$$S_0 = \hat{b} - \left(\frac{1-\alpha}{\alpha}\right)\hat{a}$$

$$\qquad (6\text{-}19)$$

$$S_0^{[2]} = \hat{b} - 2\left(\frac{1-\alpha}{\alpha}\right)\hat{a}$$

Then, starting from these initial statistics, we compute $S_1, S_2,...$ and $S_1^{[2]}, S_2^{[2]},...$ from equation 6-15 as the process unfolds. At any time T the forecast for τ periods ahead is given by equation 6-18 above.

The optimal smoothing constant for double exponential smoothing is about half that for single exponential smoothing.

E56. **Lyndon Brazos, a pigment-supply firm, has had a steady demand for the one-gallon pack of #40 black pigment, but the demand seems to be declining. Fifteen weeks ago it was estimated that the demand level was about 8500 gallons per week and that a decrease of about 230 per week could be expected. The actual demands for 15 weeks were 8722, 8933, 4375, 13,429, 12,597, 4518, 16,242, 1815, 3783, 7495, 9374, 6732, 4578, 3333, 3563. Suppose that the demand had been forecasted by each of the following methods: Exponential smoothing with $\alpha = 0.20$, moving average with $N = 9$, and double-exponential smoothing with $\alpha = 0.10$. For each method, determine what the forecasts would have been, what the forecast errors would have been, and what the sample mean and sample standard deviation of forecast error would have been. Which method would have done the best forecasting job? (To generate the first 9 moving-average forecasts, assume that the previous nine actual demands before the first week had been 16,892, 1432, 10,970, 8248, 9313, 10,112, 7569, 7796, and 4161.)**

By single exponential smoothing with $\alpha = 0.20$, the forecasts would have been the initial 8500, then (from equation 6-11) 8544.4, 8622.12, 7772.70, 8903.96, 9642.57, 8617.65, 10,142.52, 8477.02, 7538.21, 7529.57, 7898.46, 7665.17, 7047.73, 6304.79, 5756.43. The last forecast has no actual demand with which to compare. Subtracting the forecast that was made the previous week from each week's actual demand, the forecast errors would have been 222, 388.6, −4247.12, 5656.30, 3693.04, −5124.57, 7624.35, −8327.52, −4694.02, −43.21, 1844.43, −1166.46, −3087.17, −3714.73, −2741.79. These forecast errors have mean −914.52 (the forecasts are too high) and a rather large standard deviation 4331.86, as would be expected if the process persistently trends downward.

By moving average with $N = 9$, the forecasts would have been the initial 8500 followed by 7591.44, 8424.89, 7692.11, 8267.78, 8632.67, 8011.11, 8974.78, 8310.22, 8268.22, 8131.89, 8180.89, 8442.78, 7459.33, 6430, 6323.89. The last forecast has no actual demand with which to compare. Subtracting the forecast that was made the previous week from each week's actual demand, the forecast errors would have been 222, 1341.56, −4049.89, 5736.89, 4329.22, −4114.67, 8230.89, −7159.78, −4527.22, −773.22, 1242.11, −1448.89, −3864.78, −4126.33, −2867. These forecast errors have mean −788.61 and standard deviation 4321.34. Although it is typical for moving average to do a little worse than exponential smoothing, here it does slightly better.

By double exponential smoothing with $\alpha = 0.10$, the forecasts would have been the initial 8270 (not 8500; if the level is 8500, and the slope is −230, the first one-period-ahead forecast is 8270), followed by 8130.4, 8065.44, 7109.90, 8119.36, 8823.72, 7816.19, 9311.90, 7707.33, 6742.31, 6673.44, 7001.68, 6762.87, 6138.33, 5367.85, 4769.41. The last forecast has no actual demand with which to compare. Subtracting the forecast that was made the previous week from each week's actual demand, the forecast errors would have been 452, 802.6, −3690.44, 6319.10, 4477.64, −4305.72, 8425.81, −7496.90, −3924.33, 752.69, 2700.56, −269.68, −2184.87, −2805.33, −1804.85. These forecast errors have mean −170.11 and standard deviation 4301.04. The results show a fivefold improvement in average forecasting error with double exponential smoothing as compared to methods that do not forecast a trend.

Many time series are seasonal—demands for natural gas, construction materials, toys, apparel—and can be forecasted by *Winters' method*, which is the most useful seasonal forecasting method available. See *Forecasting and Time Series* (Montgomery and Johnson 1976) for a clear and complete treatment of Winters' method.

Let there be L periods in the season (commonly $L = 12$ months in a year), and let there be *multiplicative seasonal factors* $c_1, c_2,..., c_L$ that sum to L. (Thus there would be no seasonal effect if $c_t = 1$ for every period t.) Let there be three smoothing constants: α smooths the level a, β smooths the slope b, and γ smooths the seasonal factors. At time T, when an observation x_T is made, let $a(T)$ denote the new estimate of the current level, let $b(T)$ denote the new estimate of the current slope, and let $c_T(T)$ represent the new estimate of the seasonal factor for the ($T \bmod L$)th period of the season; if $L = 12$, for example, $c_1(1)$, $c_{13}(13)$, and $c_{25}(25)$ are successive estimates of the seasonal factor for the first period of the season.

To begin forecasting a time series by Winters' method, first provide estimates of initial values of parameters: $a(0)$ is the initial estimate of the level, $b(0)$ is the initial estimate of the slope, and

$\{c_i(0): t=1,...,L\}$ are the initial estimates of the seasonal factors. Remember that $a(0)$ is not where you expect the level to be at time 1, but rather is $b(0)$ less than that if $b(0)$ is positive. Also remember that if $b(0)$ is positive, a simple estimate of the c's as the proportion of previous season's amounts will tend to underestimate the early-season c's and overestimate the late-season c's.

Upon receiving observation x_T at the end of period T, we first update a:

$$a(T) = \alpha \frac{x_T}{c_T(T-L)} + (1-\alpha)(a(T-1) + b(T-1)) \qquad (6\text{-}20)$$

Next we update b:

$$b(T) = \beta(a(T) - a(T-1)) + (1-\beta)b(T-1) \qquad (6\text{-}21)$$

We update the seasonal factor:

$$c_T(T) = \gamma \frac{x_T}{a(T)} + (1-\gamma)c_T(T-L) \qquad (6\text{-}22)$$

At the end of each season we renormalize the seasonal factors by multiplying each one by L divided by their sum:

$$c_t = \frac{L}{\sum\limits_{t=1}^{L} c_t}, \qquad t=1,...,L \qquad (6\text{-}23)$$

Here t is $T \bmod L$ or any integer multiple of it. With today's computing resources, there is really no reason not to perform this renormalization at each time period rather that waiting to the end of the season; the forecasts with renormalization every period would be slightly different and theoretically should be slightly better.

The *forecast* computed by Winters' method for τ periods in the future is

$$\hat{x}_{T+\tau}(T) = (a(T) + \tau b(T))c_{T+\tau}(T+\tau-L) \qquad (6\text{-}24)$$

Here again T in the argument and subscript of c can be replaced by $T \bmod L$; the value $c_{T+\tau}(T+\tau-L)$ is the last previously updated c that is in the same position in the season as period $T+\tau$ will be.

When any forecasting method is used to forecast demand, and any demands are left unsatisfied, it is *not* appropriate to observe *sales* or *production* as a surrogate for demand. Let's say a six-selection soft-drink vending machine has too few selections devoted to regular cola, and the machine often runs out of regular cola between refills. Unsatisfied demand is either lost or diverted to other products. The forecasting system is being fed bad data—an undersestimate of the demand for regular cola and perhaps overestimates of the demand for other products. This costly, avoidable situation is unfortunately quite common in every industry. The first thing the industrial engineer should look for in setting up a forecasting system is a good way to collect accurate data on unsatisfied demand.

6.1.3.3 Dynamic Production and Inventory Models

At time zero, the start of the first of T periods in a production and inventory planning horizon, let D_t for $t = 1, 2,..., T$ be the scheduled or reliably forecasted demand for a given product in period t. For example, we may wish to provide at minimal total cost to meet demands of 76, 26, 90, and 67 units. This situation presents us with a *dynamic* production and inventory problem (dynamic means changing with time) to meet the time-varying set of demands $\{D_t : t = 1,...,4\} = \{76, 26, 90, 67\}$. If the relevant production costs and inventory costs are *convex* or *concave*, it is relatively easy to determine an optimal plan; at worst, with costs that are neither convex or concave, an optimal plan can be obtained by dynamic programming (reviewed in section 6.3.2). Linear costs are both convex and concave, and can be handled with the algorithms reviewed here or with linear programming (reviewed in section 6.3.1).

Let X_t be the number of units produced in period t and let I_t be the net inventory at the end of period t. Assuming that production and inventory costs are separable—production-related costs dependent only on production and inventory-related costs dependent only on inventory—let $K_t(X_t, I_t)$ be the cost of producing X_t units in period t and ending the period with I_t units on hand, and let $K_t(X_t, I_t)$ be separated into a production cost $C_t(X_t)$ and an inventory cost $H_t(I_t)$:

$$K_t(X_t, I_t) = C_t(X_t) + H_t(I_t) \tag{6-25}$$

Figure 6-5 gives examples of convex and concave costs. A function $y(u)$ is a *convex* function of its argument u if a straight line between two points (u_1, y_1) and (u_2, y_2) always remains on or above the curve of the function, and it is *concave* if the straight line always remains on or below the curve.

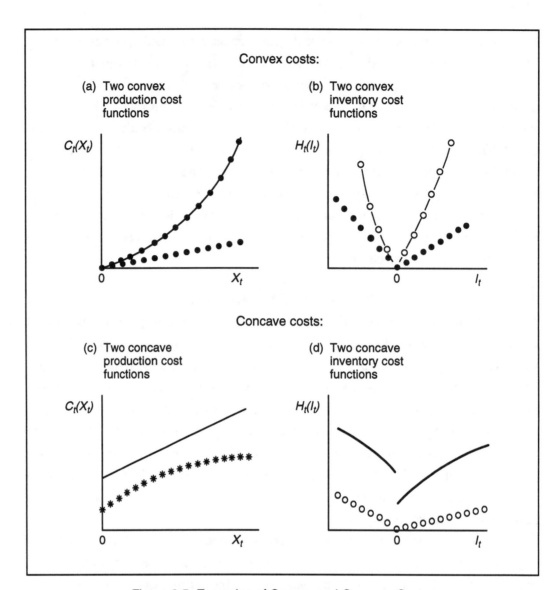

Figure 6-5. Examples of Convex and Concave Costs.

The often-encountered production-cost function that has a setup cost A_t and a unit production cost c_t, so that the production cost $C_t(X_t)$ is zero for zero units and is $A_t + c_t X_t$ for $X_t > 0$ is concave and is not convex: Note that if X_t is plotted on the x-axis and C_t on the y-axis, a straight line between the point $(0,0)$ and some other point on the curve passes *under* the curve.

6.1.3.3.1 Convex-cost Production/Inventory Model

When either all costs are convex or all costs are concave, a production/inventory model becomes easier to solve. Here is what is required for a *convex-cost production/inventory model*: $C_t(X_t)$, the cost of producing X_t units in period t, must be convex, which occurs if it is linear or involves increasing unit costs such as occur when large production rates involve overtime, additional shifts, or standby resources (it does not occur if there are setup costs or quantity price breaks). $H_t(I_t)$, the cost of holding I_t units for period t, must also be convex, both for positive I_t and for negative I_t (backlogging—filling part or all of a period's demand with production from a later period). For each unit of demand in period t there are up to T alternatives: produce the unit in an earlier period (incurring holding costs), produce the unit in the current period, or produce the unit in a later period (incurring shortage costs).

The *convex-cost heuristic* can solve complex problems easily, giving a near-optimal or optimal answer. It is based on the convexity of costs; it can give a poor answer, for example, if there are any setup costs. The algorithm is

Convex-cost algorithm:

1. For the first unit of demand in each of the demand periods, determine the cheapest way to fill it.
2. Schedule production for the cheapest filling found in step 1; there is now a reduced problem to solve (drop the filled demand units from the problem, and if all of a period's demand is filled, drop that period as a demand period).
3. If there is any remaining demand, go to step 1.

As an example, suppose demands in three periods are $\{D_t: t = 1,2,3\} = \{1, 4, 2\}$. Production of up to 3 units is possible in each period at a cost of $10 per unit plus a $2 overtime surcharge for the third unit produced in the period. Holding costs are $1.25 per unit in each period. Shortage costs are $1.10 per unit for each period that a unit is backlogged.

First, let us check whether the costs are convex. For every period t, the production costs as a function of X_t are $C_t(1) = 10$, $C_t(2) = 20$, and $C_t(3) = 32$. As the diagram shows, this is convex (a straight line between two points is never below other points). Shortage costs form an upright V and hence are convex.

Applying the convex heuristic, we find that at cost 10 (the cheapest cost appearing in the problem) we can fill 1 unit of demand in period 1, 2 units of demand in period 2, and 2 units of demand in period 3, all without any holding or backlogging. The reduced problem has 2 units demanded in period 2, and production available at cost 10 plus 1.25 holding from period 1, production available at cost 12 from period 2, and produc-

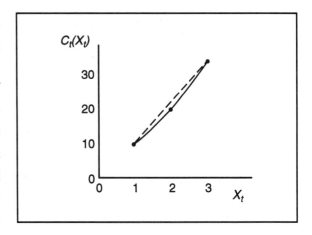

tion available at cost 12 plus 1.15 backlogging from period 3. Of these alternatives, the cheapest is to fill 1 unit of the remaining demand in period 2 from period 1. Finally, for the final unit demanded in period 2, there is production available from each of the three periods at cost 12, and the cheapest way to fill the demand is from period 2. Thus the recommended production plan is to produce 2 units in period 1, carrying 1 unit over to period 2; produce 3 units in period 2; and produce 2 units in period 3. The total cost is 73.25.

6.1.3.3.2 Concave-Cost Production/Inventory Model

When the costs are all concave, the only possibly optimal levels to leave on hand for the start of period t are $0, D_t, D_t + D_{t+1}, D_t + D_{t+1} + D_{t+2}, \ldots$. Period 1, of course, may be given a starting level over which you have no control; we assume this is small enough to affect only the first period. It is never optimal to produce in a period that has a positive starting level, except in period 1. Thus in period 1 or in a period with zero starting inventory, you choose among producing enough to satisfy D_t, or $D_t + D_{t+1}$, or ..., or $D_t + D_{t+1} + \cdots + D_T$; and in any period but period 1, do not produce anything if there is a positive starting inventory.

It is instructive to display the choices on a graph of the inventory level versus time. Figure 6-6 does this for example E57, in which the costs are concave, the demands are as shown in the figure for each of four periods, the starting inventory is 15, and the ending inventory is zero. The graph would be much more complicated if the costs were not concave. For instance, at the beginning of period 2, the graph shows entering levels of 0, 26, 116, and 183; we do not need to consider any other possibilities, e.g., a level that would satisfy demand for periods 3 and 4 but not 2. Also, with an entering level of 26 for period 2, we do not need to consider the possibility of any production in the period.

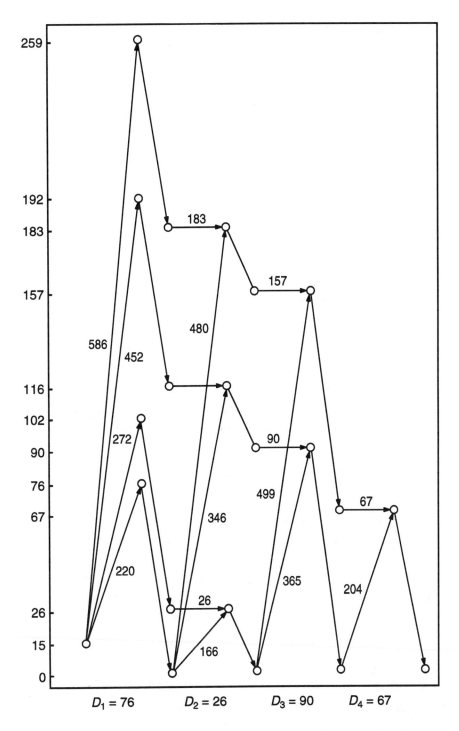

Figure 6-6. A Concave-cost Production/Inventory Planning Problem.

In a graphical representation of a production/inventory problem, each node represents a *state*, which for these problems is the inventory level at a given *epoch* or time; let there be a production epoch and a consumption epoch for each period. The directed arc from one node to another is labeled with the cost of traversing from one state to another. Specifically, the arc from a period's incoming level to a higher level during the production epoch is labeled with the *arc cost* equal to $K_t(X_t, I_t)$, that is the production cost $C_t(X_t)$ for production X_t in the period, plus the holding cost $H_t(I_t)$ for inventory I_t held over to the next period. The most common concave production-cost function is

$$C_t(X_t) \;=\; \begin{cases} 0 & X_t = 0 \\ A_t + c_t X_t, & X_t > 0 \end{cases} \qquad (6\text{-}26)$$

where A_t is the setup cost and c_t is the unit production cost. The most common function for holding cost is $H_t(I_t) = h_t I_t$. Example E57 uses these cost functions.

The solution method for a concave-cost production/inventory problem is the familiar foldback procedure or backward-pass algorithm that solves shortest-path problems (a forward-pass procedure can be used as an alternative). Let us review the backward-pass algorithm.

To solve a problem by the backward-pass algorithm, we successively label each node with a node-cost value that represents the cumulative cost from the node to the end of the graph.

Backward-pass algorithm (minimizing):

1. Label the final node with the value 0.
2. For an unlabeled node from which each arc that leaves goes to a labeled node, determine for each leaving arc the sum of its arc cost and the node cost of its destination node.
3. Choose the minimum of these arc sums. Declare one arc having the minimum sum as the *basic arc* that leaves the node. Label the node with a node cost equal to the minimum arc sum.
4. If unlabeled nodes remain, go to step 2.

The minimum total cost is the label on the initial node. The path through basic arcs from the initial node to the final node identifies the decisions and intermediate states.

E57.   In a plant that manufactures high-fidelity speaker systems, a special chromed version of the plant's nameplate is required for 76 systems next week, 26 the following week, 90 the third week, and 67 the fourth week. There are 15 on hand, and the inventory should end at zero. The nameplates cost $2 per unit to manufacture once the plant is set up to produce them. They scratch easily and get pilfered, so their holding cost is considered to be $1 per unit per week. It is difficult to work the chroming operation into the production activities when certain other activities are going on: the setup cost is $98 if any are to be produced the first week, $114 the second week, $185 the third, and $70 the fourth. Determine the minimum-cost production plan.

Figure 6-7 shows the graph with all arc costs labeled and the final node cost labeled zero, ready to begin backward-pass solution. Working backward, we label nodes with their obvious values and darken arcs to show they are basic until we get to the node that represents entering period 3 with 0 units on hand. The decision is between the arc labeled 499 leading to the node representing 157 available before the consumption epoch of the period (the node should have been labeled with a node cost of 67) and the arc labeled 365 leading to a node that should have been labeled 204. Since min(499+67, 365+204) = 566, we choose the first-mentioned arc, darken it, and label its tail node with the node-cost value 566. Proceeding thus, we end with the solution depicted by figure 6-8: at a total cost of 860, the optimal plan is to produce 61, 116, 0, and 67 nameplates in periods 1 to 4 respectively. Figure 6-8 shows the graph at the end of solution.

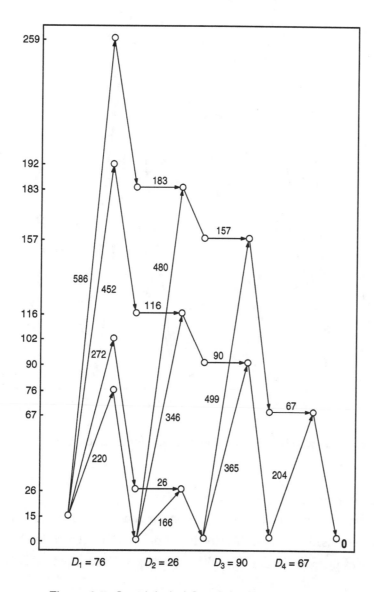

Figure 6-7. Cost-labeled Graph for Example E57.

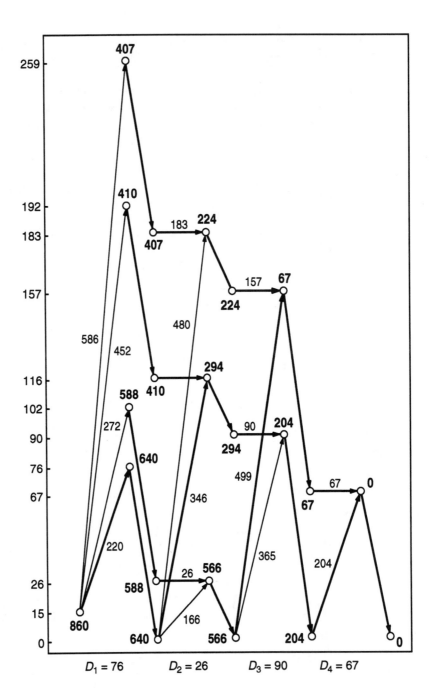

Figure 6-8. Final Solution Graph for Example E57.

6.1.3.3.3 Manufacturing Resource Planning (MRP)

For a dependent production process, where the final product is assembled from subassemblies which themselves must first be assembled (perhaps from lower-level subassemblies), production planning involves the coordination of multiple processes. For example, a bookshelf may be assembled from purchased hardware, and hardwood pieces—two sides, a top, a bottom, and three shelves—that in turn are cut from purchased hardwood slabs and lips. There is a *bill of materials* (BOM) that lists, for all levels, how many parts or subassemblies at the next lower level are required to make each part or assembly at a given level. The master BOM can be depicted in tree form (the numbers in parentheses denote the number of units required by one unit at the next higher level):

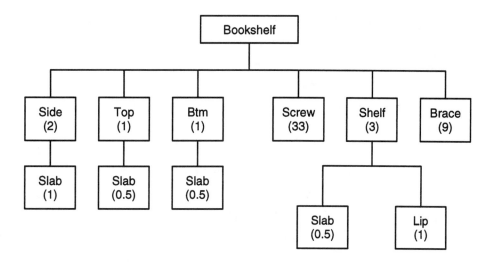

We can easily compute from the BOM, for example, that 100 bookshelf units requires 250 slabs. Such a computation is called *exploding the bill of material.*

Every part in the BOM can be assigned a *lead time*, which is the time required from releasing a batch of it to be purchased or produced to the time the batch is available for use at the next higher level. The lead time for a produced part can be estimated as a setup time plus an assembly time that consists of its lot size divided by its standard production rate. For example, the bookshelf (that is, the process of assembling a bookshelf from its next-lower-level components) may have a standard production rate of 6 units per hour, so that its lead time for a lot of 100 bookshelf units would be a setup time plus 16.67 hours. (Many engineers would round this down to 2 days, but it is recommended to round only final totals.) Continuing with the example, let us assume that the four operations that use slabs are conducted in parallel and that there are 8 working hours per working day. Suppose that the sides have a lead time of 37.50 hours, and that slabs have a lead time (say from order placement to receipt) of 24 hours or 3 working days. Thus we can compute that the slabs that go into sides for bookshelves would need to be ordered 16.67+37.50+24=78.17 hours or about 9.8 working days before we will be able to ship a batch of 100 bookshelves. Such a computation, given the due date for the final product, produces a *master production schedule* consisting of dates called *planned order release* for every component at each level. This computation, along with BOM exploding, is the heart of the methodology originally called *material requirements planning* (MRP), and its successor *manufacturing resource planning* (MRP II or MRP).

In 1993 there were about 300 vendors offering MRP II software products. Most are specialized to a particular industry and include modules to generate materials purchase orders and, for some industries, to perform detailed production scheduling, inventory control, and even general ledger accounting.

As part of the master-production-schedule calculations, MRP programs include lot sizing (EOQ) capabilities (reviewed in section 6.1.3.1). There are two options: *lot-for-lot* (LFL) calculations are commonly used for assemblies or subassemblies whose demand timings fluctuate more than their overall amounts, and *period-order-quantity* (POQ) calculations are commonly used for assemblies or subassemblies whose overal demand amounts fluctuate more than their timings.

Continuing with the example, consider the decision to make 100 bookshelves. If the decision was made on the LFL basis, then $Q* \approx 100$; the MRP system computes the time that the next lot of 100 is due, and the lot size is always 100. On the other hand, if the decision was made on the POQ basis, then $Q*/D$ is rounded to the nearest number of periods (this number is called the period order quantity or POQ); the MRP system computes the lot size required to meet demand for the next [POQ] periods, and the interval between orders is always [POQ] periods. For bookshelves, assume that customers are wholesalers who order in batches of 20 or 30 at unpredictable times; this would call for LFL planning, where we would run a lot of 100 bookshelves whenever required to keep up with demand. On the other hand, assume that the lead times for sides, tops, bottoms, and shelves differ significantly from each other, with the result that the demand for slabs is smoothed out; this would call for POQ planning for slabs, e.g., placing an order every two weeks for the amount that under the master production schedule will last two weeks.

6.1.3.4 Probabilistic Inventory Models

Two probabilistic inventory models are basic enough so that every industrial engineer should be able to use them.

6.1.3.4.1 Safety Stock from Demand over Lead Time

Recall that the EOQ models reviewed in section 6.1.3.1 assume deterministic parameters, including deterministic demand. However, if the forecasted steady demand pictured in figure 6-3 is not followed exactly, unintended shortages may occur near the end of a cycle.

Let the expected lead time be denoted L, measured in the same time units as for the other parameters. If we are ordering (P is infinite), L is the expected time from ordering a lot until it is received. Measuring time from receipt of the previous order, so that demand is predicted to bring the inventory to zero at time Q/D (see figure 6-3), let us place the next order at the approximate time $Q/D - L$, the exact time being when the level has reached DL units.

Now let us interpret D as the mean of a normally distributed random variable with standard deviation σ_D, so that the standard deviation of demand during the lead time is $\sigma_L = \sigma_D \sqrt{L}$. Let S be an amount of *safety stock* that we keep on hand (at a holding cost of $hS/2$ per period) to try to avoid shortages. Given S, the probability of a shortage is the probability that the demand will exceed its mean by S units during L, or the probability α associated with a z statistic $z = S/\sigma_L$. For example, if the mean demand is $D = 10{,}000$ units per year, and its standard deviation is $\sigma_D = 1000$ units per year, let us suppose that the lead time is $L = 0.04$ years (about two weeks), so that the standard deviation of demand over the lead time is $\sigma_L = 1000\sqrt{L} = 200$ units. Now if we choose a safety-stock level of, say, $S = 328$ units, then $z = 328/200 = 1.64$. From the normal probability table (table 4-3) we see this corresponds to $\alpha = 0.05$; a safety stock of 328 is enough to keep the shortage probability down to 5%.

Let α be selected in advance as the maximum allowable shortage probability. From Table 4-3, determine the corresponding z statistic. Then the required safety stock is $S = z\sigma_L = z\sigma_D\sqrt{L}$. To operate a system with safety stock, we place the order when the level is $DL+S$ units or less. In our example, this would be when the level is $10{,}000{\times}0.04 + 328 = 728$ units; this level is called the *reorder point*.

6.1.3.4.2 Single-period Probabilistic Inventory Model (Newsboy Problem)

The problem formerly known as the "newsboy problem" is faced by chefs, greengrocers, and manufacturers, wholesalers, and retailers of toys, apparel, or any product or service for which the main consideration is the unknown size of the immediate demand. Let x units be on hand; you can irreversibly acquire y additional units, and the $x+y$ units will either be too few, exactly enough, or too many to meet the demand D. Let D be a random variable that has a cumulative distribution function $F_D(b) = P(D \le b)$. Let c be the unit acquisition cost (there is no setup cost). Let h be the unit holding cost; if the demand D is less than $x+y$ there will be $x+y-D$ units held over, incurring a cost $(x+y-D)h$. Typically h is the loss in value from spoilage or outdating; in the classic example the value of yesterday's paper is very small, so h is large. Let p be the unit shortage cost; if the demand D is greater than $x+y$ there will be a shortage of $D-(x+y)$ units, incurring a cost $[D-(x+y)]p$. Typically p is the loss of potential revenue—the money the newsboy can't collect because he has run out of newspapers—and goodwill, as when a restaurant runs out of its specialty dish hours before closing time. We do not allow $p<c$ (why?).

Given the parameter values x, c, h, and p, and the CDF $F_D(b)=P(D\leq b)$, the optimal number of units to acquire is y^*, which is the smallest integer value of y such that

$$F_D(x+y^*) \geq \frac{p-c}{p+h} \tag{6-27}$$

For example, let a toy have a cost of $c = \$20$ and a selling price of $p = \$45$. There are $x = 2000$ on hand, and the holiday season is fast approaching. Any order with the manufacturer must be placed now. Toys that fail to sell can be warehoused for $1 and sold for $9 to a discount retailer after the season is over, so that under our definitions the holding cost is $h = -\$9$. The demand is estimated as being exponentially distributed with a mean of 10,000. How many should be ordered?

Since the CDF is $F_D(b) = 1 - e^{-b/10,000}$ (see table 4-2), the optimal number to order is y^* such that

$$F_D(x+y^*) \geq 1 - e^{-(2000+y^*)/10,000} = \frac{45-20}{45+(-9)}$$
$$\Rightarrow y^* = 9856$$

6.2 Project Scheduling and Control

6.2.1 Critical-path Project Scheduling

Project scheduling and control concerns coordination, both in planning and in execution, of a one-time set of *tasks*, also called *activities*, constituting a *project*. A project is defined by its work breakdown—its decomposition into tasks—and the task data. Let there be N tasks numbered $j = 1,2,...,N$; each task can also have a name. Each task must be completed (no substitutions or alternatives are allowed). Each task has a duration d_j.

There are precedences among tasks. If task h must be completed before task k can begin, then we say there is a precedence relationship between the two tasks in which task h is the *predecessor* and task k is the *successor*. We manipulate data only on direct precedences; if task l is a successor to task k, it is automatically an indirect successor to task k's predecessors.

A project's tasks and their precedences may be displayed graphically in two alternative forms: the *arrow diagram* (activity-on-arc diagram) that depicts each task as an arrow and represents precedences implicitly in terms of *events* that are depicted as nodes, and the *precedence diagram* (activity-on-node diagram) that depicts tasks as nodes and precedences as arrows.

Figure 6-9 gives an example of both diagrams for the following project:

> The footings of a building are to be completed in four groups of activities, one for each section of the building. For each section the activities include digging, placing steel, and pouring concrete, all in sequence. Digging of one section cannot start until digging of the previous section is complete; the same applies to pouring concrete.

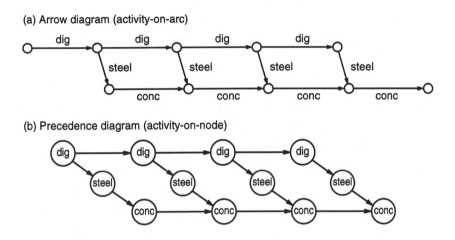

(a) Arrow diagram (activity-on-arc)

(b) Precedence diagram (activity-on-node)

Figure 6-9. Arrow Diagram and Precedence Diagram.

In the arrow diagram, each node represents an event that expresses precedences in a collective manner: all the activities whose arrows enter the node are predecessors of all the activities whose arrows leave the node. To express precedences in which a given activity is the only predecessor to one activity but is also a predecessor, but not the only one, to another activity, the arrow diagram requires *dummy* activities. (No similar difficulty exists for precedence diagrams.) Figure 6-10 gives an example for the case in which the precedences are $A \rightarrow C$, $A \rightarrow D$, and $B \rightarrow D$.

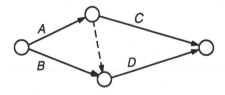

Figure 6-10. Dummy Activities.

Precedence diagrams are preferred in Europe and arrow diagrams are preferred in the United States. The events that appear in an arrow diagram but not in a precedence diagram are meaningful in controlling the implementation of a project, because they define the time when a group of activities is complete and another group can begin. In both types of diagram, it is always possible to arrange the diagram so that the head of every arrow is farther right than its tail, except for an ill-posed problem whose precedences form a loop; the diagrams should be drawn that way, to indicate the flow of time from left to right.

Given the durations and precedences of the activities in a project, the project has at least one *critical path* that is a longest path through the project's activities. The length of a critical path is the project duration. In calculating the critical path of a project, we also obtain meaningful data on individual activities and events: identification of the critical activities, early and late start times for activities (the late start time minus the early start time is the *float* or *slack* time for an activity), and early and late event times (the late event time minus the early event time is the slack or float time for an event).

To obtain these values, we perform two computation procedures: the *forward pass* and the *backward pass*. These can be demonstrated for the project depicted in the arrow diagram in figure 6-11, where the events are given letter identifiers A through G and the activity durations are shown on the arrows. Activity identifiers can be derived by the convention of naming an activity, say, *BE* if its predecessors are the activities that define event B and its successors are the activities that define event E. (Under this convention, if two activities had the same predecessors and successors, one would define a dummy activity having one of them as its only predecessor; the dummy event at the tail of the dummy activity would be given an identifier, allowing unambiguous naming of activities.)

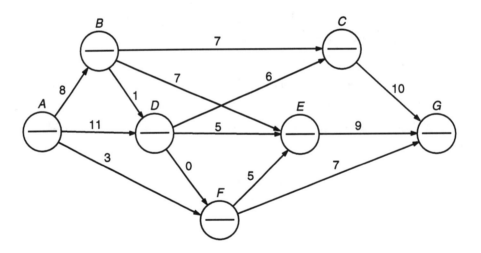

Figure 6-11. Illustrative Project for Forward- and Backward-pass Procedures.

The forward pass yields all the *early event times*; the early event time for the start event is zero by definition, and the early event time for the end event is the project duration. We start at the left, *maximizing* the time to each event. Let us record the early event times in the top halves of the event node circles. Begin with a zero for event *A*. Trivially, the early event time for event *B* is 8. Event *D* has two entering activities, and its early event time is the maximum of 8+1 or 0+11, which is 11. At each node, considering all the activities that enter the node, the early event time is the maximum of the previous early event time and the activity duration. The early event time for event *G* will be the project duration.

The backward pass yields all the *late event times*; the late event time for the end event is the project duration (from the forward-pass calculation), and the late event time for the start event will be zero if the procedure is executed properly. We start at the right, *minimizing* the time from each event. Let us record the late event times in the bottom halves of the event node circles. Begin with 27 (the project duration determined by the forward pass) for event *G*. Trivially, the late event time for event *E* is 27–9 = 18. Event *F* has two leaving activities, and its late event time is the minimum of 18–5 or 27–7, which is 13. At each node, considering all the activities that leave the node, the late event time is the minimum of the difference found by subtracting the activity duration from the downstream late event time. The numerical results of the forward and backward passes are shown in figure 6-12.

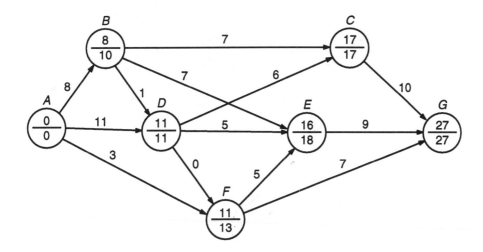

Figure 6-12. Results of Forward- and Backward-pass Computations.

E58.   Figure 6-13 depicts in arrow-diagram form a project that has 45 activities and 23 events including the start and end events. Perform forward-pass and backward-pass calculations showing the length of the critical path and the early and late times for each event.

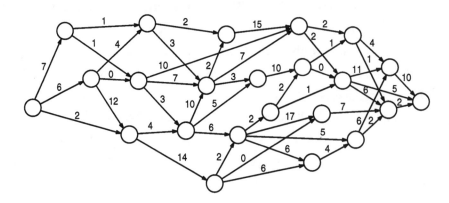

Figure 6-13. Arrow Diagram for Example E58.

The solution is shown in figure 6-14. The length of the critical path (project duration) is 72. The early event times are shown in the top halves of event circles, and the late event times are shown in the bottom halves.

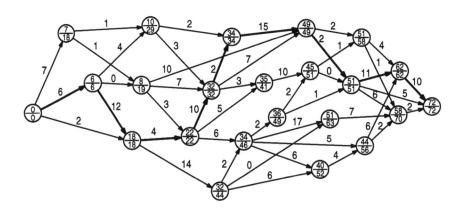

Figure 6-14. Solution to Example E58.

The *early start time* of an activity equals the early event time for the event at its tail. The *late start time* of an activity is computed by subtracting its duration from the late event time for the event at its head. An activity whose early start time and late start time are equal is a critical activity. Noncritical activities—those having early start times earlier than their late start times—are said to have a float or slack time equal to the difference. For the project in figure 6-11 these quantities are as follows:

Activity	Early start time	Late start time	Float
AB	0	$10-8 = 2$	2
AD	0	$11-11 = 0$	0
AF	0	$13-3 = 10$	10
BC	8	$17-7 = 10$	2
BE	8	$18-7 = 11$	3
BD	8	$11-1 = 10$	2
DC	11	$17-6 = 11$	0
DE	11	$18-5 = 13$	2
FE	11	$18-5 = 13$	2
FG	11	$27-7 = 20$	9
CG	17	$27-10 = 17$	0
EG	16	$27-9 = 18$	2

A time-feasible schedule, for a project whose activity durations are given, is a set of scheduled start times for all the activities. The forward- and backward-pass procedures give two specific schedules: the *early-start schedule* in which every activity starts at its early start time, and the *late-start schedule* in which every activity starts at its late start time. Schedules may be depicted in the form of a *Gantt chart*, as illustrated in figure 6-15.

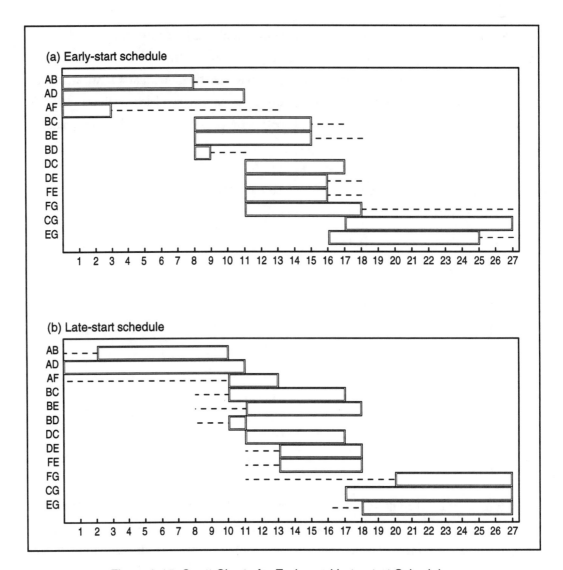

Figure 6-15. Gantt Charts for Early- and Late-start Schedules.

In a Gantt chart, each activity is represented by a horizontal bar whose width is proportional to its duration. The dashed lines are positive-slack indicators (the words "float" and "slack" are used interchangeably), showing how far the activity could be moved in time before violating precedences or the project completion time.

The early-start schedule is one that might be practical if the project manager's concern were to minimize the chance of delays. The late-start schedule is one that might be practical if the project manager's concern were to postpone expenditures as long as possible (e.g., to avoid paying unnecessary interest on construction loans). Activities can, of course, be scheduled to start at a time intermediate between the early-start time and the late-start time (in which case positive-slack indicators would be drawn on both sides—one to the left extending to the early-start time, and one to the right extending to the late-start time plus the duration).

6.2.2 Costs and Resources in Project Scheduling

When there are constrained resources, a project's shortest resource-feasible duration can be much longer than the length of the critical path. For instance, earning a college degree is a project in which the activities are courses, each with a duration of one semester. When one course is a prerequisite for another, there is a precedence relationship. But a typical college degree will have strings of prerequisites that are five semesters long at most. Therefore, if you were to use the critical-path method (CPM) techniques in the foregoing section, you would conclude that the length of the critical path is only five semesters long. But clearly a degree cannot be earned that fast.

There is a constrained resource that must be considered: student effort, which is available at a rate of one student-semester per semester. This is an example of a renewable resource. Renewable resources are usually cited in terms of their available rate (e.g., machine-hours per hour, or simply machines). Let us suppose that a 3-credit-hour course consumes student effort at a rate of 0.25 student-semesters per semester; that is to say, it is a quarter-time load, and the student therefore can take only four such courses in a semester. Otherwise the consumption of the resource would exceed the availability. But the critical-path schedule, ignoring resources, would show, say, 15 courses being taken the first semester: all the courses that have no prerequisite.

We will not review the techniques for lengthening a schedule to make it resource-feasible, but we will briefly review resource leveling and time-cost tradeoff analysis. *Resource leveling* is adjusting an early-start or late-start schedule within the activities' float times so that the maximum consumption rate of a single renewable resource is minimized. Each activity is assumed to consume the resource at a rate that is constant throughout the duration of the activity. The activity bar thicknesses (heights) in the Gantt chart can be made proportional to the resource consumption rate to show which activities are heavier or lighter consumers of the resource. A *resource consumption profile* can be drawn below a Gantt chart to summarize the total consumption of the resource by all activities as a function of time. For example, assuming that the activities in figure 6-15 all consume the resource at a rate of 1 resource unit per unit time, the resource consumption profile for the early-start schedule is as follows:

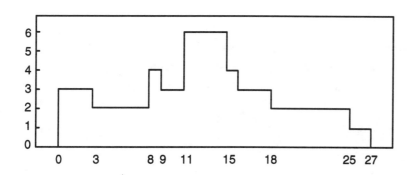

The maximum consumption rate is 6, which is the total consumption rate from time 11 to time 15. To level this, it is easy to see from figure 6-15a that activity *FG* can be shifted to the right 5 time units (delay its start time to time 16). This gives a maximum consumption rate of 5. Because activities *BC*, *BE*, *DC*, *DE*, and *FE* do not have enough slack to avoid overlapping, it is not possible to reduce the maximum consumption rate below 5.

Money is a nonrenewable resource that can act as a surrogate for all renewable and nonrenewable resources. *Time-cost tradeoff analysis* attempts to maximize the net bonus earned by reducing the project duration. The project duration is reduced by *crashing* critical and near-critical activities. In a time-cost tradeoff problem, each activity has a *normal duration* and a *normal cost*. Crashable activities have, in addition, a shorter *crash duration* and a higher *crash cost*. Although linear interpolation between durations is not the most rational interpolation method, it is customary to assume linear interpolation: there is a *unit crash cost u_j* for the *j*th crashable activity, equal to the difference between its crash and normal costs divided by the difference between its crash and normal durations. Thus the cost of crashing the *j*th crashable activity by δ time units is $u_j \delta$ dollars.

There is a *project completion bonus* of *H* dollars per time unit by which the project duration is reduced. If the project is crashed by a total of Δ time units, the net bonus is $H\Delta$ minus the total crashing cost $\Sigma_j u_j \delta$ for all the crashing necessary to achieve the shorter project duration.

For an example of a time-cost tradeoff problem, let us add the following data to the project illustrated in figures 6-11, 6-12, and 6-15:

Project completion bonus: $H = 250$ dollars per time unit

Crashable activities:

Activity	Normal duration	Normal cost	Crash duration	Crash cost	Unit crash cost
AD	11	820	8	1120	100
DC	6	660	5	780	120
CG	10	1000	7	1450	150
EG	9	930	6	1200	90

A good heuristic technique for solving the time-cost tradeoff problem is to make a network cut that passes through the critical crashable activity that has the least unit crash cost, crash the activity as far as the floats of other activities will allow, perform a new set of forward- and backward-pass calculations, and repeat. When a cut intersects n critical crashable activities, the relevant unit crash cost is the sum of their unit crash costs. The process ends when no further crashing can be done at a unit cost that is less than H.

A *network cut* is a continuous curve segment that intersects activities so as to separate the arrow diagram into left and right segments (the tails of all activities that the cut intersects must be on the same side—left—of the cut). The project can be crashed by δ time units across the cut only if all noncritical activities intersected by the cut have float times of at least δ and all critical (zero float) activities intersected by the cut are crashed by δ time units.

To illustrate, let us perform time-cost tradeoff analysis for the problem at hand.

The least unit crash cost for a crashable critical activity, ignoring the unit crash cost for the noncritical activity *EG*, is 100 for *AD*. There are two possible network cuts through *AD*: a cut through *AB*, *AD*, and *AF*; or a cut through *BC*, *BE*, *BD*, *AD*, and *AF*. Let us choose the former (it is simpler than the latter) and designate the cut as *Cut #1*:

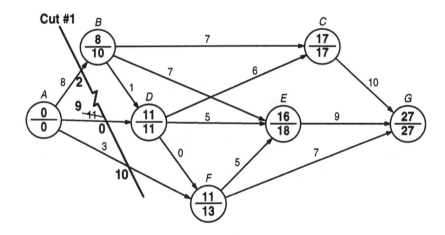

The float times of the activities intersected by the cut are marked. They allow *AD* to be crashed by 2 time units; its new duration is marked.

New forward- and backward-pass calculations give early and late event times marked in the next diagram, giving floats of 8 for *AF*, 1 for *BE*, 2 for *DE*, 2 for *FE*, 9 for *FG*, 1 for *EG*, and 0 for other activities. Since *EG* is still noncritical and *AD* can be crashed no further by itself, the least unit crash cost for a crashable critical activity is 120 for *DC*. There are three network cuts possible through *DC*: a cut through *BC*, *BE*, *DC*, *DE*, *DF*, and *AF*; or a cut through *BC*, *DC*, *BE*, *DE*, *FE*, and *FG*; or a cut through *BC*, *DC*, *EG*, and *FG*. But all these cuts intersect the noncrashable activity *BC*. This eliminates the possibility of crashing *DC*.

The least unit crash cost for a crashable critical activity is now 150 for *CG*. There are three possible cuts through *CG*: a cut through *CG*, *BE*, *DE*, the dummy *DF*, and *AF* (whose slacks would allow *CG* to be crashed 1 time unit, limited by the float of 1 for *BE*); or a cut through

CG, *BE*, *DE*, *FE*, and *FG* (whose slacks also would allow *CG* to be crashed 1 time unit, limited again by *BE*); or a cut through *CG*, *EG*, and *FG*, whose slacks also would allow *CG* to be crashed 1 time unit, limited by *EG*. However, *EG* is crashable at a cost of 90, so an additional 2 time units could be gained by crashing both *CG* and *EG* 2 time units at a cost of 150+90 = 240 per time unit, which is less than *H* and thus is profitable to do. Choose the last-mentioned cut, designate it as *Cut #2* and crash *CG* by 3 time units and *EG* by 2:

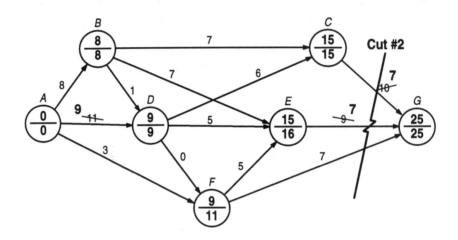

E59.   Complete the time-cost tradeoff analysis for the illustrative problem.

New forward- and backward-pass calculations give early and late event times marked in the next diagram. The remaining nonzero floats are 7 for *AF*, 1 for *DE*, 1 for *FE*, and 6 for *FG*. The remaining crashable activities are *AD*, *DC*, and *EG* (*CG* has already been crashed to its minimum duration). Let us mark all the activities that are in either of these categories with a special symbol, say a tilde (~):

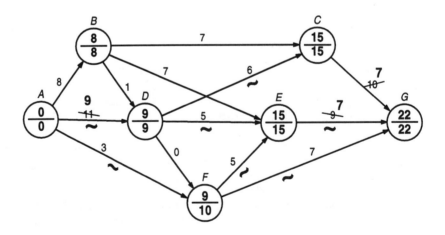

It is apparent by inspection of the diagram that no network cut can be made that intersects only activities that either have positive slack time or can be crashed further; therefore no further crashing is possible. The crashed project has a project duration of 22 compared to the original 27, thus earning a project completion bonus of $H \times (27-22) = \$1250$. The total crash cost is the sum of $(11-9) \times 100 = 200$ for AD, $(10-7) \times 150 = \$450$ for CG, and $(9-7) \times 90 = \$180$ for EG. Subtracting this $\$830$, the net bonus is $\$420$.

To check the result, we can determine the minimum potential project duration by performing a forward pass with all activities set to their minimum (crash) durations. This gives a project duration of 22, indicating that in this problem the project duration is limited by crashability, not by the cost of crashing.

6.2.3 Probabilistic Scheduling Models

Industrial engineers should be familiar with the basics of Project Evaluation and Review Technique (PERT)—both the original analytical form of PERT, and the simulation techniques that have replaced it while retaining its concepts.

6.2.3.1 Analytical PERT

The original analytical form of PERT was an early attempt to estimate the probability distribution of project completion time from the distributions of individual activity durations.

Activities are considered to have independent duration distributions. (Thus strikes or bad weather, which would delay several activities, are not represented in PERT.) There is a special approximate distribution called the *PERT beta distribution* that is customarily used to model the variability in activity durations. Recall from the brief review of this approximate distribution in chapter 4 that its parameters are

a the 1-percentile duration (the duration such that there is a 1% probability of a smaller duration)

m the modal or most likely duration

b the 99-percentile duration (the duration such that there is a 1% probability of a greater duration)

The density function of this approximate distribution is undefined, but there is a defined mean μ

$$\mu = \frac{a + 4m + b}{6}$$

and variance σ^2

$$\sigma^2 = \frac{(b-a)^2}{36}$$

From the central-limit theorem, a sequence of activities would have a mean duration equal to the sum of the mean activity durations and a variance equal to the sum of the variances, and would tend to be normally distributed with this mean and variance. A critical path, in particular, is a sequence of activities. In PERT, we define a critical path as a sequence of activities having the greatest mean duration; thus it can be identified by performing a forward-pass calculation using mean activity durations. Making the additional assumption that the probability distribution of the project duration equals the probability duration of the duration of the critical path, the project duration is estimated to be normally distributed with the mean and variance given by the sums of means and variances along its critical path. (The assumption is unrealistic if there exist other critical or near-critical paths in parallel with the chosen activity sequence.)

E60.   A project has four activities as follows, with time measured in working days:

Activity	Predecessors	a	m	b
AB	none	2	3	6
AC	none	2	4	8
BD	AB	4	7	10
CD	AC	6	8	12

Ignoring the fact that path lengths are too short for the central-limit theorem to apply, compute an analytical PERT estimate of the probability that the project will require more than 14 working days to complete.

The problem can be displayed in an arrow diagram as follows, where the labels on each activity arrow are a, m, and b:

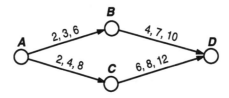

We can compute the means of the activity durations and the variances (omitting, if desired, variances for those activities that will obviously not be in a critical path):

Activity	Predecessors	a	m	b	μ	σ²
AB	none	2	3	6	3.3̄3	
AC	none	2	4	8	4.3̄3	1
BD	AB	4	7	10	7	
CD	AC	6	8	12	8.3̄3	1

The critical path consists of activities AC and CD. The critical path has an estimated length of $12.6\overline{6}$ days and a variance of 2 days² (standard deviation $\sqrt{2}$ days). Ignoring the objection to invoking the central-limit theorem for a sum of only two variates, and ignoring the influence of the noncritical path, we estimate the project duration to be normally distributed with the cited mean and standard deviation, so that the z statistic for a project duration of 14 working days is $z = (14-12.6\overline{6})/\sqrt{2} = 0.9428$, corresponding to a probability (see table 4-3) of about <u>0.17</u>.

Monte Carlo simulation has supplanted analytical PERT as the method for estimating project-duration distributions from activity-duration distributions. There is a run of experiments in which each experiment simulates one instance of the project. For each experiment, a random duration variate is generated for each activity's duration. Given all the activity duration variates for a single experiment, a forward-pass calculation is executed to determine the longest path. For example, in an experiment for the project of example E60, the variate for AB might be 3.0 days, the variate for BD might be 6.6 days, the variate for AC might be 4.0 days, and the variate for CD might be 8.2 days. For this experiment, the forward-pass calculation will reveal a project duration of 12.2 days, with path (AC,CD) being longer than path (AB, BD); in other experiments, path (AB, BD) could turn out to be the longer one.

The generation of random variates from the PERT beta distribution is done by computer and is not reviewed here.

E61. Ten Monte Carlo PERT experiments are conducted for the project of example E60, using the duration variates listed below. Ignoring the fact that the number of experiments is too small for reliable inferences, use the simulation experiments to estimate the probability that the project will require more than 14 working days to complete.

	Duration variates			
Experiment	AB	BD	AC	CD
1	3.0	6.6	4.0	8.2
2	2.9	7.1	4.0	8.2
3	4.4	7.4	3.8	6.0
4	3.1	7.0	3.0	8.0
5	2.9	7.4	7.1	8.3
6	3.0	4.5	4.9	8.9
7	3.3	7.0	4.1	9.4
8	3.8	8.9	4.3	8.1
9	3.2	6.5	3.9	8.1
10	3.1	7.0	4.0	6.8

Performing a forward-pass calculation for each experiment, we obtain the following results:

Experiment	Project duration	Critical activities
1	12.2	AC, CD
2	12.2	AC, CD
3	11.8	AB, BD
4	11.0	AC, CD
5	15.4	AC, CD
6	13.8	AC, CD
7	13.5	AC, CD
8	12.7	AB, BD
9	12.0	AC, CD
10	10.8	AC, CD

Note that in two of the ten experiments the path with the smaller average length was longer. A rough estimate of the probability of the project's requiring more than 14 days is the proportion of experiments in which it takes more than 14 days: 0.10. However, for a problem in which the paths have enough activities (say 7 or more) for the central-limit theorem to apply, a more accurate answer can be based on assuming the project distribution to be normally distributed with parameters equal to the sample mean and sample variance from the run of experiments. The sample mean and standard deviation of project duration from the experiments is 12.54±1.3818, so that the z statistic for duration 14 is $(14-12.54)/1.3818$ = 1.057, corresponding to a probability (see table 4-3) of about <u>0.15</u>.

Analytical PERT tends to underestimate the project duration and overestimate its variance. This is because when the length of the path designated as critical is very small, it is likely that another path will be longer, and consequently the project duration will be longer. As example E61 illustrates, simulation properly substitutes durations from other paths for the shortest project durations associated with the path designated as critical, and thus gives a longer expected project duration and a smaller variance than the analytical method. Simulation also gives a result that cannot be given by the analytical method: the relative criticality of activities. For example, if the simulation run in example E61 were long enough (200 to 2000 experiments is typical), we could say that activities AB and BD had a criticality of 0.20 and activities AC and CD had a criticality of 0.80; such results help warn project managers of where delays are most likely to occur.

6.3 Optimization Models

Optimization is an extensive field of mathematics generally divided into linear programming (including network flow models), nonlinear programming (including classical optimization), and integer programming or combinatorics (including dynamic programming). The IE PE Exam typically restricts its optimization coverage to a few highlights: linear programming formulation, graphical solution of two-variable linear programs, the simplex method, linear programming sensitivity analysis, dynamic programming formulation and solution, and a few techniques that lend themselves to manual solution, such as the Hungarian algorithm for assignment problems and weighted rectilinear location analysis.

Optimization problems in the IE PE Exam are necessarily small because of time limitations—often so small, in fact, that the correct answer is obvious or can be obtained without the use of formal methodology. This causes a scoring difficulty, since the problem authors are interested in testing whether you are qualified to solve a real problem, not merely whether you are able to try every possibility in a toy problem. Here are some unwritten rules to follow in solving optimization problems on the IE PE Exam:

1. Take a formal approach, not an ad-hoc one. For instance, if it is obvious by inspection that a particular constraint will not be limiting in the particular problem instance, don't simply ignore the constraint. Use the proper language: you can't say "let x_1 = bolts" when you mean "let x_1 be the number of bolts manufactured per shift."
2. Report the optimal value of the objective function, not just the values of the decision variables that make the objective function achieve this value.
3. Report the result in terms of the original problem statement: Say not only "$x_1 = 44$" but also "Make 44 bolts per shift."
4. Do not forget to express nonnegativity constraints. If x_1 represents the number of gallons of gasoline to be sold, it may be obvious to you that a negative number is inappropriate, but you must explicitly say "$x_1 \geq 0$." Texas engineer Bill Lesso tells of the time he brought computer output to a meeting only to find it recommended putting ore back in the ground at one of the mines—"selling" ore back to the mine at its production cost, which happened to be higher than the price paid by true customers.

6.3.1 Linear Programming Models

A linear program is a model in which there is a set of primary decision variables $\{x_j: j=1,...,N\}$, an objective function that is a linear function of the decision variables and represents a quantity that is to be maximized or minimized, a set of M ordinary constraints numbered $i = 1$ to M that are linear functions of more than one of the decision variables, and finally a group of additional linear constraints in only one decision variable, such as nonnegativity or other lower limits. Positive lower limits are usually handled by defining a new nonnegative variable that represents the amount by which the original variable exceeds its lower limit. Upper limits can be listed among the M ordinary constraints or treated separately. A variable unconstrained in sign is replaced by a pair of nonnegative variables, one of which represents the amount by which the original variable exceeds zero, while the other represents the amount by which the original variable is less than zero.

Formulation of a linear program from a situation statement is a tested skill on the IE PE Exam. Given a situation from which a linear program is to be formulated, the recommended procedure is

1. Identify the primary decision variables $x_1, x_2, ..., x_N$
2. Identify each constraint and express it as a linear function of the decision variables
3. Identify the objective function and express it as a linear function of the decision variables

The decision variables almost always can be interpreted as *levels of activity*. For instance, in a feedmix problem the decision variables are amounts of various materials to be put together to form a mix—how many pounds of cashews, peanuts, and so forth, are to be put into a nut mix, or how many grommets, screws, and so forth, are to be manufactured, or how many bolts of 30-in. wide cloth, 48-in. wide cloth, and so forth are to be used in making a batch of garments. The "activities" in these instances are the mixing of x_j pounds of material j, the manufacturing of an amount x_j of hardware item j, or the use of x_j bolts of cloth j. The decision variables are the quantities that answer the question "how many?" or "how much?"—x_j is the size of alternative j's share in the activity at hand.

Constraints can be of many types. Table 6-1 gives some examples.

Table 6-1. Common Types of Linear-programming Constraints.

Constraint type	Sample description	Mathematical expression
Nonnegativity	The amount of material 2 cannot be negative.	$x_2 \geq 0$
	None of the amounts can be negative	$x_j \geq 0, \forall j$
Supply or availability	Only 3 boilermakers are available (x_1 is the number of boilermakers employed per shift)	$x_1 \leq 3$
Demand	At least 1500 boxes must be sold (x_2 is the number of boxes made, and 400 already exist)	$x_2 + 400 \geq 1500 \Rightarrow$ $x_2 \geq 1100$
Sufficiency (lower limit) specification— extrinsic property	The vitamin-C content shall be at least 250 mg (x_1, x_2, are the amounts of materials that contain 40 and 33 mg per unit amount)	$40x_1 + 33x_2 \geq 250$
Upper-limit specification— extrinsic property	A unit shall weigh no more than 30 oz (weight contributed by activities 1 and 2 are $15x_1$ and $21x_2$)	$15x_1 + 21x_2 \leq 30$
Sufficiency (lower limit) specification— intrinsic property	The mixture shall have a temperature of at least 40°C (x_1 and x_2 are amounts of 25°C and 50°C water in mix)	$\dfrac{25x_1 + 50x_2}{x_1 + x_2} \geq 40$ $\Rightarrow$ $-15x_1 + 10x_2 \geq 0$
Upper-limit specification— intrinsic property	The average wealth of investors shall not exceed 10 (investors of type 1 have wealth 6, and those of type 2 have wealth 17)	$\dfrac{6x_1 + 17x_2}{x_1 + x_2} \geq 10 \Rightarrow$ $-4x_1 + 7x_2 \geq 0$
Ratio specification	At least twice as many units (x_1) of product 1 will be sold as (x_2) of product 2	$x_1 \geq 2x_2 \Rightarrow$ $x_1 - 2x_2 \geq 0$
Flow balance [out] − [in] = 0	The number of vehicles entering yard 6 from yards 4 and 5 ($x_{4,6} + x_{5,6}$) equals the number of vehicles leaving ($x_{6,7} + x_{6,8}$)	$-x_{4,6} - x_{5,6} + x_{6,7} + x_{6,8} = 0$

E62.   A linear program is to be used as a subroutine in an online computer routine that controls the making of tubing from metal plate, starting with positioning of two cutting heads that split a moving plate 1.5 m wide into two or three strips of lesser widths. The strips then go on to be formed into tubing which is sold in random lengths.

The required strip widths are approximately 3.14 times the diameter of the desired tubing. At any one time there is a batch of orders in hand, each order calling for a definite length of tubing of a definite diameter. Because the required widths do not often allow combinations that add to exactly 1.5 m, the third strip is usually "trim loss" that must be remelted later.

Formulate the appropriate linear program to decide how best to fill the following batch of orders:

> 1000 m of tubing whose diameter requires a strip width of 0.5 m
> 3000 m of tubing whose diameter requires a strip width of 0.7 m
> 2000 m of tubing whose diameter requires a strip width of 0.9 m

First we must decide what the decision variables are. To fill the orders, the operator will set the cutting-head positions to some pattern, run a certain meters of plate that way, then set the cutting-head positions to some other pattern, run a certain number of meters of plate that way, and so forth. For instance, the operator could set the heads at 0.5 and 1.0 meters from the edge, so as to make three strips each 0.5 meters wide; it would take 333.33 meters running that way to fill the first order. But since the other two orders are too wide to run side-by-side, it would take 3500 more meters with great amounts of trim loss to complete the job (1500 meters for the second order, 2000 meters for the third).

The operator would probably think in terms of *patterns* of cutting-head positions, and view the decision problem as the problem of deciding how many meters of each pattern to run. For this batch of orders, there are four patterns that make sense:

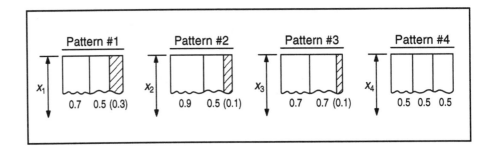

We begin the formulation by defining decision variables:

Let x_j represent the number of meters to be run in pattern j, where $j \in \{1, 2, 3, 4\}$ indicates a pattern pictured above.

Now we must define the constraints. There are three constraints that say enough plate must be run to satisfy each order in the batch. Now the number of meters of strip 0.5 m wide that is produced is the number of meters of pattern 1 that is run, plus the number of meters of pattern 2 that is run, plus three times the number of meters of pattern 4 that is run. This number of meters must be at least 1000 to fill the first order:

$$x_1 + x_2 + 3x_4 \geq 1000$$

Similarly, for the other two orders we have

$$x_1 + 2x_3 \geq 3000$$
$$x_2 \geq 2000$$

We must not forget that the decision variables are nonnegative:

$$x_j \geq 0, \; j \in \{1, 2, 3, 4\}$$

Finally, we must formulate the objective function. Evidently the aim is to minimize the total number of square meters of trim loss, which can be seen from the pattern diagrams to be $0.3x_1 + 0.1x_2 + 0.1x_3$. An equivalent and perhaps more elegant objective is to minimize the total number of meters of plate used in filling the orders:

$$\text{Minimize } x_1 + x_2 + x_3 + x_4$$

Graphical solution of two-variable linear programs, although not important in engineering practice, is sometimes tested to determine a candidate's general familiarity with linear programming theory (in the same spirit as trying fool's mate on an untested chess opponent). If the two variables are x_1 and x_2, plot x_1 on the abscissa (the x axis) and x_2 on the ordinate (the y axis). If the variables are nonnegative, plot only the upper-right quadrant, and indicate the nonnegativity by drawing bristles on the feasible sides of the axes (above the x axis and to the right of the y axis). (A full example of a graphical solution is shown in figure 6-16, which gives the solution to the next example). Plot each constraint. Inequality constraints such as $ax_1 + bx_2 \leq c$ are indicated by plotting the boundary line $ax_1 + bx_2 = c$ and drawing bristles on the feasible side. Usually the easiest way to plot the boundary line is to draw a straight line through the points $(0, c/b)$ and $(c/a, 0)$. If the constraint is of the equality type, draw no bristles since there is no feasible side (only points *on* the line are feasible). When all constraints have been plotted and the feasible region is an area, the feasible region can be identified as the area enclosed by bristles. If the feasible region is a line segment, it is that part of the segment on the feasible side of all bristles; it is customary to darken this part of the line segment to indicate the feasible region (this is illustrated in the solution to the next example).

Now plot at least one iso-objective line. Supposing the objective function to be $z = c_1x_1 + c_2x_2$, the easiest way to do this is to assume a convenient value for x_1 and assume $x_2 = 0$, and compute $z = c_1x_1$ as the objective-function value for the point $(x_1, 0)$; then another point having the same value of z is the point $(0, z/c_2)$. Plot a dashed iso-objective line through these two points. Then either plot a second iso-objective line for a different assumed value for x_1 and label both iso-objective lines with their objective-function values (the lines will be parallel), or identify and label the increasing-value side of the single iso-objective line. Finally, if the objective function is to be maximized, plot a dashed line parallel to the iso-objective line(s) and passing through the vertex of the feasible region that is as far in the increasing-value direction as possible. For minimizing, go as far in the decreasing-value direction as possible. Compute the value of the objective function at the optimal point, and report the optimal x_1, x_2, and z, not only as numbers, but in the problem statement's terms.

E63.   **There are two ways to manufacture a robot arm. One way is to buy a generic arm for $340 and expend $300 of labor and $620 of additional materials at station 1. A second way is to expend $490 of labor and $220 of materials at station 1, $240 of labor and $310 of materials at station 2, and $540 of labor and $100 of materials at station 3. There is a demand for 8 arms per working day. Materials and labor are available in unlimited supply, but no station can accommodate more than $2450 of labor per working day (this is 12 workers—more at a station would get in each other's way). Formulate as a general linear program the problem of meeting the demand at minimal total cost, and solve graphically.**

Let x_1 and x_2 represent the number of robot arms per working day manufactured by methods ("ways") 1 and 2, respectively.

The demand will be met:

$$x_1 + x_2 = 8 \tag{1}$$

The labor expenditure at station 1 cannot exceed 2450:

$$300x_1 + 490x_2 \leq 2450 \tag{2}$$

The labor expenditure at station 2 cannot exceed 2450:

$$240x_2 \leq 2450 \implies x_2 \leq 10.20833 \tag{3}$$

The labor expenditure at station 3 cannot exceed 2450:

$$540x_2 \leq 2450 \implies x_2 \leq 4.537037 \tag{4}$$

Note that constraint 4 implies constraint 3, so constraint 3 may be ignored.

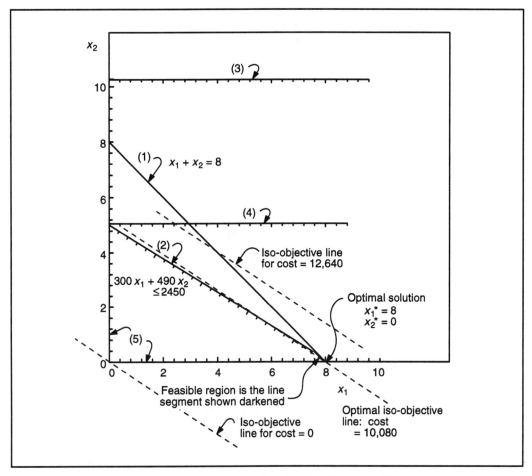

Figure 6-16. Graphical Solution for Example E63.

The decision variables are nonnegative:

$$x_1, x_2 \geq 0 \qquad (5)$$

The objective is to minimize daily total cost, which includes $340 + 300 + 620 = \$1260$ per arm for method 1 and $490 + 220 + 240 + 310 + 540 + 100 = \$1900$ per arm for method 2:

$$\text{Minimize } 1260x_1 + 1900x_2 \qquad (6)$$

The graphical solution is sketched in figure 6-16. To meet demand at minimal total cost, it is best to manufacture <u>all 8 arms per working day in the first way, and no arms in the second way, incurring a total cost of $10,080 per working day</u>.

George Dantzig's *simplex algorithm*, developed in 1947, can solve any linear programming problem in a finite number of steps, and until about 1990 was the foundation for the best methods of solving large-scale linear programs. Starting with a linear program (LP) consisting of an objective function linear in N decision variables, along with a set of M linear constraints (inequalities and/or equalities), there are three tasks in simplex solution:

1. Standard formulation
2. Finding a basic feasible solution
3. Simplex iterations

How to perform standard formulation of a linear program:

The first task, *standard formulation*, consists of reformulating the problem, usually by adding slack variables to all inequality constraints, so that the simplex algorithm can work on a set of linear equations. The second task, *finding a basic feasible solution*, consists of applying one of several techniques for manipulating the equations into a convenient form called a basic feasible solution; when the set of equations is in this form, one can tell at a glance (1) the values of one particular set of decision variables satisfying all constraints and (2) whether the solution so identified is optimal. The third task, which is the *simplex algorithm* proper, consists of applying simplex rules for proceeding step-by-step from one basic feasible solution to another, more nearly optimal, basic feasible solution, and finally stopping when the optimal solution is reached.

Any linear *inequality* constraint in nonnegative decision variables ($x_1 + 2x_2 \leq 5$, for example) can be expressed as a linear *equality* constraint by adding a nonnegative *slack variable*: $x_1 + 2x_2 + x_3 = 5$. Here x_3 represents the amount by which the left-hand side of the inequality is less than the right-hand side. Slack variables are nonnegative. In the above constraint, any nonnegative value of x_3 will ensure that the inequality is satisfied. As an illustration, let us change the set of inequalities shown below on the left to a set of equalities by adding slack variables x_4, x_5, and x_6. (*Note:* a slack variable subtracted from the left-hand side of a $\geq$ inequality is sometimes called a "surplus variable.")

Inequalities:	*Equivalent equalities:*
$x_1 + 3.5x_2 \leq 7$	$x_1 + 3.5x_2 + x_4 = 7$
$x_1 + x_2 + x_3 \geq 2$	$x_1 + x_2 + x_3 - x_5 = 2$
$2x_1 - x_3 \leq 8.5$	$2x_1 - x_3 + x_6 = 8.5$
$x_1, ..., x_3 \geq 0$	$x_1, ..., x_6 \geq 0$

The simplex algorithm works with nonnegative variables only, so when a variable, say x_7, is unconstrained in sign in the actual problem, it may be replaced in the standard formulation by a difference, say x_7-x_8. Then in a solution where the variable is positive, x_8 will be zero and x_7 will be the value of the variable; and in a solution where the variable is negative, x_7 will be zero and x_8 will be the amount by which the variable is less than zero.

How to find a basic feasible solution:

Having a set of M equations linear in N variables (here the number of variables includes slack, surplus, and other variables added in formulation), we can apply the familiar *pivoting* rules of linear algebra. Recall that the solution(s) to a set of linear equations remain unchanged when any combination of the following operations is applied:

1. Any linear equation may be multiplied (or divided) by a finite nonzero constant
2. Any linear equation may be replaced by the sum of itself (or a multiple of itself) plus another linear equation in the same set (or a multiple of such other equation)

Thus by operation (1) the equation $x_1+x_2=6$ has the same solutions as the equation $0.5x_1+0.5x_2 = 3$; and by operations (1) and (2) the following two sets of equations have the same solutions:

$$
\begin{aligned}
x_1 + x_2 \quad &= \quad 6 \\
2x_1 \quad + x_3 &= \quad 2
\end{aligned}
\qquad\qquad
\begin{aligned}
x_1 + x_2 \quad &= \quad 6 \\
-2x_2 + x_3 &= \quad -10
\end{aligned}
$$

To get the equations on the right, the second equation on the left was replaced by the sum of itself multiplied by a constant k and the first equation multiplied by a constant l, where the constants were chosen so as to eliminate the x_1 term in the second equation. (For the reader who wishes to verify this point, the values of k and l are given in the next paragraph.)

Given M equations in N unknowns, where there are fewer equations than unknowns ($M<N$), a *basic solution* is a solution which can be read from the set of equations after manipulation to isolate M of the variables so that each of them appears in *one equation only*, having a coefficient of 1 in that equation. Such variables are called *basic variables*, and the remaining $N-M$ variables are called nonbasic variables. Note that the equations on the left above form a basic solution in which x_2 and x_3 are the basic variables, and the equations on the right above (which were formed in the manner described above with $k=1$ and $l=-2$) form a basic solution in which x_1 and x_3 are the basic variables.

To read a basic solution, interpret the nonbasic variables (those appearing in more than one equation) as having the value 0 and interpret the basic variables as having their obvious values (given than the nonbasic variables are zero), which are the right-hand-side constants. For example, the basic solution on the left above is $x_1 = 0$, $x_2 = 6$, and $x_3 = 2$; and the basic solution on the right is $x_1 = 6$, $x_2 = 0$, and $x_3 = -10$.

Starting with either basic solution, the reader may wish to manipulate the equations so as to get a basic solution in which the basic variables are x_1 and x_2 (their values will be 1 and 5, respectively; the required manipulations are those described below as the *pivot operation*).

To recap: a basic solution exists when a set of M linear equations (rows) in N variables (columns) is written so that each row defines a value of one basic variable. In a basic solution each row has the following properties: 1) the coefficient of its basic variable is 1; 2) the coefficient of the same variable in all other rows is 0; and 3) the coefficient of all other basic variables in the same row is 0. If an equation is designated as the *objective function*, where there is an objective variable x_0 to be minimized or maximized, and x_0 is a linear function of the other variables, then the objective function is treated the same as other equations except that x_0 should be made basic as soon as possible and remain basic (a basic solution in which the objective function is nonbasic is meaningless).

For linear programming it is customary to display sets of equations in nonnegative variables in the form of a *simplex tableau* with the objective function as the top (zeroth) row, as illustrated here:

x_0	x_1	x_2	x_3	x_4	x_5	x_6	b_i
1					3	−4	12
			1		−5	9	11
				1	−3	5	5
		1			1	−2	2
	1				1	−1	5

The objective-function row can be read, for example, as $x_0 + 3x_5 - 4x_6 = 12$. Often the portion of the tableau to the left of the dashed line is omitted. The tableau shows variables x_5 and x_6 as nonbasic; the objective function has the value 12; the basic variables are x_1, x_2, x_3, and x_4, having values 5, 2, 11, and 5, respectively. This solution is called a *basic feasible solution*—feasible because all the basic variables have nonnegative values.

The simplex algorithm works with basic feasible solutions only. Simple algebraic manipulation can make any combination of variables basic, but some basic solutions are infeasible in that the value of one or more basic variables turns out to be negative. The simplex algorithm is designed never to create an infeasible basic solution, but one may arise before simplex iterations have begun. For example, consider the linear program

$$
\begin{array}{llll}
\text{Maximize} & x_0 = & x_1 + x_2 \\
\text{subject to} & & x_1 - x_2 & \leq 4 \\
& & x_1 + 2x_2 & \geq 3
\end{array}
$$

x_1, x_2 nonnegative

If we add a slack variable x_3 to the first constraint and a surplus variable x_4 to the second constraint, the program will appear as follows in tableau form:

x_0	x_1	x_2	x_3	x_4	b_i
1	−1	−1	0	0	0
0	1	−1	1	0	4
0	1	2	0	−1	3

Because of the −1 in the x_4 column (which arose because of subtracting the surplus variable to convert the ≥ inequality to an equation), the solution fails to be basic. It can be made basic simply by multiplying row 2 by −1:

x_0	x_1	x_2	x_3	x_4	b_i
1	−1	−1	0	0	0
0	1	−1	1	0	4
0	−1	−2	0	1	−3

Unfortunately this basic solution straightforwardly obtained from the problem statement is *infeasible*, since the required nonnegativity of x_4 is violated: $x_4 = -3$.

There are many strategies for achieving a basic feasible solution once a basic but infeasible solution is reached. The best method is to perform feasibility-seeking manipulations using rules similar to those of the simplex algorithm to be reviewed below, but oriented toward eliminating negativity rather than seeking optimality. Such manipulations are called "phase I" calculations, "phase II" being the optimum-seeking simplex iterations that begin when a basic feasible solution is achieved. In the past, it was customary to add *artificial variables* to the problem. These were nonnegative variables that represented the amount by which each nonnegativity constraint was violated. Phase I used simplex rules to eliminate the artificial variables (minimize them to zero, whereupon they would be discarded from the problem). One early method, called the "big-M method," added a large penalty (M) in the objective function for each artificial variable, thus ensuring that the simplex method would make these variables zero before changing other variables. An equivalent, numerically more efficient method, originally named the "phase I/ phase II" method, minimized an auxiliary objective function that was simply the sum of all the artificial variables, then switched to the real objective function.

Here we will review *Lemke's method*, which is a precursor of modern simplex-based methods and is convenient for manual calculation. In Lemke's method, we arbitrarily change negative right-hand-side constants to positive constants, achieve optimality for the changed problem, and use Lemke's dual-simplex rules to restore the problem to the original one.

In the problem at hand, let us change the -3 to 1, giving a first basic feasible solution:

x_0	x_1	x_2	x_3	x_4	b_i
1	-1	-1	0	0	0
0	1	-1	1	0	4
0	-1	-2	0	1	1 (changed from -3)

When all constraints are of the not-greater-than ($\leq$) type, the slack variables automatically form a basic feasible solution. Each constraint of the not-less-than ($\geq$) type gives an infeasible row. Each constraint of the equality ($=$) type can be replaced by two inequality constraints, one of each type: for example, $x_1 - 2x_2 = 4$ becomes $x_1 - 2x_2 \leq 4$ and $x_1 - 2x_2 \geq 4$. We will simply relax all the infeasibilities, perform simplex-algorithm solution of the changed problem, and recover the original problem later.

How to perform simplex iterations:

The simplex algorithm is a procedure for proceeding from one basic feasible solution to a better basic feasible solution, continuing step-by-step until the optimal solution is reached. At each step or *iteration* a variable that was formerly nonbasic enters the basis and a variable that was formerly basic leaves the basis. Starting with any basic feasible solution, the simplex algorithm does the following things to derive a better basic feasible solution:

1. Choose a variable to enter the basis (or recognize optimality by rejecting all candidates)
2. Choose a variable to leave the basis (or recognize unboundedness by rejecting all candidates)
3. Perform a *pivot operation* on each row to get the new basic feasible solution

To choose the variable to enter the basis, the simplex rule is to choose the variable whose objective-function coefficient in the zeroth row of the tableau is most negative (for maximizing) or most positive (for minimizing).

To review the reason for the simplex rule for choosing the variable to enter the basis, consider the following tableau:

x_0	x_1	x_2	x_3	x_4	b_i
1	-2	-5	0	0	0
0	1	1	1	0	10
0	-2	1	0	1	1

According to the rule, x_2 is to enter the basis because -5 is the most negative objective-row coefficient. Recall that the objective-function row actually represents the equation $x_0 - 2x_1 - 5x_2 = 0$, or $x_0 = 2x_1 + 5x_2$, where x_1 and x_2 are currently nonbasic and hence currently equal to zero. The objective function x_0 is expressed in terms of the nonbasic variables, and its derivatives with respect to them are $dx_0/dx_1 = 2$ and $dx_0/dx_2 = 5$. Thus x_0 increases faster with x_2 than with x_1; accordingly, x_2 is chosen to be the nonbasic variable to enter the basis and have its value increased from zero to some positive value.

Having chosen a nonbasic variable to enter the basis, say x_j, the simplex algorithm next chooses a basic variable to leave the basis. The jth element in any constraint row is $-dx_b/dx_j$, where x_b is the basic variable whose value is read from that row. Call the jth element in a constraint row a_j. Since $a_j = -dx_b/dx_j$ and the system is linear, a_j also represents a ratio of finite changes: $\Delta x_b/\Delta x_j = -a_j$. But if x_b is leaving the basis, it will decrease from its current amount b—the right-hand element of the row—to zero. That is $\Delta x_b = -b$. Thus $\Delta x_j = b/a_j$. This is the amount that the new basic variable must increase in order to bring the old basic variable that is defined in this row exactly to zero.

We call b/a_j for a row its *simplex ratio*. If the simplex ratio is negative, adding x_j to the basis will make this row's basic variable have a greater value. If the simplex ratio is positive, adding x_j to the basis to replace this row's basic variable will increase x_j by an amount equal to the ratio. Hence if this row's simplex ratio is not the smallest positive one, and the new variable replaces this row's variable in the basis, it will bring some other row's basic variable below zero. Thus the simplex rule for the variable to leave the basis: Choose the row having the smallest positive b/a_j ratio.

The element in the column of the variable to enter the basis (the x_j column) and the row of the variable to leave the basis is called the *pivot element*. To add x_j to the basis and remove the leaving variable from the basis, we perform a pivot operation, which is those manipulations that give the new variable a 1 in the pivot-element position, give zeros elsewhere in the pivot column, and allow the column of the leaving variable to have whatever values the manipulations produce.

To simplify the description of a pivot operation, let R represent any non-pivot row in the current tableau, including the objective-function row; that is, R is any row except the one containing the pivot element. Let R' represent the row that will replace R in the next tableau. Let P represent the pivot row, and let P' represent the corresponding row in the next tableau.

Pivot operation:

1. The new row P' is the old pivot row P divided by the pivot element.
2. The new row R' is the old row R, minus $a_j P'$, where a_j is the element of R that lies in the pivot column.

To review choosing a variable to enter the basis, choosing a variable to leave the basis, and performing the pivot operation, consider the following simplex tableau, where the objective function is to be minimized:

	x_0	x_1	x_2	x_3 ↓	x_4	x_5	x_6	b_i	
	1	−1	−3	2	0	0	0	0	
	0	1	−1	−3	1	0	0	2	
P:	0	−1	1	**3**	0	1	0	1	←
	0	0	1	2	0	0	1	3	

The greatest positive objective-row coefficient is 2 in the x_3 column, so x_3 is to enter the basis (if it were a maximizing problem, x_2 would have been chosen instead). The simplex ratios are −2/3, 1/3, and 3/2, of which 1/3 is the smallest positive ratio; call this row the pivot row P; x_5 (the basic variable defined in the row) is the variable to leave the basis. The pivot element is hence the 3 in row P.

To perform the pivot, first we divide the pivot row by the pivot element to get the corresponding row P' in the next tableau:

	x_0	x_1	x_2	x_3	x_4	x_5	x_6	b_i	
P':	0	−1/3	1/3	1	0	1/3	0	1/3	←

Notice that row P' now defines basic variable x_3, whereas its predecessor row P defined basic variable x_5. Thus x_3 has entered the basis and x_5 has left the basis. All the other rows will follow the second pivot-operation procedure listed above, where each row is replaced by the difference of itself minus the proper multiple of new row P' so as to get a zero in the new basic column. For example, the objective row minus 2 times the new row P' becomes the new objective row:

	x_0	x_1	x_2	x_3	x_4	x_5	x_6	b_i
$R' = R - a_j P'$:	1	−1/3	−11/3	0	0	−2/3	0	−2/3

The reader can verify that the new tableau is optimal and that it gives the solution $x_0 = -2/3$, $x_3 = 1/3$, $x_4 = 3$, $x_6 = 7/3$, and the other variables zero.

E64. Determine the optimal solution to a relaxed version of the following problem, where any negative variable values in the initial basic solution are changed to 1.

$$
\begin{aligned}
\text{Maximize} \quad x_0 &= -2x_1 + 2x_2 + x_3 \\
\text{subject to} \quad x_1 + x_2 + x_3 &= 4 \\
x_1 - x_2 - x_3 &\geq 1
\end{aligned}
$$

All $x \geq 0$

If you define first a $\leq$ and second a $\geq$ constraint to replace the equality constraint, add slack variable x_4 to the first of these constraints, subtract surplus variable x_5 from the second of these constraints, and subtract surplus variable x_6 from the last constraint, your first basic solution will have two infeasible rows. Arbitrarily changing the value of x_5 from -4 to 1 and x_6 from -1 to 1, you will obtain a basic feasible solution to the relaxed problem. The simplex rules will have you add x_2 to the basis and remove x_6, pivoting on the last row and x_2 column. The result of the iteration will give an optimal solution to the relaxed problem: $x_0 = 2$, $x_2 = 1$, $x_4 = 3$, $x_5 = 2$.

Inverse-of-basis method to restore relaxed constraints:

Whenever relaxation of constraints is used to force a first basic feasible solution, the simplex algorithm is, of course, working on a different problem from the original problem. It is necessary to restore the original problem, and the inverse-of-basis method does this easily. For any two tableaux—call them *initial* and *final*—there is a matrix $\mathbf{B}^{-1}$ called the inverse of the basis, that can be multiplied onto any column of the initial tableau to get the corresponding column of the final tableau. Thus if we make any changes in the initial tableau, we can simply multiply $\mathbf{B}^{-1}$ onto the changed columns of the initial tableau to get the correspondingly changed columns of the final tableau. $\mathbf{B}^{-1}$ bottles up, in one operation, all the manipulations from the initial to the final tableau.

$\mathbf{B}^{-1}$ is defined as the columns in the final tableau that correspond to the basic columns in the initial tableau. To illustrate, the initial tableau for the relaxed problem in exercise E64 is

x_0	x_1	x_2	x_3	x_4	x_5	x_6	b_i
1	2	-2	-1				0
	1	1	1	1			4
	-1	-1	-1		1		1
	-1	1	1			1	1

The final tableau for that relaxed problem is

x_0	x_1	x_2	x_3	x_4	x_5	x_6	b_i
1	0		1			2	2
	2		0	1		-1	3
	-2		0		1	1	2
	-1	1	1			1	1

In this example the basis in the initial tableau is columns 0, 4, 5, and 6, in that order; hence $\mathbf{B}^{-1}$ is columns 0, 4, 5, and 6 of the final tableau. We can demonstrate that it converts initial columns into final columns by multiplying it onto the initial x_1 column (which has elements {2, 1, -1, -1}):

$$\begin{bmatrix} 1 & 0 & 0 & 2 \\ 0 & 1 & 0 & -1 \\ 0 & 0 & 1 & 1 \\ 0 & 0 & 0 & 1 \end{bmatrix} \begin{bmatrix} 2 \\ 1 \\ -1 \\ -1 \end{bmatrix} = \begin{bmatrix} 0 \\ 2 \\ -2 \\ -1 \end{bmatrix}$$

Note that the result on the right is the x_1 column in the final tableau.

Now the original problem in example E64 has as its right-hand-side column the elements {0, 4, −4, −1} (the two negative elements were relaxed to 1 to form the changed problem). Let us use $\mathbf{B}^{-1}$ to determine the final right-hand-side for the original problem:

$$\begin{bmatrix} 1 & 0 & 0 & 2 \\ 0 & 1 & 0 & -1 \\ 0 & 0 & 1 & 1 \\ 0 & 0 & 0 & 1 \end{bmatrix} \begin{bmatrix} 0 \\ 4 \\ -4 \\ -1 \end{bmatrix} = \begin{bmatrix} -2 \\ 5 \\ -5 \\ -1 \end{bmatrix}$$

Thus the restored final tableau for the original problem is

x_0	x_1	x_2	x_3	x_4	x_5	x_6	b_i
1	0		1			2	−2
	2		0	1		−1	5
	−2		0		1	1	−5
	−1	1	1			1	−1

The dual-simplex algorithm:

Note that the final tableau for the original problem is not feasible (it has $x_5 = -5$ and $x_2 = -1$), but Lemke's dual-simplex algorithm can make it feasible. Related to every linear program is its *dual linear program*, which is the program whose tableau would be the transpose of the "primal" linear program, with the primal objective-function row becoming the dual right-hand-side column and the primal right-hand-side column becoming the dual objective-function row. Since the changed problem was minimized and the restoration affected only the right-hand-side column, there are no negative elements in any x column of the objective-function row. The restored final tableau is said to be *dual feasible*—the associated dual problem is feasible but not optimal because the primal problem is "optimal" but not feasible. Lemke realized you could turn the problem on its side and optimize by the simplex method, and the result when turned upright again would be the final answer to the primal problem. The dual-simplex method transposes the rules rather than the problem.

Recall that at each iteration the simplex method identifies a pivot element and performs a pivot. The pivot element is in the column where the objective-row coefficient is greatest (for maximizing) or least (for minimizing), and it is in the row having the least positive value of the simplex ratio. At each iteration the dual-simplex method also identifies a pivot element and performs a pivot. The only distinction is the way that the pivot element is identified.

Dual-simplex algorithm:

1. The pivot row is the row having the most negative element in the b_i column (if there are no negative elements, stop).
2. The pivot column is the column having the smallest absolute value of the dual-simplex ratio—the ratio of the element in the objective row to the element in the pivot row—ignoring ratios where the denominator is positive or zero.

Applying the dual-simplex algorithm to the restored final tableau above, we choose the row whose right-hand-size element is –5. For that row, the only dual-simplex ratio with a negative denominator is 0/(–2) for column 1. Therefore the pivot element is the –2 in the x_5-defining row and x_1 column; x_1 will enter the basis and x_5 will leave the basis.

The reader can verify that after the pivot the resulting tableau is as follows:

x_0	x_1	x_2	x_3	x_4	x_5	x_6	b_i
1			1		0	2	–2
		0	1	1	0		0
	1		0		–1/2	–1/2	5/2
		1	1		–1/2	1/2	3/2

This tableau is feasible, and of course optimal. The values of x_1, x_2, and x_3 that satisfy the original problem in example E64 are 5/2, 3/2, and 0, giving $x_0 = -2$.

The IE PE Exam sometimes covers other linear programming topics, such as sensitivity analysis, the (Hitchcock) transportation model, the assignment model, and duality theory. The appropriate level of review material can be found in any of the standard introductory operations research textbooks, e.g. those by Taha (Macmillan), Hiller and Lieberman (Holden-Day), or Phillips (Wiley).

6.3.2 Dynamic Programming Models

Dynamic programming is a powerful set of techniques for separable problems—problems that allow valid separation of the objective function and constraints into parts whose contributions to the objective function and to the fulfillment of constraints are additive or multiplicative. In *serial dynamic programming* the parts are *stages* numbered $n = 1,2,...,N$ that correspond to epochs in time, and the accounting for fulfillment of constraints is handled in terms of *states* numbered $i \in J$ for the state entering stage n and $j \in J$ for the state leaving stage n and entering state $n+1$. The state of the system at the beginning or end or both is given or constrained. There is a *decision k* $\in K_{i,n}$ at each stage. According to this decision there is an *immediate reward* (contribution to the objective function) and a *state transition* so that the state entering the next stage is a function of the state entering this stage and the decision. If the rule that determines the next state j given the current state i and the decision k is the same at each stage, the rule is called a *recursive relationship* or *transition function*. Commonly the recursive relationship is simply $j = i - k$; this is the case when the state variable represents the unfulfilled remainder of a requirement and the decision variable represents the amount satisfied at a stage. The immediate reward can be denoted $r_{i,j}(n,k)$—the reward at stage n for making decision k when the state is i, where j is the state that the transition function prescribes for i and k.

To illustrate serial dynamic programming, consider the following problem:

A shopping center has 6 applicants for Santa Claus jobs. Here are the numbers of added customers expected at each of 3 stores if given numbers of Santas are assigned to that store:

		Santas assigned (k)		
		1	2	3
	1	200	315	390
Stores (n)	2	210	310	410
	3	215	320	340

How many Santas should be assigned to each store to maximize the number of added customers for the entire shopping center and to meet the constraint that either 1, 2, or 3 Santas must be assigned to each store?

To relate the Santa problem to the quantities introduced above, imagine a bus that contains i Santas as it approaches store n; it drops off k Santas at store n and is left with $j = i-k$ Santas for the approach to store $n+1$. The table gives values of $r_{i,j}(n,k)$ for various n and k (independent of i).

Now we introduce the *fundamental value equation* of serial dynamic programming for backward solution (a similar equation is available for forward solution). Let $v_i(n)$ represent the total reward at stages n, $n+1$, . . ., N; it is the total of the immediate reward and all downstream rewards. (For the Santa problem, $v_i(n)$ is the total number of added customers expected to be attracted by the Santas assigned to stores n through 3.) The fundamental value equation is

$$v_i(n) = \begin{cases} \max_{k \in K_{i,n}}\left[r_{i,j}(n,k) + v_j(n+1) \right], & i \in J, \quad n = 1,2,...,N \\ 0, & n = N+1 \end{cases} \quad (6\text{-}28)$$

Serial dynamic programs can conveniently be solved in tabular form. There is a table for each stage, starting with the final stage N. Let there be a row for every reachable and feasible state i at the stage, and let there be a column for every allowable decision k at the stage. We can omit cells where the decision is not allowable for the state. In cell (i,k) of the table, we place the immediate reward $r_{i,j}(n,k)$ in the upper left corner, the value of the downstream state $v_j(n+1)$ in the upper right corner (this is zero for state $n = N$ and is known from the previously evaluated downstream state as the states are evaluated in reverse order), and their sum in the center. We solve the row's instance of equation 6-28 by marking the maximum sum in the row.

We begin a tabular solution to the Santa problem at stage 3 (the third store). The possible states (numbers of Santas remaining) are 1, 2, 3, or 4 (5 and 6 are unreachable since each of the previous two stores must be assigned at least one Santa from the total of six). The possible decisions are to assign $k = 1$, 2, or 3 Santas here, but not more than the number remaining. The immediate rewards are those in the last row of the data table for k (they do not depend on i, so are the same for every cell in a given column). Since this is the last stage, the downstream rewards are zero. The cell sums in a row are the possible values of the incoming state i. We choose the greatest one in row i as $v_i(3)$ and highlight it.

Stage 3

i \ k	1		2		3	
1	215	0				
	215					
2	215	0	320	0		
	215		**320**			
3	215	0	320	0	340	0
	215		320		**340**	
4	215	0	320	0	340	0
	215		320		**340**	

At stage 2 the possible states are 3, 4, and 5. The immediate rewards are those for store 2 in the data table, and the downstream rewards are the bold numbers in the rows of the table for stage 3. For example, if the decision is 2 when the state is 3, or 3 when the state is 4, the downstream state will be 1, and that state has already been found to have the value 215.

Stage 2

	k		
i	1	2	3
3	210 320 **530**	310 215 525	
4	210 340 550	310 320 **630**	410 215 625
5	210 340 550	310 340 650	410 320 **730**

At the first stage the incoming state is given as 6, the immediate rewards are from the data table for store 1, and the downstream rewards are from the table just completed.

Stage 1

	k		
i	1	2	3
6	200 730 930	315 630 **945**	390 530 920

The result of the tabular solution is that an expected <u>945</u> extra customers can be earned by assigning <u>2 Santas to store 1</u> (leaving 4 as the state for store 2), <u>2 Santas to store 2</u> (leaving 2 as the state for store 3), and <u>2 Santas to store 3</u>.

Note that in the tabular solution method the optimal value of the objective function is apparent at the end of the problem, but the optimal decisions must be traced back through the tables.

Alternatives to the tabular solution method are to solve algebraically by repeated solution of equation 6-28, and (for small problems) graphically. Recall that the solution method for the concave-cost production/inventory method, illustrated in Figure 6-6, was actually dynamic programming. The forward- and backward-pass calculations in section 6.2.1 are variants of dynamic programming. Decision-tree analysis, which sometimes appears on the IE PE Exam and is reviewed at the appropriate level in some introductory operations research textbooks and some engineering economy textbooks (such as *Modern Engineering Economy,* Young, 1993), uses a "foldback" procedure that is a particularly clear variant of dynamic programming. Example E65 will illustrate both algebraic and graphical methods of solving dynamic programs.

E65. Shippers of items of types 1, 2, and 3 pay shipping charges of 2, 3, and 4 thousand dollars per item, respectively, and the items weigh 2, 4, and 5 tons apiece, respectively. How can a cargo hold with exactly 9 tons of capacity be loaded with these items so as to maximize the shipping charges earned?

This is an example of the classical *knapsack problem*, which can be formulated as shown in equation 6-29.

$$\text{Maximize} \quad \sum_{n=1}^{N} r_n x_n$$

$$\text{subject to} \quad \sum_{n=1}^{N} a_n x_n \leq b \quad \text{(resource constraint)} \quad (6\text{-}29)$$

$$\text{and} \quad x_n \in 0, 1, 2, \dots$$

$$\text{with} \quad a_n \in 1, 2, \dots, \quad b \in 0, 1, 2, \dots, \quad r_n > 0$$

Although we will solve the problem in a simpler manner, it is instructive to note that the classical knapsack problem can be solved by the value equation

$$v_i(n) = \max_{x_n}\left[r_n x_n + v_j(n+1)\right] \quad \text{where} \quad j = i - a_n x_n$$

In this formulation there is a stage corresponding to each item type and the state at each stage is the remaining capacity. We are maximizing $2x_1 + 3x_2 + 4x_3$, subject to the constraint $2x_1 + 4x_2 + 5x_3 \leq 9$, with integer x_i.

However, since there are no restrictions on the amounts of individual types of items to be loaded (no restrictions such as $1 \leq x_1 \leq 3$), the stage (item type) is irrelevant. For each possible amount of remaining capacity i, let the decision be simply the type of the item to be loaded next. Add a null item type $n = 0$ that has no unit reward ($r_0 = 0$) and uses one unit of capacity ($a_0 = 1$), and solve the simplified value equation

$$v_i = \max_{n=0,1,\dots,N}\left[r_n + v_j\right], \quad i = 0, 1, \dots, 6$$

$$\text{where} \quad j = i - a_n \geq 0 \quad \text{and} \quad v_0 = 0$$

The value of state $i=0$ is zero, and the value of every state can be found if the values of all smaller states $j \leq i$ are known. With the numerical data, this becomes

$$v_i = \max\left[0 + v_{i-1}, 2 + v_{i-2}, 3 + v_{i-4}, 4 + v_{i-5}\right], \quad i = 0, 1, \dots, 6, \quad v_j \geq 0$$

Algebraically, the solution is as follows:

i						Load one unit of type
0	v_0	=	0 by definition			
1	v_1	=	max[0+0]	=	0	0
2	v_2	=	max[0+0, 2+0]	=	2	1
3	v_3	=	max[0+2, 2+0]	=	2	0 or 1
4	v_4	=	max[0+2, 2+2, 3+0]	=	4	1
5	v_5	=	max[0+4, 2+2, 3+0, 4+0]	=	4	0, 1, or 3
6	v_6	=	max[0+4, 2+4, 3+2, 4+0]	=	6	1
7	v_7	=	max[0+6, 2+4, 3+2, 4+2]	=	6	0, 1, or 3
8	v_8	=	max[0+6, 2+6, 3+4, 4+2]	=	8	1
9	v_9	=	max[0+8, 2+6, 3+4, 4+4]	=	8	0, 1, or 3

The maximum total shipping charge is <u>$8000</u>. Starting with 9 tons of capacity, and breaking ties by always loading the greatest of the alternative optimal amounts, the optimal loading plan is to <u>load first an item of type 3</u>; this leaves a capacity of 4 tons, and it is optimal to <u>load next an item of type 1</u>; this leaves a capacity of 2 tons, and it is optimal to <u>load finally another item of type 1</u>.

Figure 6-17 gives the graphical solution for stagewise treatment of the problem in example E65. Note that the value of the initial node is 8 ($8000); the optimal decision at stage 1 (how many units of type 1 to load) is to load 2 units (the darkened path brings the state from 9 to 5 and earns 4); the optimal decision for type 2 is to load none, and the optimal decision for type 3 is to load 1 unit (the darkened path brings the state from 5 to 0 and earns 4).

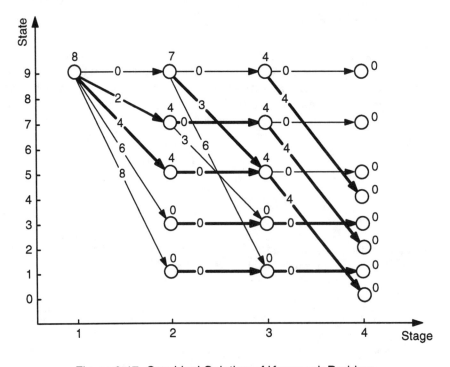

Figure 6-17. Graphical Solution of Knapsack Problem.

6.3.3 Layout and Location Analysis Models

In facility design, industrial engineers are often faced with finding the best places to put things—layout and location analysis. Much of the operations research that industrial engineers study in school is oriented toward such issues. The location-allocation model, for example, which can be viewed as a series of transportation or transshipment problems, is useful for large-scale designs such as where to put warehouses for distribution of a product throughout the continental United States, or how to lay out a mass transportation system for an urban area. Large-scale optimization models, fortunately or unfortunately, cannot be tested very well in a professional examination. However, small-scale models are often tested.

The layout technique most often tested in the IE PE Exam is based on the *activity relationship chart* introduced in R. Muther's 1973 book *Systematic Layout Planning*, Second Edition. The location analysis model most often tested is the single-facility minisum model with a rectilinear distance metric. The *assignment problem*, a special linear programming model that allows for convenient manual calculation and is useful in some layout and location applications, also appears frequently in the exam. These methods and several others will be reviewed in this section.

6.3.3.1 Layout by Activity Relationship Charts

Layout—the placement of facilities relative to each other—greatly affects several kinds of cost and effectiveness:

- material handling
- accessibility—for maintenance, for customers, for suppliers
- supervision and communication
- safety assurance and environmental control
- esthetics and public image

Any of these factors can dominate a layout. For example, 100 years ago a very important consideration in laying out a factory floor was for the manager to be able to keep everything in view (usually from an office overlooking the floor from above); similar considerations govern the layout of gambling casinos and mass transit terminals even today.

Most layouts prepared by industrial engineers are of one of the three basic types: a product layout, a process layout, or an activity-relationship layout. Often the layout within departments will be of the product or process type, while the larger-scale "block" layout of departments relative to each other will be of the activity-relationship type.

A *product layout* locates facilities according to the material flow in producing a product. The extreme example of a product layout is an assembly line. The production process follows some simple curve such as a straight line or a U-curve. For instance, a dairy can be laid out so that for 2%-fat milk the centrifuge, preheater, homogenizer, pasteurizer, cooler, inspection station, and filler all follow in a sequence. The skim-milk facilities would be nearly identical except for a heavier centrifuge, and the whole-milk facilities would be nearly identical except for lack of a centrifuge. Advantages of a product layout include flow logicality (you can walk the line along with the product from receiving to shipping, and the layout diagram looks very much like the process flow diagram), small WIP inventories, short throughput time, short material flow paths, and ease of supervision and control.

A *process layout* locates facilities according to type. The extreme example of a process layout is a job shop. Facilities of the same type are grouped together. For instance, a dairy can be laid out so that there is a centrifuge area, a homogenizing area, a pasteurization area, a cooling area, and so forth. Advantages of a process layout include better machine and labor utilization (two centrifuges might process three products), flexibility (a unique large order for one product may be processed using nearly all the facilities normally used for three products), greater reliability (equipment that normally runs a different product can substitute for equipment that breaks down), and more interesting work for operators.

Given a group of departments (or machines, or process areas) labeled A, B,..., each having a required floorspace area H_A, H_B,..., a layout that locates them relative to each other either in an existing building or on an unrestricted plane can rationally be based on interaction among departments. If the interaction is quantitatively measured, it is usually in terms of numbers of trips between pairs of departments (not material flow amounts). If the interaction is subjectively measured, it is usually in terms of Muther's interaction codes:

Code	Closeness	Rank (% below)
A	Absolutely necessary	95
E	Especially important	85
I	Important	70
O	Ordinary closeness O.K.	50
U	Unimportant	0
X	*Not* desirable	–

If there are N departments, there are $N \times (N-1)/2$ closeness ratings, one for each pair of departments. Eliminating those coded X, the rating procedure should be tuned so that approximately the top 5% of the closeness ratings are coded A, approximately the next 10% are coded

E, and so forth, according to the third column in the above table. If the importance codes are derived from trip counts, the codes should be assigned on the basis of rank as given above—the top 5% of trip counts (among those not to be coded *X*) would be coded *A*, and so forth.

It is traditional to display the importance codes in the form of a triangular chart introduced by Muther and known as the "Muther activity relationship chart." However, it is perfectly acceptable to display them simply as an upper-triangular matrix. For instance, if it is absolutely necessary for Shipping and Receiving to be close, especially important for Shipping and Packaging to be close and for Milling and Receiving to be close, important for Milling and Assembly to be close, for Milling and Packaging to be close, and for Assembly and Packaging to be close, then the activity relationship chart could be displayed in either of the following forms:

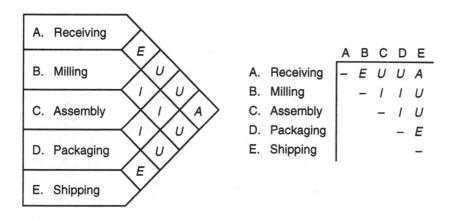

Once the activity-relationship codes are derived, the layout can be performed by a computerized plant layout package such as ALDEP, CORELAP, CRAFT, or PLANET (see the textbook *Facilities Planning* (Tompkins and White 1984)). Layout can also be performed manually.

For manual activity-relationship layout, first make a sketch of a proposed block layout. Then judge the quality of the layout. According to Francis and White (1974), a layout should be judged first on its satisfying the greatest number of *A* relationships, next on its satisfying the greatest number of *E* relationships, next on its satisfying the greatest number of *I* relationships, and finally on its satisfying the fewest number of *X* relationships. The computerized packages use a numerical scoring system. ALDEP, for example, uses 64 for *A*, 16 for *E*, 4 for *I*, 1 for *O*, 0 for *U*, and −1024 for *X*. This is equivalent to judging first on the fewest number of *X* relationships, then on the greatest number of *A* relationships, and so forth—the same as the Francis and White scheme with the glaring exception that avoiding *X* relationships is the most important criterion rather than the least important.

A layout satisfies a closeness relationship between departments Y and Z if in its block diagram there is an adequate common boundary shared by Y and Z—a common boundary adequate to facilitate whatever interactions cause the closeness relationship to be defined. Consider the following three block diagrams:

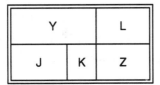 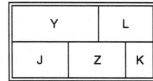 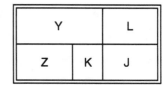

Let us suppose that Y and Z have an *E* relationship. Depending on what interactions give rise to the relationship, the layout on the left probably would not satisfy it, the one in the middle might satisfy it, and the one on the right would certainly satisfy it. The cater-cornered proximity of Y and Z in the layout on the left would be inadequate for most purposes, but if the actual requirement were that personnel in department Z would use the rest rooms in department Y, and the relationship had been given an *E* importance because of the cost of building additional rest rooms, then mere access to a corner of Y from Z should be sufficient to satisfy the requirement.

A complete activity-relationship layout problem is solved as #470 in *Problems and Solutions* (Young 1993).

6.3.3.2 Single-facility Location Models

There are several single-facility location models that have strikingly simple solution methods. One that is ideal for use in the IE PE Exam is the single-facility minisum location model with a rectilinear distance metric also known as the "median" or half-sum location problem—the problem of locating a new facility given a group of existing facilities that have known fixed locations, where the total costs of interaction between the new facility and all existing facilities is to be minimized, and these costs are a weighted sum of the rectilinear distances from the new facility to *m* existing facilities. If the new facility is to be located on the plane at some to-be-chosen coordinate (x, y), and existing facility i is located at coordinate (a_i, b_i), then the rectilinear distance between the new facility and facility i is $|x-a_i| + |y-b_i|$. That is, it is the sum of the distances in each of the two directions. Rectilinear distances are realistic for problems where the travel is along a rectilinear grid and shortcuts cannot be taken; for example, in an oil refinery where the greatest equipment cost is actually that of the thousands of pipes that connect all the equipment, almost all the pipes are constrained to go east-west or north-south in well-organized trenches and overhead pipe racks, so that even a large-diameter pipe from a piece of equipment to another that is 100 m east and 100 m north must be 200 m long rather than 141 m (the chaotic layout that would result if piping followed beelines would be even more costly than the extra distances necessitated by the rectilinear discipline).

Let w_i be the annual cost (or number of trips) per unit distance of interactions between the new facility and facility i. Then we wish to minimize this objective function for the "median" or half-sum location problem:

$$\underset{x,y}{\text{Minimize}} \quad \sum_{i=1}^{m} w_i \left(|x - a_i| + |y - b_i| \right) \qquad (6\text{-}30)$$

The solution is strikingly simple. The x and y coordinates of the new facility can be separately determined. The x coordinate must be the same as that of one of the existing facilities—the one for which the sums of the weights w_i for existing facilities to the left, and to the right, are both less than half the sum of all weights. Similarly, the y coordinate must be the same as that of one of the existing facilities—the one for which the sums of the weights w_i for existing facilities in the increasing y direction, and in the decreasing y direction, are both less than half the sum of all weights.

E66. Plotted to scale on a factory floor plan are the locations of equipment that will use compressed air to be supplied by a new compressor. Listed below each location is the estimated amount of air in m³/hr that will be demanded by the equipment at that location. The air supply lines will follow rectilinear paths. Assuming that all relevant costs are proportional to demand, determine the best location for the new compressor.

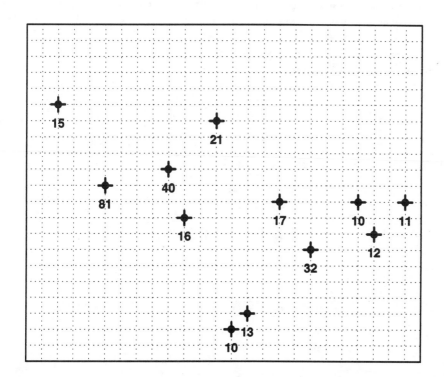

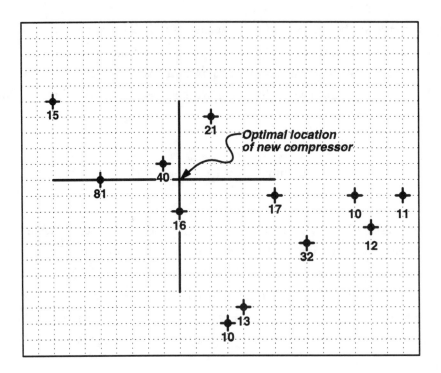

The sum of the weights is 278, half of which is 139. As we go right from the leftmost existing facility the cumulative sums are 15, 96, 136, 157,..., so x is that of the fourth facility from the left. As we go up from the bottommost existing facility the cumulative sums are 10, 23, 55, 67, 83, 121 (three facilities at this y coordinate), 202,..., so y is that of the ninth facility from the bottom.

The solution is shown in the sketch above. If the objective function were a meaningful quantity in itself, it would be necessary to report its optimal value. If it is not clear why the solution method works, imagine the weights as numbers of trips; if you moved the new compressor one unit down in the y direction, then the 121 trips below it would be shortened by one unit but the 157 trips above it would be lengthened by one unit.

When the distance metric is Euclidean (beeline) distance the same problem—locate a new facility given locations $\{a_i, b_i\}$ and interaction weights $\{w_i\}$ for m existing facilities—is called the Steiner-Weber or Fermat problem. The objective is

$$\underset{x,y}{\text{Minimize}} \sum_{i=1}^{m} w_i \left[(x - a_i)^2 + (y - b_i)^2 \right]^{1/2} \tag{6-31}$$

To solve this problem, for each of the m existing facilities compute

$$g_i(x,y) = \frac{w_i}{\left[(x-a_i)^2 + (y-b_i)^2\right]^{1/2}}, \quad i = 1,...,m \qquad (6\text{-}32)$$

Let $(x^{(0)}, y^{(0)})$ be an initial estimate of the optimal location (x, y). (A good starting solution is the "gravity" solution reviewed later in this section.) We can iteratively obtain closer estimates of x and y in iterations $k = 1,2,...$ by computing $x^{(k)}$ and $y^{(k)}$ at each iteration k as follows:

$$x^{(k)} = \frac{\sum_{i=1}^{m} a_i g_i\left(x^{(k-1)}, y^{(k-1)}\right)}{g_i\left(x^{(k-1)}, y^{(k-1)}\right)} \qquad (6\text{-}33a)$$

$$y^{(k)} = \frac{\sum_{i=1}^{m} b_i g_i\left(x^{(k-1)}, y^{(k-1)}\right)}{g_i\left(x^{(k-1)}, y^{(k-1)}\right)} \qquad (6\text{-}33b)$$

A strikingly simple solution of the Steiner-Weber problem exists for the case of four existing facilities all with equal weights. Then the optimal location for the new facility is at the existing facility that is inside a triangle formed by the others, or, if there is no such triangle, at the intersection of lines joining two pairs of existing facilities:

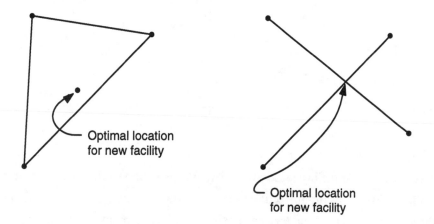

Optimal location
for new facility

Optimal location
for new facility

For any number of existing facilities and any set of weights, there is a *mechanical analog* that solves the Steiner-Weber problem. In a flat rigid sheet of plastic or plywood, drill holes at the existing *m* facilities' locations to scale. Attach *m* strings to a small washer, rest the washer on top of the sheet, put the strings through the holes, and, on each string that goes through the hole representing facility *i*, attach a weight whose heaviness is proportional to w_i to the end of the string. Then pick up the sheet, hold it horizontal with the weights dangling, and shake it to overcome friction. The washer will seek the optimal location!

When the weighted costs are proportional to the *square* of the Euclidean distance, the problem of locating a new facility among *m* existing facilities with interaction weights $\{w_i\}$ is called the "gravity" problem. The objective function for the gravity problem is

$$\underset{x,y}{\text{Minimize}} \sum_{i=1}^{m} w_i \left[(x - a_i)^2 + (y - b_i)^2 \right] \tag{6-34}$$

This problem, first solved by Lagrange, is also called the centroid or center-of-gravity problem, and its solution is simple: locate the new facility at the center of gravity of the existing facilities, where the center of gravity (x, y) has as its x coordinate the weighted average of existing facilities' x coordinates and its y coordinate equal to the weighted average of existing facilities' y coordinates:

$$x = \frac{\sum_{i=1}^{m} w_i a_i}{\sum_{i=1}^{m} w_i} \tag{6-35a}$$

$$y = \frac{\sum_{i=1}^{m} w_i b_i}{\sum_{i=1}^{m} w_i} \tag{6-35b}$$

The *minimax* single-facility location problem with a rectilinear distance metric is to locate a new facility so that the maximum rectilinear distance to any of *m* existing facilities is minimized. Given the easting a_i and northing b_i of each existing facility, compute the following quantities:

Quantity	*Interpretation*	*Governing point*
$c_{SW} = \min(a_i + b_i)$	Distance from origin to most southwesterly point	Most southwesterly point
$c_{NE} = \max(a_i + b_i)$	Distance from origin to most northeasterly point	Most northeasterly point
$c_{SE} = \min(-a_i + b_i)$	Least northing–easting difference	Most southeasterly point
$c_{NW} = \max(-a_i + b_i)$	Greatest northing–easting difference	Most northwesterly point
$c_{MAX} = \max(c_{NE}-c_{SW}, c_{NW}-c_{SE})$	$c_{MAX}/2$ is the minimax distance that can be achieved	

The minimax distance $c_{MAX}/2$ can be achieved by locating the new facility at either of the following two points or at any point on a straight line segment that connects them:

$$\left(\frac{c_{SW} - c_{SE}}{2}, \ \frac{c_{SW} + c_{SE} + c_{MAX}}{2} \right)$$

$$\left(\frac{c_{NE} - c_{NW}}{2}, \ \frac{c_{NE} + c_{NW} - c_{MAX}}{2} \right)$$

Not all m existing facilities are relevant to the minimax problem. Draw a convex hull around the set of points. Only points on the hull are relevant; those strictly within the hull may be ignored.

Here is an example of the minimax single-facility location problem with a rectilinear distance metric:

A new blood bank will have 11 hospitals in its service area. Blood-delivery ambulances will travel rectilinear paths to deliver blood to hospitals. It is desired to locate the blood bank so as to minimize the length of the longest delivery trip. The hospital locations are shown to scale on the following diagram, with distances measured in city blocks:

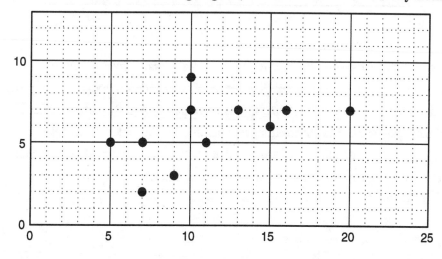

Only four of the hospitals are on the convex hull—the ones at (5, 5), (10, 10), (20, 7), and (7, 2). Call them H_1, H_2, H_3, and H_4, respectively. Calculations will be restricted to these.

Hospital	(a_i, b_i)	$(a_i + b_i)$	$(-a_i + b_i)$
H_1	(5, 5)	10	$0 = c_{NW}$
H_2	(10, 9)	19	-1
H_3	(20, 7)	$27 = c_{NE}$	$-13 = c_{SE}$
H_4	(7, 2)	$9 = c_{SW}$	-5

$c_{MAX} = \max(27-9, 0-(-13)) = 18$. Thus the minimax distance is $c_{MAX}/2 = \underline{9}$, which can be achieved by locating the blood bank at either point $(1/2(9-(-13)), (1/2(9+(-13)+18))) = (11, 7)$, or $(1/2(27-0), 1/2(27-18)) = (13.5, 4.5)$, or on a line segment that connects them.

The solution is shown in the diagram to follow. Some of the optimal blood-bank locations are (11,7), (12,6), (13, 5), and (13.5, 4.5). The reader can verify that all hospitals (including of course the ones inside the convex hull) are within a distance of 9 blocks from every one of these minimax-optimal locations.

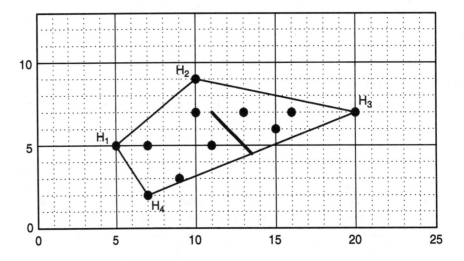

The minimax single-facility location problem with a *Euclidean* distance metric applies to such situations as locating an emergency water cache on a flat desert floor or locating a transmitter to reach a fixed set of receivers, again on flat terrain. Richard E. Rosenthal (1983) showed that this problem can be solved with arbitrary constraints (e.g., do not locate in a lake or minefield or other forbidden zone) graphically as a one-dimensional search problem. Let the search parameter be, for example, the maximum range r of a transmitter that is to reach m fixed-location receivers.

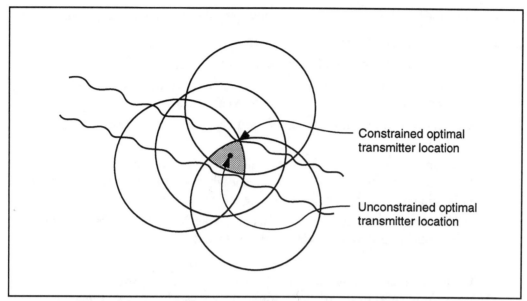

Figure 6-18. Minimax Euclidean Solution with Arbitrary Constraint.

Around each receiver, draw a circle of radius r. As r increases from zero, there will come a time when the two or three circles from the most remote receivers first contain a point in common. This point is the unconstrained minimax location and r is the required transmitter range if the transmitter is located there.

If the unconstrained optimal point is in a forbidden zone, simply keep increasing r until the area common to the two or three critical circles first contains a point outside the forbidden zone. This point is the constrained minimax point, and r is the required transmitter range.

6.3.3.3 The Assignment Problem

The classical assignment problem is this: Given a table of costs $\{c_{ij}\}$ of assigning "source" i to "destination" j, find the minimal-cost assignment plan to assign each source to a unique destination and each destination to a unique source. Contexts in which the problem arises include assigning bidders to contracts, assigning machines to locations, assigning people to jobs, and assigning tasks to resources. Let there be N sources and N destinations (unequal numbers of sources and destinations can be handled and will be discussed later).

Let the cost table have a row for each source and a column for each destination. Let an assignment plan be indicated by circling the costs of the assignments in the plan. A valid assignment plan must have one and only one circled element in each row and one and only one circled element in each column. The total cost to be minimized is the sum of the circled costs.

The assignment problem can be solved manually by the "Hungarian" algorithm:

1. Subtract the minimal element of each row from all the elements in the row.
2. Subtract the minimal element of each column from all the elements in the column.
3. Try to make a valid assignment plan using zero elements only. If successful, go to step 6. If only q assignments can be made, $q < N$, continue.
4. Cover all zeros with the minimal number of lines that it takes to cover them all (this number is q).
5. From each uncovered element *subtract* the minimal uncovered element; call this element y. *Add* y to each intersection element (element where two zero-covering lines cross). Leave the singly-covered elements unchanged. Go to 3.
6. Transfer the assignment plan to the original cost table. The total cost of the optimal set of assignments is the sum of the circled elements in the original cost table.

Appliances $\{i\}$ are at distances from electrical outlets $\{j\}$ as shown in the cost table below. To minimize total cord length, what is the best plan to plug each appliance into an outlet?

Costs c_{ij}

i \ j	1	2	3	4
1	0	2	2	7
2	3	6	6	9
3	2	5	1	1
4	2	7	6	3

Step 4:

i \ j	1	2	3	4
1	0	0	2	7
2	0	1	3	6
3	1	2	0	0
4	0	3	4	1

Step 1:

i \ j	1	2	3	4
1	0	2	2	7
2	0	3	3	6
3	1	4	0	0
4	0	5	4	1

Steps 5 and 3:

i \ j	1	2	3	4
1	1	(0)	2	7
2	(0)	0	2	5
3	2	2	(0)	0
4	0	2	3	(0)

Steps 2 and 3:

i \ j	1	2	3	4
1	0	(0)	2	7
2	(0)	1	3	6
3	1	2	(0)	0
4	0	3	4	1

Step 6:

i \ j	1	2	3	4
1	0	(2)	2	7
2	(3)	6	6	9
3	2	5	(1)	1
4	2	7	6	(3)

The resulting assignments of sources $\{1, 2, 3, 4\}$ to destinations $\{2, 1, 3, 4\}$ have a total cost of $2+3+1+3 = \underline{9}$. Note that it is suboptimal to plug appliance 1 into outlet 1, even though (since $c_{11}=0$ is the only zero cost) it is apparently right at the outlet!

For an assignment problem to maximize profits rather than minimize costs, first subtract all profits from the greatest profit. Solve the problem with the resulting cost table, then recover the final profits by subtracting costs from the greatest profit. For instance, profits 3 and 4 become costs 1 and 0 to solve the problem, them become profits 3 and 4 again.

If a destination can accept more than one source (e.g., two-plug electrical outlets), model this with more than one destination having identical cost columns. Similarly (e.g., two appliances at the same location), there can be separate identical rows for sources that have more than one destination.

If there are fewer destinations than sources, say M destinations, $M < N$, add N–M dummy destinations having all-zero cost columns. The solution will identify which sources are best left unassigned by assigning them to dummy destinations. Similarly, if there are fewer sources, add dummy sources having all-zero cost rows, and the solution will identify which destinations are best left unassigned by assigning dummy sources to them.

Chapter 7
Work Measurement,
Human Factors, and Ergonomics

The industrial engineer is specifically trained to design human work. Just as electrical or chemical engineers design electrical or chemical systems, industrial engineers design systems that have people as integral operating components. This chapter concerns work design and topics in ergonomics that support work design.

Ergonomics is the study of how people interact with their surroundings, with goals of fitting the work to the person for maximum performance and, where this cannot be done, selecting people best fitted for the work. Ergonomics draws on anthropometry (the study of human body dimensions and movement limitations), on biomechanics (the study of how the skeleton, joints, and muscles accomplish movement and react to force), on those parts of physiology (study of the human body's physical structures and mechanisms) that deal with fatigue (lessened ability to perform work), on stress (real or perceived pressure to work faster or work more), on strain (injuries and symptoms resulting from stress), and on those parts of psychology that deal with human perception and human performance. Human factors is another name for ergonomics or for its application in designing work.

Section 7.1 reviews ergonomics results that industrial engineers must be able to use in work design. Sections 7.2 and 7.3 review design lore based on ergonomics for the proper design of workstations, handtools, and controls. Finally, section 7.4 reviews work measurement techniques that industrial engineers must be able to use and methods of designing work standards that can be used to predict labor costs and establish productivity expectations that are fair to workers.

7.1 Physiology and Work Mechanics

7.1.1 The Human Body

Human body measurements are published in *Handbook of Human Factors* (Salvendy 1986). Selected measurements for American adults are also available in *Work Design: Industrial Ergonomics*, Third Edition (Konz 1990). The selected data in a textbook such as this should be adequate for the IE PE Exam.

E67a. **A door frame has a 7'1" height clearance. Approximately what percentage of American adults—males wearing 1.25" heels and females wearing 2.25" heels—must stoop to pass?**

A table gives American adult male stature as 174±6.9 cm (the ± notation means the average is 174 cm and the standard deviation is 6.9 cm) and American adult female stature as 161±6.6 cm. Body dimensions are normally distributed. A male of stature greater than 7'1" −1.25" = 83.75" or 212.7 cm does not pass. This stature is $z = (212.7 - 174)/6.9 = 5.6$ standard deviations above the mean. For females the z statistic is even more extreme, so <u>almost no percentage</u> of American adults must stoop.

E67b. **There is an ideal eye-level height zone in driving an automobile. If this zone is 6 cm high (that is, an eye level anywhere from x cm to $x+6$ cm above the floor is ideal), what range of vertical seat adjustment is required to allow 95% of American adults to drive at ideal eye height?**

For adult American males and females combined, a table gives a sitting height of 87.8±3.6 cm. The average is irrelevant to this problem. If 95% are to be within the zone, then 2.5% are to be too short and 2.5% too tall. From normal tables, $z = \pm 1.96$ standard deviations for these probabilities. The designer would center the zone at the average sitting height and would need to provide for sitting heights from 1.96×3.6 = 7.056 cm above the mean to 7.056 cm below the mean, a range of 14.1 cm. Of this range, 6 cm is allowed in the definition of "ideal eye height" and the remainder to be covered by vertical seat adjustment is 14.1 − 6 = <u>8.1 cm</u>.

Most dimensions in a table of body dimensions are self-explanatory; "popliteal" means "to the back of the knee," so the sitting popliteal height is the height from the bottom of the heel to the back of the knee while sitting, and the buttock-popliteal depth is from the back of the buttocks to the back of the knee while sitting (the height of a chair seat should not exceed the popliteal height unless there is a footrest, and the distance from the back of a chair to the forward edge of the seat should not exceed the buttock-popliteal depth).

It is common practice in most industries to design for about 95% of the relevant population. For something that can be too big for some people and too small for others, commonly $z = \pm 1.96$

for the combined male and female population, and for something that can only be too big (or too small), commonly $z = 1.64$ (or -1.64) for the female (or male) population only.

E68.   A row of seats for a new theater in Ohio is to have an aisle-to-aisle length of 5 m. Recommend how many seats should be in the row.

The seats can only be wide enough or too narrow, so in the absence of other guidance the seats should allow 95% of men to be comfortable. Elbow-to-elbow breadths are greater than hip breadths (by more than the width of an armrest) and thus govern comfort. A table gives 50.6 cm elbow-to-elbow breadth for 95th-percentile American men. If there are n seats in the 500-cm row the width of one seat is $500/n \geq 50.6$ cm, implying $n \leq 9.88$ seats. Thus we recommend 9 seats in the row. (Nothing is deducted from the 5 m for armrest widths, since elbows are above armrests.)

A qualified engineer can argue for 10 seats since the interference to be avoided occurs only with *adjacent* seating of wide people, which occurs with much less than 5% probability. A qualified engineer can argue for 8 seats by assuming a positive clearance between elbows for comfort and elbow movement, or by choosing a typically built width for a selected class of theater; in fact, 61 cm or 24 in. is a fairly typical seat width for first-class American theaters, allowing only 8 seats.

7.1.2 Metabolism

Metabolism is the body's use of food, water, and oxygen to generate energy and maintain the body. Industrial engineers estimate (or measure) metabolic rates for various purposes: to determine food and water requirements (say for agricultural work crews), to determine human-waste disposal requirements, to determine air-conditioning loads, and to judge the difficulty of work.

Below are some estimates for adult Americans' daily caloric requirements, based on data given by Stephan Konz in *Work Design: Industrial Ergonomics*. Let us consider active and sedentary adult American males and females. The daily caloric requirement will be estimated as the sum of the basal metabolism requirement, plus the daily activity requirement, plus the digestion requirement. We will assume body weights as follows:

	Active	*Sedentary*
Male	75 kg (165 lb)	88 kg (195 lb)
Female	50 kg (110 lb)	57 kg (125 lb)

The basal metabolism requirement, in watts per kilogram of body weight, is estimated as 1.28 W/kg for males and 1.16 W/kg for females.

Table 7-1. Estimated Daily Activity Requirements.

Time Interval	Active	Sedentary
8-hr workday	2.4 W/kg (more than "sweeping with hand carpet sweeper," less than "heavy carpentry")	1.1 W/kg (more than "driving car," less than "dishwashing, typing rapidly")
8-hr home and leisure	2.4 W/kg	0.7 W/kg (average between 0.4 for "sitting quietly" and 1.0 for "driving car, tailoring")
8-hr sleeping	0 W/kg	0 W/kg

The daily caloric requirement is the sum of daily energy requirements in W-hr for basal metabolism, activity cost, and digestion (estimated as 10% of 24-hr basal-plus-activity requirements) converted to kcal (kilocalories or "food" calories) by the conversion factor 0.86 kcal/W-hr:

Active male:

$$75\times[(1.28+2.4)\times8 + (1.28+2.4)\times8 + 1.28\times8]\times1.10\times0.86 = \underline{4904\ kcal}$$

Active female:

$$50\times[(1.16+2.4)\times8 + (1.16+2.4)\times8 + 1.16\times8]\times1.10\times0.86 = \underline{3133\ kcal}$$

Sedentary male:

$$88\times[(1.28+1.1)\times8 + (1.28+0.7)\times8 + 1.28\times8]\times1.10\times0.86 = \underline{3756\ kcal}$$

Sedentary female:

$$57\times[(1.16+1.1)\times8 + (1.16+0.7)\times8 + 1.16\times8]\times1.10\times0.86 = \underline{2278\ kcal}$$

Note that these estimated requirements are based on typical body weights. If sedentary people were to keep their weight down to the weights typical for active people, then a 75-kg sedentary male could eat only 3201 kcal per day, and a 50-kg sedentary female could eat only 1998 kcal per day. The Food and Drug Administration (FDA) and U.S. Department of Agriculture (USDA) agreed in 1993 on food labeling standards that are based on daily adult caloric intake of 2000 kcal and 2500 kcal. A profoundly sedentary male who burned an average of only 0.5 W/kg over the basal 1.28 W/kg during waking hours and weighed only 70 kg (154 lb) would have a daily caloric requirement of $70 \times [(1.28+0.5) \times 16 + 1.28 \times 8] \times 1.10 \times 0.86 = \underline{2564 \, \text{kcal}}$. The FDA standard caloric intakes are substantially below that of the average American diet.

All the metabolic energy generated by a worker, including basal and digestive, is converted to heat and added to the air conditioning load for an indoor worker; water is also exhaled and perspired at a rate of roughly 1.0 g/W-hr. For example, a 75-kg male who works at the "washing floors" rate of 1.4 W/kg activity cost would burn $75 \times (1.28+1.4) \times 1.1 = 221.1$ W (it is customary to assume the 1.1 factor for digestion without regard to time of day), so the air conditioning load generated by the worker would be about 0.22 kW of heat and about 0.22 kg/hr of humidity.

The heart rate of a worker can be measured directly in beats per minute. It can also be estimated from perceived exertion by Borg's scale, which has been validated by numerous studies: 60 at rest, 70 for very, very light exertion, 90 for very light, 110 for fairly light, 130 for somewhat hard, 150 for hard, 170 for very hard, and 190 for very, very hard. If R is the heart rate in beats per minute, A is the activity cost in watts (not W/kg), and M is the body weight in kg, the modified Andrews relationship is

$$R - 60 = K + 19A/M \quad \text{or} \quad A = (R - 60 - K)M/19$$

where $K = 2.3$ for work in which the legs remain still and $K = -11.5$ for work in which the legs are active (because of venous pooling in the legs, a given rate of work elevates the heart rate much more and is perceived as much harder when the legs are still).

E69.   **How much work, in watts, would a 50-kg woman perceive as "somewhat hard" if her legs could perform part of it?**

Given $R = 130$, $K = -11.5$, $M = 50$;

$A = [130 - 60 - (-11.5)]50/19 = \underline{214.47 \, \text{W}}$.

This is 4.3 W/kg, equivalent to dancing or walking somewhat fast.

7.1.3 Pushing and Pulling

It is almost always unwise to have workers work "somewhat hard" on Borg's scale of exertion (heart rate 70 beats/min. elevated over that of at rest) for more than a small fraction of a shift. Machines are much better than people for exerting mechanical power. Exercise that elevates the heart rate would actually be beneficial to the worker were it not for the fact that where there is power, there is force (power is force times distance per unit time). Force injures joints, ligaments, muscles, and nerves.

The most common force-related injuries in American industry are from manual material handling. Machines cannot load and unload arbitrarily sized and shaped things such as airline baggage or parcels and cartons being shipped and received. Injuries to the discs between vertebrae L4 and L5 and L5 and the sacrum are particularly common, because the lower back endures the greatest forces in pushing, pulling, and lifting. Knee injuries are common for workers who must step up or down while carrying a load or exerting a force.

A good reference for pushing and pulling forces is *Ergonomic Design for People at Work*, edited by S. Rodgers of the Eastman Kodak Ergonomics Group (1986). The Kodak tables and factors are reprinted in work design textbooks, including the Konz textbook cited earlier.

Where M is the body weight, a good rule-of-thumb maximum push force, in the same units as body weight, is $0.8M$. With good footing and without bracing, almost any 50-kg woman, for example, can exert at least a 40-kg force in pushing something with both hands at chest level. The amount of mass (weight) that can be pushed sideways on a level surface is, in the same units, $0.8M/\alpha$, where α is the coefficient of friction. Typical values are $\alpha = 0.4$ for wood or cardboard cartons on smooth floors or shelves, $\alpha = 0.3$ for items on metal shelves, and $\alpha = 0.1$ for carts on casters or wheels. The coefficient of friction can get much smaller for large wheels with lubricated bearings or even approach zero for air suspension or magnetic levitation. As a general rule, because of the need to accelerate and decelerate the load, a person should not push and pull a load that weighs more than 16 times the person's weight; this corresponds to $\alpha = 0.05$. Keeping this in mind, should a 105-lb woman push a 2000-lb automobile on a flat street? No, even though rolling friction for an automobile is less than $\alpha = 0.05$, unless the tires are very underinflated, but a 200-lb man could push it if the street were really flat.

When there is a grade of angle θ, such that $y/x = \tan \theta$ or $y/h = \sin \theta$, where y is the rise, x is the horizontal run, and h is the slant run, then the force required to push or pull a weight W uphill is $F = W(\alpha + \sin \theta)$.

E70. **A fairly healthy retiree is employed part-time as a mail clerk. He is expected to push a well-designed, well-oiled mail cart on flat tile floors for about 40 minutes per day to deliver mail to offices on three floors of a building. Pushing the cart into and out of elevators poses no difficulty. If the cart is loaded with 450 lb of mail, is the job too difficult?**

The male retiree very likely weighs at least 90 lb or 41 kg, and the cart's empty weight very likely weighs no more than 40 lb. For $W = 450+40 = 490$ lb, $\alpha = 0.1$, and $\theta = 0$, the required force is $F = 490 \times 0.1 = 49$ lb. The retiree can exert a force of $0.8 \times 90 = 72$ lb, so <u>no</u>, the job is not too difficult.

E71. **In an area not served directly by an elevator but which has a wheelchair ramp, how steep can the ramp be for the retiree to push the full cart up or down the ramp?**

Since pushing is easier than pulling, the cart will be brought down the ramp by gravity, with the worker pushing from the downhill side to limit the motion. $F \leq 72$ lb implies $490(0.1+\sin\theta) \leq 72$, which implies $\sin\theta \leq 0.0469$, or $\theta \leq \underline{2.69°}$. (Most wheelchair ramps are steeper than this; the retiree may need to serve this area late in the mail run, when the cart is not full.)

The Kodak tables give recommended maximum horizontal pushing and pulling forces (for the majority of workers) for various body postures. Forces are given in newtons (N). A newton is a kg-m/sec². Since the acceleration due to gravity is approximately 9.8 m/sec², a kilogram is a force of about 9.8 N. A standing worker doing such things as handling a cart or sliding rolls on or off horizontal shafts can exert about 225 N or 23 kg. But if the body position is awkward because of an obstacle, or if the work is at shoulder height or above so that mainly the arms and shoulders are providing the force, the limit is 110 N or 11.2 kg. The limit for pushing and pulling best done when kneeling is 188 N or 19.2 kg, and best done when sitting is 130 N or 13.3 kg. No references are available on pushing or pulling *behind* a worker. The very act of reaching behind oneself is potentially injurious. The worker must be allowed to turn around if standing, or to swivel if sitting, or else the workplace must be rearranged to present the work in front of the worker's facial plane.

A study of maximum voluntary strengths by Warwick, Novak, Schultz, and Berkson (*Ergonomics* 1980) implies that if a worker can push away a load with a maximum voluntary force F, the same worker's maximum voluntary force for other operations will be as follows.

Push away	Pull toward	Push sideways	Press down	Lift up
F	$0.58F$	$0.55F$	$1.16F$	$1.32F$

All force limits assume good traction, which can be interpreted as $\alpha \geq 0.75$ for the coefficient of friction between shoes and floor. To correct for slippery conditions (wet floor), assume $\alpha = 0.2$.

7.1.4 Lifting (NIOSH Standards)

The maximum weight that a strong worker (50th-percentile male) can safely pick up with one hand under the best conditions (e.g., lifting a suitcase a few inches to a platform) is about 32 kg or 71 lb; airlines commonly limit baggage to 75 lb, and parcel services commonly limit parcels to 70 lb. The "Kodak" tables on lifting allow 315 N or 32 kg for lifting an object with one hand when its handle is 25 cm above the floor; 540 N or 55 kg for pulling down on an overhead handle; 315 N or 32 kg for pulling down on a handle at shoulder height; 287 N or 29 kg for pushing down at elbow height (as in sealing a package); and 202 N or 21 kg for lifting an object to a high shelf or raising a corner or end of a shoulder-height object.

NIOSH (National Institute of Occupational Safety and Health) publishes more restrictive limits for two-handed, smooth, no-twist lifting of a compact, moderate-width load, with good grip or handles and good-friction floor support. The *recommended weight limit* (*RWL*) for lifting, in kg or lb, is given by the formula

$$RWL = LC \times HM \times VM \times DM \times AM \times FM \times CM$$

RWL applies to a workforce whose weakest members would be 25th-percentile women in their 40s. *LC* = 23 kg or 51 lb. LC, *the load constant,* is the recommended limit under ideal conditions.

The various multipliers, all of which have maximum value 1.0, each serve to reduce *RWL* below *LC*.

HM = *BIL/H*. HM, the *horizontal multiplier,* ranges from 1 when the lift is ideally close to the body, down to about 0.40 when the lift is at the functional reach limit of 63 cm or 25 in. *BIL* = 25 cm or 10 in. is the *body interference limit*. *H* is the horizontal distance from the ankle centerline to the knuckles (which horizontally span the load's center of gravity) and is estimated as $H \approx BIL - c + y$, where *y* is the horizontal distance from the front of the body to the load's center of gravity (normally half the load's distal dimension), and *c* is 5 cm or 2 in. if the hands remain at least 25 cm or 10 in. above the floor during the lift, or *c* = 0 if not. Thus $HM \approx BIL/(BIL - c + y)$.

VM = 1 - *VC*×|*V* - *KH*|. VM, the *vertcal multiplier*, is 1 when the lift starts and ends at the optimal knuckle height *KH* = 75 cm or 30 in. *V* is the height of the knuckles at the start or end of the lift, whichever is further from *KH*. *VC* is a constant, 0.003 for cm or 0.0075 for in. If the lift starts or ends at the floor (*V* = 0) or shoulder height (*V* = 150 cm or 60 in.), *VM* = 0.775. The minimum *VM* value is 0.7, for the vertical reach limit *V* = 175 cm or 69 in.

DM = 0.82 + *DC/D*. DM is the *distance multiplier*, where *DC* = 4.5 cm or 1.8 in. is a constant and *D* is the vertical lift distance. *D* is not more than 175-*V* cm or 70-*V* in., which gives *DM* = 0.8457, the minimum. If *D* is less than 25 cm or 10 in., then *DM* = 1. *Note*: A lift can be up or down; *D* is an absolute distance.

AM = 1 - 0.0032×*A*. AM is the *assymetry multiplier*, where *A* is the angular deviation in degrees, either left or right, through which the load rotates during the lift; this is the number of degrees that the lifter must turn or twist. As *A* ranges from 0 to its allowable maximum of 135 degrees, *AM* ranges from 1 to 0.568.

FM is the *frequency multiplier*, which is a tabulated quantity. (The NIOSH lifting tables are reproduced in ergonomic textbooks and handbooks.) *FM* = 1 for infrequent lifts. Typical values are {0.84, 0.60, 0.37} for {4, 8, 12} lifts per minute in short (up to 1-hr) sessions with recovery periods 120% of session length. If lifting cannot be concentrated in short sessions, the *FM* values are such that less total lifting can be done.

CM is the *coupling multiplier*, which is 1 for a good grip, 0.95 for a fair grip (e.g., lifting a box with no handles, but where the fingers can be flexed 90 degrees), and 0.90 for a poor grip (e.g., a feed sack).

E72.   Becky, a 5′2″ female, puts away her Christmas boxes in the attic. She erects a 5-ft (152-cm) stepladder under the open attic trapdoor in the ceiling, lifts a box to the top of the ladder, climbs halfway up the ladder, lifts the box up through the opening to the attic floor, and repeats until the attic-floor space around the opening, except for adequate space for her to work, is full. She climbs into the attic, whose headroom is a maximum of 4′6″, and relocates the boxes away from the opening. A second group of boxes is handled the same way. Recommend a maximum box weight.

Becky makes two overhead lifts and handles the boxes in a cramped attic. The most limiting of these three operations will limit the box weight. The first lift is from floor to head height. Letting the 30-cm dimension be distal, $HM = 25/(25 + 30/2) = 0.625$. $VM = 0.775$ since the lift starts at the floor. The lift distance is 152 cm, so $DM = 0.82 + 4.5/152 = 0.85$. $AM = 1$ (no twisting). $FM = 1$ (Becky paces herself). $CM = 0.95$.

$$RWL = LC \times HM \times VM \times DM \times AM \times FM \times CM = 23 \times 0.625 \times 0.775 \times 0.85 \times 1 \times 1 \times 0.95 = 9.0 \text{ kg or 20 lb}$$

The second lift is from ladder top to attic floor. Because Becky stands on a step of the ladder and the ladder slants away, assume an additional 10-cm horizontal reach, giving $HM = 25/(25 + 30/2 + 10)$ = 0.50. Let us assume a 9-ft attic floor height and 20-cm step spacing, so that the lift distance is 4 ft or 122 cm. The deviation from knuckle height would be half the lift distance if she could center the lift on knuckle height, and she can get within 10 cm of this by standing on the nearest step: $|V - KH|$ = 122/2 + 10 = 71 cm, so $VM = 1 - 0.003 \times 71 = 0.787$. $DM = 0.82 + 4.5/122 = 0.8569$. As before, $AM = 1$, $FM = 1$, and $CM = 0.95$.

$$RWL = LC \times HM \times VM \times DM \times AM \times FM \times CM = 23 \times 0.50 \times 0.787 \times 0.8569 \times 1 \times 1 \times 0.95 = 7.37 \text{ kg or 16 lb}$$

Handling in the cramped attic requires horizontal pushing and pulling while kneeling or seated. Recall from the quoted "Kodak" tables that the force limit for pushing and pulling best done kneeling is 188 N or 19.2 kg, and seated, 130 N or 13.3 kg. Recall that the coefficient of friction is $\alpha = 0.4$ for a box on a floor; seated, Becky could handle a box weighing $13.3/\alpha = 33$ kg or 73 lb; kneeling, she could handle a heavier box. Thus the second lift is the limiting operation, and a limit of about <u>16 lb</u> would be recommended.

E73.   40-lb ice bags are delivered to a soft-drink kiosk and must be lifted from a pallet to the top lip of a bin 138 cm above the floor. Their smallest dimension is about 18 cm. They are stacked four or five deep on the pallet and can be kicked or dragged to the nearest edge of the stack before being lifted; the worker lifts the bag next to the body and turns 90 degrees. The average lift is from a height of 58 cm to a height of 147 cm. This ocurs once or twice per shift, and the total amount of ice each time is about 320 lb. All the ice should be put away within two minutes after arriving. If slipperiness of the floor causes no difficulty, is the 40-lb bag acceptable under NIOSH standards?

One worker, we assume, is loading the entire 320 lb of ice in two minutes. If the ice comes in 40-lb bags, there are 8 bags. The horizontal multiplier for a next-to-body lift of an 18-cm bag is $HM = 25/(25 - 5 + 18/2) = 0.8621$. The 147-cm end of the lift is further from knuckle height than the 58-cm start, so $VM = 1 - 0.003 \times |147 - 75| = 0.784$. The lift distance is $147 - 58 = 89$ cm, so $DM = 0.82 + 4.5/89 = 0.8706$. The number of lifts per minute is $8/2 = 4$, so $FM = 0.84$. For the 90-degree turn, $AM = 1 - 0.0032 \times 90 = 0.712$. The grip on an ice bag is poor, so $CM = 0.90$.

$$RWL = LC \times HM \times VM \times DM \times AM \times FM \times CM = 23 \times 0.8621 \times 0.784 \times 0.8706 \times 1 \times 1 \times 0.90 = 10.6 \text{ kg or } 23 \text{ lb}$$

Certainly the 40-lb bag is <u>not</u> acceptable under NIOSH standards.

7.2 Workstation Design

A workstation is a microenvironment—the worker's immediate surroundings—that the worker stays within while performing tasks. Examples are an airplane cockpit, the chair and other furnishings and equipment surrounding an office worker or data-entry clerk, a workbench for a cobbler or other craftsperson, a symphonic musician's chair and music stand (or the conductor's podium), or a cook's station in a commercial kitchen.

There are three main criteria in designing a workstation: *facilitate the job* (provide for work to be done efficiently), *coddle the worker*, and *conserve space*. At any workstation, the worker processes materials or information or both. Given the basic job to be done (e.g., entering and verifying data at a data-entry station, controlling the flight of an airplane—particularly landing—in an airplane cockpit, placing and attaching small electric components at a circuit board assembly station) and the basic method of doing the job, the industrial engineer has design opportunities with respect to each of the three criteria.

To facilitate the job, the main design opportunities are to improve the way materials enter the workstation, improve the orientation and presentation of materials and tools to the worker, improve the presentation of information to the worker, provide decision support for the worker, improve the method of collecting informational output from the worker, improve the storage and retrieval of intermittently required materials, and improve the way materials leave the workstation (see table 7-2).

After the basic design of a workstation satisfies the "facilitate the job" criterion, the remaining criteria are to "coddle the worker" and "conserve space." The word *coddle* is used advisedly, because almost anything that can be done to make the worker more comfortable, safer, less confused, and less distracted will pay off in increased productivity and better quality. The following subsections cover two levels of design issues: The larger-scale issues of space conservation and the worker's environment while working at the workstation are dealt with by

Table 7-2. Workstation Design Opportunities for Job Facilitation.

Job facilitation opportunity	Guidelines	Examples
Improve the way materials enter the workstation.	Deliver or store materials within easy reach and in correct orientation.	Spring-loaded platform keeps top tray in stack at elbow height. Keep small parts in bins arranged in product-specific groups within reach, rather than have part kits delivered.
Improve the orientation and presentation of materials and tools to the worker.	Eliminate worker movements in retrieving and setting aside tools. Design holders and guides to keep materials and tools in place.	Hand tools hang from overhead. Location stops and guides keep work in correct position. Tools that are used only in one position are clamped in that position. Job-specific tools replace general tools. Job-specific lots of materials are presented by automatic dispensers.
Improve the presentation of information to the worker.	Provide automatic reading and display of state variables. Pre-label materials and make different materials look different. Spot-illuminate close work. Pre-mark work points on materials. Provide feedback to worker.	Roll-press indicator displays next reload time. Circuit board is printed with attachment point locations. Mirror shows incipient punch-through at back of part. Microspotlight from side makes any warpage evident. Contact beeper warns when tool touches wrong area.
Provide decision support for the worker.	Put any automated quality control tests at workstation itself. Make indicators show result, not intent. Enrich the worker's job to perform routine inspections, calibrations, and maintenance.	Videotape duplicator monitors show playback—not recording—signal. Worker—not inspector—performs solids test of yogurt batch to calibrate fruit/base ratio during run. Worker—not mechanic—performs preventive maintenance inspections.
Improve the method of collecting informational output from the worker.	Voice is the easiest human output. Recognition is easier than recall; hence worker should select from display rather than write or type.	Nurse scans barcodes rather than writing down supplies used. Press responds to voice STOP command. Video camera replaces job log. Fast food cash register has item keys, not number keys.
Improve the storage and retrieval of intermittently required materials.	Anything not always needed should be within reach but not on the work surface. Every tool and material should have a designed place and orientation for input, usage, set-aside, retrieval, and output.	Telephone work uses headsets, not handsets. CPUs are stowed below desks or tables; keyboards have a recessed niche when not in use; monitors hang, not sit; input hardcopy rests on adjustable arms; diskettes have a storage holder not on the work surface; printers are mounted overhead or below.
Improve the way materials leave the workstation.	Make blocking impossible (finished work cannot leave until next station or carry-away device is available). The last operation in a procedure must clear the station of everything not needed for starting the next job, regardless of the status of any part of the system that is not part of the workstation.	Finished goods are stacked on carts not tables, or are conveyed away. WIP inventory is designed as part of the workstation. Camera assembly station has cart for output, separate cart for rework, and scrap bin below far table edge. Covered serving dish has footlift lid device; cook steps, places ,and garnishes food with both hands, and steps away. Small item tray arrives at picker/packer station on belt, and leaves on belt.

proper selection of furnishings, dimensions, and surroundings in section 7.2.1. The smaller-scale issues of how the worker moves, reaches, and manipulates the work itself are discussed in section 7.2.2.

7.2.1 Furnishings, Dimensions, and Surroundings

Furnishings available commercially constitute ready-made solutions to the most basic design problems of providing a means for the worker to sit or stand, surfaces on which to work, storage and retrieval places for tools and materials, communication channels, and providing for illumination, noise control, and screening from visual distractions. Much good design can be done by proper selection from catalogs.

A very basic issue is whether the worker will stand, sit, or both. (Reclining, floating, etc., as in space work, underwater work, or virtual-reality control of telerobotics, are too specialized for inclusion here.) If the job itself does not dictate otherwise, always provide for the worker to both stand and sit. For non-physical work done sitting, always choose adjustable industrial chairs with adjustable height and adjustable lower back support. Chairs should not have armrests. Adjustable footrests should be provided for shorter workers.

Chairs should not have casters if horizontal forces are to be applied by the worker. They should swivel; a basic work design that calls for sideways forces to be exerted by a seated worker is usually a bad design and should be replaced rather than providing a non-swivel chair. Kneelers or saddle chairs, in which the worker tilts forward and rests the upper shins on a padded surface, are alternatives to the standard industrial chair. For both standing and sitting, consider an industrial stool.

Often the work surface height cannot be made adjustable at reasonable cost. While either standing or sitting, the top of the work should be about 5 cm below the elbow so that the wrist can be straight and the upper arms hang. The typical actual work surface height for seated American workers is about 72 cm, which is too high; a much better height is 65 cm (25.6 in.), which allows clearance underneath for the 59.3-cm knee height of a 95th-percentile American male below a thick surface. Thigh clearance is also a consideration.

E74.   **A 95th-percentile American man is to be seated at a desk whose top is 65 cm from the floor and is 3 cm thick. Recommend a seat height for his chair.**

Information from tables shows that his knee height is 59.3 cm plus, say, 2 cm footwear thickness, or 61.3 cm. His thigh is 17.7 cm above the seat and his elbow is 29.4 cm above the seat. Ideally, then, if the top of the work is not above the top of the desk, his elbow should be $65 + 5 = 70$ cm above the floor, so that his seat should be $70 - 29.4 = 40.6$ cm high. Does this allow both knee and thigh clearance? The bottom of the surface is $65 - 3 = 62$ cm high and barely clears his knees. It is $62 - 40.6 = 21.4$ cm above his thigh and easily clears his thighs. Thus he can work at the ideal seat height of <u>40.6 cm.</u>

As any cook or office worker knows, work surface area is always in short supply. This is often because the worker *stores* things on the work surface; the designer should remove this temptation by providing a place for everything. But for most mental workers, storage space for communications tools and references, including routinely consulted files, is also in short supply. The only way to provide sufficient reachable storage space is to make the workstation surround the front half of the worker. Unless the worker must confer with people across the desk, you should place shelves or suspended equipment (monitors or other displays, controls, source-document holders) should be placed everywhere within the radius of the worker's reach while sitting in place. Almost every well designed office workstation curves around the worker, providing equipment or storage directly in front above the work surface, to the sides above the work surface, and to the sides below the work surface. Resources most often used by the worker are located here; resources used somewhat less often, such as a large, flat table surface and secondary references, can be located behind the worker to be reached by swiveling the chair to face them. If a flat table is to be used primarily while standing up, it should be at least 78 cm (31 in.) high; that height can also (in an uneasy but popular compromise) serve as a surface where work is performed in a sitting position.

For a table where people do light work such as packaging computer software diskettes and manuals while standing up, the recommended surface height is 91 cm (36 in.), which is below almost everyone's elbow yet more than 11 cm (4 in.) above knuckle height for 95th-percentile males. If the typical height of the work itself is above the surface, the table should be lowered accordingly.

Work performed at a workstation is affected by the surroundings. Illumination, sound, and activity distractions in the surroundings will be discussed below.

Lighting must include spot illumination within the workstation if it has high parts that can cast shadows, even if the general area is well lighted. A good general level of illumination for an office or factory is 300 lumens per square meter of floor space, supplied by 40-W fluorescent lamps (70 lumens per watt). For example, a reception area 6 m wide and 9 m long would require $300 \times 6 \times 9 = 16,200$ lumens, or $16,200/70 = 231$ W of general lighting; dividing by 40 and rounding up, the area would require 6 40-W fluorescent lamps in or under its ceiling. Natural lighting from windows or skylights is desirable as a supplement but is not counted as meeting part of the lighting requirement. Incandescent lamps are not practical for general illumination since they supply only 20 lumens per watt.

Within the workstation, local supplementary lighting should be supplied. For each small part of the workstation that requires performance equivalent to reading a book, provide 1200 lumens of directed illumination. A 60-W incandescent (or 15-W fluorescent) lamp with an adjustable gooseneck would meet this need. Equally effective would be a 25-W fluorescent lamp mounted in a fixed place over the work. For work more visually demanding than reading a book, provide more lumens.

Glare is any distracting illumination within the field of vision. Direct glare comes from windows and lighting fixtures. There should not be a window or a lighting fixture within about 45° of the direction in which the worker looks: a window beyond a monitor, for example, or a lamp poorly placed so that the worker sees also the light source while looking at the work. Reflected glare comes from reflection off flat surfaces. A monitor, for example, should be placed so that the mirror formed by its screen does not reflect a window or a lamp. A page reflects glare, even though an actual reflected image cannot be seen. Therefore, lamps should be placed so that, if the page were a mirror, the lamp would not be seen in it.

Noise, conversation, and music are distracting when working. Noise is commonly measured in dBA units—the number of decibels displayed by the "A" scale of a sound level meter which gives the number of decibels in the range of 710 to 1400 Hz (high soprano) that would be perceived as the same loudness as the sound that is actually measured in all ranges. The "A" scale automatically corrects for the extent to which bass tones of a given decibel intensity are perceived as less loud than soprano tones of the same decibel intensity. When background noise is below 25 dBA, it is very quiet; above 27 dBA, a sound recording studio cannot function satisfactorily; 35 dBA is typical for a very quiet office; above 42 dBA an office is not considered quiet; 47 dBA is typical for busy retail stores; above 54 dBA it is hard to use the telephone; above 60 dBA people have to use raised voices if not within 0.5 m of each other and face to face; above 63 dBA it is too noisy to use the telephone or think clearly.

Plastic foam *earplugs* reduce noise by 20 dBA. When the noise level is higher than 50 dBA, it is as easy to hear and understand voices with earplugs than without them. Employees should be asked to wear earplugs if the noise level is over about 45 dBA, because it allows them to concentrate better and work with less fatigue. Continuous noise above 55 dBA can be permanently damaging to a person's hearing, although the lowest noise level for which hearing loss has been definitely established is 67 dBA. The Environmental Protection Agency (EPA) presumes that noise below 85 dBA is safe, and forbids any exposure beyond 115 dBA. The Occupational Safety and Health Administration (OSHA) allows up to 90 dBA per 8-hr shift (85 dBA for 16 hours, 90 dBA for 8 eight hours, 95 dBA for 4 hours, 100 dBA for 2 hours, 105 dBA for 1 hour, 110 dBA for 30 min., and 115 dBA for 15 min.). Although earplugs can bring almost any noise to within legal limits, earmuffs are commonly used for employees potentially subjected to more than 85 dBA; they attenuate noise by about 30 dBA, and they have the advantage that supervisors can see whether they are being used.

Conversation is very distracting for knowledge workers even at 40 dBA, because it contains information. Human beings cannot easily ignore conversation. Even if words are barely able to be made out, the conversation distracts from work. Some workers use earplugs even in quiet offices; they report that "the plugs put you in a little cocoon where you can concentrate and ignore what is going on around you." Screening from conversation is one of the advantages of a workstation that is designed to surround the worker. Portable office screens also provide the same function (as well as screening from visual distractions and for privacy), and, of course, conversation screening is one of the main functions of an office door. It is desirable to locate and orient office workstations away from sources of conversation such as break rooms and halls.

In contrast to knowledge workers, touch-labor workers may find conversation stimulating rather than distracting. If the job is not mentally demanding, workers should be allowed to converse among themselves. A special case is telephone-answering workers such as reservationists; their job is mentally demanding only while handling a call, so workstation designs such as the one at Days Inn headquarters allow workers to roll their chairs forward into a soundproofed booth to take calls and backward into a common aisle to converse with other workers during lulls between calls.

Background music helps mask conversation and also makes noise less annoying, but only in the range of about 40 dBA to 50 dBA. Below that range the music itself distracts most knowledge workers, and above that range it adds to the din. About 15% of workers find background music distracting even in the 40-50 dBA range where it is generally effective. For touch-labor workers with mentally undemanding jobs, background music is often beneficial regardless of the general noise level; the main issue, if ages and backgrounds are mixed, is what kind of music.

7.2.2 Motion and Reach

A 5th-percentile American woman either seated or standing can reach anything within 77 cm (30 in) on either side or 64 cm (25 in) directly in front, from the work surface height to head height, the distance being measured from the center of the head to the work. This includes some movement of the torso; for a still torso whose centerline remains 24 cm behind the near edge of the work surface, deduct 24 cm from the forward reach. A 5th-percentile woman can also reach 48 cm (19 in) directly above eye level, which means she can reach something 186 cm (73 in) high while standing. There should be no reaching behind the back plane of the body.

E75.   A preliminary workstation specification requires the station to have 1.0 m² of flat worktop within reach of the worker's preferred hand without swiveling and 4 lineal meters of shelf space, 30 cm high (for books or similar items), within reach of at least one hand without swiveling. Show whether this specification can or cannot be met for a 5th-percentile seated woman.

A semicircle with radius 64 cm (the forward reach of a 5th-percentile woman) has an area of $\pi 64^2/2 = 6434 \text{ cm}^2$, which is considerably less than the required 10,000 cm^2, so there is no way to meet the reachable worktop area specification.

If books are on shelves at the edge of her reach, with both tops and bottoms reachable, she can have a semicircle of books at the far edge of the worktop, with radius 64 cm; this gives $2\pi \times 64/2 = 201$ lineal cm. There can be a second semicircle 30 cm higher, but for the worker to reach the tops of the books their radius should be smaller, say 55 cm; this gives $\pi \times 55 = 173$ lineal cm for a total so far of 374 cm. With the requirement of 400 lineal cm, this leaves only 26 lineal cm, which could easily be provided at one side below the worktop, so the shelf space requirement can be met. In summary, the specification cannot be met, because a 5th-percentile woman cannot reach far enough to utilize 1 m^2 of worktop.

For workers who can step or swivel, the rule for not reaching behind the back plane of the body is moot. It is simply a version of the more general rule to avoid twisting. The following general rules for motion and reach apply more to manual workers than to office workers:

1. *Do not exceed the individual worker's physical capacity*. Requiring or allowing workers with bad knees or bad backs to perform vigorous work invites huge eventual disability settlements. This rule implies physical testing and medical examination.
2. *Avoid stoop lifting*. Train workers to lift with bent knees and straight back—squat lifting.
3. *Avoid carrying heavy loads and even human support of light loads*. Provide carts, hand trucks, jigs, positioners, or mechanical devices. It should almost never be necessary for a worker to provide the force necessary to support work against gravity.
4. *Keep physical workers on the move*. Give the worker room to adjust body positions to avoid repetitive identical motions.
5. *Provide good grips, handles, and traction*.
6. *Avoid twisting of the torso, especially when the worker is applying force or is lifting*.

7.3 Handtools and Controls

7.3.1 Handtools

Handtools allow the hand to exert forces and perform manipulation that the unaided hand cannot perform. Important design principles for handtools are:

- Keep the wrist straight
- Prefer specialized to general purpose tools; the advantage of a tool that is slightly better for the job is magnified by thousands of task repetitions
- Prefer tools that either exploit the preferred hand (and therefore must be provided in both left-hand and right-hand models) or can be used equally well in either hand
- Use hand muscles and leverage properly; use the whole hand rather than fingers if force is required; magnify hand force through leverage (long handles, gears, levers)
- Design the grip

E76a. **Two types of food scoops are illustrated. The thumb-trigger type is available in a left-hand version as well as the right-hand version shown. The hand-squeeze type feels the same in either hand. Briefly explain two advantages of the hand-squeeze type over the thumb-trigger type.**

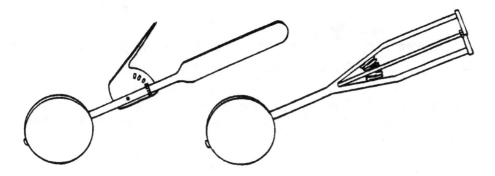

Figure 7-1. Food Scoops.

The most important advantage is that the hand-squeeze type uses the entire set of handgrip muscles, which is much stronger than the thumb-grip muscle; thus, the hand-squeeze food scoop should be less tiring, less likely to cause stress injury, and more suitable for viscous foods.

A second advantage is that the hand-squeeze type can be used with either hand, allowing the worker to switch briefly to the non-dominant hand to avoid fatigue. The same could be done if both versions of the thumb-trigger type were provided, but using them would involve extra tool cost, extra cleanup cost, and extra tool handling.

E76b. **Needlenose pliers and a claw hammer, both with handles at unconventional angles, are illustrated. Briefly explain the principle that motivates the unconventional design.**

Figure 7-2. Needlenose Pliers and Claw Hammer.

The principle "keep the wrist straight" recognizes that the most comfortable and least injury prone hand orientation is the handshake orientation, in which the wrist is straight. The two illustrated tools have their handles at unconventional angles in order to allow the worker's wrist to be straight while using the tool.

E76c.   A spatula for lifting and turning food being cooked on a hot grill is illustrated. Draw a sketch of an improved spatula and explain why your design is an improvement.

Figure 7-3. Food Spatula for Grilling.

The following two alternative designs are improvements because they keep the worker's knuckles farther from the hot surface. The second one also prevents accidental contact of knuckles with the hot surface.

Figure 7-3b. Improved Food Spatulas.

E76d.   Illustrated in figure 7-4 is a trigger grip for on-off control of a dangerous hand tool. Explain an important advantage and an important disadvantage of the trigger grip as compared to a thumb-button trigger.

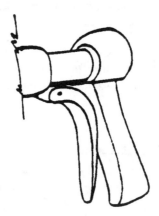

Figure 7-4. Trigger Grip for On–Off Control of a Hand Tool.

An advantage of the trigger grip is that it is less tiring because it uses the entire hand rather than just the thumb. (A minor advantage is that it allows free thumb movement.)

A disadvantage is that it is difficult to release the trigger without also losing grip control of the tool. This is an important safety disadvantage, because a common reason to suddenly turn off a tool is because it has moved into a dangerous position.

7.3.2 Controls

Controls are of two basic types: direct and indirect. Direct controls, such as a steering wheel (continuous control) or light switch (discrete control), directly affect an open-loop system, in which the control affects an actuator that joins with other inputs to the system to help determine its behavior. For example, the steering wheel of an automobile turns the wheels, which in conjunction with the tilt of the road, speed, and other factors, changes the direction of travel.

Indirect controls either affect an open-loop system in an indirect way (the floor buttons of an elevator are an example) or they affect the setpoint of a feedback controller of a closed-loop system. For example, pilots can use sticks and rudders (the stick looks like a steering wheel and moves ailerons; the rudder controls are foot pedals) for turning an airplane directly, or they can exercise indirect control by changing the compass heading setpoint on the automatic pilot.

In the steering of a car, the human driver can be considered part of a closed-loop system in which the feedback is what the driver sees and feels about the progress of the automobile. The setpoint would be the driver's intent. A closed-loop system has the following parts:

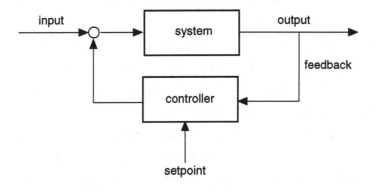

Figure 7-5. A Closed-loop System.

In using a control, the user begins with an intent for controlling the system. The control's design can be good or bad in several ways according to the answers to the following questions. First, does the user understand what the effect of the control is? Can the user easily distinguish this control from others? Does the control require too much force or awkward motion or awkward reach? Is there feedback to the user?

A powerful design concept for controls is metaphor. The task itself may be abstract, so that likening it to a less abstract task is useful. For example, deleting a computer file may be presented on a computer screen as putting the file into a wastebasket. The operation may be abstract, so that likening the control to a more direct way of performing the same task is useful. For example, the least confusing OPEN DOOR control for an elevator would be on the door itself, so that trying to open the door physically would activate it. Almost any metaphors can be useful: for example, if the gasoline tank fill opening is on the right side of an automobile, the latch that releases its lock should be on the right side of other similar controls. A light switch that goes up and down should show up for on and down for off. A knob should go clockwise for more and counterclockwise for less. A knob or lever can look like a more familiar control for the same or similar function. For example, the aileron controls for an airplane look like an automobile's steering wheel. The display associated with a menu item can be designed by a graphic artist to remind the user of the function. For example, a thermostat can look like a mercury thermometer, and it can be designed such that you increase the temperature setpoint by pushing the mercury up.

Indicators are very important in control. An indicator is a display (or sound or other sensory stimulus) that informs the human user about the output of the system. If the control is indirect, so that the human user is resetting the setpoint of a feedback control system, there is a meta-control system in which the human user is the meta-controller and indicator feedback goes to the user. For example, the record control on a tape recorder turns on a record indicator light that informs the user that recording is indeed going on. Good practice has all such feedbacks being true indicators. For example, the record indicator light should be turned on not by depression of the record control but by actual movement of the recording head to its recording position.

Before the computer age, the human-interface aspect of control design controls was restricted by being intertwined with the operation. For example, when your fingers control a flute, you are not merely entering data to tell the system what length the pipe should be, but you are actually setting the length by closing tone holes. The "muscles" used to respond to computer output are still rather primitive as of the mid-1990s, but controls are steadily becoming *gesture-collection devices* whose function is to gather information and whose design depends mainly on human factors. (Ideally, according to the gesture-collection concept of controls, physical design of the user interface should be independent of what is to be done with the information once collected.) Choice of a control for a given work function should depend, as much as possible, solely on the nature of the information to be collected and the capabilities and availability of the worker's "output channels." As an example, the bells in the University of Texas–Austin tower were once controlled (played) by pulling on ropes that hung down. Then the interface was improved by installing big wooden paddles attached to the ropes and arranged like a huge piano keyboard; now any musician could play them. Finally an ordinary synthesizer keyboard (such devices are called, appropriately, "controllers") was installed; when a key is depressed, a signal goes to a motor that accelerates the clapper.

Since talking is the easiest way for a person to output information, there will come a day when many controls will "listen" instead of being pushed, pulled, or twisted. For now, most controls are physically operated by the worker's hands, feet, or other parts of the body. Design choices are dictated by the required action characteristics and the accompanying human capability to control the required body parts in the manner required (either rapidly, consistently, smoothly, or accurately). Table 7-3 shows which kinds of controls are suitable for which action characteristics:

Table 7-3. Suitable and Unsuitable Controls for Action Characteristics.

Action characteristic	Suitable controls	Unsuitable controls
Speed of action	Switch, button, lever, pedal	Knob, crank, handwheel
Accuracy of action amount	Mouse, slide, coarse/fine arrangement	Crank, pedal
Ease of recognition of proper control in array of like controls	Any control whose shape, position, associated display, or appearance is unique and memorable	Control distinguished merely by color, or by position according to an inconsistent or unfamiliar metaphor (a line of knobs for a rectangular array of burners). Buttons in an array of them.
Need for force with moderate accuracy	Steering wheel, helm	Pedal
Need for force with little accuracy	Pedal, pull-down handle	Control using small (hand) muscles
Safety from inadvertant operation	Lever with large travel and resistance; any control in out-of-way location; arrangement needing confirmation or two simultaneous gestures; hooded toggle	Pedal; button or switch too near body; control having poor ease of recognition
Conservation of space	Toggle switch, pushbutton, keyboard	Pedal, lever, steering wheel

Some controls, such as a pushbutton or a key on a keyboard, require little force and can leave the user ignorant of whether the control has actually been activated. Thus a mechanical click or other feedback is built in. Also, all keyboards have echo. For example, you can hear the music when you play a piano, whether it is mechanical or electronic. All computer tasks also have echo, so you can see on a screen or hardcopy what you are entering into the keyboard.

Unintended activation is an important area for design effort. Controls that tend to destroy data or undo useful work can be purposely made difficult to activate, either by confirm cycles (in which a second user action is required to confirm user intent) or by concealing or recessing the control. Good layout and use of metaphor to avoid confusion helps to prevent unintended activation.

It is not only important to prevent unintended activation, but to make a system immune from it. For example, modern computer interfaces (more advanced than the Apple Macintosh interface or the Microsoft Windows interface, which are good for novice and intermittent users but bad for experts) have an undo command. A good example of immunity is the Chrysler pushbutton transmission control from the 1950s. Sometime in years of driving an automobile driver would inevitably push the reverse button by mistake. An interlock was installed to make that action have no effect if the automobile was moving forward at any appreciable speed.

E77. **A hand-held remote control for a TV set is to be designed. It is presumed that the user will pick up the control in the right hand with the thumb on the left side, the four fingers on the right side, and the palm over the lower part of the face, then shift the grip so as to be able to operate pushbuttons with the thumb while the fingers are on the bottom. Up to four pushbuttons can be located in each of the areas ULS, MLS, LLS (upper, middle, and lower left side), URS, MRS, LRS (upper, middle, and lower right side), and the numbered areas on the face:**

	1	2	3	
ULS	4	5	6	URS
	7	8	9	
MLS	10	11	12	MRS
	13	14	15	
LLS	16	17	18	LRS
	19	20	21	

The most important functions for user satisfaction are the on-off pushbutton and the mute-sound pushbutton. Recommend their placement.

Best placement for the on-off button is MLS with no pushbuttons at URS, MRS or LRS, so the user can turn the TV on or off by simply squeezing the control while picking it up. A good possible location for the mute pushbutton is LLS, again with no pushbuttons on the right side; this is the most easily reached variation on the squeeze metaphor. By the nature of the on-off and mute-sound functions, each of which is a single isolated action that would normally start with the control not already in the hand, any placement on the face would require the user to shift the grip.

7.4 Work Measurement and Standards

Industrial engineers must be competent in two types of nonautomated measurement: occurrence sampling and time study. *Occurrence sampling* is the preferred approach to determining the proportion of time a worker or machine spends in various states or conditions (e.g., idle). Rather than record the time of every change of state (continuous sampling), the observer simply observes the system at irregular times to record what state it is in. *Time study* or work measurement is the direct measurement of the time it takes to perform a task. Both occurrence sampling and time study can be *automated* by having a real-time computer system automatically collect the times of event occurrence (e.g., change of state or beginning or completion of a task), where the events are indicated by changes of monitored values or switch positions that are triggered by the occurrence of the event. If a human worker must manually indicate an event, the sampling or study is said to be semiautomated. A different kind of semiautomation is achieved by replacing the human observer with a videotape camera, producing a tape that can be analyzed later. This has the advantages that the analyst can play the tapes much faster than real time, can review tricky occurrences, and can record times by merely pressing a key while the frame containing the event is playing.

7.4.1 Occurrence Sampling

Occurrence sampling (called *work sampling* when work is observed) is more economical than *continuous sampling* when observation is not automated. For example, if a worker is always in one of five defined *states* such as idle, performing task 1, performing task 2, etc., continuous sampling would consist of recording for every change of state the time of entry and the identifier of the entered state. Occurrence sampling, by contrast, would consist of observing the worker at irregular times and recording the state identifier for each observation. Even if the analyst is viewing a videotape rather than actual occurrences, it is much easier to sample at irregular times rather than to identify each change of state.

Both kinds of sampling are vulnerable to not being representative of the population. Strata can be present both in the population itself (e.g., some crews work one way, others a different way) and in time (e.g., work sampled on Monday afternoon is different from work sampled on Tuesday morning). To get a representative sample, the observer can stratify both the sample itself and the time intervals to make sure data is collected from identifiable subpopulations and from various kinds of time interval. Stratification can be very powerful when done wisely, according to what will be used for the data. For example, in the study of congestion, if capacity decisions are to be made, one might sample only the busiest periods. It is strongly recommended not to aggregate stratified data in such a way as to destroy either stratum-defining data or the link between observed data and stratum-defining data. Also, since classification into newly defined strata may usefully be done after data has been collected, it is better to record not the stratum of a datum but the stratum-defining data for the datum. As an example, suppose small diesel trucks were one class and all others (large diesel and small and large gasoline) were another class. It would be better to note both the size and fuel of each truck than to note its defined class, because later a new class such as small gasoline trucks might be defined.

Occurrence sampling is vulnerable to failing to be representative due to periodicities, as when an observation is made every hour and the process is periodic. Periodic sampling is especially vulnerable if the period of the observed process and the period of the sampling are approximately in a small-integer ratio (e.g., 3/2, 5/3, 1/1, 1/2, 2/3). To avoid such periodicity bias, it is not necessary to sample randomly, but merely to sample irregularly.

Autocorrelation bias occurs when two samples are too close together, so that the state at the second sample is likely to be the same as it was at the first sample. To avoid autocorrelation bias, the time between successive samples should be several periods of the observed process.

For an industrial engineer performing sampling among other duties, a good scheme is to insert observations into the engineer's ordinary work schedule. For example, make an observation (or a group of observations, one for each stratum) immediately upon returning the morning phone messages, on the way to coffee break, on the way back from coffee break, and on the way to or from other activities such as meetings and lunch. Usually you can avoid getting a nonrepresentative sample without submitting to being paced by a random number generator.

The data gathered in occurrence sampling is the frequency (the count of the number of occurrences) of a state. The observed frequency divided by the number of observations is an estimate of proportion (also called percentage or ratio). If n observations are made and state i occurs with frequency f_i, so that the observed proportion is f_i/n, we are interested in the true proportion p_i, which will be interpreted as the probability of state i. When only one state or event is of interest, we call this quantity simply p, and the probability of any other state or of the event's not occurring is $q = 1 - p$. Within a stratum for which p is assumed to be constant, the binomial distribution governs the sampling probabilities; when the number of observations n for estimating p is large enough ($n > 30$), the normal distribution provides a close approximation.

The main risk of being wrong is that the process will not be the same in the future as in the past. Although that risk cannot be addressed by simple statistical methodology, the industrial engineer must be able to use statistical methods to settle the usual issues of sample size and confidence.

Given frequency f in n observations, so that f/n is the sample estimate of p, we are interested particularly in whether the sample is large enough to be confident that p is well estimated. Now if p is the probability or true proportion, the standard deviation of its sample estimate is $[(f/n)(1 - f/n)/n]^{0.5}$. For a large sample, p may be considered to be a normally distributed random variable having mean f/n and the standard deviation given.

E78.   **A workstation was observed at 50 irregular times and was found to be blocked in 22% of the observations. Could the true percentage of blocking be as great as 30%?**

The sample of $n = 50$ observations had $f = 11$ blockages, and the standard deviation of p is estimated as $[0.22{\times}0.78/50]^{0.5} = 0.05858327$. If the true percentage were 30%, then $z = (0.30 - 0.22)/0.05858327 = 1.365577$ standard deviations. It would take z of 1.64 to be 95% confident, so <u>yes</u>, the true percentage of blocking could be as great as 30%, although it probably is not.

7.4.2 Work Measurement

Work measurement or time study can be accomplished crudely using a stopwatch and a clipboard-mounted data sheet. Portable electronic recording is much more convenient and accurate. In this method, the engineer carries a programmable hand-calculator-like device that has an internal clock and allows keyboard entries (e.g., "1" for "start pour"). The device can store a few thousand words of data and can download its data into a host system. Videotaping is more expensive, requiring cameras, tripods, tape, camera placement planning, and (optionally) a professional editing-capable videocassette recorder (VCR). Many engineers who use videotaping find the audio channel convenient for recording comments. Videotaping is especially useful when one wants not only to collect time date for a task but also to diagnose its work methods.

Prerequisites to time study include methods analysis and element definition. Work measurement is meaningless unless the observed task is being done in a manner that is productive, appropriate (safe, comfortable), and likely to be continued as the established way of performing the task. Methods analysis (the work an industrial engineer does to design a task) is a prerequisite even if the purpose of the study is to contribute to further improvement of task design.

Element definition (work breakdown) is the decomposition of the task into steps. Elements should be disjoint (not overlapping) and should have well-defined beginnings and endings. The boundary between one element and the next is called the end point (EP) or termination point of the element. Defining elements is an art; the definition depends on what use the engineer intends to make of the data. Consider the example in the following table.

Table 7-4. Element Definitions for the Task of Polishing a Pair of Shoes
for a Walk-in Customer at South DeKalb Shoe Repair.

Code	Element Description	End Point
1	Greet and seat customer	Worker sit on work stool
2	Clean and scrape as needed	Pick up polish
3	Apply polish	Pick up brush
4	Brush	Pick up polish
5	Apply final polish	Pick up brush or rag
6	Brush and buff	Slap shoe with hand
7	Deprocess customer (collect)	Disengage from customer

Element 2 (Clean and scrape as needed) is an example of a variable element. Often the analysis will treat variable elements separately. The work breakdown shown in the table is appropriate for general study. However, suppose elements 3, 4, 5, and 6—the heart of the shoe polishing process—were not of primary interest. For example, if the workers are all expert shoe polishers, but some of them spend too much time in elements 1 and 7, the engineer may find it convenient to combine elements 3, 4, 5, and 6 into a single element.

Time study yields observed times. Let the ith replication of the observed time (observed duration) of element j be denoted O_{ij}, or O if only one observation of one element is under consideration. Often the observer records rating (also called *pace*), which is a subjective estimate of the pace of the work compared to a normal pace. Normal pace is defined as the speed at which a typical experienced worker would be expected to work. Rating or pace, denoted R, is 1.00 or 100% if the worker is working a normal pace while being observed. Or, for instance, R is 0.85 if the worker is working at a pace such that the number of task completions per unit time would be 85% of those at normal pace. A worker trying to make a good impression on the observer might work at a 1.10 pace or rating, while a worker seeking to avoid being held to a high standard in the future might work at a 0.90 pace or rating.

When a rating is recorded, the datum $O_{ij} \times R_{ij} = N_{ij}$ is a normal time datum. The average of these is taken as the normal time for the element, and the sum of the normal times for the elements in a task is taken as the normal task time (normal task duration) N:

$$N = \sum_{j=1}^{J} \frac{1}{n} \sum_{i=1}^{n} N_{ij} \qquad (7\text{-}1)$$

where j counts the elements, J is the total number of elements in the task, n is the number of observations of each element (if the elements are observed different numbers of times, replace n by n_j), i counts the observations, and N_{ij} is the normal-time datum for observation i of element j—the element's observed time multiplied by its rating.

E79.   The following six elements are involved in imprinting a button:
1. **Left hand retrieves a button from a box next to the machine**
2. **Left hand moves button to machine**
3. **Left hand places button and centers it in mold**
4. **Right hand pulls lever with force to impress image on button**
5. **Right hand releases lever and moves it upward**
6. **Left hand picks up imprinted button and places it in a box on the floor next to the left leg**

The operation was fitted with pressure transducers to signal the end of each element. Several hundred samples of the entire task were taken. For each session of about 50 task observations the engineer rated each element as a whole. The results for five typical task observations are recorded below in seconds:

Table 7-5. Element Observation Data for the Task of Imprinting a Button.

Element	Sample 1	Sample 2	Sample 3	Sample 4	Sample 5	Rating
1	0.6	0.7	0.5	0.4	0.6	120%
2	0.3	0.5	0.2	0.3	0.4	110%
3	0.8	1.0	0.8	0.8	0.9	90%
4	1.6	1.8	1.6	1.5	1.7	100%
5	0.7	0.6	0.5	0.6	0.8	115%
6	2.0	2.2	2.2	1.9	1.9	95%

Determine the estimates implied by these data for the normal times for each element and for the task.

For element 1, the average of the observed times in the element-1 row, multiplied by the ratings (all of which are 1.2), is 0.672 sec. This is the estimate of the normal time for element 1. Similarly, the estimates of normal time for elements 2, 3, 4, 5, and 6, respectively, are 0.374, 0.774, 1.64, 0.736, and 1.938 sec. The estimate of the normal time for the task is the sum of the estimates for its elements, which is 6.134 sec.

The formula for the z statistic of a sample estimate, illustrated in example 78, can be particularized for the common situation in which the engineer first obtains m observations of a variable, determines its m observation mean $\bar{x}$, and its m observation range r (or, more accurately, its sample standard deviation s), and desires to compute the total number of observations needed, n, for a given confidence of estimating the variable to a given relative accuracy A. For estimating the variable within ±5% of its true value, for example, set $A = 0.05$. The (two-tail) confidence interval is given in terms of the standard normal statistic z: for 90% confidence, $z = 1.64$; for 95% confidence, $z = 1.96$; for 2-sigma (95.44%) confidence, $z = 2$; for 98% confidence, $z = 2.33$. Now for a sample of size $m = 10$, the expected ratio of range to sample standard deviation is $d_2 = 3.078$ (for a sample of size 20, $d_2 = 3.735$, and for a sample of size 25, $d_2 = 3.931$). When these quantities are substituted into the formula for the z statistic of a sample estimate and the formula is solved for n, the result is

$$n = \left(\frac{zs}{A\bar{x}} \right)^2 \approx \left(\frac{zr}{d_2 A\bar{x}} \right)^2 \tag{7-2}$$

E80. **Ten observations were made of the time to install a cola dispenser. The observed times, in minutes, were 104, 132, 115, 180, 95, 96, 100, 73, 82, 113. Estimate the number of additional observations needed to be 90% confident that the average will be accurate within 10%.**

For 90% confidence, $z = 1.64$. Since the minimum and maximum in the 10 observation sample are 73 and 180, the range is $r = 107$ min. Since the sample size of the sample already taken is 10, $d_2 = 3.078$, and the required relative accuracy is $A = 0.10$. The sample mean of the 10 observation sample is $= 109.0$. When these values are inserted into equation 7-2 the result is $n = 27.36$; thus 28 observations are needed, so the number of additional observations needed is $28 - 10 = \underline{18}$.

More accurately, we can compute the sample standard deviation as $s = 30.0333$ instead of letting it be approximated by r/d_2. When s is used in equation 7-2 the result is $n = 20.41$; thus 21 observations are needed, so the number of additional observations needed is $21 - 10 = \underline{11}$.

7.4.3 Predetermined Time Systems

Predetermined time systems are useful in cases where either (1) the task does not yet exist or (2) changes to a task are being designed and not all elements of the new task or changed task are those for which normal times have already been established. In such cases no opportunity exists to measure the element time. Unfortunately, there is no scientific basis for predicting element times without breaking them down into motion-level parts called motions or therbligs.

A task consists of elements. An organization may develop its own database of normal element durations, and normal times for new or changed tasks may be predicted if the tasks consist entirely of elements whose normal times are already in the database. But new elements can be decomposed into motions, for which scientifically predetermined times exist in databases called MTM-1, MTM-2, MTM-3, and Work Factor. These databases and software to manipulate them are commercially available. To use one of them effectively requires about 50 hours of training.

Therbligs, no longer in use, are defined at an intermediate level between motions and entire elements. The word *therblig* is Gilbreth spelled almost backward and refers to Frank and Lillian Gilbreth, who were the first industrial engineers to break work down into parts. There are 17 therbligs defined by the Gilbreths and refined by Barnes (1968) before being replaced by MTM and Work Factor. The vocabulary of therbligs, MTM motions, and Work Factors is compared below:

	Therblig	*MTM motion*	*Work-Factor element*
TE:	transport empty	REACH or TURN (reach for an object with empty hand)	ARM MOTION
Sh:	search	Parameters of REACH and GRASP	Factors of ARM MOTION
Se:	select Part of GRASP	Part of GRASP	Part of GRASP
G:	grasp GRASP	GRASP (from first touch to obtaining control)	GRASP
TL:	transport loaded	MOVE or TURN (moving an object in the hand)	ARM MOTION
PP:	preposition	POSITION or REGRASP	PREPOSITION
P:	position	POSITION	Part of ASSEMBLE
A:	assemble	MOVE, REGRASP, and POSITION	ASSEMBLE
DA:	disassemble	GRASP, DISENGAGE (if resistance), and MOVE	DISASSEMBLE
RL:	release load	RELEASE	RELEASE
U:	use	Whatever MTM motions	USE
H:	hold	Not an MTM motion	HOLD DELAY
I:	inspect	Whatever MTM motions, and VISUAL ACTION	MENTAL PROCESS
AD:	avoidable delay	Not an MTM motion	Not a Work-Factor element
UD:	unavoidable delay	SIMO if due to other part of body being busy. Not an MTM motion otherwise.	BALANCE DELAY
Pn:	plan	Not an MTM motion	Not a Work-Factor element
R:	rest to overcome fatigue	Not an MTM motion	Not a Work-Factor element

It can be seen that, like therbligs, the Work Factor elements are not truly at motion level. Work Factor elements are aggregates of motions; the same is true of the elements in MTM-2 and MTM-3.

MTM-1 has a data structure containing 10 categories of motion (it is also correct to say there are 10 motions in MTM-1), each having parameters that are called cases, distances, and other category-specific names. The MTM-1 motions or categories are

- REACH
- MOVE
- TURN
- APPLY PRESSURE
- GRASP
- POSITION
- RELEASE
- DISENGAGE
- BODY MOTION
- EYE MOTION

The REACH category gives an example of cases, distances, and other parameters. REACH has five cases: A, B, C, D, and E. Case A is to reach to a fixed place, case B is to reach to an object whose location may vary slightly from cycle to cycle, case C is to reach to an object jumbled with others, case D is to reach to a small object or one that must be grasped in a precise manner, and case E is to reach for getting the hand out of the way or to balance the body. For each case, distance-specific times are tabulated. Also tabulated for case A and case B separately are distance-specific "hand in motion" acceleration/deceleration corrections. The correction is subtracted from the case-specific, distance-specific REACH time if the reach begins with the hand already in motion in the correct direction or if the reach ends with the hand not needing to stop. If both, the correction is subtracted twice.

The times (durations) for MTM motions are tabulated in TMU units. A TMU is 10^{-5} hours (100,000 TMUs per hour), or 0.0006 minute (1666.67 TMUs per minute), or 0.036 second (27.7778 TMUs per second). The distance parameters are given in cm for some MTM implementations and in inches for others. MTM users interact with the system in terms of codes such as "rR12B" for a 12 in. (or 12 cm) reach of reach case B, with an initial acceleration correction, or "M5Cm" for a 5 in. (or 5 cm) reach of move case B with a final deceleration correction. MOVE has three cases (A for the base case; B for some control of the destination position; and C for fine control of the destination position) and a system of corrections for the amounts of weight being moved.

MTM-2 is a simplified system involving only the motions Get (a combination of MTM-1's REACH, GRASP, and RELEASE), PUT (a combination of MTM-1's MOVE and POSITION),

A (apply pressure), R (regrasp), E (eye action to recognize an object or to shift view to elsewhere), C (circular crank motion), S (step), F (foot motion not moving the body), and B (bend and arise). MTM-2 has only 39 tabulated times and has been found to be nearly as accurate as MTM-1 when the engineer is experienced; it requires about 40% of the engineer's effort to analyze a task as does MTM-1.

MTM-3 is even more simplified, with elements HANDLE having two cases (A for easy, B for precision) and two distance ranges; TRANSPORT having two cases (A for easy, B for precision) and two distance ranges; SF (step or foot motion); and B (bend and arise). There are thus only 10 tabulated times. The code for an element begins with an element indictor: H for Handle, T for transport, SF for taking one pace or depressing a foot pedal, and B for bending over and arising or standing up and sitting back down. The code continues with a case indicator: A or B. Finally, for H or T, there is a range indicator: 6 for up to 15 cm, 32 for more than 15 cm. Thus, for example, HA-32 is the code for an easy Handle with range more than 15 cm. The entire MTM-3 table is reproduced in every textbook that covers motion and time study (including the Konz textbook previously cited).

The distinction in MTM-3 between HANDLE and TRANSPORT is that a HANDLE element begins with gaining control (e.g., picking an object up or repositioning the hand), whereas a TRANSPORT element does not. Both involve moving the hand and, if necessary, releasing an object it holds.

E81.   **A task requires reaching into a box 20 cm away, retrieving a spoon from the box, bringing the spoon to the work surface, rubbing its bowl 15 times, and putting it onto a moving belt at the edge of the work surface. The engineer judges that the retrieval requires precision (the spoons are jumbled in a box) but the other motions do not. The MTM-3 tables give 18 TMU for easy handling with up to 15-cm range, 34 TMU for easy handling with more than 15-cm range, 7 TMU for easy transport with up to 15-cm range, and 29 TMU for precision transport with more than 15-cm range. Determine an estimate for the normal time for the task.**

Retrieving a spoon is a precision HANDLE over a range more than 15 cm (code HB-32), so its estimate is 48 TMU; the rubbing is 15 easy TRANSPORTS with range less than 15 cm (code TA-6), so its estimate is 15×7 TMU; the placement on the belt is an easy transport with range less than 15 cm (code TA-6), so its estimate is 7 TMU. The sum is 160 TMU or <u>5.76 sec</u>.

MTM times are based on 100% pace. Work Factor times are based on 120% pace. Thus, if a task is analyzed by the Work Factor method (not reviewed here), the Work Factor duration estimate must be multiplied by 1.2 to obtain a normal-time estimate.

MTM and Work Factor analyses assume that the worker is experienced, so that there is no hesitation either within an element or between elements. Several researchers have studied the problem of how many cycles of a task are needed before the worker can perform at a normal pace. The consensus is that about 2000 cycles are needed. If a typical worker has performed a task 2000 times or more, all its motions should be up to 100% pace.

7.4.4 Allowances and Standards

The ultimate purpose of time study or use of predetermined times is to establish *standard times* (durations) for tasks and for operations that are combinations of tasks. Let N be the normal time for a task or operation. N is either a sum of observed times O multiplied by pace ratings R or a sum of motion or element times from MTM analysis, Work Factor analysis, or from a specific database for the previously observed elements making up the task or operation. Let S be the standard time for a task or operation for which N has already been estimated. S is a duration such that, in the long run, the estimated production rate per shift, F, will be given by T/S, where T is the number of time units available for work per shift and S is expressed in the same time units.

As an example, suppose producing a widget is estimated to have a normal time of $N = 12.7$ min. per widget. Further suppose that, by one of the three approaches to be described below, the standard time is set as $S = 15.0$ min. per widget, and that the time per shift available for work is set as $T = 450$ min. per shift. Then we expect a production rate of $F = 450/15.0 = 30$ widgets per shift.

If the production process were working at a 100% pace during all the shifts for every shift, we would expect a production rate of $450/N = 35.4$ widgets per shift. But the production process cannot always run at 100% pace or always run at all. Workers take breaks, handle interruptions, perform rare or minor setup or cleanup or reloading tasks not included in normal time estimates, and suffer forced idleness or slowdowns due to temporary breakdowns or slowdowns. The adjustments to convert normal time N to standard time S are called *allowances*.

Given N, there are three approaches to determining a standard time: shift reduction, shift allowance, and task allowance. Consider the treatment of lunch break, for example. Even if the enterprise does not have everyone take lunch at the same time, it is customary to omit lunch from the shift time. For example, if a shift has a 480 min. (8 hr) time span and 30 minutes is allowed for lunch, the time per shift available for work is considered to be $T = 450$ min. (7.5 hr) per shift. This is the shift-reduction approach. There is no allowance for lunch; rather, lunch is off the clock.

On the other hand, consider the treatment of morning and afternoon breaks. In the U.S., two 10 minute breaks are customarily allowed in a shift and are treated as shift allowances. If break time of 20 min. is allowed in a 450 min. shift, $20/450 = 4.44\%$ shift allowance (the shift allowance fraction is 0.0444) is said to be allowed. If break time of 30 min. is allowed, there is a $30/450 = 6.67\%$ shift allowance (the shift allowance fraction is 0.0667).

In the United Kingdom, a morning break and afternoon tea totaling 30 min. is customarily allowed, but the break allowance is treated not as a shift allowance but as a task allowance.

The distinction between shift allowances and task allowances can best be defined in terms of the defining equation for standard time, S. Let A be the total allowances for a task in the same units as the time per shift available for work, T. Then the standard time S for a task having normal time N is where A/N is

$$S = N + A = N\left(1+\frac{A}{N}\right) = \frac{N}{1-\frac{A}{S}} \tag{7-3}$$

where A/N is the task allowance fraction and A/S is the shift allowance fraction. Equation 7-3 is valid for a task of any length. In particular, it is valid for the whole-shift task whose standard time is $S = T$ and whose normal time is $N = T - A$ where A is the whole-shift total allowances. A represents the total allowances for whatever task is under consideration. From equation 7-3, the relationships between the two fractions are

$$\frac{A}{N} = \frac{A/S}{1-A/S} \qquad \frac{A}{S} = \frac{A/N}{1+A/N} \tag{7-4}$$

As an example of the distinction between shift allowances and task allowances, suppose the total allowances in a 450 min. shift were 67.5 min. On a shift allowance basis this is $67.5/450 = 15\%$; on a task allowance basis it is $67.5/(450 - 67.5) = 17.647\%$. Shift allowances are cited as percentages of the standard time; task allowances are cited as percentages of the normal time.

E82.   **The normal time for a task has been set as 33.9 min. Total allowances have been set as 72 min. in a 450-min. shift. Determine the shift allowance fraction; compute the standard time from the shift allowance fraction and from the task allowance fraction; determine the standard production rate in number of task completions per shift.**

$A/S = 72/450 = \underline{0.16}$ shift allowance fraction. $S = 33.9/(1-0.16) = \underline{40.357 \text{ min.}}$ standard task time. $450/40.357 = \underline{11.15}$ task completions per shift.

From the task-allowance viewpoint, the whole 450-min. shift consists of 72 min. of allowance time and $450 - 72 = 378$ min. of normal time; from the shift allowance viewpoint, it consists of 450 min. of standard time, including 72 min. of allowance time.

Since there are 72 min. of allowance for 378 min. of normal time, the task allowance fraction is $A/N = 72/378 = 0.190476$. Alternatively, the same answer can be obtained from equation 7-4 given A/S: $A/N = 0.16/(1-0.16) = \underline{0.190476}$. Using A/N instead of A/S, we have $S = 33.9 \times (1 + 0.190476) = \underline{40.357 \text{ min.}}$, which is the same as the standard time calculated using A/N.

As an example of the shift-reduction approach, suppose that the 72 min. of allowance time in the previous example included 15 min. of communal calisthenics, and that is was decided to move the calisthenics time off the clock. The shift duration would be redefined form 450 min. to 435 min. (this would cause the need to raise hourly pay rates by the ration 450/435, and in most jurisdictions participation could not legally be made mandatory.) The allowance time in a shift would become 72–15 + 57 min. The reader can verify that the percentage task allowance would be A/S = 57/435 = 13.1034%, the percentage task allowance would be A/N = 57/(435–57) = 15.0794%, and the standard time would be S= 33.9/(1–0.131034) (or 33.9 × 1.150794) = 39.012

min.—smaller than before because of the revised basis of time accounting. The standard production per shift would be 435/39.012 = 11.15 task completions per shift, which is exactly the same as before.

Three kinds of allowance are generally recognized: personal, fatigue, and delay. *Personal allowances* generally include standard morning and afternoon breaks plus additional time for short personal interruptions such as visiting the rest room or making a telephone call. Often the time for taking care of brief, irregular tasks such as setting up machines, getting tools, cleaning the workplace, and so forth, is added to personal allowances rather than counted separately. *Fatigue allowance* is extra time allowed to workers in difficult jobs, although few enterprises define it consistently. *Delay allowance* is extra time allowed to account for forced idleness when a worker is waiting. The usual practice is to lump all three of these allowances into a single personal, fatigue, and delay (PF&D) allowance, which also becomes the total allowance. A typical PF&D allowance in the United States is 15% on a shift allowance basis; more often than not, the same PF&D allowance is used for all jobs in a given area or shop.

When standard times are used to determine incentives or penalties, it is good practice *not* to tie incentives or penalties to working a fixed amount faster or slower than standard (for example, a penalty for working slower than 90% of the standard production rate or a reward for working faster than 110% of the standard production rate). Instead, it is better for any incentives or penalties to begin at the standard production rate and to be proportional to the ratio of actual rate to standard rate.

A more common use of standards than determining incentives or penalties is to establish labor data for cost accounting and estimating purposes. Military procurement agencies are often in the position of reimbursing contractors for costs incurred in making changes or doing additional work beyond what is in the contract. In this case, it is in the contractor's interest to have generous standards—high standard times or low standard production rates—and in the government's interest for the standards to be strict. The military specification MIL-STD-1567A for work measurement lists rules and procedures intended to keep standards from being too generous. Contractors are required to (1) show that the work method was analyzed before observed times were measured, (2) show that standard practices were followed in setting standards, (3) retain pace ratings, (4) retain observed times, and (5) retain computations of standard times, including the allowances used.

E83. **Packaging of ammunition boxes was observed on 650 independent occasions. The pace-corrected average of observed packaging times was 62.4 sec, with a standard deviation of 21.1 sec. In 90 of the observations, restocking of packaging materials was performed as an extra part of the operation; this took an average of 10.6 sec extra time, which was included in the observed times. Given 16% shift allowances, determine the standard time for packaging an ammunition box. How much confidence can be placed in the standard time estimate's being within 5% of the true average? Should the restocking be treated as a separate task?**

$S = 62.4/(1 - 0.16) = \underline{74.2857 \text{ sec}}$. The standard deviation of the average observed time statistic is $21.1/(650)^{0.5} = 0.8276$ sec. A 5% error in the average, which would be an error of $0.05S = 3.714$ sec, is highly unlikely, since there is a very small probability associated with $z = 3.714/0.8276 = 6.34$ standard deviations; we can place <u>high confidence</u> in the average observed time and hence in the standard time computed from it. The fact that the task could be subdivided into components such as packaging proper and material restocking is not a valid reason to complicate the data structure. Restocking should <u>not</u> be treated separately.

Chapter 8
Management and Safety

An industrial engineer is expected to understand basic principles of management and to be able to evaluate the safety of designs. In the management area, an industrial engineer should be able to understand the language of accounting, particularly cost accounting. Cost accounting is treated in chapter 3 (section 3.1) of this review. Industrial engineers should also understand the classical principles of management—planning, organizing, controlling, motivating, and adapting. This review covers the following key topics from the principles of management: organizational structure (section 8.1.1), motivation (section 8.1.2), incentives (section 8.2.1), and job evaluation (section 8.2.2). Although an industrial engineer obviously needs to know more about management than this, these key topics most often show up on the IE PE Exam.

Similarly, although safety engineering—a specialty within industrial engineering—requires broad skills and knowledge, this review treats only a few selected topics in the safety area that are likely to show up on the exam. Noise is treated in section 8.3.1 (and also in section 7.2.1); industrial engineering aspects of toxicology are covered in section 8.3.2; and a brief review of how to identify and neutralize safety hazards is given in section 8.3.3.

8.1 Organizations

8.1.1 Organizational Structure

Viewed from a manager's perspective, an organization is an authority-structured social entity formed to achieve definite purposes. Churches, corporations, and governmental agencies are examples. On the other hand, a person's family may lack the structure and purpose to be meaningfully viewed as an organization that can be managed. An organization has goals, which are desired future conditions. Goals can be formal (openly stated as such) or operative (ends toward which the organization's operations strive).

A measure of effectiveness of an organization is a measurable quality or quantity that helps indicate how successfully the organization meets its formal goals. Efficiency measures, on the other hand, indicate output compared to input. For example, an electronics manufacturing company may have high efficiency as measured by low unit manufacturing costs and high labor productivity (production per labor hour), and at the same time have low effectiveness as measured by low total earnings. Effectiveness is success by whatever means; efficiency is success with respect to specific means.

The authority structure of an organization is generally hierarchical and can be depicted as an organization chart. The structure is of positions (jobs), not of incumbents (employees).

E84.   The following is a partial list of jobs and employees at Blandish Industries:

Employee ID No.	Job title	Employees supervised
1	Board chair	
2	President	
3	VP–manufacturing	
4	VP–finance	
5	Manager–material control	
6	Manager–purchasing	
7	Manager–data processing	

Determine who reports to whom and display all the organization chart information in a relational table or set of relational tables.

The president reports to the board chair, the two vice presidents report to the president, the material control and purchasing managers report to the manufacturing vice president, and the data processing manager reports to the finance vice president. Thus, the third column of the above table could be filled in with 2 in row 1; 3 and 4 in row 2; 5 and 6 in row 3; and 7 in row 4. However, although the table would then express all the data, it would fail to be relational (with multiple values in the third field, it would fail to be in first normal form), and it would inappropriately express supervisory relationships in terms of employees instead of positions. (See section 5.4 for a review of relational database design.)

The following relational table, with job title as its key, would be a correct way to store the organization chart information:

Job title	Incumbent ID	Reports to
Board chair	1	(null)
President	2	Board chair
VP–manufacturing	3	President
VP–finance	4	President
Manager–material control	5	VP–manufacturing
Manager–purchasing	6	VP–manufacturing
Manager–data processing	7	VP–finance

It would also be correct to add a *job code* column that would be the key, with *job title* as an ordinary attribute; the *reports to* column would contain job code values rather than job title values.

The hierarchical authority structure is called a bureaucratic structure or function-oriented structure because people are placed in the organization according to what function they perform. Function-oriented structure works best when the goals and workload are static, that is, when the same things need to be done day after day, week after week. It works less well when the goals are to execute projects; a project, such as constructing a building or placing an astronaut on the moon, is a unique set of activities that accomplishes a unique goal. For managing projects, a project-oriented structure is possible, in which a project team is formed having its own hierarchical authority structure with a project manager at the top. Consider an engineering and construction company such as Fluor Corporation. The main business of the company is to design and construct process plants (oil refineries, chemical plants, and the like). Consider how the structure would affect a given employee, Joe, a piping designer, if a project-oriented structure were adopted. Joe might work as one of five piping designers for the project manager Henry on one project, then be the only piping designer on a team directed by Flo on the next project.

Because of the potential lack of continuity, pure project-oriented organizational structures do not exist except in temporary organizations that are formed to execute a project and then are dissolved (an Olympic basketball team or an all-star team in any sport are examples). Joe might work on one project at a time and be managed almost wholly by the project management, but he would still belong administratively to the piping design department; his boss in the piping design department, using input from his temporary project bosses, would decide on his promotions, manage his professional growth, and exert influence on his project assignments. Such an organizational structure, where for project specific purposes Joe reports to project management but for professional and administrative purposes he reports to his departmental management, is called matrix organization. Matrix organization is common not only in engineering companies but in research and development (R&D) organizations as well (e.g., drug companies that develop new pharmaceuticals).

E85.   For a research and development firm, discuss the most important advantages and disadvantages of a matrix organizational structure.

In answering a question of this type, the most brilliant snow job will fail. The problem's author is looking for a well-organized, accurate, supportable response. "Well-organized" would mean here that you discuss each advantage and each disadvantage separately, that you sort the advantages and disadvantages according to descending order of importance, and that your discussion of each advantage and disadvantage would have a transparent, parallel structure. For example, provide a brief name or description of the advantage or disadvantage, followed by a statement of why it is important (its consequences in terms of benefits, disbenefits, and costs to the organization and to the employees).

An "accurate" response to the question would mean here that you do not list two descriptions of essentially the same advantage or disadvantage and that you do not list any advantages or disadvantages that are less important than any that you fail to list. Most importantly, you must make appropriate assumptions. Here, your discussion must be about an R&D organization—not about, say, an engineering and construction firm—and you must assume that its work is mostly project work, not continuing work. You must appropriately identify the alternative to which matrix organization is being compared (here, it is "functional organization," not full "project organization"), and you must make the correct assumption about what is meant by "matrix organization"; do not confuse it with project organization.

"Supportable" in this instance would mean that you either agree with authorities (cite them) or disagree with authorities (cite them and tell why you disagree).

Suppose, for example, your available reference was the textbook, Managing Engineering and Technology *by Daniel L. Babcock (1991). On page 305, Babcock compares the advantages and disadvantages of functional organization with project organization (not matrix organization), so citing this comparison would be a mistake. On page 306, Babcock also gives a typical matrix organization chart for a consumer products firm (not an R&D firm), so displaying that chart would also be a mistake. A good response based on the material in Babcock's book would be as follows:*

I interpret matrix organization for an R&D firm (following both "Significance of Project Management Structure" by Larson and Gobeli in *IEEE Transactions on Engineering Management*, May 1989, and *The Process of Management* by Newman et al., both quoted by Babcock in *Managing Engineering and Technology*, Prentice-Hall, 1991) as an organizational structure whereby a technical person belongs administratively and professionally to a functional department but is often assigned to projects where the project manager has some degree of supervision and control over the person. Matrix organization is a two-boss arrangement, and it can be contrasted with functional organization. Under functional organization, the work on a project would be farmed out to the functional departments and supervised by the functional managers; under matrix organization, it would be performed by a project team and supervised by project managers, with functional managers perhaps assigning personnel as needed and providing advisory expertise.

Advantages of matrix organization over functional organization:

1. The main advantage of matrix management is that it provides better control over the schedule, performance, and cost of a project. In a matrix organization, technical people become immersed in and focused on their current project, and their collective attention is not divided. Larson and Gobeli found that matrix management was evaluated by managers as being better than functional management in meeting schedules, controlling costs, achieving overall project performance, and even in meeting technical performance (which may seem surprising, since in a project team the technical person works away from his or her direct professional colleagues).

2. Matrix management allows for quicker and simpler communication among members of the project team and between the project team and customers or outside consultants.

3. The continual shifting of reporting responsibilities has good effects: it keeps renewing the Hawthorne effect by having employees supported and evaluated by a succession of managers; it prevents ossified bureaucracies from forming and poisoning the professional atmosphere; and it provides ways for junior managers to prove themselves and gain experience.

Disadvantages of matrix organization compared to functional organization:

1. Uncertainty and lack of continuity of maintaining accountability in two dimensions are problems associated with matrix management. Matrix management violates Henri Fayol's "unity of command" management principle. Conflicts can arise between doing the job professionally (as would be emphasized by functional managers) and doing it quickly (as would be emphasized by project managers).

2. Matrix management may cause poor technical direction and poor technology transfer. The specialist is separated from other specialists.

3. Employees may experience discomfort from having to prove themselves over and over and from being in the shifting environment associated with Advantage 3 listed above.

A response based on different references would be somewhat different. For example, if the available reference is *Organizational Behavior* by Roberts and Hunt (1991), the response might emphasize what those authors see as the primary reason for matrix organization: to put a project under the direction of management that cares primarily about the project, rather than under a bureaucratic management that cares primarily about its own continuity and growth. (There is even a myth that matrix organization was invented by the federal government in the 1960s to enable the government, as a customer, to deal with a contractor through only one contact person with full authority for the contract, but R&D firms and engineering and construction firms made extensive use of matrix management at least as early as the 1950s.)

8.1.2 Motivation

In their role as productivity facilitators, industrial engineers must understand motivation—what makes people work harder, faster, and longer by their own volition (obedience is not motivation). As a process, motivation is synonymous with leadership, which is the process of stimulating workers to perform, but more basically, motivation involves the psychological factors that cause a person to have enough self-direction to begin work (arousal), to work well (direction), and to keep working (persistence). (In psychology, motivation is defined for any behavior, not just work.) In modern views on motivation, we also expect the well-motivated worker to work voluntarily and in a goal-directed manner.

What motivates workers is not always obvious, although several theories have attempted to clarify motivation. Almost all theories of motivation assume that workers are hedonistic (they avoid pain and seek pleasure) and rational (they make choices based on logical analysis of available information).

In the 1920s, Frederick W. Taylor articulated scientific management based on three main concepts: that what we would now call positive reinforcement (the "carrot") was better than punishment or negative reinforcement (the "stick"); that a daily pay incentive was a good motivator; and that for incentives to work there must be fair and consistent work standards, fair and consistent comparison of workers' performance with standards, and full awareness of how the incentive system works. By the 1930s, scientific management came to be viewed as dehumanizing and based too much on close supervision and the use of money as an incentive. The much-discussed Hawthorne effect gave support to this view. (Harvard anthropologists measured the response of productivity to illumination levels and other factors at the Hawthorne plant of the Western Electric Company and found inconsistent results—productivity would increase when a variable was changed, then increase again when it was restored to its previous level—finally leading to the conclusion that those workers had been motivated primarily by the amount of attention paid to them.) As a dominant management philosophy, scientific management gave way during the 1930s to the human relations movement, which tried to make employees feel valued by using such techniques as morale surveys, departmental meetings, and company newsletters. The aim was to get better performance by raising employee satisfaction.

In time, theories such as Likert's interaction influence theory (1961) arose to explain which strategies worked better than others in raising employee satisfaction. In 1967, Likert compared the following systems:

System 1:	primitive authoritarianism
System 2:	benevolent authoritarianism
System 3:	consultative management
System 4:	participative group management

Likert recommended system 4 as the management style best suited to promoting satisfaction among employees.

In 1960, Douglas McGregor published *The Human Side of Enterprise*, comparing two theories (actually sets of assumptions) about how people are motivated. Theory X assumes that people basically lack integrity, are fundamentally lazy, avoid responsibility, are uninterested in achievement, are incapable of directing their own behavior, are indifferent to organizational needs, prefer to be directed by others, avoid making decisions, and are stupid. Theory Y assumes the opposite: people have integrity, they work hard toward objectives to which they are committed, they assume responsibility, they desire achievement, they are capable of self-direction, they want their organization to succeed, they are not passive, they do not avoid making decisions, and they are not stupid. McGregor's point was that if you treat people according to Theory X or Theory Y they will behave accordingly, so a management strategy can be judged according to how well it corresponds to Theory Y.

Theory X and Theory Y are not truly theories of motivation. A theory of motivation would purport to explain how people are motivated (content theories) or how to manipulate people's behavior (process theories).

Content theories explain psychological motivation in terms of the needs that workers strive, consciously or unconsciously, to satisfy. The earliest content theories were probably the instinct theories that appeared around 1908 and tried to list the natural behaviors of workers. In 1938, Henry Murray published his "manifest needs" theory, listing needs or drives such as abasement, achievement, affiliation, aggression, and autonomy. The first content theory to have any real influence on management was Maslow's hierarchy of needs (1943).

According to Maslow's hierarchy, needs can be ordered from more to less basic: physiological, safety, social, ego, and self-actualization. A satisfied need is not a motivator. Jobholders tend to be at a particular point on the scale, with all more basic wants satisfied and all less basic wants unsatisfied. The most usual job-related examples of Maslow's scale of needs are as follows:

Physiological	Adequate pay
Safety	Job security
Social	Job status; recognition
Ego	Personal status; recognition; achievement
Self-actualization	Personal fulfillment; self-direction

One of the consequences of Maslow's concepts is that money is not a strong motivator if the worker does not drastically lack money. In general, managers should try to learn what workers perceive as their needs and try to help workers satisfy them.

E86.   A duct designer complains his job is boring and he does not get a chance to use his creativity; should the boss offer him a raise or try to give him more challenging design assignments?

Do not offer a raise, since there is no indication that the designer would be motivated by money. Obviously it is the self-actualization need that is currently motivating the designer. Find a way to offer him more challenging, less boring design assignments.

The ERG theory (Alderfer 1972) simplifies Maslow's hierarchy into three classes of need: existence, relatedness, and growth.

The two-factor theory (also known as the motivation-hygiene theory) lists dissatisficers (or hygiene factors): salaries, benefits, company policy, supervision, and working conditions. It also lists satisficers (motivators): advancement, responsibility, work itself, recognition, and achievement. The two-factor theory offers a kind of diminishing-returns approach to maximize employee motivation: improve all the dissatisficers to a neutral level, then supply satisficers to the most cost-effective extent. This is based on findings (never proven) that overall dissatisfaction is determined by the worst single dissatisficer, while overall satisfaction is determined by the sum of satisficers.

E87.   In a paint shop, salaries are low but benefits are good, and working conditions are bad. Management can provide much more advancement and responsibility at low cost, recognition at moderate cost, and improve the work itself at high cost. There is a limited budget for building worker morale. How should it be prioritized, according to the two-factor theory?

According to the theory (which is not well accepted), salaries and working conditions should be improved just enough to meet established norms. Remaining money should be spent on improving advancement and responsibility.

8.1.3 Total Quality Management (TQM)

A twin theme is shared by all modern theories of management: an organization functions best when everyone in it shares the same goals and is able to work toward those goals. Sharing the same goals may be called consensus; enabling everyone to work toward the goals may be called empowerment. Many other words and phrases express both ideas: cooperation, working together, harmony, and team spirit. The TQM movement seeks to bring about the continuing evolution of organizations to maximize consensus and empowerment. TQM is not so much concerned with the ideas themselves as with implementing them—altering the organizational culture so that people can work together effectively. The TQM movement has gained inspiration from the successes of Japanese industry and the leadership role of the American quality engineer W. Edwards Deming in helping achieve those successes.

8.1.3.1 Consensus and Empowerment

Let us suppose an organization undertakes a TQM program, hoping to change itself so that it can evolve into a more effective organization. Someone, usually a combination of outside consultants (often industrial engineers) and people within the organization (also, often industrial engineers) must organize and execute the TQM program itself. The immediate challenge for the TQM implementers is to understand existing barriers to consensus and empowerment. The most challenging barrier is adversarial relationships.

Adversarial relationships, such as union versus management, department versus department, or buyer versus supplier, are the opposite of consensus. Although TQM is intended to be evolutionary rather than revolutionary, entrenched adversarial relationships can make TQM very difficult to establish in an organization. For example, General Motors had to establish a separate Saturn division, making a new automobile in a new plant, in order to be able to give TQM a real test.

To build consensus and avoid or destroy the adversarial poisoning of relationships in an enterprise, one must first understand the constituencies involved, because everyone must be given a voice. The TQM team will use consensus-building techniques, but they will be ineffective if an important constituent group, such as suppliers or customers, is omitted. To varying extents, a consensus should be built that considers the wishes of everyone on the following list:

- Owners (shareholders, partners)
- Management
- Creditors
- Employees personally
- Unions
- Customers
- Suppliers
- Regulatory agencies
- The public, future generations, mankind

Other threats to building consensus include traditional conservative ideas of competition, fear (of all kinds, but specifically fear by subordinates of superiors), and lack of communication. Consensus-building techniques directly address these threats.

Consensus-building techniques try to create and maintain a shared vision of where the organization needs to go and how everyone should contribute to achieving this vision. The main concepts incorporated into the vision to be shared should have a source and an advocate before formal consensus building begins, because rarely can a group generate something sufficiently bold and inspiring.

A study of "Common Behavior Changes in Successful Organization Development Efforts," by Jerry I. Porras and Susan J. Hoffer (1986), identified successful change as being associated with high levels of the following organizational attributes:

- Open communication
- Collaboration
- Taking responsibility
- Maintaining a shared vision
- Respecting and supporting superiors and subordinates
- Facilitating interactions and information flow
- Employee development
- Inquiry and experimentation
- Functioning strategically

Thus, for example, a firm that helps its chemists obtain master's degrees would be expected to handle change better than one that does not.

Consensus-building techniques are varied, but they usually involve focus groups or other face-to-face meetings where employees can all be heard in a variety of nonthreatening contexts. Interviews, questionnaires, and suggestion box programs (with response to all suggestions) are used. Meetings at first should be run by outside facilitators or by employees with specific training in group dynamics. To reduce fear of frank discussion, an ombudsman may be appointed for any group that may feel threatened; this person would collect concerns and communicate them to others in a way that keeps their source confidential.

Empowerment means that employees are given the opportunity to be self-directing. Direct supervision must be made less important. The details of work procedures should be adopted by the group actually doing the work. This requires not only that management must not rule by edict, but also that employees be given sufficient time and opportunity to discuss procedures and rules.

Empowerment does not mean that all suggestions for change must originate from the work group itself, only that the group must be involved in finalizing and adopting any major changes. For example, in a Kraft Foods yogurt plant, more fruit was being used than the recipes called for. After the employees themselves improved the methods of calibrating flow instruments, improved the way of putting fruit in the vats, and improved the method of accounting for fruit losses, there was still room for improvement. An outside group was brought in. Working with the employees themselves as well as with management, the group developed further proposals: move pumps so as to leave less fruit in pipelines at flavor-change intervals, follow strict procedures for flavor changes, and have fruit room employees perform solids-content analyses previously performed by quality control personnel. Because the proposals had been developed in full consultation with the employees, they were fully accepted. With respect to the detailed procedures for flavor changes, the employees actually had a lesser degree of daily autonomy after adopting the procedures than before, but they had been empowered in the sense of first participating in the development of the procedures and finally deciding whether or not to adopt the procedures.

Employees are empowered when they can change their own work for the better. As pointed out by H. R. Hackman and G. R. Oldham in *Work Redesign* (1980), employees tend to value skill variety, task identity, task significance, autonomy, and job feedback in their jobs. That is, they want to use several skills, not just one; they want to know how the task that they perform adds value to the company's products or services; they want to know that their task is a significant one; they want the freedom to exercise responsibility and to take responsibility for the outcome of their work (autonomy); and they want knowledge of the actual results of their work (feedback). Work redesign to enhance these qualities pays off in greater self-motivation, higher quality work performance, high satisfaction with the work, and low absenteeism and turnover.

To achieve these aims of job redesign, the engineer can restructure jobs in several ways: job rotation, job enlargement, job enrichment, and group work. Job rotation is the practice of providing skill variety by having several people at the same level learn to do several jobs and rotate from one job to another. Job rotation does not really contribute much to variety, because the worker may do one boring job today or this week and do a different boring job tomorrow or next week. It does give more staffing flexibility to management, but it demands more skill from workers without rewarding them with more pay. Job enlargement is adding more variety to a job. For example, at a station where three workers assembled a door every 60 seconds, one worker did material handling, another did positioning, and another did fastening. The industrial engineer redesigned the station to employ only two workers. Only a slight increase in labor efficiency was realized, and many more stations and power tools were required, but the two jobs were far less numbing than the three previous jobs had been.

Neither job rotation or job enlargement does anything for autonomy. Job enrichment gives a worker more responsibility. For example, a worker may perform inspection tasks ("Let the worker, rather than the inspector, be responsible for quality") or perform minor equipment maintenance. In the Kraft Foods example, the fruit room employees' jobs were enriched to include performing solids analyses. The employees could now better calibrate flow control equipment, better control the quality of their product, depend less on the quality control personnel, and stay better informed about the results of their work. All these effects were positive.

Group work is the combining of jobs at the same level, allowing the workers themselves to allocate tasks among the group as they see fit. In the door assembly example, the group work solution would have been to supply more power tools, allocate to the group some planning and experimentation time, and let the three workers split up the work among themselves in any manner they chose. Group work can have highly positive effects by increasing autonomy, responsibility, recognition of significance of the work, and feedback. It can raise the employee from being a cog on a wheel to being a craftsperson. It can also fail in several ways: one employee can take over and subject the others to closer, more arbitrary supervision than they would receive from management; it can use too many resources compared to more rigid ways of accomplishing the work; and it can cause low labor efficiency if the work is such that a tightly-programmed, well-choreographed procedure would be highly efficient.

Through job enrichment, TQM offers to top-heavy organizations the prospect of eliminating the need for some management and supervisory personnel. A self-directed workforce would seem to require less supervision, but the experience of large Japanese companies suggests that the number of management and supervisory people does not decline. Instead, middle managers become expediters. The new norms that can follow from a change effort—such as faster development of new products, higher quality, and faster delivery—require higher levels of commitment, communication, and coordination, and it pays to employ managers to keep things going. TQM itself requires much care and feeding; the vision must be kept fresh, both in terms of staying appropriate and in terms of continuing to inspire employees.

8.1.3.2 W. Edwards Deming

W. Edwards Deming's famous 14 points, published in his book, *Quality, Productivity, and Competitive Position* (1982), are often cited as the roots of TQM:

Deming's 14 Points for Quality and Management of an Enterprise

1. Constancy of purpose toward continual improvement of products and services
2. Adoption of a new philosophy that does not accept formerly acceptable levels of delays, mistakes, and defective products
3. Achievement of quality by building it in, not by inspection
4. Awarding of procurement contracts on the basis of total cost (life-cycle cost), not price tag
5. Continual improvement of the quality and productivity of the production and service system
6. On-the-job training (employee development)
7. Supervision whose aim is to help people and equipment do a better job
8. Elimination of fear throughout the organization
9. Elimination of barriers between departments, so that people in research, design, sales, and production can work as a team
10. Elimination of slogans, exhortations, and targets that tend to blame the workforce for faults beyond its control, and that thus can create adversarial relationships
11. Elimination of numerical work quotas; substitution of aids and helpful supervision for quotas

12. Removal of the barriers that rob people of their pride of workmanship
13. A vigorous program of education and retraining
14. Recruitment of everyone in the organization to accomplish the transformation to a state of continual improvement

8.1.3.3 TQM Examples

In 1993, the Kellog Foundation sponsored a $250,000 TQM project by the Business School of Northwestern University to transform primary schools in the Chicago city school system. Working just as they would if they were helping to improve a business, the project facilitators (Northwestern University students and professors) began identifying the various constituencies (pupils, teachers, administrators, parents, staff people, and the school board) and building a consensus of commitment to change. The project began, as all TQM projects must, with a massive information-gathering effort featuring mainly questionnaires, interviews, and meetings guided by professional facilitators. The meetings were carefully planned with a dual purpose in mind: first, to get everyone's opinions, prejudices, and ideas out in the open, but also, just as importantly, to lay the groundwork for building a consensus. No one—not the custodian fighting a balky furnace that needs a $25 part for which there is no money (while the custodian perceives thousands of dollars being wasted frivolously on other things), not the nutritionist who is forced by rigid programs to produce unhealthy high-fat meals and who has lost the fight to exclude vending machines that sell even worse snack foods and earn profits the school never sees, not the first-grader who is frightened by high school students who use the primary school's basketball courts—will deny that their opinions were sought and valued. Everyone in the system was asked in several non-threatening contexts, "What do you think will make it better?" (where "it" is whatever aspect of the system is under discussion).

The aims of TQM here, as in any TQM project, are to build a consensus so that people can work together in harmony, to articulate a forward-looking vision that can be shared by all, and to alter the system so that all are free to work toward the shared vision.

Tom Peters, in *Thriving on Chaos: Handbook for a Management Revolution* (1987), reports on two massive improvement programs undertaken by Milliken & Co., a textile manufacturer, in 1981 and 1985. Both programs were in response to challenges from foreign manufacturers. The first program was mainly a quality improvement program. The second was a customer-responsiveness program. Both were highly successful. Peters ascribes the success of the second program to these factors:

1. Top management commitment.
2. Track record (the first program had been successful).
3. A shift from adversarial to partnership relations, both within the firm and between the firm and its customers, such as Levi Strauss.

4. Restructuring of the manufacturing organization. The span of control (number of people reporting directly to a superior) was increased from about six to about 36. The freed-up supervisors (process engineers) became expediters. Instead of supervising one small part of the process, they became in effect project managers of mini-projects such as getting out a large order, shepherding new product samples through the system, and handling customers' questions and complaints.

Just-in-time (JIT) manufacturing, in which the process of manufacturing to inventory and then filling orders from inventory is replaced by manufacturing only to specific orders, requires fast responsiveness and flexibility that cannot be achieved by a comfortable bureaucratic organization. The experience of U.S. Repeating Arms (the manufacturer of Winchester firearms) after going into bankruptcy in 1986 demonstrates how TQM attacks such problems as a shift to JIT manufacturing.

One technique used is benchmarking, which in the TQM context means observing in detail how the most successful firms solve problems. Winchester engineers visited the Tennessee plant of the Saturn division of General Motors to benchmark how Saturn handles JIT manufacturing. Another technique is cultural exchange, which in the TQM context means exchanging small groups of employees between organizations for a week or more. Winchester employees from the shotgun assembly line went to work on the cellular phone line at Motorola to see how Motorola achieves its quality control excellence. As reported in "U.S. Repeating Arms Sets Sights on World-Class Facility" (Ferguson 1993), an employee who at first saw no commonality between the two manufacturing processes later said, "I realized it was not so much the product, but how everyone takes responsibility for the quality of their work that matters. You are your own quality control person."

To change the way that people approach their jobs so that JIT manufacturing could work at Winchester, management began a TQM program. It involved, besides the consensus-building, vision-building meetings that are always part of TQM, a 30-hour training course spread over a year that focused on reducing setup times and performing statistical quality control at the line level. As Ferguson reports, the vice president of operations at Winchester, Bob Kuskowski, said, "In the past, management's perception of what needed to happen on the floor was totally wrong. At one time [Winchester's] philosophy was to 'handcuff' the operators to the machines." Operators were expected to produce perfect quality parts at 100% machine efficiency. But the machines were capable neither of running a complete shift without breakdown nor of consistently producing parts within dimension tolerances. The answer, Ferguson reports, was to "put into the hands of the worker the ability to stop the process and the ability to monitor quality before a bad part is made."

8.2 Wage and Salary Administration

8.2.1 Incentives

Incentives are recognition, additional pay, or other perquisites given to employees to motivate increased quantity or quality of work. The most commonly used incentives are merit-based promotion (advancement to a higher paying or otherwise more desirable job) and merit raises in pay. However, recognition (awards) and wage incentives other than merit raises are also widely used.

8.2.1.1 General Definitions and Principles

Associated with any incentive plan is an acceptable level of the quantity or quality being motivated, and a hoped-for incentive level. Several principles of incentives have been developed from long experience. One pair of principles is that the acceptable level should correspond to a standard and that incentives should start at the acceptable level. There have been wage-incentive plans, for example, where if the standard time to produce a widget was 0.1 hr so that the standard production rate was 10 widgets per hour, the incentives would begin at eight widgets per hour or at 12 widgets per hour. But starting incentives at below the standard has been found to depress actual production rates slightly, and starting incentives at above the standard makes for an adversarial situation and causes the employee to have to make an all-or-nothing decision about how hard to work. It has also been found that incentives should be proportional to relative improvement, and that the participation ratio should be $R = 1$, where the relative improvement is defined as follows:

$$[\text{Relative improvement}] = \frac{[\text{Actual level}] - [\text{Acceptable level}]}{[\text{Incentive level}] - [\text{Acceptable level}]}$$

The participation ratio, which applies to wage incentives but not to other incentives, is $R = 1$ if by the wage incentive the total wage is proportional to production rate. For wage incentives, the total pay is

$$[\text{Total pay}] = [\text{Base pay}] + R \times [\text{Relative improvement}] \times ([\text{Incentive pay}] - [\text{Base pay}]).$$

To illustrate these definitions and principles, consider a celebrated incentives case: Frederick W. Taylor redesigned a pig-iron handler's job to remove delays and extra motions so that it was physically possible to increase hourly production by 60%. He offered a total wage of $1.85 per day to a worker who was being paid $1.15 per day if the worker would achieve the hoped-for increase. It was an all-or-nothing deal.

To analyze Taylor's offer, let us first make a specific assumption in order to have a specific acceptable level of production with which to work. Let us assume that the elimination of extra motions alone would allow the worker to produce 25% faster at the same level of effort. Then, knowing the job was already an exhausting one, so that the delays were needed by the worker as rest periods, we can set the acceptable level at 1.25. But since delays had been eliminated by the job redesign, by working at the established pace all day long the worker could produce at the incentive level of 1.60. Let the base pay be $1.15, corresponding to the new standard production rate of 1.25. Now for $R = 1$, we can determine the fair incentive pay: from acceptable level to incentive level the production increases by the ratio $1.60/1.25 = 1.28$, so the total pay should increase by the same ratio, thus becoming $1.15 \times 1.28 \approx \$1.47$. This is the pay the worker would receive for production of 1.60.

Now suppose the worker produced 1.50. The relative improvement would be $(1.50 - 1.25) \div (1.60 - 1.25) \approx 0.7143$, and the total pay would be $1.15 + 1 \times 0.7143 \times (1.47 - 1.15) \approx \$1.38$. We can see that Taylor's offer violated most of the principles listed above. By not basing the incentive on a new standard, he was paying the worker not only for working more, but also for the improvements Taylor made to make the work easier. Taylor's incentive was an all-or-nothing deal, so the incentive failed to start at the new standard production rate; in fact, the worker would get nothing extra for producing 1.50, whereas by modern practice he would get $1.38 instead of $1.15. Taylor's scheme did, in its way, obey the participation ratio $R = 1$ principle, since the pay would be increased by a ratio 1.85/1.15, which is just slightly greater than 1.60; but if the new standard were considered, Taylor's scheme would increase the pay by more than 1.60 when the improvement due to the worker was only 1.28—a participation ratio of more than 1.25.

The principles and definitions given above apply both to individual incentives and to group incentives.

8.2.1.2 Individual Wage Incentives

Daywork pay is pay according to number of hours worked. The base rate is determined by job evaluation (see section 8.2.2); pay is determined by multiplying the base rate by the number of hours worked. It is customary to multiply the base rate by 1.50 for overtime, which is customarily defined as more than 40 hours per week, and to multiply the base rate by 2.0 for overtime work performed on holidays. For regularly scheduled work on second ("night") shift (afternoon through approximately midnight) or on third ("graveyard") shift (approximately midnight through morning), there is no customary shift differential, but pay is often about 15% higher than on first ("day") shift.

Measured daywork pay is pay according to the number of hours worked, plus periodic opportunities (often annual) for merit raises and/or bonuses based on performance reports. To produce performance reports, the quality and/or quantity of work is measured and compared to standards.

Modern piecework incentives are structured as in section 8.2.1.1 above, but the term "piecework" often refers to more primitive plans in which the worker is literally paid by the piece rather than by the hour. Pure piecework pay is outlawed for most workers in the U.S. because it has been abused as a way of circumventing minimum-wage laws. Legal piecework pay plans have a guaranteed base rate in dollars per hour. The piecework rate in dollars per piece is calculated as follows:

$$[\text{Piecework rate}] = [\text{Base rate}] \times [\text{Standard time per piece}]$$

Many piecework plans define the expected output, which is simply the reciprocal of the standard time per piece, and compute the piecework rate by dividing the base rate by the expected output. The total pay is

$$[\text{Pay}] = [\text{Piecework rate}] \times [\text{Number of pieces completed}]$$

but it cannot be less than

$$[\text{Base rate}] \times [\text{Number of hours worked}]$$

For example, let the base rate be \$10/hr, and let the worker work an 8-hr day, charging all time to task X. Let the standard time for task X be 0.75 min./piece. Then the piecework rate is \$10/hr$\times$(0.75÷60) hr/piece = \$0.125/piece. Alternatively, the expected output is 1/(0.75÷60) = 80 pieces/hr, and the piecework rate is 10/80 = \$0.125/piece. Now suppose the employee produces 720 pieces in the 8-hr day. The pay is \$0.125/piece$\times$720 pieces = \$90. But if the employee had produced only 600 pieces in the 8-hr day, the pay would not be only \$75; instead, it would be the base rate multiplied by the number of hours worked, or \$10/hr$\times$8 hr = \$80.

The standard hour piecework pay plan is equivalent but with more convenient definitions. The earned time is defined as

$$[\text{Earned time}] = [\text{Number of pieces completed}] \times [\text{Standard time per piece}]$$

but it cannot be less than the number of hours worked. The total pay is defined as

$$[\text{Pay}] = [\text{Earned time}] \times [\text{Base rate}]$$

In the above example, if the worker produced 720 pieces in the 8-hr day, the earned time would be 720 pieces $\times$(0.75÷60)hr/piece = 9 hr, and the pay would be 9 hr$\times$\$10/hr = \$90. But if the employee had produced only 600 pieces in the 8-hr day, the earned time would be not 7.5 hr but the 8 hr actually worked, so that the pay would be 8 hr × $10/hr = $80. The standard-hour version of piecework pay gives exactly the same results as the other versions, but it is more convenient because its database stores only standard times rather than piecework rates (which are computed from base rates and standard times and hence must be kept separately for each base rate, which may change from time to time or from worker to worker).

Disadvantages of piecework plans and other individual incentives are that employees may produce barely acceptable quality work and may skimp on allowance-covered work such as workplace cleanup and material restocking, and that adversarial relationships may develop as workers and managers quibble about standards or issues not covered by allowances, such as undertaking special assignments or helping train other workers.

8.2.1.3 Group Incentives

Group incentives avoid the aforementioned disadvantages by letting each person in a group earn an incentive based on output or performance of the group as a whole. Group incentives can be based on any variables for which motivation is desired: safety, quality, and, of course, production rate. Immediate group incentives can have all the structures reviewed above, where the data and calculations are for the group rather than for an individual. However, it is more common for group incentives to be long-term. We will very briefly review the most important classes of long-term group incentives.

Profit-sharing plans pay a predetermined share of operating profits to employees in the form of cash, retirement plan contributions, or capital stock (ownership) of the enterprise.

Funded incentive plans have designs that set up incentive funds out of which incentives are paid. The funds are self-sustaining. Given that performance will be better than the acceptable level in some years and worse in other years, and that negative bonuses will never be paid, these plans set aside some of their accumulation in good years. Three of the commonly encountered plans are Scanlon plans, Rucker plans, and Improshare plans.

Scanlon plans, introduced by Frederick G. Lesieur (1958), are plans that measure labor productivity above a baseline and share the associated profits with workers, usually on a 75% worker, 25% company basis. Bonus reserve funds, usually 25% of the potential bonus, are set aside to keep the plans afloat in bad years. In philosophy, Scanlon plans are based on "Theory Y" (see section 8.1.2).

Rucker plans are trademarked by the Eddy-Rucker-Nickels Company, Inc., based in Cambridge, Massachusetts. Introduced in 1962, they are based on value added. Value added in an operation is the increased value of the output over that of the input, less all production costs. In Europe, value-added accounting is widely used because taxation is largely on the basis of value added rather than on income. If the cost accounting system already maintains value-added data for each operation in a company, Rucker plans are more convenient to administer than other plans.

Improshare plans, trademarked by Mitchell Fein, Inc., in Hillsdale, New Jersey, compare actual to standard production to calculate "Improshare hours," which are analogous to "earned time" as defined in section 8.2.1.2 for piecework incentives. A 30% ceiling is placed on bonuses. Improshare hours above the ceiling are "banked" to be used for low-productivity periods. If banked hours consistently accumulate, the company and employees negotiate a buy-back rate for them; a cash sum is paid to each employee and the standard is raised to the point where the next bonus is expected to be 30%.

8.2.1.4 Recognition Incentives

Recognition, given in the form of awards and designations, can be a motivator. It often carries tangible rewards; for example, an engineer who wins a recognized award or designation such as fellow or senior member in a professional society can turn the award or designation into a greater salary or higher consulting fees or access to better consulting clients. Like other incentives, recognition is given for past performance, not as a reward for hoped-for future performance. The same general principles apply as for other incentives, but there are differences. One difference is that internal recognition (recognition within the organization, as opposed to external recognition seen by the public) is, unlike money, a currency that depreciates with use. For example, "employee-of-the-month" programs are ill-advised. Why? They violate the principle that an incentive should start at an acceptable level of performance; no incentive is earned except by the person who performs at the highest level, so only the best few candidates are motivated by it and the employees who need motivation the most are untouched. The value of the recognition also depreciates. Suppose, for example, Emma is the best waitress and wins the award for waitress of the month. The first month, everyone says, "How nice. She deserves it." After she wins four months in a row, everyone resents her, and she perceives the award as a negative motivator. Good recognition programs recognize everyone who improves. Like any incentives, award programs should be carefully designed to achieve the most motivation for the least cost.

E88.   **In a state that has 8 million residents, a statewide business association decided several years ago that the educational system was turning out high-school graduates who made poor potential employees because they were poorly educated. The association blamed the poor education on insufficient academic emphasis and motivation, and therefore proposed to improve the situation by starting an award program for student achievement recognition (STAR). Each year, the student in each of the state's 11,000 high schools who earned the highest score on the SAT (Scholastic Aptitude Test) was designated the school's STAR student and honored at a 100-person banquet by principal, administrators, community leaders, and business leaders. Then, the student with the highest SAT score among all high schools in the school district was similarly honored as the district's STAR student. Continuing, 10 regional banquets followed, and at each of these the region's STAR student was given a $500 scholarship, a $100 inscribed silver tray, and a place in a 14-day tour of regional STAR students around the neighboring states, with all expenses paid. Finally, there was the state STAR banquet, at which the state's STAR student received a $10,000 scholarship. Critique this incentive program and suggest improvements.**

The reason for the incentive program was that most of the students were not well educated. Therefore, a reasonable goal for the incentive system would be to motivate most of the students to become better educated. However, this program touched only the very best students, not the majority. It is difficult to think of any way in which the STAR awards program would motivate a typical student. It violates the principle that incentives should start at the acceptable performance level.

Another difficulty is cost effectiveness. If we assume, for example, that every banquet has 100 guests, that the cost of a banquet is $7 per guest, and that there are 1,200 school districts (the result will not be sensitive to the specific numbers), the cost of banquets alone would be $700 \times (11,000 + 1200 + 10 + 1) = \$8,547,700$. Regardless of where the money comes from, this represents at least $1,000,000 profit given to vendors rather than to students. If the $1,000,000 could be spent on $500 scholarships, it would provide 2,000 of them; if it could be spent on $50 cash awards, it would provide 20,000 of them, or nearly two for each high school. (A further issue is whether SAT scores really measure aptitude, but discussion of that issue would be beyond the scope of this review.)

The program should be restructured to reach as many students as possible. If we defined the acceptable level as a score not too far above the median for the state, then a majority of students could aspire to be designated as STAR students. The very top ones could be super-STAR students and receive additional recognition. The reward system should be scaled to provide whatever is considered the minimum motivationally-relevant amount for the students at the lowest award level, with awards increasing modestly in value for students at higher levels.

8.2.2 Job Evaluation

Besides motivation and incentives, other considerations affect how much a worker should be paid. Seniority—the length of time since the employee joined the organization—is an important consideration in most economies; a worker should be promoted and paid partly on the basis of length of service. The seniority criterion rewards loyalty, since seniority is broken when an employee changes jobs. Arguments to justify using seniority as a basis for pay and promotion often stress the intangible benefits to the employer of the employee's experience. Other justifications are that seniority is easily measured and compared, it gives an employee a promise of future progress, and it cannot be easily abused by an employer. Merit—an employee's history of productivity or usefulness to the organization, compared to that of employees who do similar work—is another consideration. Merit is measured in job-specific ways: sales volume can be used for salespeople, number of lines of code written without callbacks (complaints that the code does not work) can be used for computer programmers, results of student evaluations can be used for instructors, and awards won or certifications earned can be used for many kinds of workers. Seniority and merit, which are attributes of the worker and job, not of the job itself, are usually superimposed as modifications to what is considered the basic worth of a job.

Job evaluation is estimation or determination of the basic worth of a job, based on two broad considerations: benefit of the work to the company and demands of the work on the employee.

It is not acceptable to pay and promote workers according to an arbitrary standard that cannot be audited. If a class of employees can show that its members are being paid or promoted worse than another class for equal work, the organization or its management can be vulnerable to bad will, civil action, and even criminal sanctions. There are four formal approaches to job evaluation that can be used to produce wage scales that can be defended as equitable:

- Job classification (e.g., civil service grades)
- Job ranking (pairwise comparisons of jobs)
- Job-factor comparison
- Job point plans

Job classification is not quantitative and is not a method in which industrial engineers are expected to be competent. Job ranking is based on subjective pairwise comparisons (should this job be paid more or less than that one?) and thus is not really quantitative; it is also quite inefficient.

E89. **An organization has 250 different key job titles. Compare the number of estimations required to produce a set of pay rates using two job-evaluation methods: job ranking and factor comparison using five factors.**

By job ranking the number of pairwise comparisons is $249 \times 250 \div 2 = 31,125$. *Note:* If there are N jobs, the first one must be paired with $N-1$ others, the second with $N-2$ others, and so forth, so that the total number of pairwise comparisons is the sum of $N-1$, $N-2$,..., 1, which by Pascal's formula is $(N-1)N/2$. The comparisons yield a ranked list but not pay amounts; 250 of these must be estimated. The total number of estimations in the job ranking method is hence 31,375.

By factor comparison, there must be an estimation of the value of each factor for each job; this requires $5 \times 250 = 1250$ estimations. In addition, if the factors are not all weighted equally (but usually they are weighted equally), there would be five more estimations. The total for factor comparison is either 1250 or 1255—much less than that for job ranking.

Regardless of the specific method used for job evaluation, not every job title is evaluated. Jobs are aggregated into job classes, each of which has a key job title. All jobs within a job class are assumed to have equal worth. A few dozen job classes are needed at most for all but the very largest organizations.

8.2.2.1 Job-factor Analysis

Job-factor analysis is performed by a job-evaluation committee whose first task is to define job factors that are associated with difficulty to the worker, benefit to the employer, or both. Factors should be of the job, not of the worker, and must be nondiscriminatory. Factors should also be as orthogonal as possible; this means they should measure separate aspects of difficulty and benefit to the organization. It is seldom necessary to define more than 10 job factors.

E90.   **A job evaluation committee is considering a draft of a list of job factors. The list contains skill required for the job, mental effort required, balance (the extent to which employing the worker contributes to the organization's minority and disability hiring goals), responsibility, supervision (number of employees directly and indirectly supervised), appearance (degree to which special grooming or dress is required, as for a receptionist job), working conditions (how bad they are), and noise level in which the employee will work. Improve the list.**

Balance must be removed, as it is an attribute of the employee, not the job. Supervision is not orthogonal with responsibility; it is largely correlated with responsibility and should be removed. It is better to remove supervision than to remove responsibility, because responsibility includes supervision but also includes such non-supervisory aspects as the criticality of high quality work. Appearance is a questionable factor, even though it is appropriate to give higher pay to people who are required to wear expensive clothes or be particularly well-groomed; it can be perceived as discriminatory, as when a corporate receptionist job may be highly paid relative to other receptionist jobs because a highly decorative person is expected to hold it. It would be appropriate to remove this factor; the working-conditions factor can include the notion that a job that requires close contact with the public is more demanding than one that does not. Noise is just a part of the working-conditions factor and should be removed. Physical effort is not on the draft list and certainly should be a factor for all blue-collar jobs. The improved list would be *skill*, *mental effort*, *responsibility*, *working conditions*, and *physical effort*. For an organization in which some jobs are dangerous, *risk* may optionally be considered separately from working conditions. For jobs where the organization is willing to pay extra because qualified workers are scarce, *competition* can be a factor.

After adopting job factors, the committee must select key jobs. Job-factor evaluation should be done for actual jobs, each considered typical of its job class, rather than for hypothetical jobs. How should key jobs be selected? Most importantly, the selected set of key jobs must cover the ranges of all factor values as evenly as possible. If, for example, there are no jobs with moderate physical effort in the set, the set does not provide for accurate evaluation of any job that involves moderate physical effort. Also, the key jobs must be well-documented, mature jobs with well-established responsibilities and performance expectations and a stable demand and supply.

The third and most difficult task for the committee is to assign a money-apportionment value to each factor for each job. A money-apportionment table is built with a column for each factor and a row for each key job. Row values must sum to a number proportional to the base pay for the job; usually the row values sum to the base pay itself. Column values must be such that if a job is considered more demanding or beneficial than another with respect to the column's factor, it must have a greater money-apportionment value. Unless otherwise noted, the values are in dollars per hour.

E91. **A job-factor money-apportionment table has five factor columns. The values for two key jobs are shown:**

Key job title	Skill required	Mental effort	Physical effort	Responsi-bility	Working conditions
Tool and die maker	6.00	4.72	1.06	2.56	1.28
Drill press operator	3.50	3.22	0.97	1.78	1.22

Interpret the values and determine the basic pay rate for each of the two key jobs.

The values are probably in $/hr units. They can be interpreted as the amount of money per hour the employer is willing to pay for each factor. For example, the skill required by the tool and die maker's job is "worth" $6/hr and its mental effort is "worth" $4.72/hr. The basic hourly pay rate for tool and die maker is $6.00 + 4.72 + 1.06 + 2.56 + 1.28 = \underline{\$15.62}$. The basic hourly pay rate for drill press operator is $3.50 + 3.22 + 0.97 + 1.78 + 1.22 = \underline{\$10.69}$.

The final task for the committee is consistency checking. A common method of consistency checking is to perform a separate analysis such as ranking the jobs informally or formally or obtaining old job evaluation data or data typical for the industry. The results of the job-factor analysis imply a rank order that can be calculated simply by sorting the rows in descending order of basic hourly pay rate. If the separate data also allows the jobs to be ranked, the two rankings can be compared. In example E91, if the drill press operator job had paid more in the past than the tool and die maker job, there is an apparent inconsistency. In resolving it, factor values for the two jobs can be compared, and the committee may decide to revise some of the money-apportionment values, especially if they bring the basic hourly pay rate more in line with the available separate data.

The consistency checking process can be illustrated as follows: A committee member said she felt job A47 (shrinkwrap operator) paid too little. Asked why, she said, "Well it's so hot and noisy at the shrinkwrap machine, and the operator is continually being interrupted to help with shipping and receiving." She suggested a $0.20/hr increase in the money-apportionment value in the working conditions column for this job to recognize the heat and noise. But other members of the committee pointed out that a raise this large would put job A47 ahead of two other jobs with clearly worse working conditions, including heat and noise. The committee finally settled on a $0.12/hr increase in the working conditions value, so that the working conditions for this job seemed in line with those for other jobs. But there was one glaring exception: Job C28 clearly had about the same working conditions as job A47 yet paid even less for this factor than job A47 had paid before the question was brought up. The working-conditions money-apportionment value for job C28 was then raised to bring it in line. Finally, there was a discussion about interruptions. The committee remembered having increased the mental effort value for a job where interruptions tended to make an operator lose count in a delicate procedure and be forced to start over. It was decided that for job A47 the interruptions did not contribute to the job's requirement for mental effort, and that the operator may even welcome them, depending on his or her personality and level of boredom with the repetitive shrinkwrap operation.

Job-factor analysis allows for normalization by multiplying every money-apportionment value in the table by a normalizing multiplier. For example, an across-the-board 5% pay hike would be expressed by multiplying by 1.05. As another example, a new textile mill in eastern Tennessee used job-factor analysis to establish pay scales for 1250 workers who were to fill 60 distinct job classes. After the first round of meetings established a preliminary set of basic hourly pay rates for all 60 job classes, the rates were found to infer a total payroll 17% lower than had been projected. The projected total payroll had been a point of negotiation with local authorities and constituted an obligation. To normalize the rates, all the money-apportionment values were simply multiplied by $1/(1 - 0.17)$, so that the total payroll was raised to the projected amount.

8.2.2.2 Point Systems for Job Evaluation

Point systems use predefined job factors similar to those in job-factor analysis, but they assign predefined numbers of points to defined levels of the factors. For example, one factor may be working conditions, having five defined levels:

- 1 (excellent) = absence of disagreeable conditions
- 2 (good) = occasional exposure to disagreeable conditions
- 3 (fair) = one disagreeable condition continuously or several occasionally
- 4 (poor) = several disagreeable conditions continuously
- 5 (harsh) = particularly disagreeable working conditions

The "disagreeable working conditions" include exposure to dust, dirt, heat, fumes, cold, noise, vibration, and so forth.

The Midwest Industrial Management Association (MIMA) publishes two point-system plans—one for office jobs and one for shop jobs. The entire MIMA plan for job shops is reprinted in Konz's textbook cited earlier. The MIMA shop job plan cites the following five "degrees" (levels) for each of eleven factors.

MIMA Job Factors for Shop Jobs

SKILL	1.	Education or trade knowledge
	2.	Experience
	3.	Initiative and ingenuity
EFFORT	4.	Physical demand
	5.	Mental and/or visual demand
RESPONSIBILITY	6.	Equipment or process
	7.	Material or product
	8.	Safety of others
	9.	Work of others
JOB CONDITIONS	10.	Working conditions
	11.	Hazards

In the MIMA system the points for SKILL-education or trade knowledge are 14, 28, 42, 56, and 70 for levels 1, 2, 3, 4, and 5. SKILL-experience is the most heavily-weighted factor; for level 1, for example, it has 22 points, and for level 5 it has 110 points. The smallest point score possible for a job is 100, which would be earned by a job that was least demanding for every factor; for factors 1, 2,..., 11, respectively, it would earn 14, 22, 14, 10, 5, 5, 5, 5, 5, 10, and 5 points. The greatest score possible for a job is 500, which would be earned by a job that was most demanding for every factor; for factors 1, 2,..., 11, respectively, it would earn 70, 110, 70, 50, 25, 25, 25, 25, 25, 50, and 25 points. In practice, no job would earn less than about 140 total points or more than about 360 total points.

Pay rates can be made proportional to point totals, but it is more common to convert point totals to grades and establish a pay rate range for each grade. In the MIMA system, there are 12 grades, ranging from grade 12 for the lowest scores (below 140) to grade 1 for the highest scores (above 359). Let S be the MIMA total score; then the grade G is computed by adding 14 to S, dividing by 22, rounding down to an integer, and subtracting from 18.

$$G = 18 - \lfloor (S+14)/22 \rfloor$$

E92a.   **Under the MIMA system, a certain job is in level 3 for job factor 1; in level 5 for job factors 2 and 3; and in level 1 for all other factors. Determine its point score and its grade.**

This job demands great skill but little effort and responsibility and is performed under excellent working conditions. It earns 42 points for job factor 1, 110 points for job factor 2, 70 points for job factor 3, and 10, 5, 5, 5, 5, 5, 10, and 5 points, respectively for job factors 4,...,11. The total is <u>272 points</u>, which puts the job in <u>grade 5</u>.

E92b. **The holder of the abovementioned job apparently does not supervise anyone. Why? If the job were changed so that it carried very heavy responsibility for supervising others, would it have a higher grade under the MIMA system?**

The job is at level 1 for RESPONSIBILITY–work of others (factor 9), so apparently it is not a supervisory job. It earns 5 points for factor 9. If the job were changed so that it was at the highest level for factor 9 (level 5), earning 25 points for the factor, the revised point total would be <u>292 points</u>, which still puts the job in <u>grade 5</u>; it would <u>not</u> have a higher grade under the MIMA system. *Note:* The grade brackets are 22 points wide, so a 20-point increase would usually put the job in the next higher or lower numbered grade; but this job starts out barely in grade 5.

8.3 Noise, Toxicology, and Safety

8.3.1 Noise

Please see the last part of section 7.2.1 for a discussion of noise as measured in dBA for typical office noise levels and oral communication, and for ear protection. Here we deal with estimating the articulation index for communication adequacy in a noisy environment using 1/3-octave band measurements. (The dBA scale uses full-octave bands, which are too coarse for accurately estimating speech intelligibility).

Human factors textbooks such as *New Horizons for Human Factors in Design* (Huchingson 1981), *Human Factors: Understanding People-System Relationships* (Kantowitz and Sorlein 1983), and *Human Factors in Engineering and Design*, Fifth Edition, (McCormick and Sanders 1982) explain the articulation index in full.

Speech intelligibility depends upon the signal-to-noise ratio in each of 15 frequency bands. The signal for a band is the peak level of speech reaching the listener in decibels. The noise for a band is the steady-state noise level in decibels. The signal-to-noise ratio is (because decibels are on a logarithmic scale) the difference between the peak speech decibels and the steady-state noise decibels. For example, if in the 1/3-octave band centered on 400 Hz the peak speech level is 68 dB and the steady-state noise level is 40 dB, the signal-to-noise ratio for that band is $68 - 40 = 28$ dB.

Two corrections to the signal-to-noise ratio are made before computing the articulation index. First, since a signal-to-noise ratio of more than 30 dB in any one band does not enhance intelligibility any more than one of 30 dB, each signal-to-noise ratio that exceeds 30 is corrected to 30. For example, if in the 1/3-octave band centered on 200 Hz the peak speech level is 64 dB and the steady-state noise level is 30 dB, the band's signal-to-noise ratio is corrected from 64 − 30 = 34 to 30. Also, since a signal-to-noise ratio of less than zero is no worse than zero, each negative signal-to-noise ratio is corrected to zero. For example, if in the 1/3-octave band centered on 4000 Hz the peak speech level is 53 dB and the steady-state noise level is 57 dB, this band's signal-to-noise ratio is corrected from 53 − 57 = −4 to 0.

If we let the raw signal-to-noise ratio in band j be denoted S_j, the corrected signal-to-noise ratio can be mathematically described as $C_j = \min[\max(0, S_j), 30]$.

The final step in estimating the articulation index is to multiply each S_j by a band-specific weight a_j and to sum the results. The weights are published in tables given in the references cited above. Then a speech intelligibility score, published in a plot or table in the references, is assigned for each value of the articulation index. For example, if the articulation index is 0.30, the associated intelligibility score is 90%. Interpretations of the intelligibility scores are also given in the references; 90% is minimally acceptable for speech communication.

E93. **A public-address system is to be installed to relay instructions and data by voice to workers on a noisy factory floor. Steady state noise levels have been measured and peak speech levels from the system's speakers have been estimated as follows:**

Band center frequency (Hz)	Steady-state noise level (dB)	Peak speech signal level (dB)	Band center frequency (Hz)	Steady-state noise level (dB)	Peak speech signal level (dB)
200	30	64	1250	52	60
250	32	65	1600	54	59
315	34	66	2000	55	59
400	40	68	2500	56	57
500	42	65	3150	62	55
630	44	63	4000	57	53
800	46	61	5000	47	50
1000	51	60			

Determine the articulation index for the system; determine and interpret the intelligibility score for spoken sentences.

The first three bands have corrected signal-to-noise ratios of 30 dB; the bands at 3150 and 4000 Hz have corrected signal-to-noise ratios of 0 dB; other bands have the differences (e.g., the band at 630 Hz has 63 − 44 = 19 dB). When these are multiplied by the band weights given in the references, and the products are summed, the result is an articulation index of 0.30. From the references, the corresponding speech intelligibility score is 90%, which is interpreted as minimally acceptable.

8.3.2 Toxicology

A toxin is, in the narrowest sense, a poisonous substance having a protein structure, secreted by an organism, capable of causing toxicosis (a pathological condition resulting from poisoning), and also capable of inducing the body to produce counteragents or antitoxins to remove it. An example of a counteragent is a phagocyte, which is a mobile cell such as a leukocyte or microphage that engulfs and digests cells, microorganisms, or other foreign bodies in the bloodstream and tissues.

For the industrial engineer, a more general definition of toxins is appropriate: chemical substances, biological agents, or radiation capable of causing acute or long-term (chronic) harmful effects on the body. Toxicology is, for our purposes, the knowledge of how toxins affect the body, how they are produced, and how to prevent them from reaching or affecting human beings, particularly workers.

In general, there are several lines of defense against toxins. The most desirable strategy, where possible and cost effective, is to limit toxins at the source. For example, carbon monoxide (CO) is a poisonous gas that arises from incomplete combustion, and the process that produces it should be improved so as to produce less of it, if possible. Next is the strategy to isolate or remove toxins so they cannot reach people. For example, one can, at great expense, run flue gases (exhaust from combustion) through scrubbers to remove CO and make it harmless; another example is the cigarette filter, which removes tar and nicotine from cigarette smoke so that the toxins will eventually reach a landfill rather than a person's lungs. Less desirable is to disperse toxins so that low doses will be received. This is the smokestack strategy, and it works better than would be predicted by the simple mathematics of dilution, because there are many natural removal processes for most toxins. Final defense strategies (before getting to the last resort of medical treatment) include protective devices such as breathing masks, exposure-duration limitations, and avoidance training.

Unfortunately, some exposure to toxins is unavoidable in industry. The industrial engineer should be familiar with how toxins enter the body, how they are eliminated, and what standards should be met for protecting workers and limiting their exposure to toxins.

Most toxins are ingested through breathing. Faced with airborne contaminants and no opportunity to limit them at the source or isolate them, the industrial engineer's first instinct should be to provide better ventilation. Let the worker breathe fresh air, not contaminated air. Other ingestion routes are by mouth (workers whose hands or tools may be contaminated should be trained not to touch their face or should be provided with masks) and through the skin (provide protective gloves or some other kind of protective clothing).

Most toxins are eliminated by the kidneys and liver, and low exposure levels can be safe if poisons enter the body at a rate not greater than that which the body can eliminate them. Heavy metals, such as lead, are particularly dangerous because they are eliminated slowly and tend to build up. Little's Law applies here: If a toxin enters the body at rate λ and dwells an average time W as it passes through the body before being eliminated, then the long-run average amount of it in the body is $L = \lambda W$.

Particulates are an important class of contaminants in the air. Their diameter is measured in μm (microns). The diameter of a human hair is about 100 μm. The smallest visible dust motes are in the 5 to 10 μm range; the concentration of particles in the air by weight is greatest in this range, but the concentration by number of particles is much greater for smaller particles. The greatest numbers of particles are near 2 μm in size. Particles of 4 μm diameter or less that are inert (not microorganisms or proteins) are particularly harmful, because not only do they get through the nose, trachea, and bronchial tubes into the lung itself, but also they cannot be digested by the microphages that engulf them; the microphages die, forming scar tissue and loss of lung surface area for absorbing oxygen. Silica particles (dust from earth and sand) and fly ash particles (inert combustion products and tars) are particularly numerous in the 1 to 3 μm range; secondhand cigarette smoke is a kind of fly ash. Particles 10 μm and greater in diameter are nearly completely caught by the nose and upper airways; sputum containing them is eventually swallowed or spit out. Particles in the 5 to 10 μm range are fairly efficiently removed; about 40% by weight reaches the lungs. Particles smaller than 4 μm get past the nose and upper airways and enter the lungs.

Gases that contaminate the air are individual molecules that range from harmless to very harmful depending on chemical properties. Important harmful gases include carbon monoxide (CO), chlorine (Cl_2), hydrocarbons, and sulfur dioxide (SO_2, which becomes sulfuric acid upon contact with mucus). The concentration of gases is measured in ppm (parts per million), which is a volumetric measure of concentration—the number of molecules of the gas per million molecules of air-gas mixture, or, what is essentially the same, per million molecules of air. By weight, gas concentration is expressed as mg/m^3 (milligrams per cubic meter). If c_v is the concentration of a gas by volume in ppm, c_w is the concentration by weight in mg/m^3, and M is the molecular weight of the gas, the relationship between c_v and c_w is

$$c_v = 24.45 c_w / M$$

For example, if a worker is exposed to 150 ppm of chlorine gas, which has a molecular weight of 70, the corresponding weight concentration is

$$150 \times 70 \div 24.45 \approx 429 \text{ mg/m}^3.$$

Exposures of workers to toxins are regulated by the Environmental Protection Agency (EPA), the Occupational Safety and Health Administration (OSHA), and state agencies. Most such regulations are based on the Threshold Limit Values (TLV) set by the American Conference of Governmental Industrial Hygienists in Cincinnati, Ohio. This conference publishes revised TLVs every year. There are three different TLVs:

- **TLV-TWA** (time-weighted average) is the maximum average concentration allowable for a 40-hr work week (8-hr per day, 5 days per week).

- **TLV-STEL** (short-term exposure limit) is the maximum 15-minute average concentration allowable for any 15 minutes of the workday. There can be up to four periods approaching this concentration, separated by at least one hour.

- **TLV-C** (ceiling) is the maximum allowable peak concentration that should never be exceeded.

E94a.   **Acetone has TLV-TWA = 750 ppm and TLV-STEL = 1000 ppm. Is it permissible for a worker to be exposed to acetone at 500 ppm for 4 hrs, 750 ppm for 2 hrs, and 1500 ppm for 2 hrs?**

$$\text{TWA} = [(500 \times 4) + (750 \times 2) + (1{,}500 \times 2)] \div 8 = 812.5 > 750 \Rightarrow \underline{\text{No}}$$

Not only is TWA > TLV-TWA, but since the worst 2-hr average is 1,500 ppm, there must be a 15-min period that exceeds 1,500 ppm, which is greater than TLV-STEL, so again <u>no</u>.

When a worker is exposed to more than one contaminant, the exposures are assumed to be additive; the total of the proportional exposures must not exceed 100%. The proportional TWA exposure for a contaminant is its TWA divided by its TLV-TWA; the proportional STEL exposure for a contaminant is STEL divided by TLV-STEL; and the proportional ceiling exposure is the peak concentration divided by the TLV-C. The TLV-C additivity does not depend on simultaneous exposure. Thus, for instance, a worker cannot be exposed briefly to 60% of the peak allowable concentration of H_2S at one time during the day and to 41% of the peak allowable concentration of CCl_4 at another. The TWA and STEL proportional exposures, unlike that for the peaks, are for simultaneous exposure only.

E94b.   **For 15 minutes a worker is exposed to 15% of the TLV-STEL for acetone, 35% of the TLV-STEL for acetaldehyde, and 12% of the TLV-STEL for butanol. Is this permissible?**

The total proportional exposure to the three contaminants is 0.15 + 0.35 + 0.12 = 62% ⇒ <u>yes</u>. *Note:* Even if the proportional exposures added up to more than 100%, it would be permissible for the exposures to occur at different times; they are treated as additive because they all occur over the same time period.

E94c. **Acetic anhydride has TLV-STEL = 2 ppm and TLV-C = 5 ppm. For 15 minutes a worker is exposed to a varying concentration of acetic anhydride, averaging 1.5 ppm with a peak of 6 ppm. Is this permissible?**

No, because 6 > TLV-C.

E94d. **Carbon monoxide has a molecular weight of 28. How many ppm of carbon monoxide is 4 mg/m³?**

$24.45 \times 4 \div 28 = \underline{3.493 \text{ ppm}}$

8.3.3 Safety

Safety engineering is a specialty within industrial engineering, but there are some basics that every industrial engineer should know. In this review, we are concerned with worker safety (as contrasted with public safety, food and drug protection, and product liability). In the U.S., federal legal requirements for worker safety are regulated by OSHA, which enforces workplace safety and health conditions; the National Institute for Occupational Safety and Health (NIOSH), an agency of the Department of Health, Education, and Welfare, sets workplace safety and health and publishes guidelines. (For example, see section 7.1.4 for NIOSH standards concerning lifting effort.) The National Safety Council, whose members include most major insurers and employers, promotes safety and compiles and publishes safety statistics and accident-prevention manuals. The American National Standards Institute (ANSI), which provides technical standards for tests and measurements of many kinds, provides some definitions widely used in safety work. (It is usual in safety work to use "days" and "hours" to mean mandays and manhours or person-days and person-hours; we will use all three sets of terms interchangeably.)

8.3.3.1 Injury Frequency and Severity

The frequency statistic defined for disabling injuries (known more commonly as lost-time injuries) by ANSI standard Z16.1 is known as the Z16.1 frequency rate:

$$[\text{Z16.1 frequency rate}] = \frac{[\text{Number of lost-time injuries}] \times 1,000,000}{[\text{Number of manhours worked}]}$$

This is the number of disabling injuries per million manhours and is the accepted frequency measure for comparing safety policies or workplaces. For example, if there were 320 workers at a paper mill employed an average of 2,000 hours per worker in 1983, and there were five accidents in which a total of eight workers suffered lost-time injuries for a total of 72 mandays of lost time, the Z16.1 frequency rate is

$$8 \times 1,000,000 \div (320 \times 2,000) = 12.5 \text{ lost-time injuries per million manhours}$$

The corresponding severity statistic is

$$[\text{Z16.1 severity rate}] = \frac{[\text{Number of lost-time mandays}] \times 1,000,000}{[\text{Number of manhours worked}]}$$

The paper mill experienced a Z16.1 severity rate of

$$72 \times 1,000,000 \div (320 \times 2,000) = 112.5 \text{ lost mandays per million manhours}$$

There are three important things to note about the number of lost-time mandays. First, only full lost days are counted, so visiting the doctor or resting for a few hours does not count; for example, if Joe was injured Thursday morning and returned to work Friday afternoon, then zero lost-time mandays were charged. Second, weekends, holidays, shutdowns, and other potential days of work are counted; for example if Ahmad was injured Thursday morning, could not work Friday, could not have worked Saturday but would have been off, could have worked Sunday but was off, and returned Monday, then two lost-time mandays (Friday and Saturday) were charged. Third, ANSI standard time charges exist for death or permanent total disability (6,000 mandays for either) and loss of various body parts (e.g., 20% loss of the use of a thumb at the proximal joint is charged at 20% of 6000 mandays, or 1200 mandays). Thus, the permanent-injury charges far overshadow the actual lost mandays in the Z16.1 severity rate, and a medium-sized company that experiences one on-the-job death may have its severity statistic jump by a factor of 1000.

These statistics are used in setting insurance rates, identifying unsafe workplaces, and judging overall safety levels for many purposes such as administering safety competitions. Note that the number of accidents is not one of the statistics; however, the National Safety Council publishes a measure called "average days charged per injury," which is the ratio of severity rate to frequency rate but can also be computed as the ratio of number of lost days to number of lost-time injuries, without regard to the number of hours worked. Note also that minor accidents (those where there is no lost time) are not counted; not only would statistics be unreliable for minor accidents (temptation to overlook them) and the frequency rate inflated by including unimportant data along with important data, but also a requirement for recording statistics on minor accidents would discourage first-aid treatment.

Many other safety statistics are in use; all have definitional difficulties. For example, the number of deaths per appropriate activity unit, such as millions of vehicle miles traveled or million hours of travel, is used in the transportation industries. An example of the definitional difficulties can be seen in the familiar statistic of approximately 50,000 annual automobile deaths in the U.S. This statistic, and ones that relate deaths to passenger miles or passenger hours, is a tip-of-the-iceberg statistic, because the number of tragic nonfatal injuries is so much greater than the number of deaths. Still, the number of deaths is a useful comparative indicator of the safety level within a limited subject area such as traffic hazards because the related nonfatal measures such as hospital days are roughly proportional to the number of deaths.

8.3.3.2 Goals of Safety Engineering
The main goals of safety engineering are:

1. To reduce accident frequency
2. To reduce injury frequency
3. To reduce injury severity

These goals are in decreasing order of cost effectiveness. An accident is defined as an unexpected, undesired incident. Some accidents cause injury. It is usually more cost effective to remove the cause of accidents than to try to make them less traumatic. For example, if a window air-conditioning unit hangs out over a sidewalk such that the bottom is 180 cm (71 in.) above the sidewalk, short people may walk under it but tall people may bump their head. It would be better practice to bring two columns down from the corners so that people cannot walk under the overhang (reduce accident frequency) than to cushion the overhanging corners (reduce injury frequency and severity). However, after opportunities to prevent accidents have been exhausted, the other goals become important. Air bags for automobiles, for example, do nothing to prevent accidents but do reduce injury frequency. The third goal, to reduce injury severity, is largely attained by accident-response systems and procedures. For example, an eyewash fountain, actuated by stepping on a foot pedal, can be provided in areas where a worker risks getting chemicals in his eyes. Other examples are fire-evacuation plans and drills, first-aid kits, and procedures to provide fast emergency medical or paramedical attention.

8.3.3.3 Hazards and Safe Design
To achieve these safety engineering goals, the industrial engineer must learn both how to recognize hazards and how to design safe facilities and procedures. Every plant has its own set

of hazards, but they fall into categories. Possible hazards should be systematically searched. In nearly all plants, there are:

- Tripping hazards
- Head hazards
- Energy-release hazards, including electrical shock, steam or compressed air, reactive chemicals or explosives, pressure vessels no matter what the contents
- Touch hazards
- Fire hazards
- Pinching or entrapment hazards
- Air-contamination hazards
- Falling hazards
- Chemical hazards
- Engulfment hazards
- Moving-equipment hazards

There are common preventive measures for each kind of hazard. For tripping hazards, the engineer should avoid unnecessary changes in floor level and provide lighting, handrails, and warning signs where small changes in level are unavoidable. Stairs must have identical rise for every step and identical run for every step. Head hazards are dealt with by eliminating head-level overhangs, preventing the possibility of things dropping from overhead (using nets if a better way cannot be found), and insisting that hard hats be worn.

Energy-release hazards are of many kinds, but for most of them it is best first to try to eliminate or substitute for the energy source, second to isolate the source (as by keeping live electricity out of areas where workers can go, and providing interlocks to interrupt electricity if a worker enters the area), and third to reduce exposure (as by insulating). These three strategies correspond to the main goals of safety engineering listed earlier. The same three levels of approach can also be expressed in terms of the classic safety problem of an open manhole.

Safety Approaches for an Open Manhole

The engineering approach:	provide a manhole cover
The guarding approach:	provide a guardrail around the manhole
The warning approach:	provide a warning sign

As this vignette makes clear, the engineering approach is better than the guarding approach, which in turn is better than the warning approach.

Touch hazards, such as hot flanges or whirling blades, require similar measures to those of energy release: keep the hot flange out of reach (above 8 ft overhead or 5 ft to the side), insulate, or guard. A warning would never be enough.

Fire hazards require first eliminating flammable materials if possible, then isolating them, and then providing sprinklers or other firefighting facilities. (Electrical fires, petroleum-fuel fires, and chemical fires cannot be fought with water but require CO_2 or foam.) Safety engineers need to know the combustion process; a fire requires both flammable material and oxygen, and most fire fighting involves smothering—keeping air (which is 21% oxygen) away. Common flammable gases such as CH_4 (methane), natural gas (mostly methane), LPG (liquefied petroleum gas, mostly butane and propane), and fuel fumes will explode when in medium concentrations in the air; if the concentration is too low or is high enough, they will not. Much money is spent on explosion-proof gear (even explosion-proof telephones and computer terminals) that prevent sparks in areas where flammable vapors may be present, but this is a last-ditch strategy.

Pinching or entrapment hazards are those such as getting a hand caught in a belt or set of rollers. Loose clothing is forbidden around machinery that can pinch or entrap the worker. (In the 1930s, workers wore ties, and there were many cases of choking or head injuries when ties became entangled.) Where a pinching or entrapment hazard cannot be removed, guards or interlocks are commonly provided. For example, a simple cover guard may prevent a worker's hand from entering the danger area, or a trigger may immobilize the dangerous parts when a worker's hand gets too close.

Air-contamination hazards are treated in some detail in section 8.3.2. The last-ditch protection for large-particle dust is the breathing mask, which should be used by workers who must sweep, engage in such activities as cutting grass or handling dry animal feed, or perform work that grinds or pulverizes any material or creates dust (a lathe or metal saw, for example, creates metal dust). Breathing masks are useless for 5-μm or smaller particulates such as result from combustion. For fine particles and for gases, the last-ditch protection is a respirator (gas mask), which filters breathed air. A respirator can remove great amounts of hydrocarbons, Cl_2, CO_2, and CO from air. Of course, this would be after the engineer had provided better protection to the maximum practical extent: a wet process to keep dust down, ventilation hoods, or vapor-recovery collection devices.

Most falling hazards can be completely prevented with guard cages or handrails. Ladders should be fixed, not portable, and should reach only 12 ft between landings. Chemical hazards are a specialized area, requiring more knowledge of chemistry than can be reviewed here. Engulfment hazards, such as sinking into a pile of loose material or having snow, liquid, or loose material fall on a worker, can be prevented by commonsense methods. First, the worker should not have to go into an engulfment hazard area. Next, there should be positive footing or a safety line (rope attached to the worker) or other means of positive removal, and, of course, vigilant help should be quickly available to haul the worker out.

Moving equipment hazards include such things as being hit by something small like a robot arm, by something larger like a fork truck or a load being handled by a crane, or something very large like a truck, gantry crane, or other large vehicle. All equipment is required to beep when going in an unexpected direction such as reverse. Workers are assumed to be able to keep out of the way of large moving objects; for example, workers can freely walk around an active train yard or truck yard without being in real danger, because large equipment is slow and visually and aurally obvious. But such hazards as loads swinging from cranes are more dangerous. Particularly dangerous are robots, because they can move unexpectedly. An industrial robot is a machine that has a fixed base; a mobile arm articulating from the fixed base, usually an articulating joint in the middle of the arm; and a tool such as pincers, a welding head, or a spray nozzle at the "hand" end of the arm. The usual safety measures for robots are to fence off the area that any part of the robot can reach and to provide interlocks so that opening the gate in the fence (necessary for access by maintenance personnel) shuts off power to the robot.

Most safety questions on the IE PE Exam test the examinee's ability to recognize hazards and propose cost-effective strategies to neutralize them.

E95a.   **Your plant stores a combustible material in silos that are 28 ft (8.5 m) in diameter and 70 ft.(21 m) tall. Employees occasionally have been required to go into the silos to dislodge material from the walls.**

(1) **List the safety hazards.**

(2) **Recommend procedures to create a safe working environment.**

From the problem statement, it can be assumed that the material is not very hot, very cold, poisonous, radioactive, nor harmful to the skin upon brief contact. However, no assumptions can be made about the material's form and consistency beyond its tendency to adhere to silo walls. In particular, it is not known whether it can support being walked upon; it may have the consistency of dirt, gravel, logs, sticks, tar, coal, dust, moss, quicksand, apples, corncobs, wheat, flour, molasses, or sugar.

Hazards include:

— Fire and/or explosion (explosion if the combustible material is dusty).

— Engulfment. There may be a hazard of suffocation or immobilization by the worker's sinking into the bulk or by material's falling from the wall.

— Lung or eye damage. The air within the silo may be unfit to breathe.

— Mechanical injury. There may be a hazard of mechanical injury from dislodged materials falling on the worker, from the worker losing footing on the surface, or from the material suddenly shifting underfoot.

Less important but acceptable items in the hazard list include noise (if the material is dislodged by hammering metal walls), clothing damage, and long-term injury to skin, nose, throat, or ear canals.

Recommended procedures include:

— Engineering solutions. It is very doubtful that the situation could require plant employees to enter the silo to the exclusion of allowing substitutions: mechanical dislodgment or, at worst, long-handled tools allowing the worker's body to remain outside the silo.

— Protective clothing. Against each hazard, there is the possibility of correction by clothing: for fire (brief exposure), for engulfment's suffocation hazard (breathing apparatus), for lung or eye damage, and even for mechanical injury (armor).

— Vigilance and positive removal. The plant can provide for someone to be in continual visual or audio contact with any worker in the silo. There should be a hoist, a rescue plan, or a standby rescuer to assure that a worker can be removed from the silo if incapacitated.

Less important but acceptable items in the procedures list include ventilation, air testing, and training.

E95b. A chemically non-hazardous, crushed rock ore is in the form of small boulders that weigh less than 15 lb and are less than 5 in diameter. Your company is presently using large front-end loaders to move the ore a distance of 500 ft. You are investigating the possibility of eliminating the loading operation by using an existing conveyor-belt system now located in another part of the plant.

(a) List the possible hazards to investigate.

(b) Describe how each hazard could cause injury.

(c) Describe procedures or equipment modifications that could be used to eliminate or mitigate the hazards.

(d) Identify the procedures or equipment modifications that are potentially most damaging to the economic feasibility of reusing the conveyor.

Table 8-1. Solution to Example E95b.

(a) Possible hazards	(b) Injuries	(c) Procedures or modifications
Structural incapacity: belt or supports not adequate for the loads (the reused equipment was not designed for this job)	Mechanical failure; load could be dumped suddenly, endangering nearby workers	Perform structural and dynamic design as if the equipment were being specially designed for this job. Take deterioration of used equipment into account. Specify any needed modifications, replacements of worn parts, or additions.
Material falling off sides of belt (the reused equipment may not have been designed to carry rock even if strong enough)	Injuries to legs or feet or from boulder-littered ground	Design containers to carry rock on the belt (and procedures for loading and unloading the containers), or design side guards to keep rock on the belt
Driver (assumed to be electric motor) could be too small for load, and hence run hot and shut itself down; it could be too exposed to personnel or too exposed to dust from the rock (previous use may have been in closed area)	Injuries from sudden stoppages (e.g., rock surging at load or unload end), from electrical fire (fumes, flames), from shock hazard	Make sure motor is adequate for job; isolate it from personnel and from dust
Moving machinery hazards: pinching by belt or rollers	Pinching injury to hands or by being pulled by clothing into moving parts	Isolate moving parts from workers (e.g., guardrails)
Dust and noise, which are hazards that also exist with front-end loaders	Respiratory and lung damage, hearing loss, indirect injury from loss of verbal communication	Make sure dust and noise are not worse than with front-end loader; require breathing masks or ear protection if necessary
Material handling at loading and unloading ends of conveyor; it is likely the discharge is into a rock crusher, and workers afoot may be required to dislodge jams formerly handled by front-end loader	Being pulled into crusher or bin at discharge end of belt; engulfment or injury from falling rock while working at either end	Design for human intervention to be from a distance, as it now is with the front-end loader

The modifications most likely to make reusing the conveyor economically infeasible are structural modifications necessary if the conveyor is inadequate to handle the load. Note that the load for which the conveyor must be adequate is not merely the load implied by the material flow rate; it is that implied by the maximum amount of rock that can be put onto the conveyor. This is because it is unreasonable to assume that workers will never allow rock to be piled onto it as high as possible.

8.3.3.4 Productivity and Workmans' Compensation

In any enterprise that employs workers, the industrial engineer is responsible for achieving the highest human productivity not only by providing for the safety and comfort of employees, but also by protecting the employer from false or invalid claims of injury, disability, or illness. Never cut corners on safety or employee comfort; never disallow a valid complaint or take unfair advantage of an employee. Employee perception that management is uncaring or unfair poisons the atmosphere and ruins productivity in many ways, none of which management can do anything about except by slowly regaining employee confidence. Always work for safety and employee comfort; always treat employees fairly. And always be open and visible in doing so. Make a positive show of concern for employees' well-being.

Workmans' Compensation is a program, administered by state government and different in various states, that pays workers' claims for job-related injuries and disabilities. It is financed by employer contributions, and employers pay more when their workers have a history of making more claims.

Workmans' "Comp" is fraught with opportunities for abuse on both sides. Many employers illegally discourage reporting of incidents. Many employees illegally file false or overblown claims. Many occupational medicine clinics illegally make false diagnoses, encourage unjustified disability claims, and bill for phantom treatment. Claims follow fashion. California added mental stress injury as a category and started a goldbrick's gold rush; mental stress injury is now the most costly category in the San Diego area. Legislators in other states, who would like to provide somehow for real job-related mental damage, dare not follow California's lead and open a Pandora's cashbox.

Carpal tunnel syndrome is both truly endemic and fashionable. Compare modern data entry to keypunching as formerly performed, or modern word processing to typing as formerly done. The work is no longer automatically relieved by tasks such as physically pulling a manual typewriter's carriage-return lever, physically loading paper or carbon paper or punch cards, getting up to deliver or copy finished work, physically erasing or correcting errors, or walking or at least reaching into an in-basket to get source material. If the work arrives electronically, is processed electronically and leaves electronically, the employee does nothing but tap keys. If this is done with poor posture, poor placement of the keyboard, bent wrists, or slight twisting of the body, trouble will ensue. The industrial engineer can provide adjustable chairs, wrist rests, foot boards, reading stands, and adjustable monitors, but even the best static work position is harmful if employees fail to move occasionally.

Arthritis, ganglion cysts, metabolic neuropathy, toxic neuropathy, heart attack, thoracic outlet syndrome, or anything else that causes numbness in the fingers can be confused with carpal tunnel syndrome. All would be covered by health insurance, but only toxic neuropathy (poisoning that affects the nerves) would be likely to have anything to do with one's job and justify a Workmans' Compensation claim.

The following vignette illustrates how simply some cases of repetitive injury can be prevented simply by getting workers not to stay in the same position all the time:

> An occupational physician saw similar cases of wrist overwork and back pain in all three taco-folding employees on a food-preparation line. He visited the site and found the workers standing to the side of the waist-high line turning each taco—flip, flip, flip, flip, 80 per minute—with the right hand, facing upstream with the left arm hanging down. He told them, "Hey, this ain't rocket science! Turn around facing downstream and do it with your left hand for awhile." They got up to speed with the non-preferred hand within the first shift. The extra cost (for sanitary gloves and stopping to change gloves) was negligible. Complaints ceased.

What can be done, beyond good design and training, to keep Workmans' Compensation claims from mushrooming? According to occupational physicians, it is important that doctors prescribe modified work programs when dealing with cases involving on-the-job injuries. In modern occupational therapy, nearly every treatment is exercise of some kind (often very gentle); bed rest or immobilization is rarely best except in the very first stage of treatment. Merely being at the workplace, doing whatever is prescribed by the doctor, is never harmful and is always better than staying away from work. Modified work leads to recovery; a doctor's excuse from work leads to disability. But the doctor must understand how to prescribe modified work: for example, if a bricklayer injures her hand and the doctor tells her not to lift anything heavier than 5 lb (without saying how often), then, since a brick weighs 3 lb, she might find the employer returning her to her full job because of the doctor's failure to understand the precision required in prescribing a treatment.

The occupational physician must also be able to communicate with the patient. If the patient has to wait, is treated rudely, or is greeted with open skepticism, the patient may shop around for a doctor who will listen to him—maybe a doctor who views the goal as milking the system rather than getting the patient back to full functioning.

Affecting 43 million Americans, the Americans with Disabilities Act of 1992 tries to remove barriers to the employment of people with disabilities. According to its provisions, employers can no longer just say no. It is illegal for an employer to ask about injuries or illness, but a physician can ask, so you can still legally screen potential employees. That is important, because the best predictor of costly claims is the candidate's five-year history of work injuries. Also, hiring a double-jointed person for a job that carries a risk of tendonitis or hiring a person with a history of asthma to paint walls can be avoided.

Appendix
Glossary of Computer
and InformationTerms

array N-dimensional data structure. $N = 1$, see *vector*. $N = 2$, see *matrix*. $N = 3$: collection of $L_1 \times L_2 \times L_3$ words, where L_m is the length of the mth dimension of the array. If the dimensions are called *page*, *row*, *column*, the word in the ith page, jth row, kth column is identified by a triplet (i,j,k).

ASCII code   A one-byte code that represents a character, e.g., the ASCII code for the @ character is 64. Codes 0 through 127 (the original ASCII codes) represent the English alphabet, numerals, punctuation marks, and a few control characters; codes 127 through 255 are the extended ASCII character set, including European, graphics, and scientific characters.

ASCII file   A file consisting entirely of ASCII character codes, able to be imported by a different system from the one that produced it. For example, whereas a document file produced by a word processor would contain a special code to center a heading, an ASCII file of the same document would replace the centering code with the equivalent sequence of ASCII space-bar codes, so the document could be read in that form by almost any system.

baud rate
Serial communications rate in bits per second (bps). (Parallel communications between N-bit devices are N times greater.) A baud is one bit per second. Net data transfer rates in characters (bytes) per second are about 1/10 of the baud rate. Serial communications rates over telephone lines via modems are limited to 56,000 baud (56 kbps) until fiber optics completely replaces copper, allowing 96,000 baud and higher.

binary search
To search for an item in an ordered or indexed list by accessing the middle item, then stopping or repeating according to whether the accessed item is seen to be the sought one, or above the sought one, or below the sought one.

bit
Binary digit, the smallest unit of information. A boolean or zero-one (0,1) variable's value is one bit in length.

byte
Eight bits, which in communication can hold seven bits of information, the eighth being a parity bit.

**cardinality
(of a relationship)**
A relationship between A and B has a maximum cardinality at A or either *one* or *many*, meaning that the maximum number of instances of A for one instance of B is either one or many. A relationship between A and B has a minimum cardinality at A of either *zero* or *one*, meaning that the minimum number of instances of A for one instance of B is zero or one.

CD-ROM
Compact disk, read-only memory. A high-capacity 350 megabytes or more) portable optical data-storage device, about 5 inches in diameter, that has supplanted the diskette.

**central
processing
unit (CPU)**
The hardware component that executes program instructions by processing data and controlling other components. Informally, "CPU" is sometimes used to mean the computer itself (the hardware package that includes the actual CPU and disk drives) as opposed to keyboard and monitor.

**choose
(or select)**
To press a key, or provide input by any designated means, in order to indicate selection of a displayed item that is highlighted, usually by a cursor that can be moved by mouse, arrow keys, or another input selection device.

consequential	Data that is a consequence of (is derived from) more basic data. Archiving it along with basic data risks data integrity; archiving it instead of basic data foists data processing out of the system ("Do not give the computer what it should give you").
CSMA/CD, carrier sense multiple access with collision detection	A message control scheme used in LANs, whereby any device can begin transmitting if there is no signal on the network. Since a short time elapses between checking for a signal and beginning transmission, more than one device can start at almost the same time. When this "collision" is detected by each device, it stops, waits a random time, and tries again. CSMA/CD is used in Ethernet and broadcast networks. Compare with *token passing*.
cursor	In an interactive user interface, a displayed symbol whose position in a display is controlled either by the user to indicate selection of a displayed item or by the system to provide a designated place for data entry to be echoed (to echo is to display what is entered) or indicate what object or function is currently active.
database	A set of records that is integrated so that all applications access the same version of data. A *relational* database is not only integrated but is also self-describing.
database management system, DBMS	A software product that provides utilities to define and manipulate a *database*. A relational DBMS, which has largely supplanted other types, provides utilities to define and manipulate a *relational database*; utilities often include menu, forms, and report generators. Programs that perform mostly data manipulation, with trivial computational and logical requirements (e.g., warehouse management programs) can be programmed without a driving program. With a separate driving program, the DBMS performs the equivalent of READ and WRITE functions, perhaps managing data entry, perhaps managing menu selection, and perhaps managing report generation. Newer DBMSs are fully integrated with a programming language so that the driving program need not be separate.

data integrity   Avoidance of loss of data from integrity insertion or deletion anoma-
                          lies due to poor data design, or inconsistencies due to redundant storage
                          of both basic and derived data.

datum (singular),   Representation of information as a computer word (datum) or words
data (plural)   (data).

deletion anomaly   Inappropriate restriction on ability to delete information due to poor
                          data design, e.g., the price of a widget is lost if the only widget sale
                          transaction in the database is deleted.

derived data   Data that can be fully reconstituted from other data and is therefore
                          redundant to save. See *consequential data.*

disk   Storage device for permanent archiving of data. *Hard disk:* large, permanent
                          magnetic disk having capacity measured in megabytes or gigabytes.
                          Diskette (formerly *floppy disk):* small, portable magnetic disk (3.5-in.
                          diameter, 1.44 mb capacity), supplanted by CD-ROM. *Disk drive:* hardware
                          that reads from and writes on disk.

enter   To type data into a system through an interactive user interface, ending
                          by pressing the ENTER or other designated key or (not recommended)
                          by filling the provided data-entry field. Compare with *choose.*

field   Subdivision of a record into which one datum fits.

file   Collection of records.

file server   Computer and storage system in a server network, serving other
                          computers as if they were their own disk drives.

gigabyte, gb, gig   230 = 1,073,741,824 bytes, or approximately one billion bytes

GUI, graphical   An interface (e.g., Windows 95) that uses dialog boxes, pop-up
user interface   menus, and the like to collect and guide menu-driven user actions.

import   To transfer data wholesale from some source to a target system. For
                          example, a spreadsheet may be imported into a relational database.

information   Amount of uncertainty, measured in bits. If a set of possible values has H bits of information, a series of answers to H yes-no questions can identify the actual value. $0 \leq H \leq \log_2 N$, where N is the number of possible values. Also, reduction of uncertainty, in the sense that to reduce H is to gain information.

input (noun)   Data that is entered or imported. (verb) To provide data values, such as by entering or importing.

I/O   (noun) Input and output. (adjective) Pertaining to an interface that accepts input and displays or distributes output.

insertion anomaly   Inappropriate restriction on ability to enter information due to poor data design, e.g., the price of a widget cannot be entered except as part of a widget sale transaction.

K   kilobyte, as in 512K memory or storage. Also 1000, as in 20 K$ = $20,000.

kilobyte, kb, $2^{10} = 1024$ bytes, or approximately one thousand bytes.
K (as in 20K)

knowledge base   The most nonvolatile data, maximally protected from being changed.

LAN, local area   A communications network that connects local computers with other
network   computers and peripheral devices over short distances (tens of meters). Network control and file serving are usually handled by a personal computer or workstation.

matrix   Two-dimensional array where the value of the (i, j) word is kept in row i, column j.

megabyte, mb, meg $2^{20} = 1,048,576$ bytes, or approximately one million bytes.

nonvolatile

Not often changing, as in *nonvolatile data*. Not lost when power is lost, as in *nonvolatile storage*.

parity bit

A bit whose value is 0 or 1 depending bit on whether the sum of preceding bits is even or odd.

PC; personal computer *or* **programmable controller**

A personal computer is a computer with personal power below that of a workstation-class computer; a 486-class, DOS-type PC, for example, could handle light computer-aided design tasks but would bog down for animation. A programmable controller is a computer with a real-time operating system, ability to accept a heavy flow of input (feedback) data from a running process, and calculate and transmit corrective signals based on comparing the feedback data to setpoint (desired) data.

record

Collection of fields or subdivision of file, or collection of values kept one per field.

relation

A set of rows or tuples containing data for an instance of an object or relationship, each datum being a value of a specific *attribute* for the instance.

relational database

A database that is a collection of *relations* and is manipulated via a *database management system* that is relational.

relationship

Between entities or relations, the fact or requirement that one or more instances of an entity or relation must or may correspond to one or more instances of another entity or relation. Indicated formally by a link between entity or relation symbols showing maximum and minimum cardinality of the relationship in both directions.

save

To cause a file to be written on a disk or other storage medium. Compare with *store* or *retain*.

store

To cause a value to be kept in memory (or to be kept in storage). Synonym: *retain*. Compare with *save* and with *enter* or *input* (verb).

structured query language (SQL)	A standard language for defining, filling, querying, updating, and controlling a relational database. SQL is available on every modern, high-quality relational DBMS.
terminal	Keyboard and monitor (or other I/O device set) separated from other components of a system and serving as a remote user interface for it.
token passing	A means of message control in LANs whereby a "token" code circulates rapidly and a device waits for it when ready to transmit, catches it, transmits, and lets it go. No collision can occur. Used in IBM LANs. Compare CSMA/CD.
value	Number or character string that identifies a specific instance of a datum. For example, the *value* of "name" may be "Joe."
vector	Collection of words numbered 0, 1, 2, ..., $L-1$, where L is the length. Also, the collection of values kept in the words. One-dimensional array.
volatile	Often changing, rapidly disappearing, or susceptible to loss when power is lost. *Volatile data* can be data whose values must often be changed, or (as in *volatile memory*) data that disappears when power is turned off or interrupted.
word	Unit of memory or storage, having lengths commonly of 8 bits, 16 bits, 32 bits, 64 bits, or 128 bits.

References

Chapter 1

Kennedy, William J. 1992. New professional engineering exam format for 1993. *Industrial Engineering*: Norcross, GA: Institute of Industrial Engineers. December.

National Council of Examiners for Engineering and Surveying (NCEES). 1989. *Analysis of Professional Activities and Requirements of the Engineering Profession*. Clemson, SC.

Young, Donovan, editor. 1993. *Problems and Solutions to the Principles and Practice of Engineering Examination for Industrial Engineers*, Second Edition. Norcross, GA: Industrial Engineering and Management Press.

Chapter 2

None cited.

Chapter 3

Ostwald, Phillip F. 1992. *Engineering Cost Estimating*, Third Edition. Englewood Cliffs, NJ: Prentice Hall.

Young, Donovan. 1993. *Modern Engineering Economy*. New York: John Wiley & Sons.

Chapter 4

Dodge, H. F. and H. G. Romig. 1959. *Sampling Inspection Tables*. New York: John Wiley & Sons.

Chapter 5

Geoffrion, Arthur M. 1987. Introduction to structured modeling. *Management Science*, Vol. 33, No. 5, May.

National Council of Examiners for Engineering and Surveying (NCEES). 1989. *Analysis of Professional Activities and Requirements of the Engineering Profession*. Clemson, SC.

Chapter 6

Hiller, Frederick S. and Gerald J. Lieberman. 1990. *Introduction to Operations Research*, Fifth Edition. Oakland: CA: Holden-Day, Inc.

Malcom, D. G., et al. 1959. Applications of a technique for R and D program evaluation. *Operations Research*, Vol. 9, No. 5.

Montgomery, D. C. and Lynwood A. Johnson. 1976. *Forecasting and Time Series*. New York: McGraw-Hill.

Muther, R. 1973. *Systematic Layout Planning*, Second Edition. Boston: Cahners Books.

Ravidran, A., Dom T. Phillips, and James J. Solberg. 1987. *Operations Research: Principles and Practice*, Second Edition. New York: John Wiley & Sons.

Rosenthal, Richard E., et al. 1983. Interactive graphical minimax location of multiple facilities with general constraints. *IIE Transactions*, Vol. 15, No. 3.

Special Projects Office, Bureau of Naval Weapons, Department of the Navy. 1958. *PERT Summary Report, Phase I*. Washington, D.C.

Taha, Hamdy A. 1992. *Operations Research: An Introduction*. New York: MacMillan Publishing Co., Inc.

Tompkins, J. A. and John A. White. 1984. *Facilities Planning*. New York: John Wiley & Sons.

Young, Donovan, editor. 1993. *Problems and Solutions to the Professional Engineers Examination for Industrial Engineers*, Second Edition. Norcross, GA: Industrial Engineering and Management Press.

———. 1993. *Modern Engineering Economy*. New York: John Wiley & Sons.

Chapter 7

Konz, S. 1995. *Work Design: Industrial Economics*, Fourth Edition. Scottsdale, AZ: Publishing Horizons, Inc.

Rodgers, S., editor. 1986. *Ergonomic Design for People at Work*. Eastman Kodak Ergonomic Group.

Salvendy, G. 1986. *Handbook of Human Factors*. New York: John Wiley & Sons.

Warwick, Novak, Schultz, and Berkson. 1980. Maximum voluntary strengths of male adults. *Ergonomics*, Vol. 23, No. 1.

Chapter 8

Alderfer, Clayton. 1971. Quoted in Babcock, 1991.

Babcock, Daniel L. 1991. *Managing Engineering and Technology*. Englewood Cliffs, NJ: Prentice Hall.

Deming, W. Edwards. 1982. *Quality Productivity and Competitive Position*. Cambridge: MIT Press.

Ferguson, Gary A. 1993. U.S. repeating arms sets sights on world-class facility. *Industrial Engineering*. Norcross, GA: Institute of Industrial Engineers. March.

Hackman, H. R. and G. R. Oldham. 1980. *Work Redesign*. Reading, MA: Addison-Wesley.

Huchingson, R. D. 1981. *New Horizons for Human Factors in Design*. New York: McGraw-Hill.

Kantowitz, D. H. and R. D. Sorlein. 1983. *Human Factors: Understanding People-System Relationships*. New York: John Wiley & Sons.

Konz, S. 1990. *Work Design: Industrial Ergonomics*, Third Edition. Worthington, OH: Publishing Horizons, Inc.

Larson and Gobeli. 1989. Significance of project management structure. *IEEE Transactions on Engineering Management*. May.

Lesieur, Frederick G. 1958. *The Scanlon Plan: A Frontier in Labor Management Cooperation*. Cambridge: MIT Press.

Likert. 1961. Quoted in Babcock, 1991.

——. 1967. Quoted in Babcock, 1991.

Maslow. 1943. Quoted in Babcock, 1991.

McCormick, E. J. and M. S. Sanders. 1982. *Human Factors in Engineering and Design*. New York: McGraw-Hill.

McGregor, Douglas. 1960. *The Human Side of Enterprise*. New York: McGraw-Hill.

Newman, et al. *The Process of Management*, quoted in Babcock, 1991.

Peters, Tom. 1987. *Thriving on Chaos: Handbook for a Management Revolution*. New York: Alfred A. Knopf.

Porras, Jerry I. and Susan J. Hoffer. 1986. Common behavior changes in successful organization development efforts. *Journal of Applied Behavioral Science*, Vol. 22.

Roberts and Hunt. 1991. *Organizational Behavior*. Boston, MA: PWS-Kent.

Index

B
Babcock, Daniel L., 340
Background music, 315
Backorder, 230
Backward-pass algorithm, 244-245, 252-254, 259-260
Balance delay, 222
Bar-codes, 166
Barnes, 329
Baseline, 68
Base rate, 352
BASIC programming language, 207
Baud rate, 165
Bayes' Theorem, 43-44,120-122
BCNF. *See* Boyce-Codd normal form
B/C. *See* Benefit/cost ratio
Before-inflation. *See* Indexed dollars
Benchmarking, 350
Benefit/cost ratio (B/C), 79, 81
Benefit estimating, 67-68
    double counting, 64, 67-68
    exhaustive benefits, 67
    riders, 67
Bill of materials(BOM), 247
Bill of materials(BOM),exploding, 247
Binary number, 149-151
Binary search, 149-150
Binomial distribution, 43,101
Biomechanics, 301
Bit, 148,151
BOM. *See* Bill of materials
Book value, 89
Boolean logic, 123-126
Borg's scale, 306
Boyce-Codd normal form (BCNF),193,197-198
Breakeven analysis, breakeven assertion, 85
Breakeven analysis, breakeven parameter, 8485
Breakeven parameter, 8485
Buttock-popliteal depth, 302
Byte, 148

C
Caloric requirement. *See* Metabolism
Candidate key, 197-198
Capacity balancing problem, 220
Capital efficiency, 81
Capital expenditure, 89
Carbon monoxide (CO), 364365203
Cardinality, 184, collision
Carrier sense multiple access with detection control scheme (CSMA/CD), 165
Cash flow diagram, 69
Cash flow set, 68-73
CDF. *See* Cumulative distribution function
Cell, 159
Central limit theorem, 104
Central measure (statistics)
    expected value, 97-99,101
    mean, 97
    mode, 97

Central Processing Unit (CPU), 159,166
Characteristic, 203
Chebyshev's Theorem, 100
Chemical hazards, 370-371
Chi-square distribution, 111 - 114
    chi-square statistic, 112-114
Chlorine (Cl_2), 365
Chrysler, 322
Closed-loop system, 319
Cl_2. *See* Chlorine
Codes and standards, 4
Coefficient of variation, 103
Column, 156,159-160
"Common Behavior Changes in Successful Organization Development Efforts", 346
Common life, 78
Composite escalation rate, 83
Computer hardware, 4,147,166-167
Computer information systems, 52-57,147-215
Computer programming, 147
Computer software, 4,147,167
Concave, 239
Concave-cost production/inventory model, 242-246
Concave production-cost function, 244
Concept, 202
Concordance, 185
Conditional probability, Bayes' Theorem, 120-122
Conditional probability, joint probability, 120
Confirm cycle, 322
Consensus, 344348
Consistency checking, 359
Constituencies, 345,349
Constraints, linear programming, 265-267
Consumer, 132
Consumer's risk, 132
Content theories of motivation, 343
Contingency, 60
Continuous control, 319
Continuous probability distribution, 102
Continuous production system, 218-219
Continuous sampling, 323
Continuous timing convention, 78
Continuous uniform distribution, 102
Control chart, 126-132
    lower control limit (LCL), 29,31,126-132
    out-of-control condition, 126-132
    p chart (proportion), 29,31,127
    R-chart (range), 127
    s-chart (standard deviation), 128
    upper control limit (UCL), 29,31126-132
    $\bar{x}$-chart(average), 127
Controls, 50-52, 319-322
Conversation, 314
Convex, 239
Convex-cost heuristic, 241-242
Convex-cost production/inventory model, 241
CORELAP, 289
CO. *See* Carbon monoxide